In the same week of September 1956 that Elvis Presley rocked and shocked the nation with his TV debut on *The Ed Sullivan Show*, Martha Kostyra landed on her feet in the hallowed halls of Nutley High School and never stopped running. Like Elvis, Martha was to become an icon one day. But for now she had made a conscious decision to become the best, the most active, and the most famous member of the Nutley High class of '59.

"I sat next to her in the front of Margaret Gerdinick's French class," said a pal, Barbara Rubin Oliver, who recalled Martha's modus operandi. "We'd come into class on a day we were going to have a test, and she'd *still* be studying. As far as I was concerned and our friends were concerned, we had studied the night before. But Martha would study right up until the very last *second* before the exam and then say, 'Oh, I don't know *any* of this.' And then of course she'd get an A. She was disciplined—always one step ahead of the rest of us."

Barbara Viventi Howard, voted the girl "Most Likely to Succeed"—she later became a prominent microbiologist and the president of a research institute—felt there was something extraordinary about her close friend Marty, as some called her. "She had a focus that was extremely unusual for Nutley High School girls of the fifties. Martha was highly ambitious and competitive."

Just Desserts

THE UNAUTHORIZED BIOGRAPHY
Martha Stewart

JERRY OPPENHEIMER

AVON BOOKS ◆ NEW YORK

AVON BOOKS
A division of
The Hearst Corporation
1350 Avenue of the Americas
New York, New York 10019

The William Morrow edition contains the following Library of Congress
Cataloging in Publication Data:

Oppenheimer, Jerry.
   Martha Stewart—just desserts: the unauthorized biography / by Jerry
Oppenheimer
      p. cm.
1. Stewart, Martha.   2. Artisans—United States—Biography. 3. Busi-
nesswomen—United States—Biography.   I. Title.
TT140.S67064 1997   96-53261
338.7'6164'92—dc21   CIP
[B]

First Avon Books Printing: May 1998

AVON TRADEMARK REG. U.S. PAT. OFF. AND IN OTHER COUNTRIES, MARCA
REGISTRADA, HECHO EN U.S.A.

Printed in the U.S.A.

WCD   10 9 8 7 6 5 4 3 2 1

For C.W.H.

Preface

The first time I ever saw Martha Stewart she was starring in a TV commercial that showed her lining a swimming pool with credit cards. A few days later, at an airport newsstand, I spotted her visage plastered on a rack of magazines named after her. Not long after, in a bookstore, I noted that same smiling face staring at me from a whole section devoted to her best-selling oeuvre. That same night, while channel surfing, she popped up on my TV screen once again, this time hostessing her own show. Everywhere I turned, it seemed, I encountered her hawking good living.

Martha Stewart appeared to have a monopoly on all things domestic. This media juggernaut had come in low under my journalistic radar and struck hard. Though she had burst onto the national scene with her first book in 1982, it wasn't until late in 1994 that Stewart finally crept into my consciousness.

Although late, her timing was perfect: I was searching for a new subject, having just completed a biography of Ethel Kennedy, and Martha Stewart appeared to be at the top of her game, thus making her a likely prospect. She had all the right stuff: success, wealth, power, popularity. Strong, enigmatic women like Barbara Walters, about whom I'd also written a biography, intrigue me. So I started to poke around.

I read everything in the public domain about Stewart, and it quickly became apparent from the mound of clips that little was really known about this woman who came out of nowhere to become an icon virtually overnight. One story read much like the other, as if the material had come from a press release.

It was not until I thoroughly scrutinized every issue of Stewart's magazine, *Martha Stewart Living*, and each of her books that I was convinced she would be my next subject. It was in her own material that I saw a fascinating story. Stewart writes in great detail about her perfect childhood, her perfect family, her perfect education, her perfect marriage, her perfect motherhood, her perfect career, her perfect husband, her perfect daughter, her perfect house. Taken as a whole, it seemed all *too* perfect. In her chatty, autobiographical style, she names names, dates, and places; she describes incidents, serves up anecdotes.

She had laid out an intriguing trail for me to follow. My investigative juices began to flow. If her stories were true, I foresaw a book about a perfect woman who had brought perfection to the masses. If her stories were not true, I foresaw a book that would shatter myths that were well constructed.

For me, Martha Stewart's world was virgin territory. I cared little about cooking, had no interest in gardening, decorating, or the fine art of entertaining. Since I'd only recently been introduced to Martha through her multimedia appearances, I had no strong feelings about her, except that she'd make an interesting study. I had no ax to grind. I was neither fan nor foe (though I'd quickly learn as I began my research that feelings about this woman ran high: People either loved her or they hated her).

In any case, my goal was to write an objective account of her life, piecing it all together through the experiences of those who knew her best.

During the course of two years, I followed the trail Stewart had provided in her writings. Along the way, there were many roadblocks: Early on she told people not to cooperate with me (most ignored her request), and she declined to sit for an interview. There were detours, dead ends, and mazes to weave through. At one point, a relative told me that Martha had instructed certain people to tell me falsehoods. That piece of intelligence served only to intensify my scrutiny.

In public appearances (on *Larry King Live,* for instance, and in a forum with Charlie Rose), she curiously referred to my work in progress as "stupid." In a newspaper interview, she said, "What could he possibly know about me that hasn't already been written? . . . I'm more concerned about the privacy of my family than me. That's what makes me sick to my stomach. It's unauthorized. Why would a reputable publisher pay for it?" I found her comments odd since it was Martha herself who introduced her family to the public in her books and magazine, thus making them known to a wide audience. As for unauthorized biographies, they are considered a reputable and popular literary form.

In all, I conducted some four hundred interviews with siblings, relatives, close friends, past and present, former and current associates, employees, and colleagues. Writers of independent biographies are used to having doors slammed in their faces, and phones hung up on them. With Martha Stewart, just the opposite happened. The general response was, "Ah, someone's finally going to tell the real story."

By the end of my research, I had been able to penetrate the inner circles of all stages of Stewart's life, from childhood to the present. By then, Martha had made quiet attempts to prevent the book from being published. When that failed, she sicced her attorneys on my publisher in an unsuccessful attempt to control the book's contents. What, if anything, was Martha Stewart trying to hide from the millions who idolized her?

—JERRY OPPENHEIMER

Acknowledgments

This book could not have been written without the gracious help of some four hundred of Martha Stewart's friends, colleagues, associates, employees, acquaintances—present and former—and relatives who agreed to be interviewed. Their candor, perception, guidance, insights, and remembrances were remarkable, especially since most agreed to talk on the record about often controversial incidents and events.

A minority, for personal or professional reasons, requested and were granted anonymity. Not everyone is willing to put careers on the line or to jeopardize relationships. Most, if not all, of the information provided by those unnamed sources—and by all others interviewed—was cross-checked for accuracy with a number of other sources. My goal was to portray Martha Stewart in the truest and most objective light, and I believe my sources helped me to fulfill that end. I'm grateful to all of you who opened the door.

At the office where the digging, transcribing, filing, and researching began and ended, I'd like to express my thanks to a team of fine typist-transcribers, headed by Edna Turner. And once again my chief researcher, Caroline Howe, tracked down those sources who seemed to have dropped off the earth, and then got them to talk.

Finally, I'd like to express my sincere appreciation to everyone at William Morrow who helped bring this book to fruition, especially Paul Bresnick, my editor, who made certain my vision—from text to title to jacket design—was realized. My gratitude also goes to my literary agent, Stuart Krichevsky, who always keeps the ball rolling. And I owe a special thanks to Liza Dawson, who got it from the start.

Contents

There are no skeletons. There are no secrets.

—MARTHA STEWART
March 26, 1996

PART ONE

Cooking Up a Gingerbread Family

Fatal Attraction

It was after midnight when Martha Stewart arrived at her Westport, Connecticut, farmette, Turkey Hill, still raging, still furious, still seething. In a frenzy she had stormed through the lovingly restored 1805 farmhouse filled with antiques and *objets,* but devoid of life, and headed for the garage apartment in back, where her friend Kathy Tatlock was staying.

Not long before, Martha's life had spun irrevocably out of control when Andy Stewart, her lawyer-publisher-handyman husband, had fled the life they had carefully fabricated during more than a quarter century of marriage.

Andy's sudden departure had come at a very inauspicious time for Martha, who was riding high, with her career in a period of enormous growth. America was suddenly bullish on the once-poor girl from New Jersey whose fearsome drive, ambition, and unrivaled creativity had parlayed a relatively obscure catering business into what was fast becoming a multimedia juggernaut based on the simple premise of living well. Martha had recently signed a highly lucrative deal to become a spokeswoman for Kmart. She had also just starred in her first holiday television special on PBS and was preparing for her second. All her books, beginning with the first in 1982—the groundbreaking lifestyle guide *Entertaining*—were blockbusters. Corporate America was hurling offers at her. Thinking even bigger, wanting even more, she had dreams of starting a Martha

3

Stewart magazine and starring in her own regularly scheduled Martha Stewart television show. Martha saw herself as Betty Crocker, Julia Child, Miss Manners, Emily Post, and Rupert Murdoch all rolled into one juicy pie.

From all appearances Martha Stewart, Inc. was running on all four burners. But now "that stupid Andy, that idiot," as Martha often called her husband, had gone ahead and thrown a wrench into the works.

Besides being inopportune, the timing of Andy's escape was ironic. He had walked out while Martha was on the road aggressively pitching her latest book, *Martha Stewart Weddings,* which she had dedicated to him.

For years Andy had stood by his wife like a scared little boy with a mean stepmother, absorbing the shock of her abusiveness, her acid tongue, her intolerance, her anger, her drive for more, more, more, while at the same time inexplicably aiding and abetting her unabashed ambitions as her de facto legal, business, and creative adviser. He had tried to ward off the inevitable day of reckoning, but all his efforts to save the marriage, nudging Martha into marriage counseling and therapy, had failed. Martha wouldn't change, wouldn't admit wrongdoing, showed no remorse. Andy couldn't endure another minute of her. After much soul-searching he sat down one spring morning and drafted a "Dear Martha" letter at the big wooden table in their famous kitchen, then walked out the door.

Known as a control freak to her intimates, Martha was livid that Andy had on his own flown the coop. If the marriage were to end—and Martha herself had brought up the subject on numerous occasions, telling Andy what a dud he was as a husband—she would have wanted to be the one to end it. For once Andy had the balls to beat Martha at her own game, and she was furious.

Martha's reaction to Andy's flight appeared to have nothing to do with lost love, which made Andy hurt all the more. Her immediate concern was over the impact the split, and any possible scandal, might have on the Kmart executives who had chosen her in part because of her wholesome image.

Then Martha's fierce anger had kicked in, and she started

harassing Andy, to show him precisely how she felt about what he had done to her.

"I want you to see what that bastard made me do!" Martha shouted, pounding on the door of Kathy Tatlock's quarters above the former garage turned TV studio–kitchen. Martha had roused Tatlock from a troubled sleep to recount one of what were to be a number of confrontations between her and Andy.

Tatlock was exhausted after having undergone another emotionally grueling day, dealing with Martha's outbursts, fury, and deepening depression. A struggling, talented film and television director, widowed early with two daughters to feed and clothe, Tatlock had been lured to Turkey Hill by her friend of more than twenty years with the promise of a fifty-fifty split to produce a series of Martha Stewart home videos. In mid-production Andy had walked out, and Tatlock, trying to be Martha's "Rock of Gibraltar," was feeling the brunt of her anger and frustration.

"Martha was very agitated," Tatlock recalled. "She felt Andy had betrayed her with other women. She felt she had had plenty of opportunities to experiment with other men, but she said she had been faithful. So she felt doubly betrayed." Unknown to Tatlock, though, Martha had taunted Andy over the years with a few real, or invented, stories about flirtations and indiscretions of her own.

Martha told Tatlock that earlier in the evening she had met with Andy in Manhattan and once again they had argued over his leaving. Andy, on the other hand, had told a friend it was more of a frightening confrontation than a simple argument.

"He told me Martha was angry, that she was *imploring* him to return, *ordering* him to return, *demonstrating* how important it was that he cancel his plans to separate," the friend revealed. "She became so distraught that Andy feared for his own safety. He said, 'Had Martha had a gun or a knife in her hand my guess is she might have threatened me.'"

Instead Martha had turned her fury on herself.

"She came into my room, and she just exploded," Tatlock stated. "She launched into this whole thing about having seen Andy and his having been so horrible. She said it made her so furious. She said something about being so upset that she wanted to tear the hair out of her head.

"I was being sympathetic and said, 'Yeah, I've felt like that a couple of times myself.' And Martha said, 'No, I *really* did it.' Then she showed me a patch of scalp where she had actually pulled out her hair in front of Andy. It was terrible. I was alarmed. I suggested that she get some help.

"Martha said, 'Oh, I've already tried that, and it doesn't work for me because I'm always smarter than the shrink. I can always outsmart them.' I said, 'Well, isn't that self-defeating?' And she responded, 'Yeah, but it just doesn't work that way for me. I'm different.' "

Into the World

Martha Helen Kostyra was born seemingly happy and healthy at 1:33 P.M. on August 3, 1941, a warm, sunny Sunday, at the Margaret Hague Maternity Hospital, named after the mother of Frank Hague, the "Boss" of Jersey City, New Jersey, where the Kostyras lived. A week or so later the cute brown-eyed infant was christened at St. Ann's, the neighborhood Polish Catholic church.

Martha was the second child, the first daughter, of Edward Rudolf Kostyra, a handsome twenty-nine-year-old Jersey City public school physical education teacher, and Martha Ruszkowski Kostyra, a plain-looking twenty-six-year-old housewife, who also had a teaching degree.

For those who take astrology seriously, Martha would prove to be a perfect Leo like her father: egotistical, strong-willed, self-centered. In later years, after becoming a publishing mogul and media star, Martha believed strongly enough in her astrological sign, and its meaning, to throw a "Leo birthday party" for herself and two female friends.

Despite the *Jersey Journal*'s forecast of beautiful weather, a pall hung over the grimy industrial city on the Hudson the day Martha came wailing into the world. Because of Nazi hostilities across the Atlantic, and provocations by the Japanese in the Pacific, Jersey City was being placed on a near-wartime footing. Though the United States would not officially enter World War II for another four months, the mayor imposed a gasoline curfew to take effect at seven o'clock, some five hours after Martha's birth.

Leaving his car at the hospital, Eddie Kostyra had decided to walk the two miles to his home. At brightly lit Journal Square he stopped to buy a nickel cigar in honor of his new baby. Looking up at the movie marquees, he thought about catching a show. *The Bride Came C.O.D.*, with Jimmy Cagney and Bette Davis, was showing at the Stanley; Clark Gable and Rosalind Russell were in *They Met in Bombay* at Loew's. But he chose instead to continue homeward. Times were tough, and he knew he couldn't afford to splurge, what with another mouth to feed.

The best Eddie Kostyra could afford on his thousand-dollar-a-year teacher's salary was a tiny ground-floor flat in a two-story cracker box of a house, home to three other families, at 33 Stagg Street. There was no garden, no porch, just one step up to the front door. If one had to pick a house that *didn't* look like a Martha Stewart house, that would be it. The place was just two blocks from Liberty and Spruce, where Eddie Kostyra's hardworking Polish immigrant parents, Frank and Helen, operated Kostyra's Tavern.

The Sparrow Hill section of Jersey City Heights was a melting pot of struggling immigrant families, mostly Poles, like the Kostyras. Residents who lived on the eastern side of Sparrow Hill could see the beckoning possibilities of Manhattan, across the Hudson. The Kostyras' view, in the opposite direction, was of odoriferous Jersey garbage dumps, burial grounds for the odd bullet-riddled mobster.

Eddie Kostyra went to sleep that night presumably dreaming of all the opportunities that awaited his newborn. Surely, he must have thought, life would be better for her than it had been—and would be—for him.

At the hospital Martha Kostyra rested, weary from the hours it had taken to deliver her namesake. Luckily there had been nothing untoward about Martha Jr.'s birth, as there had been with Martha Sr.'s firstborn, Eric. The events surrounding Eric's birth on May 13, 1938, were a closely held family secret, one that would have embarrassed the very private and prideful Mrs. Kostyra had it been revealed.

For years no friends—and very few relatives—knew the secret. It wasn't until decades later, when Martha Sr. celebrated her eightieth birthday on September 16, 1994, that the cat was let out of the bag at a fancy Martha Stewartish bash.

Remembering the moment and its aftermath, Estelle Kostyra Bukowski Burke, Eddie Kostyra's sister, became livid. "It was just horrible," she sputtered. *"Horrible!"*

The trouble started when Eric, who years earlier Americanized his last name to Scott, arrived at the party at his famous sister's club, the tony Fairfield Hunt Club, and was told by another sibling that he'd be required to toast the matriarch of the Kostyra clan. "My sisters and brothers had handwritten notes of things to say about Mom," said Scott. "No one ever gave me advance warning, so I had to speak off the cuff to eighty people and kids. I thought, 'What am I going to say?' So I just stood up and said, 'Well, I guess the reason you're all here is because of me.' They looked at me, and I said, 'Yeah, if it wasn't for me, my mother wouldn't have gotten married.' "

An embarrassed silence fell over the gathering. The smile froze on Martha Sr.'s face. Her sister-in-law Estelle Burke, for one, was in "a state of shock," thinking, "I kept that secret from the time my brother Eddie and Martha were married. I never told my children. I never told *anybody*!"

Her married daughter Diane Carey said she had "guessed" the secret years earlier. "I knew Eric was conceived out of wedlock, but he wasn't *born* out of wedlock. I just didn't say anything, and nothing was said, so I thought it was dropped—until my aunt's party.''

Another cousin, Rudy Krukar, came rushing up to Eric. ''If your grandmother [Helen Kostyra] was alive today,'' he said, infuriated, ''she'd be so upset with you for saying that because her Eddie could do no wrong.''

''Well, he didn't do wrong,'' Eric responded wryly. ''He married her.''

For the Kostyras and the Ruszkowskis, the shotgun wedding was scandalous. Staunchly Catholic, the two families were the kind that had their houses blessed every Easter by the local parish priest, so an out-of-wedlock pregnancy was against everything the Bible and the church taught them.

Eddie had met Martha, daughter of a Polish immigrant ironworker from Buffalo, at a Polish heritage summer session on the bucolic western Pennsylvania campus of Alliance College, founded and sponsored by the fraternal Polish National Alliance and funded by the Tadeusz Kosciuszko Foundation.

But from what everyone who claims knowledge of their meeting has said, the Kostyra boy and Ruszkowski girl apparently were more interested in the birds and the bees than learning about polkas and pirogi.

''They ran off and eloped,'' said Martha Sr.'s younger sister Clementine Ruszkowski Carriere.

''Dad joked that he spent his marriage night behind bars because they were getting married by the justice of the peace at the local jail in some town between Buffalo and New York City,'' Eric Scott said. ''By the time they got around to having a church wedding, which was demanded by the parents on both sides, Mom was already pregnant with me. In those days, if a woman was three weeks premature, right away all the old women had their calendars out counting days.''

Estelle Burke remembered the story somewhat differently. ''Eddie and Martha said they had to get married in a hurry, and they wanted me to be their witness. I couldn't go, so my cousin Rudy's father, who ran a deli in Jersey

City, went. They were married down at city hall in Jersey
City. Then around Christmas there was a small church wedding in Buffalo. I was the maid of honor.''

Whichever way it happened, it's clear that Martha Stewart's mother became pregnant with her first child in the late
summer of 1937. On September 7, nine days before her
twenty-third birthday, she and Eddie Kostyra were wedded
in a civil ceremony. That December the couple shuffled off
to Buffalo to take their formal vows at the Ruszkowskis'
Catholic church. Five months later Eric was born.

It was bad enough that Eric Scott had revealed the family
secret in front of a hundred or so guests. But his sister
Martha's next move absolutely floored relatives.

By the time of her mother's eightieth birthday, Martha
had soared to the level of genuine American icon. Her most
lucrative venture was a two-hundred-million-dollar multimedia partnership with Time Warner that included a hugely
popular magazine that had her name and usually her picture
gracing the cover, a feat no one in publishing could rival.

As the magazine's domineering editrix Martha had a
hand in choosing every story, picture, and caption that appeared in *Martha Stewart Living*. Thus she had decided to
report on her mother's party in a signed introduction to
Special Occasions: The Best of Martha Stewart Living, a
compilation of menus, recipes, and entertaining ideas. (She
also dedicated her 1994 book *Martha Stewart's Menus for
Entertaining*, ''To my mother, Martha Kostyra, on the occasion of her eightieth birthday.'')

Martha's devoted fans had become familiar with Kostyra
family lore from her books and from a page in the back of
her magazine where Martha often waxed nostalgic about
growing up in the little town of Nutley, New Jersey. Martha
Sr. had become like a character in a soap opera or a comic
strip being penned by her daughter. Those stories gave
readers the *perception* of familial warmth that was a key
ingredient in Martha's product and they helped make Martha seem more human and lovable.

''1994 was an important year in our family's history,''
Martha informed her readers. Falling into her inimitable

chummy style, she told how the party had taken months of planning, how her mother had told her that she wanted "a bash with all my friends and family that everyone will remember." Martha described drawing up the guest list, dividing party chores with her siblings, using tissue-lined envelopes for the invitations that "greatly enhanced the look of the card," planning the menu, baking the "tiered yellow pound cake with black-currant filling," enlisting the piano teacher of one of her nephews to play the Steinway, having the entire event videotaped as an "important memoir" for the grandchildren. The article described a picture-perfect Martha Stewart party, chock-full of Martha Stewart tips for Martha Stewart wannabes to use for their own Martha Stewartesque special occasions.

However, there was one ingredient that Martha left out of her recipe for a successful party: If one can avoid footing the whole bill, one should do so. And that's just what Martha did, according to her brother Frank Kostyra.

"Martha *sponsored* the party," Kostyra asserted. "Mom actually paid for it. It was Mom's party, and Mom requested it. Martha just followed up."

Kostyra, who had been feuding with his sister for years, claiming emotional and physical scars to prove it, said he'd received a bill from Martha Stewart, Inc., his sister's company, for fourteen hundred dollars to cover his share of the party costs, and he assumed that the other siblings had gotten similar invoices.

With her description of the joy and happiness, the fond embraces and smiles of everyone present, Martha could easily have ended her published remembrance of her mother's milestone eightieth on an upbeat note. Instead, inexplicably, she decided to spill the beans and make public the whole sordid mess, letting at least 1.2 million readers in on her mother's deepest and darkest secret. "Our parents had eloped before the real wedding," Martha wrote, "and Mother was actually pregnant when she had the formal ceremony."

The family went ballistic.

"She said it was a shotgun wedding, and that's what kills me," declared Estelle Burke, Martha's aunt and godmother.

"After I read it, I called Martha Sr. to tell her what little Martha did, and she said, 'Oh, Martha wouldn't do that.' I said, 'Don't bet on it!' " I sent her a copy of the article, but she never responded. She must have been furious.

"My feeling is Martha will do anything to feather her own nest. Who got benefit from that? Nobody except Martha Stewart."

From Poland with Love

If Martha inherited her epicurean and entrepreneurial talents, her imperial manner, and hard-nosed business style from anyone, that person might well have been her paternal grandfather, Franz Josef Kostyra.

Sailing past the Statue of Liberty into New York Harbor in 1905, Franz Kostyra looked far different from the tired, poor, huddled masses arriving from all over Europe during that great wave of immigration. At twenty-six, Kostyra was a man of strength, bearing, and vigor who towered over his sickly looking fellow travelers. When snow fell in the old country, Kostyra gleefully doffed his clothing and danced in the white stuff. Imposing at well over six feet, he had served in the military honor guard of his namesake, Emperor Franz Josef of Austria, a member of the ancient ruling family of Hapsburg.

The earliest Kostyras lived in the medieval kingdom of Poland, which was partitioned among Prussia, Russia, and Austria-Hungary in the late eighteenth century. When Franz Kostyra was born in 1879, the Poles under the rule of Franz

Josef fared somewhat better than those under the Prussians or Russians. The emperor adopted relatively liberal internal policies, giving Poles some semblance of self-government, even permitting them to form their own political parties.

Because of his height, equestrian talents, and the fact that the Kostyras had come from a line of warriors dating back to the Crusades—family lore tells of a crest emblazoned with broken spears and arrows—Franz Kostyra had been recruited into the emperor's honor guard and participated in many colorful parades, proudly riding one of the famed Lippizaner horses.

But young Kostyra, who had no real formal education, was determined to learn a trade that would put bread and butter on the family's table when he returned to civilian life. Volunteering for training as a cook, he found his calling. Kostyra learned everything from baking to running a mess hall. By the end of his enlistment he knew the meat and potatoes of food preparation and restaurant management, all of which served him well when he landed in America.

Kostyra, who arrived in New York with a survivor mentality—one that his granddaughter Martha would inherit—started at the bottom at Childs, a cafeteria chain that had white tile walls to emphasize cleanliness and discourage loitering. By the time he got a job behind the steam counter, Childs was starting to boom, aided in part by temperance pressure against taverns. Demonstrating ambition and drive, Kostyra, who now called himself Frank, quickly moved up the Childs food chain. Before long he was overseeing the opening of new restaurants, developing recipes, hiring and training kitchen workers.

One night at a Polish social club he met Helen Krukar, a pretty teenager eleven years his junior, and they fell in love and were married after a short courtship. After they had tied the knot, she got a job working in the household of a wealthy New York City family, the Oppenheimers, and the newlyweds moved into a crowded apartment building on Madison Avenue, between 107th and 108th streets, where other Krukars lived. Unlike the Kostyras, the Krukars had a difficult time assimilating. Helen often recounted

the story of how back in Galicia a family of storks had
established a nest on the chimney of the Krukars' thatched-
roof cottage. The storks' decision to take up residence
there, the Krukars believed, was a good sign, a lucky omen,
and the family made no effort to force the birds to leave.
But Helen's belief in that old wives' tale was severely
shaken with the birth of her first child in America. The
baby, a girl whom the happy parents named Stacia, was
taken seriously ill and soon died. Helen was devastated.
The memory of Stacia's inexplicable death haunted Helen
Kostyra for the rest of her life.

Despite this tragedy, she became pregnant again, and on
August 21, 1911, the apple of her eye came into the world.
He was a beautiful baby with bright blue eyes and a shock
of blond curly hair. The Kostyras lovingly named him Edward Rudolf. For Helen Kostyra, Eddie's birth had reaf-
firmed the peasant story about the goodness of the stork.

But, like Stacia's, little Eddie's health was poor too. He
suffered from innumerable childhood illnesses and ailments, including frequent nosebleeds that caused Helen
enormous concern. Because of his problems and her memory of Stacia, Helen coddled, spoiled, and nursed the future
father of Martha Stewart. Despite the fact that Helen had
two more children—Estelle in 1917 and Henrik in 1922—
Eddie was always her favorite. "She babied him along all
through his life," Henrik ("Hank") Kostyra observed.

Unlike his wife, however, Frank Kostyra was a stern
taskmaster, who didn't believe in coddling the boy.
"Grandfather would hold a lit cigarette under Dad's elbow
to force him to keep his arm up when he was practicing
the violin," Eric Scott offered. "*That* was Grandfather."

By 1920, at the age of forty-one, Frank Kostyra had been
with Childs for fifteen years, and the chain had plans to
name him manager of its flagship restaurant on Fifth Avenue, but tired of being a working stiff, he decided to strike
out on his own. That year he moved the family across the
Hudson to Jersey City, where Kostyra saw greater opportunities for himself.

With the city's large Polish population, and a mayor who
was a benevolent despot much like Emperor Franz Josef,

Kostyra immediately felt at home. Even Jersey City's cops—tough Irishmen and Poles who were required to stand at least six feet tall—reminded Kostyra of the emperor's honor guard, in which he had proudly served.

Because of his expertise in the food business, Frank Kostyra decided to open a butcher shop, specializing in cut-to-order prime meats. Money to start the business wasn't a problem. Kostyra had socked away virtually every penny he had ever earned, frugality being another family trait. "Dad worked hard for his money, up early in the morning and working until late at night," said Hank Kostyra. "Very seldom did we have a vacation. We're all the same—all the Kostyras. We work hard, and we hold on to what we have."

Kostyra paid cash for the little butcher shop at 730 Newark Avenue from a fat wad of dough with a rubber band around it that he kept in his hip pocket. He called the business Kostyra's Meats. The family moved into a three-story apartment house two blocks south of the store, at 3041 Hudson Boulevard, and joined the local parish church, St. Ann's. The kids, Eddie, Estelle, and Hank, went to nearby public schools, and their father joined the Society of Sons of Poland Group III—a fraternal organization.

But his most important move as a newly arrived businessman was to become allied with Mayor Hague's powerful Hudson County Democratic Association, the machine that kept the Irish Catholic political boss in power for a mind-boggling three decades, without his ever once getting indicted for a political crime or misdemeanor. Though Hague's mayoral salary was modest, he somehow managed to buy a fancy house on the Jersey shore, enjoy a posh apartment on Manhattan's Park Avenue, and winter at his chic place in sunny Florida. And every year he took a European vacation.

"Dad was very active with Hague," Hank Kostyra said. "They were buddy-buddy."

To stay in favor, Frank Kostyra always made certain that the finest cuts of his shop's primest meats were on the mayor's dinner table and that his campaign contributions were in Hague's pocket. Solid citizens and supporters like

Kostyra, who were on the mayor's A list, were generously rewarded for such civic-mindedness and generosity.

Once, when Hank Kostyra was out playing in a vacant lot, he fell on a broken bottle and required specialized treatment for the injury that could have resulted in the loss of a hand. "Dad called Hague, who called the hospital, the Hague Memorial Center, and told them I needed help," Kostyra said. "Hague said, 'Send him up there, we'll get him treated.' I went up there, and they gave me a room and the best doctors. We never got a bill. Hague was a good guy."

Frank Kostyra's Buick eventually sported a very low Hudson County license number. "If you had below ten, you didn't have to worry about anything. You could park anywhere without getting a ticket. Dad had tag number eight or nine," Hank Kostyra recalled. "The traffic cops stood on these little pedestals in the middle of the street, and when they saw Dad's tag coming, they'd salute. When he took his car for service, he'd go next door to the precinct house and borrow a police car and use it for the rest of the day. That's the kind of deal he had with Hague."

By 1925 Kostyra had tired of the butcher business and sold the shop to a brother-in-law. "By that time my father also had a couple of butcher shops up in Union City," Hank Kostyra said. "He would buy different businesses. He bought and sold property. Dad was a speculator. He took chances. He'd buy a business and run it himself for a while, and then he'd put it up for sale. He'd say, 'I'll turn it over to you, and you run it for a month or two, and if you decide to keep it, you pay me off on it, and it's yours.' Before the guy even had a chance to change his mind, my dad would get the guy's money in his hand."

Frank Kostyra also made a nice dollar by lending money and charging interest on the loan. Even though Kostyra charged hefty rates, the borrowers thought of him as a benevolent man because no one else would give them credit. The borrowers were working stiffs like the big black man who showed up unexpectedly one afternoon at the Kostyras' front door, scaring Helen half to death, to repay a loan he had received from her husband. "He didn't have me sign *no* papers, just a handshake,'' the black man told Helen Kostyra when he handed her the money.

Despite Prohibition, Frank Kostyra traded his butcher's apron for a barkeep's garb and bought Billy Marx's Tavern, at 153 Liberty Avenue, which he renamed Kostyra's Tavern. The slogan on his business card read: ''Good Beer Served Here . . . All Kind of Best Wines and Liquor.'' Kostyra was free to sell all the booze he could because the mayor never seriously enforced the national law on the sale of beer, wine, and liquor.

''I guess we had the largest bar in Jersey City until somebody bought another place and made the bar a little longer,'' Hank Kostyra said.

The Kostyras took up residence in an apartment above the tavern; the place was big enough for the two brothers, Eddie and Hank, to share a room and for their sister, Estelle, to have one of her own. It was a comfortable apartment, and the family resided there for almost two full decades—through the Depression and most of World War II.

Being the Man

Eddie Kostyra's family believed he was a boy genius, and he certainly had acted the part. If he wasn't buried in a book, he was at center stage, reeling off what he knew to anyone who would listen. He appeared to be an expert on everything, though some thought of him as a bit of an oddball or a boorish braggart. Because of all the attention, especially from his mother, he grew up believing he was special, and he had the extraordinary ability to convince others of his uniqueness, a trait his daughter Martha inherited and utilized with far greater success.

Usually at his mother's side because of his early illnesses, Kostyra had learned housewifery skills that most boys his age would have fled from. With enthusiasm he took up cooking and had a flair for gardening and an eye for fashion and design. Sewing fascinated the boy, so much so that Helen Kostyra's lady friends were green with envy over the way little Eddie wielded a needle and thread. The boy also was artistic and creative, with a penchant for drawing and writing.

But there was nothing effeminate about him. In fact, once over his childhood ailments, Eddie, who physically took after his father, grew into a handsome and strapping young man of six feet two, with curly blond hair and flirtatious blue eyes. He was athletic, became an equestrian and a handyman. He enjoyed learning how things worked and discovered how to fix them when they stopped working. "He had what you'd call a photographic mind," Eddie's brother, Hank, stated. "Eddie was a walking encyclopedia," said his sister, Estelle. "You mentioned a word, and he'd tell you what it meant. I thought he swallowed a dictionary."

Martha Stewart's brother Frank Kostyra, who was named after his paternal grandfather, firmly believed that all the children in his family, *especially* Martha, had inherited their father's mind power: "We have a talent for looking at something just once—like watching someone bake a cake or lay bricks—and being able to do it right away. We could walk into someone's kitchen and smell something cooking on the stove and pretty much know what the ingredients were and go home and duplicate it. It's in the blood. It's in the genes."

At Jersey City's William L. Dickinson High School, where his pals called him Curley, Eddie Kostyra was the sole drum major for the marching band and sang with the glee club. Following in his father's path, Kostyra had taken up horseback riding and was accepted into an elite cavalry outfit, the Essex Troop, which had a reputation for smart appearance and high military standards on the order of Emperor Franz Josef's honor guard. When the troop was ordered to help quell a mob of angry strikers, Kostyra was in the center of the action, and for years he kept a newspaper photo of himself in uniform on horseback galloping after a frightened picket.

In June 1929 Kostyra graduated from Dickinson High with a general curriculum diploma. While there was no mention of any academic achievements in his yearbook, *The Gnome,* someone wrote: "Music hath its charms especially when played by Ed, who was interested in almost every musical organization at school." Another yearbook photo noted: "The Band will lose its tall, handsome Drum Major, Eddie Kostyra, through graduation."

From day one the Kostyra family saw great things for their Eddie, and there was talk about him becoming a doctor, a perfect profession for a young man who possessed a steel trap for a mind. But that was not to be. A high school gym teacher had advised him that the future was physical education, not medicine. Kostyra, who was a decent, if unspectacular, athlete—he entertained family and friends by balancing with one hand on a Coca-Cola box and juggling Indian clubs—took the teacher's advice.

With money from his parents to cover an annual tuition of $275 ($290 in his senior year), Kostyra enrolled at a small school called the Panzer College of Physical Education and Hygiene, in nearby East Orange. The school was in the business district, in a two-story building that had several classrooms, a laboratory, and a gymnasium. Since there was no campus, the students played outdoor sports in nearby public parks. When Kostyra enrolled, Panzer offered three years of training, but it became a four-year college when he was a junior, allowing him to earn a bachelor's degree in physical education. Granted, Panzer wasn't the Harvard School of Medicine, and Helen Kostyra's boy genius wouldn't be performing brain surgery, as she had dreamed, but he was the first Kostyra to earn a college degree.

At the height of the Depression Kostyra seemed to be

living the life of a rich college boy, riding horses, playing tennis, and driving to school in a new Ford Model A roadster with a rumble seat that his father bought him at the insistence of his doting mother. Eddie had promised his father that he'd earn part of his keep by using the car to deliver telegrams for Western Union, but he usually had more pleasurable pursuits. So he had found an out. "Eddie would go pick up the telegrams," Hank Kostyra said with a chuckle, "but I'd wind up delivering them."

At Panzer Kostyra's reputation as a bookworm continued. "Everything he read, he took in that brain of his," his brother said. "In college he had to draw pictures of the torso, the muscles, and hell, they looked better than photographs. Besides his studies, he had a real artistic ability." Those drawings also underscored Kostyra's perfectionism and his obsession with detail, both success-oriented traits that failed him but were passed on to Martha, who used them with great success.

While Kostyra's aesthetic side was highly visible in his work at Panzer, his athletic abilities didn't shine on the playing fields. "Eddie just wasn't much of an athlete," remembered classmate Hazel Wacker. "He had more artistic traits. We took English, sociology, psychology, and he liked those kinds of things more. We had basketball, baseball, and soccer teams, but he never went out for those. The whole time Eddie was there the only team he was on was track, and he was a member of the badminton club. He was not a strong athlete. He was more of a scholar and a dreamer."

To broaden his cultural horizons, Kostyra decided that a European trip was mandatory for his education. With his father picking up the tab, once again at his mother's insistence, young Kostyra spent a summer break touring the Continent, a luxury unheard of at the peak of the Depression, when millions of American families were on the relief rolls.

Kostyra returned home with hundreds of snapshots of his odyssey abroad—photography was one of his passions—and with a doozer of a story. "He said he met the king of Sweden and that the king had invited him to play tennis,"

Hank Kostyra recalled. ''Eddie told us he was beating the king and that during a break in the match they told my brother it was customary for the king to win. So Eddie let him win.'' Kostyra's tale of the royal tennis match—undoubtedly embellished, if not made up out of whole cloth—underscored his penchant for exaggeration, another facet of his personality that Martha Stewart inherited.

In 1933 Kostyra was among about a dozen Panzer students who were the first to graduate from the college with bachelor's degrees in physical education. His yearbook picture showed a handsome, serious young man in a three-piece suit. The caption, written by the yearbook staff, read: ''The race is not always to the swift. Time reckons with all men. Eddie started slowly, but there is that indescribable idealistic air about him that makes it almost impossible to know where his accomplishments match his artistic leanings. Such a man bears watching.''

Finding a Mate

By the time Eddie Kostyra met Martha Ruszkowski, his bride-to-be, at that summer of 1937 Polish heritage seminar in Pennsylvania, he had been working as a gym teacher in the Jersey City public school system for several years.

Not many other Panzer graduates could make that claim, it still being the Depression. Kostyra's college classmate Hazel Wacker, for one, recalled, ''There weren't an awful lot of jobs available for us. I didn't have a real job for three years after I graduated.'' But Kostyra didn't face bleak unemployment like others. Right out of Panzer he landed a teaching job because of his father's pull at city hall.

But spending eight hours a day instructing sweaty adolescents on how to climb ropes and hang from rings without falling on their heads wasn't Kostyra's idea of career heaven. He had come to the realization that his high school gym teacher had given him a bum steer. Kostyra wanted bigger things for himself.

At night he took college credit courses in a variety of subjects, hoping to move into a more lucrative and interesting career. He saw himself as a man of many talents and with a great future. But Martha Ruszkowski's unplanned pregnancy, and their sudden marriage, stopped him dead in his tracks.

"Eddie tried to make the best of a bad situation. They both did," observed a Kostyra family member. "But Eddie had a lot of resentment in him. He felt his life was over before it had really started. Eddie's dreams were definitely shattered, and it made him a bitter and angry man through much of his life. Martha Senior wasn't really happy either. She had wanted to teach and not jump into marriage and have kids right away. But she was able to handle life's slings and arrows more realistically than Eddie. He always had those visions of greatness, and he possessed that inflated ego, and it always got in the way."

Unlike the Kostyras, the Ruszkowskis were not entrepreneurs. As one Ruszkowski family member observed, "Eddie's father had his own business, and Martha's father was a laborer. But everybody worked hard. There really wasn't that much difference between both families."

Martha's parents, Joe Ruszkowski and Franciska Albeniak, were of the farming class. They had come to America before World War I from towns near Warsaw and Lublin where the Albeniaks were fortunate to own a small parcel of land and Ruszkowski's father was believed to have been the *Bürgermeister* of a tiny village. "Actually, our parents lived fairly close together in Poland but didn't know each other until they came to this country," said Clementine Ruszkowski Carriere, Martha Sr.'s younger sister. "Father came to this country because he was scheduled to go into the Russian Army and he did not want to do this because there was so much hatred between the Russians and the Poles.''

Joe Ruszkowski, who had left behind a younger brother, knowing he would be excused from military service because he was the family's sole surviving son, settled in Buffalo, New York's large Polish community, where he knew someone from his hometown. Arrangements had been made by the Albeniaks for Franciska to move to the community of Perry, New York, where a job was supposed to have been waiting for her. But when she arrived, there was no work, so she too migrated to Buffalo, where she found menial labor. ''They didn't know English, other than a few words,'' Carriere said of her parents. ''They met when both of them moved into the same boardinghouse. My mother was supposed to have been here for only a year. But then she met my father and decided to stay permanently.''

Joe Ruszkowski became an ironworker, a job he held for the rest of his life. Between 1914 and 1925 his wife brought four children into the world: two girls and two boys. The firstborn, named Martha, would be Martha Stewart's mother.

All the children were raised in a two-story wood-frame single-family house, at 42 Guilford Street, on Buffalo's predominantly Polish East Side. ''We always had tenants either upstairs or downstairs from us,'' Carriere said. Because of the Ruszkowskis' poor circumstances, Francis worked as a seamstress in her spare time to bring in extra money, and she taught her daughters how to make their own clothing. Martha became skilled at dressmaking and sewing, a talent she passed on to her namesake.

Years later Martha Kostyra wrote to her son Frank and told him of the hardships she had endured. ''She talked about her early childhood, growing up with nothing, sharing a bedroom with her sister, and the two brothers sharing another bedroom. The house had central heat: one coal stove in the center. She grew up with nothing, and the first time she had something was when my parents married.''

The Ruszkowskis had scrimped and saved for their children's education. One son became a lawyer, another an engineer, and Martha got a teaching degree. She was scheduled to welcome her first class in September 1937, in the town of Slogan, New York, but that was before she became pregnant and eloped with Eddie Kostyra. Despite the fact that her life had suddenly been turned upside down, Martha fulfilled the teaching contract she had signed, working while pregnant. She then moved to Jersey City, where she and her husband rented the little apartment on Stagg Street where Eric was born. Several years later Martha came along, and then the others, six children in all.

"It was boy, girl, boy, girl, boy, girl," family members said. With a growing brood to care for, Martha Ruszkowski Kostyra's dream of a teaching career went up in smoke. She did not return to the classroom until the last child, Laura, was in kindergarten, in the early sixties.

On a lazy Sunday morning in December 1941, four months after Martha's birth, America entered World War II when the Japanese attacked the U.S. naval base at Pearl Harbor. Soon, tens of thousands of able-bodied men were enlisting and being drafted every day to serve in the armed forces. Among those going off to fight was the Essex Troop, of which Eddie Kostyra had been a proud member. On April 6, 1942, the unit became a fully mechanized armored cavalry regiment, and it did valiant battle in the European theater. Eddie Kostyra's brother Hank enlisted in the navy and served from 1943 to 1946 as an aviation machine specialist.

Somehow, though, Martha's father was able to remain at home. The way Hank Kostyra remembered the situation, his brother avoided conscription because "of the kids" and "because he was a teacher." But through most of the war the Kostyras had only two children. It was odd that Kostyra avoided the draft since millions of healthy men with small families like his were called to bear arms.

Frank Kostyra, Eddie's second son, the third of the children, who was born on February 3, 1945, about six months before the war ended, said, "When I asked Dad what he did in the war, he said he was in the cavalry, and it was his duty to patrol. He said, 'Some went, some didn't. I was chosen not to go.' But it was never very explicit about why he did't go overseas.''

In any case, Kostyra did serve his country on the home front, working at the federal shipyard and dry dock, in nearby Kearny. "When he started there, Eddie told me he made suggestions to his supervisor for speeding up production,'' Hank Kostyra said. "Ed said the supervisor asked him, 'Well, how the hell do you know that? Are you a college graduate or something?' My brother said, 'Well, I happen to have *several* degrees.' And so they took his suggestions and made him superintendent of outfitting and rigging. Ed told me he was able to get the destroyer escorts out way ahead of schedule. He said he even took the ships on test runs to look for problems.''

The senior Kostyras, Frank and Helen, continued to operate their tavern through the war years. But the patriarch's death from pneumonia the day after Christmas 1943 turned the family's world upside down. All the Kostyras had relied on his strength and support, and now he was gone. He died without leaving a will. Letters of administration valued his estate at twenty-five hundred dollars.

After her husband's death Helen Kostyra, then sixty-three, tried to make a go of running the tavern herself. "Mom took it over for a couple of years,'' Hank Kostyra said. "It was nothing but hardship because if you don't keep the family in it, you get robbed to death. I caught one of the workers carrying out a bundle of garbage, and I looked in it, and it was full of bottles of booze. So it didn't pay to run it anymore. It was too much for her.''

The widow moved in permanently with her daughter, Estelle, who was now married and living a few blocks from the family tavern. Estelle was to support her mother for the rest of her life, a sensitive issue that caused dissension between her and her brother Eddie for years to come.

Meanwhile Eddie and Martha Kostyra, with two children and a third on the way, had decided that they wanted to leave the growing urban blight of Jersey City and move out to the suburbs, where the air was fresh and the grass green, where he could have a garden.

With the down payment given to him by his devoted

mother, Kostyra bought an asbestos-sided, two-story, three-bedroom, one-bath Depression-era house, with a full basement, a small sun room, a tiny sewing room, and an unfinished attic, for eight thousand dollars.

Martha had just turned three that fall of 1944 when the moving van pulled up in front of 86 Elm Place, in the town of Nutley, a quiet and pleasant community, a short bus ride from Manhattan. Cowgirl Annie Oakley had once been a resident, Mark Twain used to summer there, and Jacqueline Kennedy Onassis's father's family, the Bouviers, once owned a house there. The town was known for its gracious parks, good schools, and the development of the antianxiety drugs Librium and Valium. Today its claim to fame is that it's the place where Martha Stewart grew up.

A Dysfunctional Family

With the end of the war and the start of defense plant cutbacks, Eddie Kostyra suddenly found himself out of a job. Whatever fantasies he'd had about entering a *real* profession had all but faded. Now he faced the empty prospect of finding a new line of work to pay the bills for his growing family. Martha was five years old and about to enter kindergarten when her father decided to become a salesman.

"It was the perfect job for Eddie," said a relative. "He was a bullshit artist. He was a storyteller. He had the ability to embellish and overstate. He could be charming. He knew how to make a presentation. He was bright, quick, and articulate. Most important, he believed in whatever he sold, and he believed in himself. As it turned out, Martha, of all of Eddie's children, turned out most like him.''

Because his parents had wanted him to become a doctor and because he had a passing knowledge of chemistry, biology, anatomy, and health issues from his courses at Panzer, Kostyra decided to hustle pharmaceuticals. His first job was with Pfizer Inc., which had been propelled into the modern drug business when the company was asked to mass-produce penicillin for the war effort. Kostyra got a base salary, commissions, and a company car. For Martha it was a happy time, because every summer Pfizer hosted a family day at Coney Island, and she could go on the amusement rides for free.

But that wasn't enough of a perk to keep her father on the payroll. Over the years he held a succession of medical and hospital drug and supply sales jobs. For Ayerst Laboratories, for instance, he pitched cod-liver oil, vitamins, and female hormones. "But if another company bettered the offer, and gave him a nicer car, he'd take it," Hank Kostyra noted.

Like the fictional Willie Loman, Kostyra had an overblown view of his salesmanship and was knocked for a loop whenever he was passed over for a promotion or, worse, lost a job. "At one company Dad was director of sales for a certain district, and he could call all the shots," recalled Eric Scott. "Then the company manager hired his cousin and bumped Dad." That, Scott remembered, was a difficult time for the family. To help make ends meet, Martha Sr. had to find work. "She had a teaching degree, but she did not have a teaching certificate at the time in New Jersey," her son said. "She became a parochial school teacher for a time until Dad found a new job."

Kostyra loved to see his name in print, and whenever he secured a new position with a prestigious-sounding title, he made sure the Nutley *Sun* gave him a mention, such as the time he was promoted from "special professional service representative" to "eastern regional manager" of a firm that manufactured anti-infection aids for hospitals.

Always intellectually curious, Kostyra set up a small lab

of sorts in the basement and experimented with different drugs in hopes of finding a formula to grow giant tomatoes in his yard. But he experimented on humans too. "Dad doctored us up with a lot of the samples that he had," Frank Kostyra recalled. "We were always taking new drug inventions."

Eddie Kostyra boasted that local physicans regularly sought his advice on dispensing drugs to their patients. On one occasion he claimed he had saved the life of a neighbor's father, a heart patient, by spotting a wrong prescription that a doctor had written for him. Kostyra crowed that the prestigious *New England Journal of Medicine* had become aware of his work and had once made mention of him. (A check of the journal's index shows no such reference.) Another story involved saving the lives of a herd of valuable cows badly burned in a fire and how afterward the grateful farmer had delivered free dairy products to the Kostyras' door for months.

Despite his claimed successes, Kostyra felt frustrated that he wasn't more than a poor salesman whose top salary and commissions added up to thirteen thousand dollars in his best year. "Eddie felt he never reached his potential," Martha Sr.'s sister, Clementine Carriere, sadly observed. "He was a very smart man, but nothing seemed to gel for him."

Eddie Kostyra's feeling of failure and frustration with his lot in life often manifested itself in an uncontrolled fury that erupted at home, an anger that verged on abuse.

"Dad was physical with us," Frank Kostyra asserted. "He had a fiery temper, and when we misbehaved or got out of line, we got the stick or the belt. Martha resented Dad. She *hated* him in many respects. I know she never forgave him for kicking her in the back one time on the front sidewalk for some incident. She said, 'I'll *never* forgive him.' "

Kostyra said that his mother also was a victim. "Mom denies it and says, 'Oh, it never happened,' but there was some beating going on between the two of them, and I was in the middle trying to push them apart. There was pushing and slapping around. Mom had a lot of her own opinions that clashed with Dad's, and sparks flew. They spoke Polish when they got heated, so we couldn't really tell what they were fighting about. That's the only reason I think they never taught us the language.

"One time they were in the little alcove between the kitchen and the living room and they got into a squabble and were going at it hot and heavy. I was maybe eight years old, and Martha was around twelve. They were smacking each other. It was a severe disagreement, and I remember crying out, 'Why don't you just go and divorce him?' I don't know where I got that from. Maybe Mom was saying, 'If you continue this, I'm going to divorce you.' I used to be afraid of that."

Eddie Kostyra also enjoyed teasing his wife with talk about other women. "My father fancied himself a ladies' man, which he wasn't, but he always talked about how, when he was traveling, the stewardesses were always looking at him," Eric Scott recalled. "He was a good-looking guy, and he played up on that. Mom would hear stories, but she would let things go by the by. Maybe he was trying to piss her off because he liked a lot of attention. He always wanted to get a rise out of somebody and always at *their* expense."

The Kostyra Brothers' description of their father—and life at 86 Elm Place—is far different from the happy family portrait that Martha Stewart has painted in her magazine and books. Beginning in 1982 with the publication of *Entertaining*, Martha has regaled millions of readers with delightful stories about the warm and loving family members who nurtured her talents and taught her skills—particularly her father.

As Martha has portrayed them, the Kostyras were truly an idealized family: Ed and Martha Sr., the picture-perfect, hardworking parents, bursting with love, wisdom, and support; Martha, Kathy, Laura, Eric, Frank, and George, the devoted, industrious, creative children. Then there were all those wonderful aunts, uncles, and cousins and the wizened grandparents from the old country—in all, a truly close-

knit and loving nuclear family, the kind almost everyone
would want to have.

According to Martha's account, the Kostyras were virtual
mirror images of another well-known family, the idyllic all-
American Andersons: Jim and Margaret and their squeaky-
clean brood—ponytailed, saddle-shoed Betty, better known
as Princess; adolescent car- and girl-crazy Bud; and little
button-nosed Kathy, affectionately dubbed Kitten. The Andersons of course were fictitious, brought to life by a troupe
of talented actors: Robert Young, Jane Wyatt, Elinor Donahue, Billy Gray, and Lauren Chapin. On the other hand,
the Kostyras were real. Perhaps, then, it's purely coinci-
dental that the Kostyras seemed so much like the Andersons
of *Father Knows Best,* the ultimate hi-honey-I'm-home
family situation comedy of the vanilla Eisenhower and
Kennedy eras, when Martha was growing up. Perhaps not.

According to childhood friends of Martha's, *Father
Knows Best* was one of her favorite TV programs, one that
she began watching religiously at the impressionable age
of thirteen. *Father Knows Best* lasted from October 1954
to April 1963, roughly the Nutley years that Martha has
written about and described so effusively.

"In many ways Martha was a clone of Betty Anderson,"
recalled a pal from those days. "She was cute and perky,
mature and active. If Martha ever had a role model from
TV, it would have been Betty Anderson. Martha loved that
show and probably fantasized about being in a family just
like the Andersons—because the Kostyras were far from
that ideal, despite what Martha has written. Today, when I
read Martha's books and magazines and those family reminiscences of hers, I have to wonder whether she's still
fantasizing about the Andersons. But it works. It *sells.*"

Like the fictional Andersons, the Kostyras of Martha's
vision personified everything that was right about mid-
1950s–early 1960s American family values, key ingredients
in the lifestyle recipe that Martha has marketed so successfully. Eddie Kostyra, according to the way Martha has described him, was much like Jim Anderson: wise, thoughtful,
responsible, rational, a loving role model and mentor. To
underscore her feelings, Martha dedicated *Entertaining* in

part to: "My Father, for instilling in me a love for all things beautiful."

In *Martha Stewart's Gardening,* published a decade later, she acknowledges her father "for being my first teacher of gardening. His love of growing things was transferred to me through our gardening together. I will remember what he taught me forever."

Her most vivid memories of childhood, Martha told her readers, was of planting seeds indoors with her father and of spending long hours with him during Christmas vacation "poring over seed catalogues . . . and carefully filling out the order forms."

To assure readers of their closeness, Martha boasted that "I was the only one of my father's children who took naturally to the garden—I never minded the hours in the blazing sun, weeding and cultivating."

In *Martha Stewart's New Old House* (1992) she describes the family homestead on Elm Place as "modest, but friendly," and waxes on about the narrow yard that "Dad had beautifully terraced."

In the introduction to *Martha Stewart's Pies & Tarts* (1985) she writes of her father's love of the earth and how he was forced to cut down the family's old apple tree because its large shadow cast too much shade over his other beloved plants and flowers. Martha recalled studying garden books with him, "choosing what we would like to have on an imaginary estate, as well as what we could actually afford to have and take care of."

Martha has said that she owes her "self-confidence and self-worth" to her father. She said he "drilled into my head on a regular basis" his credo, which she described as "Work hard, try hard, and most of your goals will be realized. Don't limit yourself."

At home, pickle making became "an art form." For research, father and daughter visited Orchard Street, on Manhattan's Lower East Side, to study the various varieties of dills. Besides pickles, the two enjoyed fishing together, according to Martha. "Dad fished for food more than sport," she recalled. Once, out on Captain Charlie Dodd's party boat with her father, Martha won a seventy-seven-dollar pool for catching "so many fish we had to give them away."

In a "Remembering" essay entitled "Of Easter Bonnets and Easter Suits," Martha reminisced about Easter food shopping at "Dad's favorite purveyor" of kielbasa and about his driving the family and friends after Easter Sunday mass into New York for the parade and then documenting those happy times with "his Rolleiflex. . . . These pictures are our family's visual history."

Like any father, Ed Kostyra wasn't always Mr. Nice Guy, Martha has acknowledged. He could, she has suggested, be strict and demanding. However, in the many mentions of him in her books and magazine, there were only two that indicated a darker side to the man. Regarding his strictness, Martha wrote that she and her siblings were once "severely punished" by him for sampling Valentine's Day chocolates he'd bought for Martha Sr. As for his being demanding, Martha recalled that her father "really liked" her mother to hand-iron his pima cotton shirts, even though she had her hands full with kids and other domestic chores.

Despite those minor flaws, Martha boasted to the readers of her magazine that she had inherited many of her father's traits, "including his fiery temper."

Over the years Eddie Kostyra has been a member in good standing of the cast of family members appearing in "Remembering" and "A Letter from Martha," both popular features in *Martha Stewart Living*.

Though Martha has become *the* expert on entertaining, she rarely entertained friends at the Kostyra house when she was growing up. When pals were invited to spend time at 86 Elm Place, they felt uncomfortable there, describing the household as cold and forbidding. The warm and convivial atmosphere that Martha later described so delightfully didn't exist, they maintained.

Some friends, such as Gail Hallam Charmichael, said they spent as little time as possible at Martha's because they were afraid of her father. "He was a real ogre," Charmichael said emphatically. "He was a tyrant." Charmichael was a pal of Martha's and the best friend of Martha's sister Kathy. The prettiest of the three Kostyra girls, Kathy was the Kostyras' fourth child, the second and middle daughter, born in January 1947, five and a half years after Martha. "If you were over there sitting around and Mr. Kostyra decided that Martha should be doing something, he'd send the friends home and send Martha into a room to read," Charmichael recalled. "When he hollered, we all ran. We all scrammed. We all went home. It was you-don't-stick-around time.

"He had a little library just off the living room that was filled—*just filled*—with *National Geographic*s, and I remember him throwing books, throwing things, throwing *National Geographic*s, when he got angry, and that's when you decided it was time to go home. The girls—Martha and Kathy—would just go upstairs to their rooms. It was like everyone walked on eggshells around him.

"I remember one confrontation between Martha and her father, and it was scary. They were fighting. There was shouting. Kathy and I went to hide somewhere—maybe in the bathroom. I remember Martha ran into her bedroom and blocked the door with her dresser so her father couldn't get in.

"But you never saw any emotion from the girls. If Martha or Kathy cried, it would have been to themselves. They would not have complained to anyone."

In her "Remembering" column, "A Good Cry," Martha noted that she was "guilty of perpetuating the family philosophy," which was, she acknowledged, " 'Don't Cry.' " However, she did admit to sobbing "late into the night, under my quilt." She attributed those tears not to her father's rage but rather to sad novels she had been reading. The real-life trials of the Kostyra household, had she revealed them, would not be conducive to the cheery world of *Martha Stewart Living*.

Charmichael said that while she enjoyed reading Martha's remembrances—"It's all so nostalgic"—the kindly portrait she has painted of her father was upsetting to her. "That really bothered me because I knew what he was *really* like."

About five years after the Kostyras had moved to Elm Place, Eddie's mother, Helen, who always idolized her son, followed suit, moving from Jersey City with her daughter, Estelle Burke, and her family. The Burkes bought a house at 66 Elm Place, just five doors away from the Kostyras.

Martha bonded with her first cousin Diane, the elder of the Burkes' two daughters. Though Martha was a year ahead of Diane in school, they were constantly together. "We walked to school together," Diane Carey said. "We played together. We had clubhouses. When we got a little older, we both baby-sat, and if Martha couldn't make it, I'd sit in for her. We were in and out of each other's houses all the time. We were family."

As youngsters the two girls, at Eddie Kostyra's behest, used hammers to knock down a wall between the pantry and the breakfast area of the Kostyras' kitchen so he could install a small powder room. "Martha's mother was quite upset because there was plaster dust all over the place. We did nothing to protect the rest of the house. We just took hammers and started going," Carey said, chuckling at the memory.

Because of their blood ties and close proximity, Carey got a close-up view of life at Martha's house, and she didn't remember it as being very pleasant—certainly not the way her cousin has described it in her writings. "Her father was *very* stern," Carey maintained. "I never felt that there was a great deal of love there either [between father and daughter]. So what Martha writes now is so unlike what I remember. When we read these pages in the back of her magazines, sometimes we laugh because it's just so unlike what the relationship was between the two of them."

Carey said she "disliked" Martha's father for another reason too. "He was *not* caring toward his own mother," she observed. "He would come down to our house for five or ten minutes and talk to her—but not offer to do anything for her."

In her books and magazines, though, Martha has written lovingly and expressively about Babcia Helen, as she called her grandmother, and told readers of the important place she had held in the Kostyra household.

Though the Kostyras lived on Elm Place for years, they were relatively private and not very social. There were greetings on the sidewalk and back-fence gossiping—the homey, small-town atmosphere that Martha has described so nostalgically—but little else. In an essay entitled "Celebrating Differences," Martha described Elm Place as a melting pot of Jews, like the Mendelsons, and Gentiles like the Mauses, the jolly retired German bakers, whom she has cited numerous times in her writings. "We were friends. Mothers were on borrowing terms. . . . Children played on one another's stoops. . . . Families shared information, recipes, gardening tips. . . ."

But there was little, if any, *intimate* contact that would have publicly bared the Kostyra family's dysfunctions. Some longtime neighbors, such as Miriam Mendelson McRob, whose family lived two doors from the Kostyras—the same Mendelsons mentioned in Martha's essay—couldn't recall having *ever* been in the Kostyra house. "You didn't see Martha's parents, and that would be when my mother said, 'Oh, they work so hard. They don't relax. We never see them.' "

McRob, however, had become aware that Kostyra "was a taskmaster—that he really made those children toe the line. When we got out of line a little bit, my father would say, 'Do you want me to be strict like Mr. Kostyra?' "

But outside the home Eddie Kostyra put on a cordial face. A religious Catholic, he proudly led his handsome-looking family to mass every week at Our Lady of Mount Carmel Church, where he was a member of the Holy Name Society. When his sons joined the Cub Scouts, Kostyra became active and, before long, was Nutley's premier Scouting leader, a position he held for some seventeen years.

"When I was in Scouting, Dad produced a series of minstrel shows, and these were fund-raisers that were put on for three straight nights for several years running in the auditorium at Nutley High School," Eric Scott recalled vividly. "The Scouts wore blackface and white gloves. Today that's frowned upon. Dad wrote, produced, and directed the shows and arranged for the funds. He took songs from *Porgy and Bess* and from vaudeville and used poetry. I sang 'I Got Plenty o' Nuttin'.' It was quite a real professional production. Everybody in town turned out for those shows.''

But because of the adversity at home, the relationship between father and son was severely strained. The intensity of those feelings was underscored when Eric, just a few merit badges shy of the pinnacle, becoming an Eagle Scout, suddenly quit the troop to spite his father. "I did it because he was pushing me a little too hard," Scott acknowledged years later. "It got to a point where I said, 'Hey, that's it. I'm not going to be a Scout anymore.' He was upset. I don't exactly remember what his response was. I blocked it out."

At eighteen Eric left home for good, moving to Buffalo, where he lived with his maternal grandparents while working his way through college and dental school.

Of course none of these Kostyra family contretemps were generally known to the local citizenry, who, because of Eddie Kostyra's pleasant public persona, thought of him as a loving father, dedicated husband, and concerned citizen— a perfect Nutleyite. Public image always was a priority to him, as it would be for his famous daughter.

However, stress and anxiety weighed heavily in the Kostyra household, causing violent arguments among the children, particularly between Martha and Frank. "Martha and I fought a lot," Kostyra asserted. "Martha claims she still has a scar below her belly button where I bit her. Until a few years ago I still carried the lead mark in my finger where she stabbed me with a pencil and broke the lead off in my hand trying to get me."

And Martha developed what Frank Kostyra called a hate syndrome. All her life, he maintained, her favorite words were "I hate," followed by someone's name. "She would say, 'I hate Uncle Henny . . . I hate Uncle Al . . . I hate Aunt Stel . . . I hate this, I hate that . . . I hate Mom . . . I hate Dad.' It was a thing that she concealed in her nature. It was one of her eccentricities, and it was with her since I've known her. It's why we fought about stupid things. She had to have her way, and I had to have mine. That was one of Dad's principles—be a leader, get out there and lead, head of the pack—and we followed his philosophy."

When probed by journalists after she became famous, Martha alluded to the problems that existed between her and her father, but for the most part she put a positive spin on their relationship.

Acknowledging that he was a "very difficult, very demanding man," she maintained at the same time that he had a positive influence on her creativity. "I think my father had a lot to do with it, because he always wore—I can remember his clothes so well—Harris Tweed suits and pima-cotton shirts," she said. "I mean, when we made dresses, we made them out of very fine fabric. Even though we were not wealthy people, I still had my first formal dress made out of ice-satin peau de soie with underskirts of pink silk net. I mean, we didn't skimp on the fabric. We looked for bargains. We went to 38th Street [New York's garment district]. But I knew all about good feelings, good food, and good taste."

Another time, however, she hinted at her father's strictness: "My father took me under his wing, and I learned everything. He taught me how to garden, how to use all his tools. He helped me with public speaking. Mother may be the better teacher, because he taught by *'I'll beat it into you,'* and my mother did it in the more *normal* fashion. But I was receptive to that kind of teaching. I didn't mind at all."

Still later she described her father as a "crazy force in the family . . . not always likable."

Eddie Kostyra's anger and temperament had an enormous psychological impact on Martha, according to family members and friends, and left her with emotional scars that impacted on virtually all her relationships later in life. As Frank Kostyra maintained, "Because of Martha's perceptions and her treatment in early life—I imagine by Dad—I think she became a man-hater. She didn't like male authority then, and she doesn't now."

School Days

Though Martha has described her mother as warm and loving, she was, according to others, a chilly and dispassionate figure. Her stolid and austere personality, combined with her husband's frustrations and temperament, made for a gloomy household with few, if any, demonstrations of parental love.

"Martha Senior was a sweet and nice person, but there was a certain distance between her and other people," a Kostyra family observer noted. "She was not physically affectionate with her kids. As an adult Martha expressed that fact and confronted her mother on whether she held or kissed her much, and Martha Senior admitted she hadn't. Martha didn't learn at home how to be affectionate."

Frank Kostyra expressed the belief that their mother's reserve was attributable to her own bleak childhood. "When I would read Martha writing about how affectionate her mother was, I would think, 'Boy, that's *not* the Mrs. Kostyra I remember.' I remember her as being *very* stern," said one of Martha's close childhood friends, Judy Churchill Stothoff. "She stood very erect and was imposing and had that immigrant-stock look. I don't have too many warm, fuzzy-type feelings about her. I was rather afraid of both her parents. I just remember wanting to get in and out of Martha's house. It was not a very friendly, welcoming place. The whole atmosphere was pretty stern."

Escaping from the harsh realities of Elm Place, Martha

found a safe harbor in school, where she quickly jumped on the fast track. By the third grade she had become one of the shining stars at Yantacaw Elementary School, dubbed "Stinktacaw" by the kids.

There Martha developed a bond—one that was to last a lifetime—with Irene Weyer, a teacher who took a keen interest in the skinny, serious-looking Kostyra girl, who wore her brownish blond hair in a cute bob, held in place with barrettes, and came to school each day in colorful handmade dresses; a store-bought wardrobe was out of the question for the struggling Kostyras.

To Martha, Weyer looked and acted differently from all the other teachers, the stern old maids of the day. Her style, mannerisms, and personality were distinct and alluring and caught the keen-eyed child's attention. Pretty and vivacious, the petite Weyer cut quite a stylish figure, sporting expensively tailored suits, with a colorful corsage in the lapel, stockings, high heels, and makeup.

Years later Weyer was still in Martha's mind's eye. She was "beautifully groomed," she recalled fondly in a column called "School Days." "She was loving. . . . Her classroom . . . was full of laughter and fun. . . ."

Judy Churchill Stothoff observed that Weyer's "attractiveness and femininity" were probably things that Martha liked. "You wouldn't look at Mrs. Kostyra and think, 'What a feminine woman'—not facially or physically—and she really was not fashion-conscious," she noted. "Nor was my mom, who was a Greek immigrant. Miss Weyer was our first teacher who had *any* femininity."

Having Irene Weyer as a friend, teacher, and confidante, and her classroom as a refuge, was a blessing for the affection-starved Martha, who quickly became Weyer's prize pupil and her pet. Martha's drawings and paintings were tacked up on the corkboard around Weyer's classroom, and the teacher always called on Martha to assist her in handing out papers and supplies. She also chose Martha over others to play a singing doll in a class production of *The Little Engine That Could*. Wearing a frilly bonnet her mother made for the event, Martha and the class bad boy held hands onstage and sang a duet.

Already competitive and an achiever, Martha desperately wanted to play the better-speaking role of the clown, but that part was won by Judy Churchill Stothoff, whom Weyer was helping overcome a stuttering problem. "Since Martha didn't get a speaking part, I remember Miss Weyer saying, 'Well, you can be a doll, dear, and you can sing.' It was one of the few times I beat Martha," Stothoff observed.

Martha also was among a handful of pupils who consistently earned perfect scores in Miss Weyer's weekly spelling tests, exempting her from the ominous fifty-word exam. Because of her exemplary work, Martha was permitted to make up the sentences for the words used in the test and to stand in front of the class and administer the examination as Irene Weyer watched adoringly from the side of the room.

Even at that young age, entertaining was on Martha's mind. On a number of occasions she invited Weyer home, ingratiating herself even more with the teacher. "I remember getting up extra early on those days Miss Weyer was coming to lunch to set the table and make a flower centerpiece," Martha wrote. "Mom would cook something special, and the forty minutes we spent together eating and talking were invaluable in cementing the family-teacher relationship."

Over the years their bond grew stronger. Martha had private visits with Weyer, returning often to see her when she was in junior and senior high schools, and their friendship reached a point where confidences about personal matters and problems in their lives were exchanged and discussed— something Martha couldn't do at home.

Martha came to view the teacher as a counselor, even a surrogate mother at times.

Years later, still active at the age of eighty-five, Irene Weyer remained captivated by her former student. "Martha was a very bright, friendly, caring child," she said. "She was a child of superior intelligence. She would make such lovely pictures. Her English, her grammar, her whole makeup showed that this child loved to learn and was creative. I'll never forget the way she carried herself, the way she spoke. She was really a little lady—and she was *so* pretty.''

But the ''pleasant'' lunches at the Kostyras gave Weyer little if any insight into the Kostyra family dynamics. She saw Martha Sr. as ''reserved'' and Eddie Kostyra as ''always very quiet.'' Taken together, they were ''hardworking people who brought out the best in their family,'' she believed.

But if Martha had revealed any of the problems that existed at home, Weyer wasn't talking. ''People have a way of telling me things that maybe they wouldn't tell somebody else. If Martha had confided something about her family, I would not repeat it.''

At the Kostyras', meanwhile, finances remained tight, causing continual tensions, turmoil, and frustrations. If Martha didn't go home for lunch, she brought a bologna sandwich wrapped in wax paper in a brown bag to school. Often she didn't have the luxury of an extra few pennies to buy an ice cream for dessert in the cafeteria. After school she watched enviously as other kids dug into their pockets for the seven cents to buy Popsicles from the Good Humor man. Every penny was carefully counted. As Martha has acknowledged, she was brought up with a ''save for the morrow mentality.''

In her remembrances Martha has often written about the homey Kostyra kitchen and the marvelous concoctions whipped up by her mother and grandmother—with no mention made of bologna on white. Millions of Martha's readers could almost smell the pies and tarts and breads coming out of the Kostyra oven. ''At Sunday dinner, my mother would present ten different vegetables and five fresh fruit desserts . . . my early memories are bound up with mushroom soup and pierogi. . . .'' Martha writes in *Entertaining*.

But Martha's close friends from that time had a different memory. ''From reading the first issue of *Martha Stewart Living* I thought, 'This doesn't sound like the 86 Elm Place that I remember.' When we were in grammar school, we ate *mustard* sandwiches every day,'' Stothoff revealed, ''which is kind of a far cry from Martha's gourmet meals.

It was Gulden's mustard on white bread—never anything but white bread—which we'd wash down with a soda or milk. That was our afternoon snack—every single day."

Martha, however, claimed higher culinary aspirations, even at that young age. She maintained she had an early interest in cooking and baking, which she credited to an elderly German couple, the Mauses, who lived next door. Martha first revealed the existence of the Mauses in *Entertaining*, telling readers: "From the time I was four until I reached ten, when Mr. Maus died, I found excuses to visit them. I was welcomed as an apprentice and as a taster . . . [I] sifted flour, helped stir, and sampled breads and cakes. . . ."

In *Martha Stewart's Pies & Tarts*, she describes the Mauses as "our best friends . . . my time was spent . . . in the Mauses' flour-covered basement, learning how to make pie crust, kuchen doughs, yeast breads. . . . The Mauses wanted me to know how to make the best cherry pie and the finest peach tart."

But once again, childhood friends, neighbors, and relatives have contradicted Martha's assertions, saying they didn't recall the kind of special relationship that she has claimed. "She had *nothing* to do with Mr. Maus," declared Estelle Burke, Martha's aunt, a blunt woman, who was also a neighbor and friend of the Mauses'. "It was Frankie [Martha's brother]. *That's* the truth. Frankie used to follow Mr. Maus around like a shadow. Mr. Maus didn't teach Martha a damn thing. She embellishes everything."

In *Entertaining*, Martha says: "As tangible proof of the strength of their [the Mauses'] art, and my memories, I retain Mrs. Maus's dough bowl, and a stash of recipes." But Frank Kostyra claimed, "The bowl that she mentions was *my* bowl. The Mauses gave it to me."

Even Martha's description of the Mauses as "jolly Bürgermeisters" who had "commercial-style gas ovens . . . installed in their basement" may also be up for question—if there's any truth to a shocking story told by Eddie Kostyra to his son Eric.

"Dad said Mr. Maus had nationalistic ties to the German-American Bund and was a supporter of Hitler. I remember as a kid marching down the street with the American flag, celebrating D-Day, or V-J Day, and my father called me over and told me that the FBI had been watching Mr. Maus throughout the war.''

Around the time of her infatuation with the Mauses, according to *Entertaining*, Martha made her first foray into catering, a career that one day launched her into iconic status in the world of entertaining, cooking, and something called lifestyle. ''When I was in grade school,'' Martha wrote, ''I used to organize all the birthday parties in our neighborhood, just for the fun of arranging little dramas.'' Later she told an interviewer that she was ''inspired'' by the need for money to cater those events. ''Well, because you're making 50 cents an hour as a baby-sitter in those days. So that wasn't quite enough money—I didn't think so—so if I did extra-special things, I would get paid more.''

But if anyone got competitive with the budding Martha Stewart, watch out.

''I guess I was the only other child in the neighborhood who had similar interests,'' recalled a childhood chum. ''One summer Martha heard about caterers, and right then and there she said, 'That's what I'll be.' Martha went home and began soliciting neighbors. She had it down from the beginning: how much she'd charge, what she'd serve, the whole nine yards.''

Martha's friend thought, ''What a neat idea,'' and decided to take up catering too, never contemplating the consequences of her decision. ''Martha came over to my house one afternoon and said she'd heard that I was also catering little parties, and did I need any advice or help? 'That's what friends are for,' she said. I needed a recipe for a chocolate cake I'd promised someone I'd bake—my mom was really going to do it—and Martha told me not to worry, that she'd share her very favorite recipe with me. I remember thinking, 'What a pal.'

''Well, when I opened the oven, and this was like an hour before I had to deliver the cake, it was flat and hard as cardboard, a total disaster. I was crying, and I called this woman to tell her that there wouldn't be a cake. But she said, 'Oh, don't worry, there's a cake coming in the door right now. Martha Kostyra called me a few minutes ago and told me she just took one out of the oven.' I was stunned. That night I asked my mother to look at the recipe Martha had given me, and we discovered she had left out a key ingredient. I still wonder to this day whether she did it on purpose. Later, when I asked Martha about it, she said, 'Oh, I'm sorry. I must have made a mistake.'

"Every time I recall that story, I think of that wicked little girl Rhoda in *The Bad Seed*. Looking back on Martha now, I guess she was all sweetness—with a killer instinct. And that's how she is today from what I hear. Same girl, different cake."

Puberty and Privacy

By the time Martha entered seventh grade at Nutley Junior High, in September 1953, she had gone through an uncomplicated puberty, and had blossomed into a beauty: tall and thin, with coltish legs, tiny breasts, a Pepsodent smile, and high cheekbones.

But in the crowded Kostyra household Martha had little of the kind of privacy a pretty and precocious adolescent required. The only bathroom in the house, which had "very annoying" hot and cold faucets, a minuscule medicine cabinet, and no electrical outlet, was used by the entire family. Martha bitterly complained that she never had a moment of privacy. Years later she still was bothered by the fact that she had been forced to wash her hair in the kitchen sink because the one in the bathroom was used by the whole family for brushing teeth.

And the Kostyra family never seemed to stop growing. The fifth Kostyra, George, who was born on Washington's Birthday in 1952, was only a year old when Martha entered junior high. As the eldest daughter she was enlisted by her mother to help with the additional household chores. A few years later more responsibility would be thrown on her when the the sixth and last Kostyra, the unplanned-for Laura, was born when Martha Sr. was forty-one. As one relative noted, "Laura's birth caused a *major* upheaval in the family. The last thing in the world Eddie needed was another mouth to feed."

And the last thing Martha needed as the eldest daughter was another baby to help care for. "I was like a second mother," she said later.

Martha and Laura, whose life has been troubled and tragic at times, have had a stormy relationship. Some observers believed that Martha harbored resentment toward her baby sister for the burdens that her birth imposed upon her when she was a teenager.

The added responsibilities in those teen years ignited in Martha a growing anger and frustration, but she remained steadfast, always trying to be the consummate, mature daughter, seeking her father's elusive praise, her mother's reserved love. Martha studied hard, earned superior grades, and performed all the chores assigned to her without grousing too much.

However, with all those pressures she had begun to exhibit personality quirks that were to remain with her. For one thing, she became obsessive about cleanliness. "I was forever dusting. . . . Even then I was a compulsive cleaner," she acknowledged later. She was a perfectionist in everything she did, always trying to be absolutely correct, beyond criticism or fault. She'd also become an insomniac. She'd go to sleep at ten and be up at midnight, sitting in the kitchen with her father eating onion sandwiches— "white onion on white bread and butter"—playing Scrabble, or talking into the wee hours. Before long Martha was getting only three or four hours of sleep a night despite busy, intense days at home and at school. Being somewhat wall-eyed, the fatigue gave her a slightly crazed look, which continued into adulthood.

Her aunt Clementine Ruszkowski Carriere remembered how overpowered Martha felt during those difficult years. "She was staying with me for a couple of weeks, and she was griping about her younger sisters and brothers. She just looked at me very seriously and said, 'I don't know why my Mom couldn't have stopped with two children.' I guess she felt she had to give up something because she had all those brothers and sisters."

Martha, who dreamed of a frilly bedroom for herself, was required to share a cramped Spartan one with her younger sister Kathy. And with little or no money, it was impossible for her to indulge herself with the latest fashions, cosmetics, and other luxuries demanded by teenage girls. One complaint she later aired in her magazine was that she was forced to use her small bedroom dresser for whatever cosmetics, costume jewelry, and other personal effects she could afford to buy.

Years later, when she owned almost as many houses as the Elm Place homestead had rooms, Martha confessed that she had been jealous of her girlfriends' possessions, admitting, in one instance, that she had "coveted" their "skirted, kidney-shaped dressing tables. . . . I never had one of my own. . . ."

Nutley Junior High, unlike Yantacaw, drew students from all over town. For the first time Martha was exposed to upper-middle-class affluence, for a number of her classmates were the daughters of executives, lawyers, bankers. Martha was drawn to this elite crowd like a gourmand to Beluga caviar. Her fascination with social status was born in those years. It was around this time that Martha haughtily declared to her aunt Estelle Burke, "When I grow up, I'm going to have three dogs and two maids to walk them."

Martha also longed to have a closet filled with the latest fashions that her well-to-do classmates were wearing. In seventh grade the outfit to die for was a pastel sweater-skirt set that was being featured at Hahne & Company, *the* exclusive Newark department store, where Martha could only afford to window-shop. The Kostyras shopped instead for bargains at discount stores; their favorite was a place called Two Guys from Harrison.

When Judy Churchill Stothoff received the "in" outfit as a Christmas gift from her parents, Martha turned green with envy. And when Stothoff wore it to school before the holidays, without her parents' knowledge, Martha squealed on her, touching off a curious chain of events that left Stothoff feeling betrayed and still wondering years later about Martha's motivations.

"Martha saw me wearing the outfit and went right home and told her mother," Stothoff said. "Mrs. Kostyra called me. I was scared. I knew I was in trouble. She told me that what I had done was appalling, that my mother and father had worked hard to earn the money to give me a nice gift, and it really was horrible that I had worn it before Christmas. She told me I was ungrateful, that I was awful. How dare I do that? And she ordered me to tell my mother what I'd done. I had not a doubt that if I didn't tell her, Mrs. Kostyra would. That's the kind of woman she was."

Stothoff's mother *was* furious and punished her by not allowing her to wear the outfit to school the first week after the holidays.

"I never confronted Martha," Stothoff said years later. "I never said, 'You weaseled on me. Why did you rat on me?' It was just kind of accepted. I don't know why Martha told on me. It's an unanswered question in my mind."

An avid reader, Martha spent a good part of her free time at the Nutley Public Library, pedaling there on an old Schwinn. By the time she got to junior high, she had read her way through the children's and young adult sections and was given permission, with her mother's approval, to borrow from the adult shelves, where, she later wrote, "my appetite for reading was whetted even further." She has written of her love for Hawthorne, Jane Austen, Dickens, Sir Walter Scott, Edith Wharton, Tolstoy, Henry James, George Eliot, among others.

"Already curious about the writer's craft," she told her readers, "I sought to discover the key to good literature, sometimes reading several books on the same subject just to figure out how one was better than the next.''

While Martha may have digested literary classics, her favorite reading was really more pulp than Pulitzer. From a pal whose father was in publishing, Martha borrowed review copies of simple teenage girl adventure novels, which she passionately devoured. ''They were more her style,'' a close friend observed. ''If she read classic literature, she never mentioned it to me.''

Initially the *Nancy Drew* series had caught Martha's imagination. Once she polished those off, she discovered a similar series, about a girl named Cherry Ames. One after another, Martha read *Cherry Ames, Student Nurse; Cherry Ames, Navy Nurse; Cherry Ames, Army Nurse; Cherry Ames, Indian Reservation Nurse.* She found the books upbeat and lively and was thrilled when, in one of the stories, Cherry Ames actually kissed her boyfriend.

The book that Martha read and reread, a teen novel about twins who fooled a young man about their identities, was titled *Double Date.* The publisher's daughter brought the book to school, still unread, and when Martha saw the cover and read the jacket, she knew she had to have it. She pestered her pal until she finally lent it to her.

Like others in her class, Martha hungrily consumed the steamy commercial best-sellers of the mid-fifties: *Peyton Place, Not as a Stranger,* and *Battle Cry.* She used brown paper, backed with glue—it was years before she discovered the glue gun—to disguise the covers of the controversial books so that she could read them in class and at home without getting caught. When the film version of *Battle Cry* came to Nutley, Martha was one of the first in line, but she found the movie disappointing; all of novelist Leon Uris's profanity had been cleaned up by Hollywood. Still, she liked teen heartthrob Tab Hunter's looks.

For the most part, though, Martha didn't have teen idols the way her friends did. There were no posters on the wall or stacks of movie magazines in the closet. ''Martha's room was very sterile,'' a girlfriend recalled.

Martha had her earliest formal cooking training—aside from whatever she learned in her mother's kitchen—in a stuffy home economics classroom lined with white ranges. But the class bored her stiff.

"Martha had about as much interest in cooking as any of us did—zero," maintained a classmate. "Cooking or at least helping her mother cook was one of Martha's *chores* at home. She *had* to do it or she would have gotten hell. If home economics hadn't been mandatory, Martha wouldn't have come within a hundred feet of that classroom."

But four decades later, on her 1995 hourlong CBS prime-time special, *Martha Stewart's Home for the Holidays,* she fondly recalled that same junior high cooking class. "These are little almond crescents [cookies]," Martha told millions of viewers. "I got this recipe years ago when I was in eighth grade from . . . my home economics teacher, and this recipe has really held up."

Back then, however, Martha thought of the teacher's projects as insane, the way some critics came to view many of Martha Stewart's cooking projects years later.

"The teacher used to have us cut maraschino cherries into *eighths* because that way we could see how color added to the dish we were making," a classmate recounted. "It was *crazy*. Martha *hated* spending her time doing it. One day the teacher was late, and we opened up every jar of cherries and gobbled them down so we didn't have to stupidly cut them up. Martha was grinning from ear to ear and had cherry juice dripping down her chin, but she denied any wrongdoing when the teacher showed up. She lied and blamed it on the class before us.

"Martha once said something I'll never forget in light of who she's become. She said, 'That's all my mother does, stand in front of a hot stove cooking. And what does she have to show for it? She works like a peasant. I want more out of life, and I'm going to get it.' "

High School Days

In the same week of September 1956 that Elvis Presley rocked and shocked the nation with his TV debut on *The Ed Sullivan Show*, Martha Kostyra landed on her feet in the hallowed halls of Nutley High School and never stopped running. Like Elvis, Martha was to become an icon one day. But for now she had made a conscious decision to become the best, the most active, and the most famous member of the Nutley High class of '59.

"I sat next to her in the front of Margaret Gerdinick's French class," said a pal, Barbara Rubin Oliver, who recalled Martha's modus operandi. "We'd come into class on a day we were going to have a test, and she'd *still* be studying. As far as I was concerned and our friends were concerned, we had studied the night before. But Martha would study right up until the very last *second* before the exam and then say, 'Oh, I don't know *any* of this.' And then of course she'd get an A. She was disciplined—always one step ahead of the rest of us."

Barbara Viventi Howard, voted the girl "Most Likely to Succeed"—she later became a prominent microbiologist and the president of a research institute—felt there was something extraordinary about her close friend Marty, as some called her. "She had a focus that was extremely unusual for Nutley High School girls of the fifties. Martha was highly ambitious and competitive."

Martha got her first formal writing and editing experience

on the staff of Nutley High's literary quarterly, the *Gauntlet*, a consistent first-place winner in the Columbia Scholastic Press Association's annual contest.

However, her pieces were considered simplistic and colorless. And when she served as the *Gauntlet*'s art director, the drawings and photographs were thought to be pedestrian and uninspired.

The *Gauntlet* issue for Summer 1958 carried two articles by Martha. One, titled "Annual Swim Campaign," dealt with a program sponsored by the Nutley Red Cross Chapter. ". . . Many high-school students successfully complete the lifesaving and Water Safety Aide courses, enabling them to offer their services as life-guards and assistant instructors . . ." she wrote. "It is hard work, but loads of fun. . . . We think it is necessary for everyone to learn to swim correctly, so why don't you take advantage of the Swim Campaign?"

The other piece, a recommendation for summer reading, was a review of Thoreau's *Walden*, which Martha described as "a story of happiness, a story of a contented, satisfied man, unhampered by needless luxuries and comforts. . . . He believed that the woods, books, enough solitude, and the simplest food and clothing were prerequisites for successful leisure." She declared it "truly a classic of American literature" that "offers us an escape from the toils of everyday life. . . ."

In a later issue Martha reviewed Thackeray's *Vanity Fair*, which she panned as "shallow reading . . . overlong . . . too involved with affected language, and certainly dated." She described Vanity Fair as "a wicked, foolish, very vain place." (Throughout her review the words "villain" and "villainous" were misspelled.)

Martha was a student in Honors English, a demanding course taught by Maxine Hoffer, one of the *Gauntlet*'s advisers. A woman of extraordinary intelligence and creativity, Hoffer, a graduate of Barnard, which Martha later attended, was considered one of the best teachers in the Nutley school system. "I tried to show my students that literature was simply one expression of the kind of spirit that was being demonstrated in architecture, painting, and music," Hoffer said. "My class was a gathering of the school's best and brightest, so to speak."

While Hoffer found Martha an able student, she said she "never thought of her as a standout" and recalled nothing extraordinary that she had ever produced in class or in the *Gauntlet.* "But Martha was very competent and very efficient," stated Hoffer, still scrupulous and pointed at age eighty-five. "She got her papers in on time, and that was always a pleasure for a teacher. Martha was always busy doing other things, *lots* of extracurricular activities, and *always* on the run. But I never felt I could get a handle on her. She never opened herself up. She was a bit reclusive despite how active she was. She was her own mistress, and she did what she felt was necessary and good at that particular moment."

On the college-bound fast track, Martha could have gotten away with only two years of math. But she elected to take four, pushing her way into what had been an all-male calculus class with her buddy Lynn Sherwood Kaneps, daughter of a wealthy and prominent Nutley family.

"A lot of our friends just did the required two years and then thanked God they were finished," recalled Kaneps, who went on to teach advanced economics in high school. "The calculus class was the only class that Mr. Assmus, the principal, taught, and it was quite difficult. But Martha enjoyed the competition. *Thrived* on it."

Eddie Kostyra had warned Martha that the family didn't have money to send her to college, that she should do everything in her power to win scholarship money, and that one way to impress scholarship committees was to be involved in lots of extracurricular activities. Martha took her father's advice. By graduation she had been in more clubs and held more offices than just about anyone in her class.

She served as a gym helper, dean's helper, guidance helper, and main office helper; was a Red Cross representative, home room representative, and general service representative; belonged to the Art Club, the Girls' After-School Sports Club, the Latin Club, the Ushers Club, Debating Club, and Chemistry Club; and was secretary of the Bowling Club. Along with working on the *Gauntlet,* she also served on the *Exit* yearbook art staff and was a class treasurer.

Most of her activities took up little actual time, but they *looked* impressive on paper, and that was her goal, friends noted. Sometimes she even had assistance from her father. "He helped her with school projects," said her brother George Christiansen, who took his wife's maiden name. "For the junior prom they decorated the gymnasium together. All the creative stuff was happening between them, working toward her college education. She has a lot of him in her. They are both Leos. Strong-willed individuals, you know."

Because of her academic load and extracurricular schedule, Martha had little time for just plain fun. However, there was one activity that she seemed to savor, even though it was a tad sadistic. "In the winter, when there was ice on the ground, we'd be standing outside school, and you'd see Martha quietly sidle up to somebody who was standing huddled with other people to keep warm, and she'd get engrossed in a conversation with them," recalled a classmate. "Then, when they least expected it, she'd use her foot to kick their feet out from under them, and they'd go down on the ice. At the time it appeared funny, especially when you knew she was going to do it to someone other than yourself. But it was meanspirited, and people did get angry."

Martha also relished terrorizing a friend by forcing her onto a small carousel in the park and pushing it as fast as she could, knowing her pal feared speed and would become dizzy and nauseous. "I'd scream, 'Stop it! Stop it!' I just hated that. But she'd laugh and laugh."

Though Martha had never tried out for the cheerleading squad, she did work hard on football Saturdays. Manning a little stand, the future arbiter of fine cuisine hawked lukewarm hot dogs on soggy buns to hundreds of cold and hungry fans of Nutley High's Maroon and Gray eleven. She also participated in feeding the hungry players before the big games. A hearty Saturday morning breakfast for the team, given at a different home each week, was a Nutley tradition. Assisted by a group of the school's most active and popular girls, the mother of the house oversaw the pregame feast.

However, reminiscing about that activity in *Entertaining*, Martha appeared to take sole credit for the one and only football breakfast that was ever held at 86 Elm Place. "My first 'catered' party," she writes with bravado, "was a breakfast of heroic proportions for the Nutley High School football team."

That's not quite the way members of Martha's inner circle remembered it. Barbara Viventi Howard acknowledged that such a festive feed was in fact held at the Kostyras'. But Howard maintained that "Martha's mother, *not* Martha," was the actual caterer. "Martha's mother thought nothing of having thirty guys in and feeding them because she was a very efficient, high-energy kind of person," Howard noted. "I remember that breakfast because I was just so impressed that she could serve so many people. Her mother did all the preparation, although I'm certain Martha and other girls helped."

Another close high school friend, Eleanor "Ellie" Watts Flavin, said, "I recall reading Martha's description of that breakfast in *Entertaining* and thinking to myself, 'I wonder where I was when she was doing that.' Martha wasn't any more outstanding than the rest of us. But then she started getting those modeling jobs and—phew! All of a sudden it was really exciting!"

The Model Hustle

When Martha began modeling around 1958, the half dozen or so biggest agencies in New York had combined bookings of only five million dollars, a drop in the bucket compared with today's revenues, and top models at the time were earning thirty-five hundred dollars a week, a far cry from the ten thousand dollars an hour some generated in the age of the supermodel.

But for a pretty teenager like Martha who possessed classic all-American looks, the return could be quite handsome—far more lucrative than the pittance her friends were earning working summers at New Jersey Bell or at Hahne's—and it was certainly more glamorous.

Martha has claimed that she got into modeling after a neighborhood girl, who was a model, introduced her to an agent. But none of her friends or family remembered such a scenario.

Instead all evidence points to Eddie Kostyra—always looking for a new way to make a buck—as the brains behind Martha's modestly successful modeling career, a hustle to help put her through college.

"Dad pushed Martha into modeling," asserted Frank Kostyra. "It was because of his insistence, coaching, lecturing, and enthusiasm. Martha was sort of reluctant, but Dad was a salesman. He could see that Martha's looks had a retail value, and he wanted to market them.

"He had a Rolleiflex and a darkroom, and he took hundreds of photographs of her. She spent *hours* posing for him: 'Smile . . . turn your face that way . . . turn your face this way . . . the light's not right . . . wait for the light!' "

Always very private about what she was up to, Martha allowed only a few close friends to know she was trying to become a model. Most others found out by chance and were surprised when they came upon her in a print ad or a TV commercial.

One of those in on Martha's secret from the start was Lynn Sherwood Kaneps, who accompanied Martha by bus to Manhattan when she was searching for an agent. "I went with her as a chaperone because her mom didn't want her to go alone," Kaneps said. "Martha had been given a list of modeling agencies to see—by whom I don't know—and she went to four or five and was interviewed. I don't think we were knocking on the doors of the top-notch agencies, like Ford. But the message they gave her was that she had to get a portfolio together. One or two of the women who interviewed her gave her names of professional photographers.

"I was amazed, and surprised, and a little apprehensive that we were doing this, not knowing whether we were walking into dens of iniquity. But she was determined. She was confident from the start that something would happen. Martha wasn't scared or nervous about anything. For the portfolio photographs, she borrowed some of my clothes, a wide variety of outfits, because she didn't have much of a wardrobe."

While Kaneps saw a confident Martha, Barbara Viventi Howard said she had gotten the impression that Martha was reluctant and anxious about her chances for a modeling career. "Martha wanted to do it, but I think she was worried about the competition," Howard observed. "She didn't have any inside pull; her family had no connections. She was doing it all on her own, so she *was* worried. I can remember watching her juggle her courses, her homework, all the club activities because she had to go into New York City by bus, sometimes several times a week. It was hard on her, but she kept at it."

For the girl from Nutley, the glamorous world of New York fashion modeling was an eye-opener and was not without its bizarre episodes, for Martha quickly realized there were those in the business who would do almost anything to cash in on her good looks. One such agent seriously suggested that she needed to lose her classic features and get a look more like Twiggy. He recommended she have all her teeth extracted, for that sunken-cheek effect, and he even offered to have false teeth made for her to wear when she wasn't posing.

But Martha's wholesomeness paid off in her junior year in high school, when a small but respectable Manhattan agency, Foster-Ferguson, took her on as a client. "I remember modeling at Bonwit Teller on Saturdays," Martha said. "They had these little girls modeling these high-fashion dresses. I can remember thinking, I should probably be at the football game or something. But it was fun."

Martha got her first big break when she was chosen at a

casting call to appear in a Lifebuoy soap commercial. The spot premiered on one of America's most popular prime-time shows, *Have Gun Will Travel*, an Old West melodrama about a suave gunslinger named Paladin, who, ironically, was a Martha Stewart wannabe: He savored epicurean meals, entertaining, antiques, and literate company—when he wasn't bumping off someone. For under thirty seconds Martha's wholesome, Lifebuoy-scrubbed face was seen in millions of homes from coast to coast between nine-thirty and ten on Saturday nights. In homes all over Nutley TV sets blazed the night her spot premiered.

"She was seen climbing a ladder, and it was showing how natural she was, which was perfect for her," recalled Gail Hallam Charmichael. "Just the natural kind of girl who does everything."

But there was something amiss. "We all thought, 'That's not Martha. Where's her voice?' " remembered Eleanor Watts Flavin, still laughing about that moment years later.

It seems that while the commercial makers were smitten with Martha's "look," her "Joisey" accent was considered déclassé. Her face and her voice, they concluded, went about as well together as white bread and mustard.

"In Nutley in those days we all talked fast and talked New Jersey talk—Martha included," classmate Barbara Rubin Oliver pointed out. "Back then Martha didn't have that wonderful kind of Waspy way of speaking that she developed later when she created herself. Now she articulates. Her speech patterns were different back then. That's why I get a kick out of watching her on TV now."

To fix the problem, the commercial producers dubbed her words, using a professional with a melodious voice. "It struck us so funny," noted Flavin, "because when her mouth opened up, it wasn't her voice, and we chuckled. But we were excited for her, and we were very impressed with the fact that she had gotten this job. We knew she didn't come from a lot of money and that this would help."

Judy Churchill Stothoff's *Gauntlet* gossip column "Senior Peephole" ran a blind item asking, "Say, who is that tall, blond girl who's been modeling in the Big City lately?

Perhaps we'll see her in *Mademoiselle* soon!''

Martha, who was initially low-keyed about her burgeoning career, became more boastful. Her friend Mike Geltrude, a math wizard, varsity football player, and senior class treasurer who was voted "Most Talkative," said, "We'd be in math class and Martha would lean over and whisper, 'Mike, I'm going to be on Saturday night, *Have Gun Will Travel*. Try to watch it.' She was proud of what she was doing. I used to say to her, 'Martha, how do you do it? How do you get such good grades and still have time for modeling and everything else?' She said, 'Mike, it's tough.' She used to go into New York, and I asked her whether she was afraid. She said, 'No, I protect myself. I always make sure I'm in a position where nobody can bother me.' She was very confident of herself and what she was able to do."

Meanwhile Martha's growing success sparked envy among some of her classmates. "Everybody was in awe of her," recalled fashionable LeAnne White Ritchie, a member of Martha's clique, who was voted the "Best Looking" girl in the class of '59. "Martha's modeling was a big thing, and everybody was suddenly talking about it," added another friend, Mariette Vandermolen, who shared activities and clubs with Martha. "All the girls were *very* jealous of her and thought she was the most beautiful thing going and wanted to do what she was doing. But Martha was aloof and cool about it."

Whatever their feelings, Eddie Kostyra had proved that father did indeed know best. As he had suspected, Martha in and of herself was a very marketable commodity.

High School Boys

$\sim\!\!\sim$

While a number of her girlfriends were going steady, Martha seemed to have little interest in boys. Naturally her pals had wondered why. With her good looks, they thought her date book should have been filled for months in advance. But it wasn't. Was Martha afraid of men? Did her relationship with her father negatively influence her feelings about the opposite sex? At the time Martha's chums chalked up her indifference to her busy schedule. Later they placed the blame on the father-daughter relationship and Kostyra family problems in general.

"Martha was very closemouthed about what went on at home," stated Nancy Teischman DeGrote, whose mother and Mrs. Kostyra were close friends. "Martha kept a lot to herself. I don't know if anyone could really get real close to her."

Once, when DeGrote overheard her own parents arguing, she became so upset that she sought Martha's guidance. "I was absolutely devastated. I said, 'Martha, I think my parents are getting a divorce. I've never heard them talk like this before.' And I remember Martha saying very coolly, 'Nancy, don't worry about it. My parents fight and say things like that *all* the time.' "

Lynn Sherwood Kaneps said she was aware that Martha had problems with her father, as Frank Kostyra has also asserted. "I'm always surprised when, on her TV shows or in odds and ends that I've read, Martha speaks lovingly of her father," she said. "Instinctively I knew that there was something wrong. As kids we all had strict fathers. I always thought my father was the strictest. But maybe under it all Martha's was the worst because *we* would talk about it, but *she* wouldn't talk about it. And instinctively we realized that there might be a problem there. She would never have said, 'My dad hit me, my dad kicked me, my dad hit my mom,' because maybe it was something much more serious.''

Martha's seeming uninterest in boys didn't preclude the fact that she did on occasion go out with them. But they usually found her cold and intimidating.

"She didn't flirt, and she didn't project a whole lot of personality,'' observed Kaneps.

"She was *too* attractive, and she was *too* intelligent, and she was *very* cold,'' maintained handsome Ansis Girts Kaneps, a member of Martha's class who later married Lynn Sherwood.

"The guys didn't think much of Martha,'' asserted Gail Hallam Charmichael. "Having three brothers, I used to listen to them and the guys on the football team talk when they came over to our house. They would laugh and call her a cold fish. And they would talk about her having no boobs, or whatever expressions they used.''

But Charmichael also remembered the evening Martha and a boy steamed up the Hallams' kitchen making out, breaking the ironing board Martha was leaning against while in a passionate embrace. "The rest of the guys were kind of astonished that maybe she wasn't as cold as they thought,'' she said.

Mark Hallam, one of Gail Charmichael's older brothers, was one of the few Nutley High boys who actually dated Martha. Like her, he was among the school's elite; he was president of the Student Council in senior year and a jock. Both were in a preppy clique and shared many of the same college-bound classes and extracurricular activities. Hallam also met Martha's standards for social acceptability: He was good-looking and came from a good family—his father was a banker and the Hallams lived in the best part of town. Plus, he was one of the few boys who owned a car, a '49 green Studebaker convertible, and Martha enjoyed being seen around town in it—even if it was only for an evening at the Bowlero and a pizza afterward.

"My folks *loved* Martha," remembered Hallam, who went on to earn degrees at Amherst and the University of Pennsylvania and developed a successful practice as a veterinarian. "To them she was the ideal girl. She was intelligent. She was beautiful. She was well mannered. They couldn't ask for more.

"But she wasn't real warm, so she wasn't a real desirable date as a romantic mate in those days. She had blond hair and a cute face, but she didn't have a great figure. She was kind of a beanpole—skinny and no breasts. I didn't have great expectations when I went out with her. Back in those days there were a few girls in the school where you anticipated something more than making out a little bit and a good night kiss. You knew that at best you were going to kiss Martha a couple of times, maybe make out a little, but that was going to be as far as it would go. Martha was goal-oriented. She had a lot of drive. She wasn't about to get tied up in any kind of relationship."

The search for eligible young men sometimes took Martha and her pals far afield of Nutley. The Ivy League campus of Princeton University, about an hour south of town, for instance, was occasionally their hunting ground, especially on fall weekends when there was a football game and Doreen Sawyer Skök had her Ford. "We were not looking for academic boys," recalled Lynn Sherwood Kaneps. "I don't think we looked at anybody and said, 'What's your grade point average?' We would go strictly to see what was available. The criteria were: sophisticated, rich, good-looking."

"Martha immediately took to the Waspy Princeton scene," a friend said. "It fulfilled a fantasy for her, an escape from her poor roots. And she fitted in so well."

Not long after her initial visit, Martha made it known to her friends that she had been invited to attend a weekend house party on the Princeton campus. "It was supposed to be very glamorous, and we were all kind of envious that she was doing this sophisticated, glamorous thing," said a member of Martha's clique.

"Martha came back from the party with a glow. She said

she had the most marvelous time ever. But the story that Martha put out for general consumption was different from what actually happened,'' said her pal. ''Once you're in college, once you've been to those house parties, you find out they're nothing more than drunken orgies. I don't think the party Martha went to was an orgy, but it *wasn't* sophisticated and wonderful like she expected and like she said it was. I asked her, 'Why don't you say what really happened? Why don't you tell the truth?' And she finally admitted that she didn't have as good a time as she had claimed.

''She said her mother had told her *not* to say she didn't have a good time. Why would her mother tell her that? Because Martha was doing something the rest of us hadn't done. Mrs. Kostyra felt that if we were envious of her, we should remain envious. It's what I call revisionist history, just like her published memories about Nutley. It's what she *wished* had happened as opposed to what *did* happen.''

Martha's one ''hot'' romance during high school was with a transfer student from St. Benedict's, in Newark: Peter Farabaugh, a six-foot-four, blue-eyed, square-jawed son of an obstetrician-gynecologist.

''*I would study,*'' Farabaugh acknowledged in the Nutley High yearbook, ''*but me oh my, these women drive me crazy* . . . Pete likes girls, 'Mostly Martha . . .' ''

The handsome, easygoing Farabaugh swept Martha off her feet, or she seduced him, depending on who was telling the story. Others suggested that Martha had lured Farabaugh away from her pal Doreen Sawyer Skök. They remembered that Doreen had been dating Farabaugh, and when she went away for the summer, Martha had suddenly started seeing him.

''Martha kept things pretty much to herself. And if Peter and Martha did date, it was not being talked about because Doreen was our friend,'' said Lynn Sherwood Kaneps. ''If they were seeing each other, it would have been very much on the sly.''

That fall a photo appeared in the *Gauntlet* of Martha and Farabaugh, smiling and holding hands, at the Miss Gauntlet of 1958 dance held in the Nutley High gymnasium. Martha's pal LeAnne White Ritchie had been chosen as queen, and

Martha was one of the four runners-up, which got a mention in the *Gauntlet*'s gossip column, "Senior Peephole."

But true to form, the relationship between Martha and Farabaugh ended rather abruptly. After about five months, the two stopped dating. According to friends, Martha's father was behind the breakup. He didn't like Farabaugh, they said, nor for that matter did he like any other boy with whom she went out.

"Peter used to laugh about that," recalled Farabaugh's first wife, Peggy Mylod Farabaugh, also a Nutley High grad. "Martha's father was rather strict, and Peter had to get her home on time. It would be worth your life if you *didn't* get Martha home on time. All the boys used to laugh about how strict he was. They used to say they'd just slow down in front of the Kostyra house and tell Martha to jump out of the car because Mr. Kostyra would be waiting out front. It was the same no matter whom she went out with."

Eddie Kostyra believed that a steady boyfriend would take away from Martha's pivotal senior year studies, her efforts to get into a good college, her need to win a scholarship, and her budding modeling career. He put his foot down, and Farabaugh was suddenly out of the picture.

From what friends recalled, there was no argument from Martha, whose goal was to get out of Nutley and into a good college. "She thought Peter was cute and fun but had nothing upstairs," said a member of her circle. "Martha was much more sophisticated than Peter. She had bigger fish to fry."

It was actually Peter Farabaugh's best friend, William Craig Carey, who probably benefited most from taking Martha out. Though he lived in Nutley, Carey commuted daily to New York City, where he attended Xavier High School, an exclusive private Jesuit military academy. With the school's annual military ball scheduled for early in November 1958, he had decided that the girl he escorted should be a knockout and classy enough to be voted queen of the hop. From Farabaugh, Carey learned about the teenage model from Elm Place. Carey, who stood an inch or two shorter than the five-foot-nine Martha, took one look and told her she was a definite contender and that he would submit her pictures to the school. If she won, she'd have to be his date for the evening.

The ever-confident Martha, looking down at Carey, said, "Why not?"

Carey, a shrewd go-getter who later became a lawyer, had picked a winner.

Under the headline CADET CHOICE, the New York *Journal-American*, on Sunday, November 9, 1958, ran a photograph whose caption read: "An honor guardsman salutes with sword as Martha Kostyra, 17, of 86 Elm Place, Nutley, N.J., escorted by 2nd Lt. William Carey, enters New York City Hall to invite Mayor Wagner to Xavier High School's Military Ball tomorrow night at the Hotel Statler. Martha will be crowned Sweetheart of the Xavier Regiment."

Martha, who basked in the publicity, added the clipping to her scrapbook, the kudo to her high school résumé, and put the photograph, which showed her wearing a conservative suit, into her modeling portfolio.

The next evening Carey, a personable Irish American with an ironic sense of humor, arrived to pick up Martha wearing several extra pairs of socks in hopes that it would make him look taller next to his willowy date.

"Martha made the dress she was wearing to the ball, and when Craig came to pick her up, I was upstairs hemming it like Cinderella," recalled Martha's cousin Diane Carey. "That was the night I met Craig, who became my husband. He called me the following week to go out for a date. We got married seven years later. I guess it never panned out between them."

Though Martha was a teenager during the golden age of rock and roll—the mid to late fifties—the music had little fascination for her. Unlike many of her classmates, who were beboppers—some even making the pilgrimage to Philadelphia to dance on *American Bandstand*—Martha thought rock and roll was garbage, possibly because her father wouldn't permit her to play it at home. "Unlike my house," said Diane Carey, "I don't remember rock and roll being blasted at Martha's. My uncle played the violin, so he was trying to instill that into the kids."

The other issue was money. Martha, who was socking away every penny she earned for college, wasn't about to shell out eighty-nine cents for a 45 rpm record, the way her friends did. "For Martha, the basic thing in high school was *money, money, money*," Carey observed. "She put it in the bank. She wasn't one to go out and blow money by any means."

But Martha, always on top of popular trends, kept up on who was on the hit parade. And when she discovered that her pal Doreen Sawyer Skök was a friend of Concetta Franconero's brother, George, Martha shifted into high gear in hopes of meeting *her* through him.

At the time the Franconero girl, better known as Connie Francis, had had a number of hit songs: "Who's Sorry Now," "Stupid Cupid," "Fallin,' " and "My Happiness." Connie, who was twenty, was raking in big bucks for herself, for the Franconero family of Belleville, a predominantly Italian enclave next to Nutley, and for MGM Records. Her money, her power, and her popularity impressed and fascinated Martha, and she was determined to get to know Connie Francis. It couldn't hurt.

Martha decided that the best way to meet the singer was to become friends with her brother, so she decided to throw a party in his honor. She also arranged to have Doreen Sawyer Skök put in a good word for her. The Sawyers and the Franconeros had summer homes at Lake Mohawk, a tony North Jersey vacation spot.

Although Martha later became America's premier expert on entertaining, she had never thrown a real party at the Kostyra house during her high school years until the Connie Francis opportunity came along.

"Connie Francis's brother's presence was *very* important to Martha," Nancy Teischman DeGrote said. "She was socially aware of that sort of thing even then—of being with the *right* people. Martha was *very* aware of social things."

Martha tossed the bash when her father was out of town. Otherwise he never would have permitted it. But the party apparently had little impact on the Franconero boy, who never introduced Martha to his famous sister. Without Connie Francis in the picture, Martha's interest in George Franconero quickly faded out, and the friendship ended. As one high school chum observed later, "I always got the impression that Martha only liked a guy if there was something in it for her."

High Honors

By senior year, all of Martha's hard work and planning had been amply rewarded. Her hustling had combined to earn her at least partial scholarship money and admittance to Barnard, one of the nation's finest women's colleges.

"I had little choice of where I could go to college because I had to live at home," she said. "NYU gave me a full scholarship. Barnard offered me only a very partial scholarship, but I was modeling and I knew I could make enough money to pay for my education, so I chose Barnard."

When friends and family members read those words in a magazine profile in 1991, they were surprised. None of them was aware that Martha had *ever* been offered a full-tuition scholarship. "If she had, Eddie damn well would have demanded that she accept it," a relative commented. "Eddie would have never let Martha turn down something like that."

The only scholarship that Martha was known to have won was a partial scholarship awarded by the Nutley Rotary Club. TRIBUTE FIVE "ROTARY SCHOLARS," declares the headline over a photo of Martha and four of her classmates on the front page of the Nutley *Sun*—READ EVERY WEEK IN 96% OF NUTLEY HOMES—on June 25, 1959.

"The five Nutley High School 'Rotary Scholars' were

guests of the Nutley Rotary Club at its weekly luncheon last Thursday at Casa Capri,'' the caption reads. The photo shows a beaming Martha, wearing a waist-length double-breasted plaid jacket, a faux pearl necklace, and a summery skirt. She was standing with class president Sandy Stoddard, bound for the U.S. Naval Academy; her close pals Ellie Watts, who chose Elmira College, and Barbara Viventi, who was off to Bryn Mawr with a four-thousand-dollar National Newark and Essex scholarship; and Martha's onetime boyfriend Mark Hallam, headed for Amherst. "Each of the five received special Rotary medallions for scholarship and leadership, at N.H.S. graduation exercises . . . with one of the quintet being awarded a sixteen-hundred-dollar scholarship. The actual winner of the scholarship was not made known.'' Years later Martha's uncle Hank Kostyra discovered a copy of that article among his family memorabilia. On the clipping someone had written that the scholarship had been worth four hundred dollars a year to his niece.

Martha was overjoyed at the prospect of going to Barnard. In Ellie Watts Flavin's yearbook, Martha wrote triumphantly: "Dear Ellie, I've just been accepted at Barnard, and Barnard here I come!''

Recalled Flavin: "It was real excitement in her, and I know there had to have been some concern about payment for tuition because that was not a cheap school. Barnard was her first choice, and it also was one of those late-admissions things, like a mid-April kind of thing, so it was a matter of her hanging on and hoping that it would happen.''

"Stairway to the Stars'' was the theme of the class of '59's senior prom, and the prom committee had huge plans to transform the smelly gym into what the *Maroon and Gray*, the school newspaper, described as "a silvery summer night, a fairyland of billowing clouds and twinkling lights.'' The Souvenirs, a nine-piece orchestra, had been hired, and "lucky couples'' were being offered door prizes that included "two Pig's dinners at Bonds.''

The girls had been preparing for the prom for months— all of them except Martha. Once again she was without a date, this time for the most important social event of her high school career.

When Lynn Sherwood Kaneps learned of Martha's fix, she set to work arranging a date for her with Peter Lanken, the school's lanky, bashful film-projector operator, a member of the Rifle Club, a big fan of TV's *Maverick*, and a swimmer.

"Like Martha, Peter Lanken didn't date anybody," said Kaneps. "So I fixed them up. I was the manipulator behind it because Peter was *painfully* shy—it got to be a challenge to get Peter Lanken to even talk to you. Somehow or other I convinced him that he *had* to go to the prom, and that Martha would like to go with him, and I told Martha the same thing. I pulled off some stunt like that."

Once Martha agreed, she set about making her own prom dress from a *Vogue* pattern. All of the girls were wearing pastel gowns, but Martha used a rich brown fabric. "She wanted to stand out," observed Diane Carey. "She wanted to be different."

Martha was graduated in the top 10 percent of her class. Her only award, despite all her activities and high grades, was High Honors in English, based on her having had all A's in the subject.

Her yearbook picture made her look like Doris Day. " 'Marty' . . . likes reading, eating, English, and swimming . . . would like to see Darkest Africa . . . and when she hears 'Somebody Loves Me,' she says 'Ohhhhhh . . .' " the caption said.

Martha's personal inscription confidently declared: "I do what I please and I do it with ease."

Barnard, Bermudas,
and *Glamour*

"**M**y best friend during my freshman year at Barnard College was Wendy Supovitz," Martha wrote in her magazine. "Her family lived in Shaker Heights, Ohio, and whenever her parents came to New York to visit they took us to Trader Vic's for drinks and dinner. It was then, in 1960, that I was introduced to the pleasures of Polynesian cuisine. . . ."

Martha has used the "Remembering" column in *Martha Stewart Living* as a segue for colloquies about various subjects having to do with the cosmic product of lifestyle. "Foreign Affairs" was the title of the piece that mentioned Ms. Supovitz, an essay not about Martha's first-year social life at Barnard but rather about her early experimentation with exotic foods.

When Wendy Reilly, née Supovitz, read that particular column in Martha's magazine, her first reaction was one of euphoria. Out of the blue there she was, her name unexpectedly appearing in one of America's most popular magazines and linked to one of America's most extraordinarily successful women. "It was really exciting," she said later. "I couldn't believe it." Then, after rereading the brief mention, she shook her head, thought, "Shaker Heights? . . . What?" And burst out laughing.

A residential suburb of Cleveland, Shaker Heights is one of the most affluent communities in the country, a place that would make a perfect backdrop for a Martha Stewart layout. But Wendy Supovitz Reilly *wasn't* a Shaker Heights girl.

"Martha knows I'm from Steubenville," she said. "I guess Shaker Heights looked and sounded better to her than Steubenville."

Reilly said it *was* true that on several occasions the Supovitzes had visited New York and had taken her and a few of her college chums to dinner. "We could go to any restaurant we wanted, Pavilion, for example. But I don't remember ever going with my parents to Trader Vic's. And I don't remember that we ever took Martha there."

The daughter of a well-to-do businessman and Martha became instant friends during freshman orientation in September 1959. "Martha was tall and blond, and I was tall and blond," Reilly said. "It wasn't real deep, but that's what brought us together."

Martha began college at the dawn of one of the most tumultuous decades in America's history—a montage of momentous and minor events, one replacing the other so quickly that they all seemed to swirl together like images in a kaleidoscope: the civil rights movement; the space race; the Cuban missile crisis; Elvis, and Marilyn, and Charles Van Doren; the Twist; Vietnam; the assassination of John F. Kennedy.

Barnard was a highly politicized school. As early as Martha's freshman year, classmates were joining peace marches or traveling South to protest segregation.

But Martha was no activist, and the Kostyras were not liberals though they did support Kennedy. The civil rights movement was as invisible to Martha as black people were in Nutley, a mostly white community, with African Americans relegated to the ghettos of nearby Newark. Martha never had a black friend, never knew any blacks until she entered Nutley High, where there were only a few. In her graduating class there were four African Americans, and the yearbook showed them in a stereotyped light: One girl, "Says 'Goodness'" and "hopes to own a Cadillac." Another's ambition was "to graduate," and a third "likes dancing and Chuck Berry. . . ." The most popular black in Martha's class was Clinton A. Taylor, a star athlete, known affectionately as Goose, whose favorite phrase was "You betchum." One yearbook photo showed an unidentified white boy standing with his arm around Taylor, whose face and hair were covered with what appeared to be whipped cream. "Taste good, Clint?" the caption asked.

Martha's world always was white. Her many books, her magazine, and her TV show ignored the tastes and lifestyles of even the most upscale black Americans, a fact that was underscored somewhat embarrassingly by Martha during a December 1995 appearance on *Larry King Live*. Asked by a caller whether she had any holiday decorating tips for Kwanzaa, Martha asked, "What's Kwanzaa?"

While Martha didn't march for equality in Alabama or Mississippi or hand out "Ban the Bomb" flyers in Washington Square, she did become enmeshed in one campus political controversy known as the Bermuda Shorts Ban.

It all started in the spring semester of Martha's freshman year, when Barnard president Millicent McIntosh, despite her staunch feminist views, established a dress code, still referred to years later in the *Barnard Alumni Magazine* as the "Dress Code Horror." McIntosh caused a furor among a certain faction of the student body, mainly Martha's preppy crowd, when she ordered that Bermudas, which were highly popular at more traditional Seven Sisters schools like Smith and Vassar, could not be worn on her sophisticated Manhattan campus.

The ban became a cause célèbre when *The New York Times* and the *Herald Tribune* ran prominent page one stories. Reporters and photographers from all over the country descended on the college.

Enter Martha Kostyra, her pal Wendy Supovitz Reilly, and an unidentified Japanese young woman wearing a traditional kimono and clogs. Martha and Wendy were looking *très* preppy in their banned Bermudas, button-down oxford cloth shirts, and white sneakers as they stood talking to the Japanese woman. A news photographer, covering the fuss, shot the tableau, and Martha's picture appeared in newspapers around the country.

"Martha and I were totally unaware of President McIntosh's proposal," Reilly swore. "We weren't wearing our

Bermudas as part of any protest. Actually we had been off campus shopping for *new* Bermudas the day that photo was taken. We just didn't know we weren't supposed to be wearing them.''

What really angered Martha most about the whole controversy, though, was not the rights issues raised but rather the angle of the photo of her that appeared in the New York *Daily News* and other newspapers across the country.

''The camera was to Martha's back,'' Reilly said. ''Martha was furious because the picture showed my face—and *not* hers.''

An art history major, Martha seemed undaunted by the heavy academic load and intellectual demands that Barnard placed on her. She had no choice but to be on the five-course system, which meant she had to take a minimum of five subjects per semester, equal to fifteen credits or more. Competition was keen, and the professors rarely gave out A's. But Martha was used to working hard. However, unlike her high-profile status at Nutley High, she now was lost in the crowd, a small fish in a big sea of many extremely bright, driven, ambitious, and attractive women.

The heavy hitters, the two who became the best known of the class of '63—at least until Martha Kostyra reinvented herself as *the* Martha Stewart—were a talented dancer, Twyla Tharp, and an ambitious writer, Erica Mann. Years later, Martha and Mann, better known as Erica Jong, were antagonists in a private feud of potentially explosive and scandalous proportions.

Students who lived in the dorms kept their lights burning, studying late into the night, rarely leaving campus, the academic pressures being so great. They often arrived at early-morning classes wearing nightclothes under their raincoats, having studied right up until the last minute. But Martha was placing even greater physical and emotional demands on herself as a commuter working her way through school. Her daily grind often began before dawn, when she boarded the bus in Nutley, bound for the Port Authority terminal, in Times Square, where she jumped onto the crowded subway to the campus, at Broadway and

116th Street. The trip often took two hours, time she used to study.

After classes, and sometimes in between, she worked, squirreling away every penny to supplement her scholarship. "I lived home my first year and commuted, and I had so many jobs," she said. "I modeled. I worked in Bamberger's in Newark selling chocolates at Christmas."

Recalled a classmate, Caroline Fleisher Birenbaum, who became active in the art world: "Martha's life wasn't glamorous, even with the modeling. The modeling was a grueling piece of work that she had to squeeze in before she did her homework. When she went out on modeling interviews, I'd see her racing off campus wearing a beautiful gray coat dress that she had made herself. It was a hectic life."

Sometimes the pace became too much, and Martha would crash on the floor in Wendy Supovitz Reilly's dorm room in Hewitt Hall. But usually she required little sleep, had infinite energy, and seemed to thrive on the stress, even volunteering to help design costumes for Barnard's annual Greek Games, a weekend festival of artistic and athletic events.

"Martha was very knowledgeable about the sewing and construction of costumes, and we tried to design and make a historically accurate costume by doing research," said Marlene Lobell Ruthen, an American history major who commuted from Yonkers. "When we didn't win the costume designing award, Martha was *very* disappointed. She felt the judges didn't appreciate our design."

Next to her classes, though, Martha's focus remained on her modeling career. She had started getting jobs at Bendel's and Bergdorf's, and her face was showing up frequently in magazines. For a "very short time," she was a Ford model.

In order to go out on interviews, Martha often resorted to borrowing clothing from friends because her wardrobe was still nearly bare. "Martha didn't have a lot, so she borrowed mine," said Wendy Supovitz Reilly, whose dorm closet was bursting with expensive things from Saks and Bonwit's. "She'd say, 'Let me take this, let me take that,' and she went in and took them. My clothing even showed up in a number of magazine layouts. After she won the *Glamour* thing, the French magazine *Marie Claire* did a profile on her, and she wore my outfits in that layout too.''

The *Glamour* ''thing'' was a major milestone in Martha's modeling career. Every fall *Glamour* magazine selected the ten best-dressed college girls in America. Martha, ever confident, felt she had a shot at being chosen, so she sent in her application, attaching photos of herself wearing borrowed dressy, casual, and business outfits.

The formal announcement of her selection appeared in *Glamour*'s big back-to-school issue. IT'S A GRAND NEW FLAG, declared the headline over *Glamour*'s sappy text.

> There is, suddenly, nothing old under the sun. Art, science, politics—in each, we have tried to imagine the unimaginable new frontiers that will be met, and crossed, by today's college girls, in tomorrow's world. Things no longer mean what they used to mean: all at once, they mean far less— or infinitely more. That's why, with little or no apology to blueberry pie, we first photographed the ten young women you meet on the next pages, Glamour's best-dressed college girls of 1961, with the star-spangled space-sign of freedom; the newly meaningful, soberly magnificent, freshly waving American Flag. Now, one by one: the winners.

A full-page photograph showed a pert Martha, wearing an A-line coat, gloves, and medium heels and carrying an alligator handbag. The layout described her as a young woman of ''Tenderness'' and ''Vitality.''

> An expressive face. Both shy and sure, a flicker of fun in her eyes and mouth. . . . Life pleases her . . . in particular, a young man named Andy, art and architecture, heroes, composer Bartok, Churchill, playwright Christopher Fry; she cooks, too. . . . She wears ''TIGER BRIGHTS''—orange-tropical extract . . . here in a fluffy coat, first semi-fitted then flared—in front a waist and shirred, in back no waist and smooth. Scarf: paisley print.

Barbara Stone, *Glamour*'s model editor at the time, later Martha's agent, said the magazine's contest was "a very big deal in those days. It was something young college girls really vied to get in. Colleges all over the country were hoping to be selected, girls were hoping to be chosen. But not every girl had actually been modeling like Martha. She was ahead of the game when she entered the contest."

The winners' chaperone that year was a stunner. "Tall and slim as a sapling with streaky brown hair and level blue eyes," was the way *Glamour* described just-married Norma Collier, one of 1960's ten best-dressed college girls, a cum laude, and Phi Beta Kappa, from Wilson College, a small Presbyterian school in Pennsylvania.

"Martha was excited about having won," Collier recalled. "She liked the opportunity, but she was certainly not starry-eyed about it. After all, she was a Barnard girl. She was too sophisticated. She hadn't come from a little school in Kansas."

Martha and Norma were to have a close relationship that lasted for decades. "We became very good friends right away," she said. "Martha was the godmother of my children, and I was her daughter's godmother. We had keys to each other's houses. We spent holidays together. We were very close, like family."

Over the years Norma Collier was a prime-time player in the many private dramas in Martha's life. She also was one of the many friends and associates who fell victim to Martha's increasingly rapacious, calculating, manipulative, exploitative, and sometimes frightening behavior.

Few College Men

In describing her collegiate love life after she became famous, Martha claimed that "my boyfriends had been fun-
seekers—boys from South America and Europe with big
allowances who took me dancing at El Morocco."

Once again, Martha's assertion was somewhat exagger-
ated. For a very short time she ran around with a few
wealthy Argentinian boys, and they took her nightclubbing.
But the glamorous life of the sexy college girl she was
trying to portray didn't really exist.

As in high school, Martha had few, if any, dates at Barnard, and classmates usually had to arrange escorts for her
because most young men were turned off by her cold and
intimidating manner.

"I was not as beautiful as Martha," said Wendy Supovitz Reilly. "But I was tall and blond and outgoing and liked
to go out and have a good time, so I'd often have to get
Martha a date for Saturday night. Boys were afraid to ask
her out. If there was an event going on, I would call guys
and ask them to call her, and they'd say, 'I'm afraid. But
thanks anyway.' Or, 'I can't go with her. It would be too
much.' They seemed kind of overwhelmed by her."

Reilly couldn't recall Martha's dating the playboys she
has described and maintained that any dates Martha did
have were with traditional college boys whom she met at
mixers.

In the early sixties many college girls—especially at so-

76

phisticated schools like Barnard—began experimenting with sex and drugs. Martha's college years heralded the Sexual Revolution, the "Swinging Sixties." Helen Gurley Brown's *Sex and the Single Girl* had become required reading. "Nice girls should do it, too," the *Cosmopolitan* editor advised. The Pill, which the Food and Drug Administration approved in Martha's freshman year, had become available by prescription by her junior year.

For some of Martha's classmates, sexual experimentation and "pot parties" became de rigueur. "There could well have been those kinds of parties," said Reilly, "but I was still coming from that midwestern wholesome orientation, and Martha was the same way. She was too wholesome to smoke pot."

While Reilly didn't think Martha participated in any of the shenanigans, she did remember taking her to hip parties at the Greenwich Village pad of a friend. An incident during one of those excursions on the wild side still struck Reilly as curious years later. "I had a friend from Steubenville who came to study at NYU," Reilly said. "She was very promiscuous, but it was fun to visit her, and it was kind of a big open house at her apartment, a walk-up on West Tenth Street. We all knew she was kind of wild, and the kinds of things she was doing one wouldn't do in public.

"I went with Martha and it was late at night and I guess we were heading back to Barnard when a carful of boys started following us, and they definitely weren't the kind of boys we wanted to meet. So out of the blue Martha whispered, 'Hold my hand, and we'll pretend we're queer, and they'll leave us alone.' So we held hands, and they stopped bugging us. In that day *that* was really something. Martha was *not* naive."

Another close friend of Martha's during freshman and sophomore years, Rosemary López Roca, daughter of a high-ranking diplomat from the Philippines, attributed Martha's sexual conservatism to her Catholicism and the high goals she had set for herself. "Martha was very picky and choosy about men," Roca recalled. "She thought the other girls would go out with *anyone,* and she felt that was very déclassé. Martha believed one had to be more discriminating. Actually I don't remember Martha dating at all.

"Other girls were experimenting with the freedom their parents gave them. Martha was not. The kind of sexual activity the other girls were partaking in was not acceptable to her. Martha believed a girl was less desirable if she had to do *that* kind of thing just to get a date or to be popular. She was convinced she could be popular *without* doing those things. Martha and I both felt that if boys really liked us, we could get dates without having to *do* anything. Martha was Catholic, and so was I, and we shared those beliefs, which gave us something in common. We did not have sex, and we looked down on girls who did. We thought they were cheap and vulgar. Martha's view was that you got engaged and got married."

Roca, whose first marriage after college was to the heir to the United Philippines Lines' fortune, maintained that Martha also wanted to find a wealthy man.

Wendy Supovitz Reilly, a close friend of Roca's, agreed: "Martha wanted to marry well. She knew what was available in the world, and she wanted to get some of that for herself. I wanted a guy who was cute or was a good dancer. Martha wanted somebody who was rich, who would give her a certain kind of lifestyle. She knew what she wanted, and she wasn't going to take any risks to not achieve her goals. That was obvious."

It began in a Greek art class in the spring of 1960, near the end of Martha's freshman year. The slender, elegant brunette art major noticed Martha the instant she walked into Associate Professor Virginia Harrington's class and was struck by her looks: tall, slim, blond, very clean-cut. "How attractive," Diane Stewart Love thought. "How nice."

Recently married to Stanley Love, who was to make millions in children's wear, Diane (pronounced Dee-Ann) always had an eye out for a pretty woman who might make a suitable date for her big brother, Andy Stewart, who was in his first year at Yale Law School.

But playing Cupid for her brother in the past had been a disaster. On previous occasions Diane had attempted to fix up Andy with friends, but in each instance the chemistry wasn't there. It wasn't as if Andy, a handsome, six-foot-four, charming, and erudite young man, needed his sister's help. He did quite well on his own with the opposite sex. But he appreciated her efforts and tried not to discourage her because he never knew whom she might come up with next.

Not long after she had spotted Martha in class and made a mental note of her, Diane Love was working in the library when she saw the Kostyra girl browsing through the stacks, and on impulse approached her. "Excuse me, but I have a very nice brother. Would you like to meet him?" She showed Martha a picture of Andy that she kept in her wallet and told her what a swell guy he was and asked how he could get in touch with her. Martha was intrigued, but more with Diane than her brother. Years later she noted, "Diane was such an interesting person. She drove a Jaguar and dressed in Dior and Balenciaga coats."

"And so Martha gave me her number, and I gave it to my brother," Diane Stewart Love recalled later. In hindsight she had mixed feelings about making the introduction. "I guess I was only looking at the cover of the book. My interest was my brother's happiness, and that's what motivated my behavior and actions."

PART TWO

*Frosting the
Wedding Cake*

Andy

Though he was to play a pivotal role in Martha's literary and business successes and control three creative and dynamic publishing houses, Andy Stewart as a youth had never really read a book or spent much time in a library. Until he got into college, he considered himself semiliterate.

Blame it on his parents, George and Ethel Stewart, an eccentric couple who had moved from apartment to apartment, city to city, state to state, country to country so often that Andy never was in one place long enough to have an orderly education. For the boy, and later the man, chaos, commotion, and turbulence seemed to follow him like a shadow—and even more so after his marriage to Martha Kostyra.

Like most average families in the postwar years the Kostyras anchored themselves firmly in an affordable house with simple comforts, whereas the far more affluent Stewarts were adventurous nomads. And unlike Eddie and Martha Kostyra, who were college-educated but rather parochial, the Stewarts were extremely worldly but had no formal higher education.

George Stewart had an obsession with travel. He'd hear or read about an interesting place and decide to pull up family stakes and go there.

Similarly, Ethel Stewart had a preoccupation with decorating. "She explored decorating, she loved it, and she once even bought an apartment just to fancy up, but not live in," said a family friend.

While they were loving parents, they were impractical when it came to raising their children. In many ways they had never grown up themselves. Later, Andy and Martha would virtually mirror the Stewarts' unsound parenting techniques with their own child.

George Stewart was from a large brood. His strict immigrant parents, Jews from Russia, never permitted him to speak at the dinner table. Because of his stern upbringing, he grew into a quiet, closed dreamer, a modern-day wandering, nonpracticing Jew from Brooklyn.

An impressive-looking man who stood over six feet and weighed more than two hundred pounds, Stewart derived his greatest pleasure from his career, which was playing the stock market. He was a risk taker who used curious investment systems.

In his heyday, between December 1953 and June 1957, he owned a seat on the New York Stock Exchange, entitling him to transact business on the trading floor. Because of a good deal, he had paid only thirty-eight thousand dollars for trading privileges, and his two partners supposedly financed the purchase. At the time Stewart was a principal in a firm called Spring, Stewart & Company, with an office at 25 Broad Street, in the financial district. In 1957 Stewart left the firm and gave up his seat on the exchange; the reason was never clear. He then formed George Stewart & Company, with an office in the Empire State Building. That was the little firm he was running when his son met Martha Kostyra.

Years later the daughter of Stewart's principal partner in George Stewart & Company said it was her understanding that Stewart had taken her father, Emanuel J. Matkowsky, a certified public accountant, for a ride. "My father had been very impressed by this man," she stated. "My father had worked his way up to be a certified public accountant without ever going to college. His passion had always been the stock market. Of course he could never dream of having a seat on the New York Stock Exchange himself. So George Stewart came along and offered him this partnership, and then something turned sour. My mother remembers that as soon as they went into partnership, George and his family took off for a long trip to Europe and left my father to run the place. My father had trusted George Stewart completely. But then a Canadian stock deal turned bad, and I think my father was left holding the bag. He then had to go back to his CPA practice. Afterwards we felt that my father was just a little naive in this Waspy world of big business.''

Because of his Wall Street cachet, George Stewart gave people like Matkowsky the impression that he had come from old money or at least had lots of new money. In fact Stewart's small retail brokerage house was beset by financial problems, and Stewart family life was often a scary fiscal roller-coaster ride. But whereas Martha's family worried about putting milk on the table, the Stewarts sometimes wondered where their next tin of caviar was coming from.

Ethel Stewart, née Gilbert—her roots were in England—was a tall, elegant East Side dowager type known for being outspoken and domineering. She also was a devout Christian Scientist whose beliefs, not her husband's Judaism, predominated in the Stewart household. Some people believed Andy Stewart was Jewish, but that was not the case.

Around the time Ethel Stewart's daughter, Diane, introduced Martha to Andy, the Stewarts were living in a three-room apartment that, in Ethel Stewart's words, ''looked like a sultan's palace.'' However, a Stewart family friend said that the apartment, in the elegant Ritz Tower, ''was bizarre'' and that Ethel Stewart was idiosyncratic.

''Ethel put up these huge, heavy valances and curtains which completely obliterated the view,'' she recalled. ''She installed a mirrored floor, and you'd hear her cracking across it in her stiletto high heels. Andy used to laugh about that.

''I have this great image of this elegant New York lady wearing very expensive clothes, and her red lips, and her makeup, in this dark, curtained house with the mirrored floor.''

Ethel Stewart once declared, ''Other than my family,

nothing has ever been as important to me as my homes. I am comfortable with grandeur.''

Andy Stewart was born in New York City on February 8, 1938, three and a half years before Martha. While Andy was growing up, the family lived in at least nine Manhattan apartments that had been decorated by his mother. Andy sometimes didn't recognize his own home after being away because of Ethel Stewart's decorating jones. For the most part he found apartment life confining, if not suffocating.

Much later—probably *too* late—he discovered that his mother and the woman whom he took for his wife had a commonality when it came to decorating. ''You could practically not sit on anything,'' Andy told a confidant after his divorce, ''because it was all *so* precious.''

There were other odd things about his childhood. For instance, the family never exchanged birthday presents, and it wasn't until Andy got into college that he received his first birthday gift—from his roommate.

When Andy was just a child, his father got a whim to see the entire country, so the Stewarts took a motor odyssey through the forty-eight states, with an eight-month layover in Florida, where the family rented a nice home in Miami Beach. Andy was sent to the Lear School, a private academy catering mainly to the sons and daughters of affluent northerners who wintered there. One such student was Barbara Walters, whose father operated the Latin Quarter nightclub. Andy's days were spent sitting around umbrella-covered picnic tables gazing at Biscayne Bay. He hated the school.

Right after the war ended, George Stewart decided that a European jaunt was in order. At the expense of his children, he uprooted the family once again, and they sailed to Europe on the *Île de France*. Andy and Diane were left to fend for themselves in the Gothic environment of an old *école* for boys, the Lycée Jacard, operated by a stern Swiss headmaster, on Lake Geneva near Lausanne. After some months the Stewarts returned for their offspring, and the family traveled together through most of Europe and to Egypt and North Africa.

The experience left Andy bewildered. He felt his formal

education was being stunted by his parents' whims. But his mother thought the travel was a marvelous opportunity to discover exotic decorating ideas—the main reason she allowed her husband to keep her on the road so much. "I don't like to be a copycat [when decorating], I value originality," she said. "We used to stay at the Plaza Athénée—not for days, not for weeks, but for months."

The Stewarts were on the last leg of their long European jaunt, staying at the Hôtel de Paris in Monte Carlo, when Andy's mother struck up a conversation with another traveler who mentioned that she had a nephew who had gone to a wonderful school in the mountains of Vermont, the Putney School. Andy, who loved nature and working with his hands—he had a talent for fixing broken radios and building the Eiffel Tower with his Erector set—was overjoyed at the prospect of living in the country instead of his mother's stifling apartments.

After a year at the very liberal North Country School, in Lake Placid, New York, where Andy spent a happy eighth grade, he was old enough to be enrolled at Putney, an even more progressive coed school, where in tenth grade he had his first girlfriend.

Putney was a working farm with classrooms in former outbuildings. Indeed the dormitory Andy lived in for four years had once been a carriage shed. Along with academic subjects, he learned to work the land, use tools, build things, milk cows—skills that came in handy during his marriage to Martha.

Though the school didn't release grades to the students, Andy knew by the time he reached his senior year that he stood near the top of his class, a fact he learned one afternoon when a friend stood on another classmate's shoulders, peered into the headmaster's window, saw the class order, and passed the good news on to Andy.

By the time he was ready to graduate in June 1955, Andy had high academic aspirations. Just like one of the Kennedy boys, Bobby, Andy wanted to go to Harvard but had to settle for the University of Virginia.

From the day he arrived on the Charlottesville campus as a member of the class of '59, he felt out of place: Andy was politically liberal, most UVA boys came from conservative families; Andy was a civil rights advocate, UVA had few blacks; Andy favored work clothes, his classmates wore khakis, cord jackets, and rep ties.

In class he discovered he could barely write a coherent sentence and got a D minus on his first paper. Facing the threat of failing, Andy hunkered down and began to flex his intellectual muscles. He took a strong interest in cosmology and was accepted into an unusual program, philosophy honors, with philosophy as his major. He was fascinated by epistemology and devoured the writings of Hume, Berkeley, Locke and Kant, Russell and Whitehead. For his honors program he wrote a thesis on human equality.

But Andy didn't completely lose himself between the covers of his books. He was equally adept between the sheets, a talent that became a sore spot at the end of his marriage. Andy had a driving interest in the opposite sex. From adolescence he had a succession of girlfriends. In his last three years at UVA, living with two buddies in a converted garage off campus, he had an intense relationship with a tall, beautiful girl from an upper-middle-class Cincinnati family. She wanted marriage; Andy wanted more girls. They broke up.

In June 1959 he was graduated with a Phi Beta Kappa key, membership in several honor societies, and a degree in philosophy. He turned down a fellowship to study philosophy in graduate school because it required that he teach, which he couldn't stomach.

The draft now hung over his head. "None of us wanted to go," said a college pal of Andy's. "So we had a big reason for staying in school even though we might not have liked it." Still feeling that he had a fuzzy grip on the real world, Andy decided that studying law might get him more organized, even though he wasn't sure he would ever practice. He applied to the best schools, got accepted at all of them, and chose Yale.

Meeting Andy

The summer before he started classes in New Haven, Andy lost his virginity. He soon found other young women who were willing to go all the way. They thought he was a big, lovable bear and ate it up when he played his guitar, quoted poetry, or spouted philosophy. As Jack Rosenblum, his roommate at Yale, recalled, "Andy was always looking for women. He was successful without being a womanizer. He was introspective, and vulnerable, and very sincere. In those days part of dating was trying to get laid, which wasn't easy. But Andy did okay."

When his sister approached him with Martha's telephone number in mid-April 1960, Andy was reluctant to call her. The last blonde she introduced him to had been a dog. But Diane kept telling him this one was different. One evening in May, while he was down from New Haven having dinner at the Loves' Forty-seventh Street apartment, his sister nudged him again. At the time Andy was playing the field, dating a girl from Wellesley, along with a few townies, but he figured what the hell. He dialed the number Martha had scribbled on a scrap of spiral notebook paper, and they arranged to have dinner the next evening.

There had been a major change in Martha's life beginning in January 1960, the start of the second semester of her freshman year. Because of her rigorous academic and work schedule and a desire for more independence, she had moved out of Elm Place into Manhattan. Except for one brief period, she never lived at home again.

College friends of hers thought she had made the right decision. A few who had visited Elm Place felt the tension that existed between Martha and her father. Wendy Supovitz Reilly, who became a psychotherapist, said, "I never heard Martha complain or make derisive comments. But I sensed he was a harsh person—rigid and decisive in what he expected of her."

In order to help finance living in Manhattan, Martha applied at the Barnard job placement office and accepted a position as a full-time maid and cook for a pair of finicky widowed sisters who had a huge apartment on Fifth Avenue in the Nineties, a place crammed with mementos from family travels. "I lived in the servants' quarters," Martha said years later. "It was kind of fun, but depressing."

Martha made an impressive housekeeper who was obsessed with cleanliness. When she discovered a flake of food on top of a kitchen cabinet that had gotten wormy, she was so horrified that she cleaned the *entire* kitchen until it gleamed. Friends found it admirable and remarkable that Martha wasn't ashamed of earning a living doing menial work. "She wasn't embarrassed at all," recalled Reilly. "She needed the money. It was just another thing she had to do to get herself where she wanted to go."

From the moment Andy saw Martha standing in the doorway of her employers' apartment he was wild about her. She was everything his sister had told him and more. Then Martha shut the door in his face, leaving him standing in the little vestibule near the elevator while she finished getting ready for their date.

Andy was not feeling tiptop. Earlier in the day he had had a terrible toothache, had gone to the dentist, and, just before leaving to pick up Martha, had swallowed a handful of aspirin to deaden the pain, all of which he blurted out to her on their way to dinner at his favorite Armenian restaurant. His whining struck Martha as cute, and she joked about it, at one point pushing him flirtatiously, a sudden intimacy that surprised and excited Andy. Enthralled, Andy quickly forgot about his throbbing molar. Easily infatuated with women, but not very perceptive about them, Andy found Martha to be sharp, honest, open, and direct.

The next day the twenty-two-year-old Yalie anxiously telephoned the eighteen-year-old Barnard freshman, and they made another date for that night. And then another. And another.

"We fell in love the first date, that kind of thing . . ." Martha stated. "He was shocked that I always accepted every date. I hadn't read any F. Scott Fitzgerald novels and I didn't know that girls were supposed to lead men on."

For most of that summer, between Martha's freshman and sophomore years, Andy traveled abroad, a trip long planned. There had been some discussion about Martha's joining him—by that point they couldn't bear to be apart—but it was out of the question because of her financial situation.

Martha spent the summer working for her elderly employers, but a problem had developed. They had a nephew, an odd duck in his forties, who had his eye on her. At first she was somewhat flattered by his seemingly innocent advances, but she became alarmed when she walked into her room and found him sitting on her bed. Concerned, she told her close friends. "I think the ladies actually wanted to take her over for their rather strange nephew," recalled Wendy Supovitz Reilly. "Martha told me they were trying to make some kind of arrangement. He definitely was very weird, but they were hoping something would work out. Obviously Martha had no interest in him, and she wasn't going to have any part of it."

His first night home Andy called Martha, and they picked up where they'd left off. Whenever Martha had a free moment, they were together in those few weeks of summer break before Andy was due back in New Haven. The more he saw of her, the more he admired her strength and courage, especially after she told him that she had been paying her own way since the age of thirteen.

In September Andy returned to Yale, and Martha began her sophomore year at Barnard. She continued to live in with her employers and take modeling assignments, some of which were on Seventh Avenue, which made Andy ner-

vous. He imagined short, fat, balding guys in silk suits paw-
ing his girl. But Martha, who was commuting to New
Haven virtually every weekend that fall and winter, told
him not to worry. She knew how to take care of herself.

Some weekends Martha didn't show and gave Andy
vague excuses. When he probed, she admitted she couldn't
afford the seven-dollar train ticket, so he began paying her
fare. He got additional evidence of her financial plight when
he took her to dinner and watched as she scarfed down an
enormous meal. It turned out that the woman who one day
was known for her fancy cooking had been subsisting on
cottage cheese and lettuce most nights.

By now Andy had moved out of his dorm into a funky
little first-floor apartment in West New Haven with his
skirt-chasing sidekick Jack Rosenblum. Sometimes a cur-
mudgeon, Rosenblum had taken an instant liking to Martha.
"She started coming up to the apartment. Martha hung out
with us just about every weekend." It was during that period that Rosenblum became a coconspirator in Andy Stewart's deflowering of Martha Kostyra.

"A lot of our man-to-man talk during the week was cen-
tered on 'What should I do to be successful sexually with
Martha?' Andy was very attracted to her and was asking
me what he could do to make it with her. And I gave him
advice which I'm ashamed of and embarrassed about and
which does not reflect well on me. Basically my advice to
Andy was to tell Martha that he *loved* her, which he did,
and he *was* successful.

"Andy came back from the big weekend and related to
me what happened. Sometimes you have to say the words
'I love you' to find out that they are true. There's an ex-
istential thing about it. You tell somebody you love them,
and you find out if it's true or not. And it was for Andy.
It turned out that he wasn't making it up."

Among a select circle of friends, Andy's deflowering of
Martha has come to be known as the "Martha-I-love-you-
now-let's-fuck" story. Martha was not quite twenty and a
sophomore when she lost her virginity. One of Martha's
Barnard pals remembered her returning to campus after the
momentous event, expressing elation, anxiety, and guilt.

"She talked nonstop about it, and there was a lot of emotion. There was fear," the friend said. "She felt good and bad all at the same time. She worried about pregnancy. She worried that maybe she really didn't love this guy and had gone way too far with him. And another concern was how her father would feel or what he would do if he ever found out."

Nevertheless Martha and Andy became lovers.

"Their relationship went to a different level," observed Rosenblum. "You don't go backwards. But Andy and I had plenty of discussions about how one way to fuck up your life was to knock up somebody."

Martha and Andy installed a black privacy curtain so they wouldn't disturb Rosenblum, who was frequently in the apartment studying while they were making love.

"They had their own privacy, and I just assume they were screwing all the time." The former roommate chuckled. "Andy was happy they had a physical relationship. It became part of the fabric of their relationship. Andy obviously cared for and loved Martha."

A Shaky Engagement

Despite their intimacy, issues involving Martha's strong religious beliefs, along with a certain lack of communication on her part, began to upset Andy, posing a threat to their relationship at a time when he was seriously considering proposing marriage.

Early in their relationship Andy had not been aware of

Martha's rigid adherence to, and beliefs in, the rituals and tenets of Catholicism. He felt that Martha had accepted Catholicism blindly, and that bothered the contemplative former philosophy major who had grown up in a household where religious and philosophical thought and discussion were promoted.

Martha had been raised in an entirely different spiritual and intellectual environment. As she has acknowledged, "I was raised a strict Roman Catholic." In *Entertaining* she writes, "In my childhood home, a religious tradition influenced the rhythm of our [Easter] holiday. It is a custom in the Polish Catholic church for the priest to visit each parishioner to bless the Easter food."

Her brother Eric Scott said, "There was church every Sunday. There was catechism class for all of us. We were all friends of the parish priest, and he was a friend of the family, and he used to come over for dinner at times."

Martha's friend Ellie Watts Flavin said, "The Catholic Church was important to her. There were a few of us Catholic girls—Martha, myself, and Lynn Sherwood [Kaneps]—who would get together on the important occasions like Holy Thursday, when we would go to church together and pray."

A major family trauma occurred during that time when Martha's brother Frank, at the age of twelve, rebelled against the Kostyras' Catholicism while undergoing training to become an altar boy. "I was kneeling down in a cubicle where there was a statue of Mary and the little Christ child," he said. "Suddenly an inner voice spoke to me, saying, 'Get up. You're not to bow down to statues.' From then on, I refused to go back to church. Instead I would ride my bicycle down into the woods near our home on Elm Place, and I would pray to an unknown deity. Dad caught me, and when I told him I wasn't going to go back to church, I was severely reprimanded. Some whippings occurred—he used a strap and a yardstick—and there were other chastisements."

Frank's conversion had caused a major imbroglio within the Kostyra family and had angered Martha. Knowing that he couldn't make a life with such a religiously parochial woman, Andy confronted Martha but found her unresponsive, uncommunicative. Ironically, it was during this period of confrontation that Martha had made her college acting debut as a martyred French Revolution nun, in Georges Bernanos's *Dialogue of the Carmelites*.

"Andy had many discussions with Martha, usually one-sided, about religion, and God, and the nature of the universe, and cosmology, and Andy made his views clear to Martha quite a few times," a member of their college circle recalled. "Early on Martha resisted, refusing to address the issues he was raising. He probably realized she was even more parochial in her thinking than he had initially thought, and certainly *not* introspective. He clearly told her that if she didn't change, their relationship wouldn't work. And Martha did start to change. She began to tell Andy what was on her mind. She softened on the ritualistic aspect of religion. Eventually she stopped practicing Catholicism altogether."

Around Christmas 1960 Martha took Andy home to Nutley for the first time to meet her family, and he was warmly welcomed by Martha Sr. and by Martha's siblings. But Eddie Kostyra was clearly upset. Looking for any excuse to denounce the man he feared was stealing his favorite baby away, Kostyra irrationally accused Andy of acting too affectionate when he picked up little Laura and put her on his knee. Kostyra's accusation caused a terrible row within the family, and when Andy heard about it from Martha, he felt sick to his stomach.

Despite all those undercurrents, Andy proposed marriage to Martha in late February 1961, catching her completely off guard. To his amazement he didn't get the answer he had expected. Martha didn't say no, but she didn't say yes. She was cautious and reluctant. She reeled off a litany of excuses: Marriage was the last thing on her mind; she was too young; he was too young; she wanted to continue with her modeling career; her father would be furious.

Andy's decision to propose was prompted by a fear of losing her. Martha had told him that there was a strong possibility she'd get a chance to go to Paris to model, the result of the *Glamour* award and of a feature story on her that had appeared in the French magazine *Marie Claire*, portraying her as the ideal American young woman. Andy had no doubt that if Martha went to Paris and was successful, he'd never see her again.

"We were young and innocent," Andy said many years later. "We never had the experiences we might have had if we were married four or five years later. But Martha might have changed and I would not have wanted her."

Martha later claimed that Andy had raced down from New Haven when she mentioned the Paris possibility. "He stood outside my window throwing stones at one in the morning," she boasted. "Finally I snuck out of the dorm in my bathrobe. He drove around and around Central Park telling me I should marry him."

But Martha may have been exaggerating just a bit. By that time she'd left the employment of the elderly sisters and had moved into a ten-dollar-a-week room, on an upper floor of a student building, on the Columbia University campus. Stones would have never reached her window, and Andy probably would have been arrested for vandalism. However, the essence of her story was true: Andy did show up unexpectedly at Martha's door, and he took her for a drive in Central Park in his old cream-colored Mercedes sedan, and he talked marriage with her again.

A few weeks later, she finally relented, and in early March 1961 they became engaged.

Eddie Kostyra naturally was incensed. He ranted and raged, warning Martha that marrying would ruin her chances for success. He gave himself as an example of how marriage could destroy someone's potential. "He told me I was crazy," Martha said. "But I decided to go ahead because Andy was honest and extremely serious."

Kostyra also was infuriated because Andy wasn't a Catholic. The fact that he was "that half Jew," as he began to refer to his future son-in-law, made his daughter's choice even more intolerable to him.

"Eddie certainly was anti-Semitic," a Kostyra family confidant asserted. "Anti-Semitism was ingrained in him. While he wasn't a fanatic, he made his views pretty clear, and it was something that Martha heard while she was growing up. It was all the stereotypical stuff: that the Jews killed Christ; that the Jews had all the money; that the Jews were to blame for everyone else's misfortunes.''

In Jersey City's large and close-knit Polish-Catholic community, anti-Semitism had flourished when Kostyra was growing up. Philip Roth documented that fact in his autobiographical novel *Portnoy's Complaint,* which was published to critical acclaim only a few years after Martha and Andy's marriage.

> We moved from Jersey City because of the anti-Semitism. Just before the war, when the Bund was feeling its oats, the Nazis used to hold their picnics in a beer garden only a few blocks from our house. When we drove by in the car on Sundays, my father would curse them, loud enough for me to hear, not quite loud enough for them to hear. Then one night a swastika was painted on the front of our building.

Estelle Burke said her brother was so upset by Martha's choice of a man with Jewish blood that he feared telling their mother, Helen Kostyra, ''because she would have said, 'Martha *has* to marry a Catholic!' ''

Martha's sister Kathy told her pal Gail Hallam Charmichael, '' 'You know my sister's getting married, and his name is Stewart, and he's Jewish, and my father is not happy about it.' '' According to Charmichael, ''It was a hush-hush thing. We didn't talk about it in the Kostyra house because her father was so upset. The Kostyras were Polish Catholics, and this was not what you did: marry a Jew.''

In the 1930s, when fascism and anti-Semitism were on the rise abroad and in this country, Andy's father had decided that being a Jew was not in his best interests, so he buried his roots by changing his last name to the Waspish Stewart. He felt safer and more comfortable in the closet, and he did a good job at passing.

''I *never* knew that George Stewart was Jewish,'' said the shocked daughter of one of Stewart's former stock brokerage partners. ''That is the surprise of the century to me. The impression we got was that he was a well-educated, very elegant, urbane WASP.''

After she had married Andy and was still modeling, Martha saw the value of the Stewart moniker as a selling tool. When she was chosen by the very Waspy Crane stationery of Dalton, Massachusetts, to be in a full-page Sunday *New York Times* advertisement, Martha insisted that the name she was photographed signing on a piece of Crane's exquisite writing paper be "Mrs. Andrew Stewart."

A longtime friend recalled asking Martha at the time about her use of the signature. "She said she felt the name alone would sell more of the company's product. It was also kind of a private joke, a complex assertion that she had arrived in an upscale, elegant, Waspy way. Martha firmly believed her married name emphasized that."

For Martha, George Stewart's choice of a new last name to cover his Jewish heritage was like a gift from heaven. Like the name Betty Crocker, the name Martha Stewart had a perfect ring to it, evoking images of Yankee simplicity and understated WASP elegance. The Jew from Brooklyn had done well for his future Catholic daughter-in-law, a fact that Martha took note of some years later. "Can you imagine my real name, Martha Kostyra? I think it would be very hard to say *Martha Kostyra's Gardening*. It all fits . . . it's all been very fortuitous [*sic*]."

While Andy's Jewish roots were never an issue during the Stewarts' marriage, Martha for some reason chose to make them public long after Andy had left her. In the winter–spring 1996 issue of the *Martha Stewart Living* special weddings issue she writes, "We were raised Catholic, but I had married a Jewish man. . . ." In the magazine's December 1992–January 1993 issue she says, ". . . when I married Andy Stewart, who was Jewish, my family cheerfully included him in our holiday celebrations, and I looked forward to being included in his family's observances. . . . As it happened, Andy and his family (except for his father) did not practice their religion." For whatever reason, Martha chose not to state the true facts: that Christian Science, not Judaism, was the predominant religion in the Stewart home, and that George Stewart was a Jew only by birth. Andy's only concession to his father's religious heritage was pledging a Jewish fraternity while at UVA at the behest of his roommate, Gene Levy.

Many of Martha and Andy's closest friends were shocked after reading Martha's words. Why, they wondered among themselves, did Martha claim that Andy was Jewish when she knew that he wasn't? Norma Collier, for one, said, "I didn't know for *years* that Andy was part Jewish; he was kind of nothing." And Judaism was never a part of Martha and Andy's household. As Martha herself has acknowledged, "We decided to raise [Alexis, their daughter] in no single religion but to educate her about all of them. We invented our own holiday rituals, and as time went on, they became very important to me. . . . We attend no services; family gatherings have become the central holiday rituals, the cornerstones of our lives."

Though Martha has always had a number of Jewish friends and business colleagues and has dated Jewish men since her divorce, she has been known to make comments about Jews when not in their presence. "I don't think she ever used a word like 'kike,' " a confidant said. "But she would say things like 'Well, that's just the Jewish mentality. . . .' I never thought Martha was prejudiced against Jews, but there was some drop of poison there left over from her father."

Besides Andy's Jewishness, an issue that caused some controversy and gossip after Martha accepted his marriage proposal involved the state of the Stewart family's finances. While it *was* true that the Stewarts were in a different league from the Kostyras, everyone misconstrued that to mean that Andy was heir to a family fortune and that his father was a Wall Street baron of sorts.

"I knew Martha was looking for a rich boy to marry— some of the girls even used the words 'gold digger' when they referred to her—and when Andy came along, I had the strong impression, which I'm certain I got from Martha herself, that his family was loaded and that she was set for life," a college friend recalled.

From Kathy Kostyra, Gail Hallam Charmichael had heard that " 'Andy was well fixed and had a good name,' and that meant Martha was moving up in the world. And that bothered me," Charmichael said, "because at that age you're looking for the wonderful prince on the white horse."

To celebrate their engagement, Martha and Andy went "to a romantic cabin" in Vermont. For the first time in her life on skis, Martha fell and twisted her knee, and she spent the rest of the weekend hobbling around. She blamed it all on her family, who, she later wrote, didn't have the money or the time to teach her "social" sports. "Mother and Dad had to struggle so much just to feed the family that these expensive and time-consuming sports—tennis, skiing, water-skiing, sailing—had no place in our lives."

After the ill-fated ski trip Martha's future sister-in-law, Diane Stewart Love, threw a festive dinner party in honor of her brother's engagement. After all, it was Diane who single-handedly had arranged for their meeting, and now she felt like a successful matchmaker. In *Entertaining*, Martha points to Diane's party as her "introduction to grown-up entertaining." She writes: "I remember white damask cloths, silver candlesticks, and a tiny crystal bell that was tinkled after each course and whenever I dropped my napkin."

Meanwhile, to Eddie Kostyra's chagrin, plans were set in motion for a small, nondenominational wedding, scheduled for the summer of 1961.

Tying the Knot

Their first squabble was over the ring. Martha hated it.

Andy had gone to Harry Winston and selected a small quality diamond, which had set him back more than a thousand dollars, a present from his folks. But when he slipped the stone in a simple setting on Martha's finger, she wrinkled her nose and said she didn't want it. She complained that it wasn't big or elegant enough, that it wasn't *anything* she would ever wear on the fourth finger of *her* left hand. She wanted something nicer, and she wanted to choose it. Andy had no other choice but to return the ring the next day.

Through a friend of a friend, Martha and Andy found their way to a midtown diamond wholesaler, where Martha selected a slightly larger diamond in a more interesting setting and *hondled* a better price. "That incident should have set off an alarm," a lifelong friend of the Stewarts observed. "How many women would do something like that? It was a bad omen."

In Nutley Martha and her mother began the enormous task of designing and making her wedding ensemble—the gown, the veil, even the Jackie Kennedy–style pillbox hat that she planned to wear on the big day.

Hearing that she was engaged, some of Martha's high school friends decided to toss a wedding shower. "We found out at the last minute that she was getting married because we were scattered around the country at different colleges," recalled Lynn Sherwood Kaneps. "So Ellie [Watts Flavin] and I rounded up as many people as we could. We just said to Martha, 'Come over, we're going to celebrate your upcoming marriage.' It was *so* low-key. Not many people showed up. It was not a formal, dress-up affair—no decorating the dining-room table, no fancy cake. It was beer and pretzels in the basement recreation room. Through Ellie's mom, who worked in the bridal department at Hahne's in Newark, we got a discount and bought Martha a peignoir set because we figured that maybe this was something that she did not have." But none of those in attendance at the shower remembered Martha expressing excitement about the nuptials or about Andy.

A few of her friends saw Martha, in the final hours leading up to the wedding as she put the finishing touches on her dress in the Kostyra kitchen. "Martha was sewing hundreds of little buttons on the back of her dress and making the little loops for the buttons," said Ginny Stager Diraison. "I was thinking, 'My goodness, to go through all that! It is *so* painstaking.' But she was a very detailed person. Martha didn't do anything halfway."

The wedding of Martha Kostyra and Andy Stewart took place on July 1, 1961. Only immediate members of both families were invited. And Martha kept Andy waiting at the altar. "I was late . . . really late," she admitted. "My father was so nervous, and Andy was standing there, and they played [the music] about ten times before I walked down the aisle. I was just procrastinating."

In the preface to *Weddings* Martha remembers the momentous day in great detail. She said she "did" her wedding herself (meaning without a Martha Stewart–type consultant telling her what to do and how to do it) "in a bit of an unsophisticated haze. . . ." She noted that she married a man "of a different religion, which was a more complicated matter in the 1960s."

She said that she had "the desire for a classic, beautiful wedding. But had no time, had no money, and little self-awareness," possessed, she hoped, by the brides and Martha Stewart wannabes who bought and read *Weddings*.

I was a naive nineteen-year-old, still a student at Barnard, and Andy was beginning Yale Law School [he actually was in his second year], so it seemed appropriate to be married in St. Paul's Chapel at Columbia in an Episcopalian service, mainly because we didn't have anyplace else to go.

Our families were somewhat overcome at the prospect of our marriage. But we were strong-willed enough to just go off and do it. Andy chose the music (Purcell's "Trumpet Voluntary") and in the three weeks after final exams, my mother and I made my dress from embroidered Swiss organdy we found on West Thirty-eighth Street in New York's fabric district. We fashioned four layers of fabric into the gown, and then saved a length to cover a pillbox, the hat Jackie Kennedy had made so fashionable at the Inaugural earlier that year. I carried a bunch of field daisies. There were no formal invitations (I wrote little cards to the family), and no formal portraits.

I had arranged a simple lunch for eighteen in the Barberry Room of the Berkshire Hotel that ended with an ice-cream cake. . . . I suppose it was very basic, but I didn't feel that way. I felt very special.

Guilford Hiatus

Immediately after the wedding the newlyweds left for a quickie honeymoon in Vermont, which coincided with the long Fourth of July weekend. "We both had summer jobs," Martha said, "and I had to be at work on Monday." For three glorious days they stayed in an inexpensive cabin, in a plain vanilla motel, and they used the fourth day to move furnishings from Andy's place, in New Haven, to their first apartment, in Manhattan, a knockout Upper East Side penthouse with terraces and a view that Martha swore allowed her to see Nutley across the Hudson if she squinted.

But alas, it was only a temporary abode, lent to Andy for two months by a well-to-do school friend.

That summer Andy worked as a law clerk for the prestigious New York firm of Breed, Abbott & Morgan, and Martha took whatever modeling jobs she could get. The Stewarts were pinching pennies; money, they knew, would be tight until after Andy graduated from law school. While he didn't have a plan for their future, Andy told friends at the time that he "had a crazy fantasy" that Martha would model for a while and then become a schoolteacher after she got her degree. He saw them having a quiet, uneventful, and traditional life together.

Before the end of the summer of 1961 the Stewarts took a second rushed honeymoon. They drove to Martha's uncle Hank Kostyra's house in Florida and then hopped over to the Bahamas, where they stayed in a modest Nassau hotel. For Martha, who had rarely ventured farther than Manhattan and had never gone out of the country, the brief trip to the touristy island was a glamorous first in her life. "They parked their car in my backyard to avoid having to pay weekly parking tolls," Hank Kostyra recalled. "When they came back, they told me how expensive everything was. Martha complained that breakfast cost seven bucks. But they came back wearing straw hats and looking happy— typical tourists."

During the honeymoon period Martha had been riddled with self-doubt and anxiety about what to do come September, when she was scheduled to begin her junior year at Barnard. One of the issues her father had raised—the impact of marriage on her continuing education—had in fact become a nerve-racking reality for her, and now she had to face it head-on.

Because Andy still had another year of law school and because they didn't want to be apart, Martha reluctantly agreed to interrupt her education for Andy's. It would be a sacrifice she never quite got over. Not only would she be forced to miss a year and not graduate with her class, but she also would have to continue working—hustling modeling jobs in New York—to help support both of them. At the same time, in order to keep up with her schooling, she planned to take courses at the Columbia School of General Studies, which made her life even more of a grind. All this would make the difficult first year of any marriage even more stressful for the Stewarts.

To add to this already explosive mix, Andy had decided that he and Martha should set up communal housekeeping with another attractive young couple, John and Kyra Carswell.

A bohemian and an iconoclast, Carswell reminded friends of a character out of *Easy Rider*. Andy had met him during their first year of law school, and they had instantly bonded. Unlike the other phlegmatic and pedantic law students at Yale, Carswell was in many ways like Andy: romantic, literate, and funny. They had a mutual admiration society. Carswell thought of Andy "as the man I most liked and cherished. . . . Our chemistry was just great. I cherished the look on his face, with that great smile. He was a special and good friend."

After a year Carswell had decided that he hated the law and wanted to write, so he dropped out and enrolled in the graduate program in comparative literature, a move Andy thought took a lot of guts. Carswell became even more of a hero in his eyes.

Carswell's wife, Kyra, was a stunning, extremely bright undergraduate at Pembroke College. Together the Carswells were considered "a cool couple." But they weren't Martha's kind of people, and tensions boiled to the surface.

The couples rented a small house on thirty acres with a lake in back, just outside the quaint town of Guilford, Connecticut, a quick drive for Andy to the Yale campus. The Stewarts took the upstairs front two rooms for sixty dollars a month, and the Carswells the rear two for forty a month. Downstairs was a living room and kitchen, where the Carswells subsisted mostly on nineteen-cent Swanson's frozen chicken pies and bread. The Stewarts ate a little better, but not much; Martha wasn't yet much of a cook. She mentioned her lack of skills at the time in one of her "Remembering" columns, called "Giving Thanks."

She said she "braved" the Kostyra family's "critical palate" by inviting the Nutley clan to Guilford for a "country" Thanksgiving. The day before the big day she made pies, cooked vegetables, bought a thirty-pound turkey, and set the alarm for three in the morning, when she got up to put the bird in the oven. "I went back to sleep only to awake to a house full of black smoke—the turkey was burning. My husband ran downstairs and I timidly followed, thinking how embarrassing it would be to serve a Thanksgiving dinner without turkey. . . . I started to cry." Luckily she was able to find another turkey at the last minute and served dinner at 7:00 P.M. instead of the scheduled 1:00.

Despite the fact that Carswell was a great chum of

Andy's, Martha made it clear that she didn't like him, which made their nonconformist living arrangement rather uncomfortable. "I'm sure Martha would look back on that year and say, 'Oh, yeah, I had problems with him,' " Carswell said later. "It had to do with Martha's and my chemistry. We didn't click. Her recollection of me would be less than overwhelmingly complimentary. Sparks didn't fly, but it wasn't a mutual admiration society.

"In those days I had somewhat corrosive verbal qualities. I knew how to drop somebody in their tracks with a line, and I don't think she took too kindly to that. I had a quick tongue, I was caustic, and I don't think that was particularly pleasing to her. In those days I was at the peak of my jaundice. But I'm sure Andy appreciated it. Martha was probably thinking, 'Here's my new pleasant husband spending male-male time with this goddamn guy who has this mouth on him.'

"My overriding sense of Andy vis-à-vis Martha, though, was that he was a man in love, that he cared for Martha deeply, that he cherished her and really felt devoted to her, and that in the nine months or so that we all lived together his world sort of turned on her. I always thought it was kind of dear and tender how much he loved her. The word 'doting' has a slightly pejorative sense to it, but yes, he doted on her."

While Carswell found Martha physically attractive—"I could see why she would be able to succeed in the modeling world because she had a particular sort of *je ne sais quoi* in her face"—Carswell's underlying feeling was that his best friend's wife was conventional and not very interesting.

As for Kyra Carswell, she said, "I had very little contact with Martha. We didn't stay up and have great talks. We weren't real chummy."

114th Street

In June 1962 Andy graduated from Yale with his law degree. Martha was elated. She couldn't wait to escape Guilford, flee the Carswells, and return to New York to her own
studies.

Andy had gotten a job for the summer doing legal writing and research for four dollars an hour at gilt-edged Webster, Sheffield, Fleischman, Hitchcock & Chrystie. In
September he was to begin three semesters of studies at
Columbia for a Master of Laws degree and work part-time
at Webster, Sheffield. Between the two of them they were
bringing in little more than a hundred dollars a week.

With little money they were forced to store Andy's old
Mercedes in the New Jersey garage of a Kostyra family
friend for fifteen dollars a year because they couldn't afford
the car's upkeep. Often they took the long subway and bus
ride to Nutley in order to have one of Martha Sr.'s meals.
"But," a family member recalled, "Eddie [Kostyra] made
Andy feel he was imposing upon them, that he was eating
all their food, and Andy felt self-conscious."

Meanwhile the only apartment the Stewarts could afford
was in the drab building at 609 West 114th Street, near the
Columbia campus. Simply put, Martha and Andy's first
permanent home was, a college friend remembered, "a miserable little dump with roaches. That place depressed Martha. She absolutely hated it."

Apartment 96 consisted of three small rooms, facing a

rear court, in a gray, dingy, odoriferous, crowded building, whose other tenants were a mix of struggling university people and blue-collar workers.

To help out, Andy's sister donated some old furniture that included a smelly foam rubber–filled sofa. To make the place cheerier, Andy jury-rigged a desk out of a door and two small tables. He and Martha put their books on boards supported by bricks, and they paneled one wall with pine, severing an electrical line in the process. To hide the lifeless scene outside, Andy covered their window with a handmade latticework screen of Martha's design, and the two of them painted the walls white. The place looked as if it had been furnished with orange crates, Martha's uncle Hank Kostyra recalled.

To brighten the colorless environment, Martha also became the unofficial Bird Woman of West 114th Street. She picked up an old cage in a junk shop and filled it with a succession of pet shop parakeets, and named two of the birds Ivan and Ethel Twig.

"It took some thought to find the right animal occupant for a three-room apartment near Columbia University whose owners were not always home . . . the three pale-blue birds were perfect," Martha noted. "While we studied, they could fly freely through the apartment. They shared bits of our meals and liked to sit on my pencil as I took notes. We could easily leave for a day or two without concern."

However, she didn't tell the whole story. All the birds met with various fatal accidents: slamming into doors, flinging themselves out of the window. In the end the birds brought little joy to the depressing apartment.

Years later Martha's terrible memories of the flat and that period in her life apparently still haunted her. She was giving a lecture at the Boston Junior League when a young woman stood up to ask about the elegant Martha Stewart lifestyle and how it applied in real life to someone like herself who lived in a one-room apartment and didn't have a thing. Showing her irritation, Martha declared: "When I was *your* age I lived in three *miserable* rooms overlooking the rooftops of 114th Street, and I still had time to plant some herbs on my windowsill, and still had time to go around to junkshops and collect some pretty things. And I made my life nicer. I worked for everything I have. I'm twenty years older than you are. Can't you see that?''

The young woman must have thought, "Hey, Martha. *Chill.*''

The only thing Martha liked about the apartment was the bathroom. "The tub was so long I could actually lie down flat on the bottom,'' she wrote, "and the pedestal sink so huge that I could arrange pretty bowls of cotton balls and Q-tips. . . .''

Nevertheless Martha was so unhappy during that period that she became noticeably depressed, the first of a number of emotional lows that she suffered through the years and that caused Andy concern.

"Just a year into her marriage Martha clearly was unhappy and feeling depressed, and it probably had to do with living in that dumpy apartment and having no money,'' a confidant recollected. "She had all sorts of dreams, and it was hard in the beginning for her and Andy to make any of those dreams come true.''

Martha meanwhile buried herself in her studies to make up for the Guilford hiatus. She took a course in Russian history and politics and wrote an exceptional paper on an esoteric British invasion of Siberia at the end of World War I. Required to take a science, she chose chemistry, a subject she had done well in during high school. Classmates recalled that while Martha had some problems with theory, she did brilliantly in laboratory work. "It's interesting,'' a Barnard friend observed, "because Martha showed in lab how well she could put things together—mix things—a gram and a half of this, twelve and a half centimeters of that, and she would be right on the nose.''

Outside classes Martha was vigorously pursuing her modeling career but was getting mostly low-paying editorial work, typically fifteen dollars an hour. Often she would go on one "go-see'' after another and be turned down. That was the depressing side of the business, particularly for someone like Martha, who despised any form of failure or rejection. She complained vociferously about the modeling game, expressing discouragement and disappointment. Weeks would go by without a job. Then, suddenly, she'd get a lucrative assignment. A before-and-after hairstyling ad for Clairol, for instance, was one that paid extremely well. Another big-money gig was a spot for Tareyton cigarettes. A nonsmoker, she had to learn how to inhale, but the fee was a godsend for the Stewarts, who were living hand to mouth.

In January 1964 Andy finished his graduate law program. Scheduled to graduate from Barnard that June, Martha had only a paper to write in order to fulfill the requirements for her B.A. To celebrate, the Stewarts decided to take an extended tour of Europe. When Martha Sr. mentioned that she wanted to buy a new Volkswagen, Martha suggested that it would be less expensive if she and Andy picked up the "Beetle" in Germany. The Kostyras readily agreed, and that permitted Martha and Andy to drive through Europe for free in a new car.

While Martha has never mentioned how the trip was financed, she has on several occasions written with great enthusiasm about that first European jaunt with her husband. In *Entertaining* she explains that the trip was the beginning of her "serious culinary education." On the street, in cafés and restaurants, "we ate with enthusiasm, and with great innocence, for we had not planned our travels for the sake of meals. . . . But in Italy and Germany, and particularly in France, the climate, the soil . . . the attitude of mind . . . the smells . . . all made food far more than a filling. I kept mental notes . . . I asked, 'What is this, and how do you cook it?' "

Readers of *Martha Stewart Living* were told: "My actual diary records each day's itinerary, expenses, and personal observations. . . . Hotel rooms were $2.30 a night in Athens, $3 a night with breakfast in Sorrento. . . . Gasoline for our Volkswagen Bug, which we bought at the Wolfsburg factory for $900 new, cost $1 a day. . . ."

But Martha's published memories painted a happier picture than what really transpired. In many ways the Stewarts' grand tour was troublesome, both emotionally and physically.

One extremely upsetting incident occurred while they were staying at a small inn in Florence. At dinner Martha struck up a conversation with a handsome young Englishman, and the threesome broke bread and drank wine together. By eleven, with everyone a little bit tipsy, Andy suggested that they call it a night. But Martha balked. Upset and angry, Andy went to bed alone while Martha went off with her new friend. Long after midnight she returned, claiming they had gone to midnight mass at the cathedral.

While it had been clear to Andy that Martha was attracted to the man, he was inclined to believe her story. But her actions that night raised questions in his mind about how much she really cared for him and whether she was emotionally committed to him.

The next day Martha became ill with nausea, chills, headache, and sore throat. By the time the Stewarts reached Valencia a week or so later, her condition had worsened. She became semidelirious, with a temperature of 103, panicking Andy, who rushed to the U.S. Consulate. A physician was recommended, but he declined to examine Martha fully or to administer medication. Luckily Andy had run into an English couple—the woman was a nurse—at the hotel who gave Martha an injection, and Martha was quickly nursed back to health. Once she was well, the Stewarts continued their European odyssey. But the events of the past few weeks had made them both tense.

They arrived back in New York in time for Martha to do the last of her class work, and in June 1964, a year behind schedule, she graduated from Barnard with a degree in art history. At that point the Stewarts decided to give up their place on 114th Street. They spent the summer living in Martha's old room on Elm Place while they hunted for a new apartment.

Riverside Drive

In the fall of 1964 the Stewarts made a dramatic change in their lifestyle, renting an elegant six-room apartment with a river view in a genteel Riverside Drive building. While the $250-a-month rent was staggeringly more than they could afford, Andy and Martha—both driven and confident—saw no reason to wait. They wanted it all . . . *now*.

"Martha had big dreams," a member of the Stewarts' circle stated. "She wanted more in her life than she grew up with, and she didn't believe in waiting to get it. Andy liked nice things too. He'd grown up surrounded by them. So they fed each other's hunger and drive for more and better. They were the original yuppies." Money, and the pressure to make more of it, quickly became a priority in their lives, one that drove them throughout their marriage.

The apartment needed work, and Martha and Andy spent the first few months sanding floors, painting, and plastering; do-it-yourself projects eventually consumed virtually all their time and were, some observers thought, the cement that held them together.

At the same time they wanted to fill the apartment with beautiful things as quickly as possible. "We were trying to find inexpensive, useful, attractive furniture," Martha acknowledged. "We had a formal dining room with a big wall, and Ethel Stewart, my mother-in-law, had seen a huge Federal sideboard she was sure no one would want because of its size. It was at Sotheby's, the preeminent auction house in New York City. We thought it looked good, like something in the American Wing at the Metropolitan Museum of Art. Since I observed auction selling only in movies, I had no idea of what to bid or how to do it. Ethel gave me a quick lesson on getting a number and pacing my bidding. For some reason, I could not attend that particular auction, but Ethel was right: The sideboard was one of the last pieces to be sold, when the crowd had thinned and interest had waned. There were no other takers, and she bought it for the opening bid—$50, a steal. It cost $100 to cart it to our apartment, where we enjoyed it immensely as both an antique and a utilitarian object.''

The Stewarts subsequently restored the piece, and sold it for a seven-hundred-dollar profit.

Andy's mother had picked up other *objets* and furnishings for her son and daughter-in-law: an elegant chandelier here, a beautiful piano there. Before long the Stewarts' apartment was ''crowded'' with furniture, including ''huge country trestle tables'' in the living room.

While Martha loved the stuff, all of her mother-in-law's attempts to bond with her failed miserably; the two women would never be close. A mutual friend commented, ''Martha's and Ethel's personalities just didn't click, and Martha wasn't interested enough in trying to make it work.''

But Ethel Stewart had infected Martha with antiques and auction fever. Martha became ''wrapped up in the excitement'' of bidding and lusted for ''the sound of the gavel assuring me of my purchase, my prize. . . .'' She began feeding her obsession by foisting herself off as an antiques dealer in order to obtain trade discounts. She traveled the country auction and flea market circuit, transporting her finds in an old Land Rover that Andy had picked up for the venture.

In order to pay for it all, Martha had abandoned vague thoughts of becoming a chemist or going to graduate school to study architecture and was devoting all her time to modeling. Andy meantime had been hired full-time at Webster, Sheffield and was studying for the bar exam.

But Martha's modeling career was not advancing as she

had hoped. Her dream had been to work the runways in the world of high fashion. Finally, she took a stab at it: Leaving Andy behind in New York, she flew to Paris alone to see if she could succeed.

"In those days if you went to Paris and you made it big, you were assured of being successful in New York," said Martha's friend Norma Collier, who did model successfully in Paris until the mid-sixties. "But somehow Paris didn't work for Martha. She stayed about a month and didn't get many assignments. I'm assuming she didn't make it because Martha is large-boned—she has the kind of body where sideways she's very slender, but head-on she's broad—and in those days they liked small-boned girls, with fine features.

"But Martha didn't express the view that she had failed. Martha didn't talk like that. She made excuses that *she* didn't like the French and that *she* didn't care about modeling in Paris. Martha was not someone who would ever admit defeat. But she was hoping that it would happen because it would bring her the two things that Martha was really interested in: money and fame."

Martha and Collier were represented by the same agencies: Stewart (no relation) and Plaza Five, which were among the biggest in New York and were run at various times by their mutual friend the former *Glamour* editor Barbara Stone, who had discovered Cybill Shepherd and Cheryl Tiegs.

All along Stone sensed that Martha wasn't Paris fashion model material. "Was Martha destined to be a star? No. Was she able to earn a nice living? Yes," Stone said. "There is that certain something that makes a model stand out, the ones in the top twenty. And then underneath that are many girls like Martha who are terrific-looking, do well, work well, and make nice livings.

"Martha was a bright, strong-willed person who was in it for money. The ego of being in pretty pictures wasn't the driving force with Martha. She knew her limitations. I don't think she suffered any illusions that she was on her way to being a supermodel. She was a businesswoman even then, and she approached modeling as a business. Martha really is, and always has been, more or less what you see. She laughs all the way to the bank.''

At the height of her modeling career Martha claimed annual earnings of as much as thirty-five thousand dollars, which in the mid-sixties wasn't peanuts.

''That's another one of Martha's exaggerations,'' asserted Norma Collier. ''Thirty-five thousand dollars was a *lot* to be making as a model in those days, and Martha didn't make that much. I know she didn't because I did, and I worked at least four times as much as she did. I would say she made closer to twenty thousand—the absolute most.''

In any event Martha's modeling career was winding down. The New Year 1965 was celebrated by the Stewarts with the joyful news that Martha, at twenty-three, was pregnant.

A Little Stewart

The Stewarts had talked from the start about having a family, but no real planning was involved. When Martha missed her period, she went to the doctor, got the good news, and then she and Andy instantly threw themselves into what they loved to do best: renovating, decorating, and furnishing—in this case a nursery, in preparation for Martha's late-summer due date.

According to members of the Stewarts' circle, the decorating project seemed to give Martha more pleasure than the prospect of having the baby. ''On a purely intellectual basis and as a woman, Martha wanted to be a mother,'' said a longtime friend. ''But emotionally I think she could have done without ever having a child. As a teenager she had helped her own mother with the younger siblings. In Martha's mind, she'd already done the mothering thing. But she *acted* pleased.''

Luckily for Martha, the woman across the hall, Florence Libin, a friendly, vivacious mother of two, also was pregnant—her third was due around the same time as Martha—so they spent much time together. The Libins—Paul Libin was a theatrical manager and producer—and the Stewarts became good friends, often dining and sometimes spending country and beach weekends together.

''There was nothing dramatic about Martha's pregnancy,'' Florence Libin said. ''Martha didn't look overly pregnant or heavy, and she had no fears; Martha never had fears about anything. She was a healthy young woman with a lot of energy, and she paid no special attention to the fact that she was pregnant. There was no kvetching. She handled it all with aplomb.''

Awaiting her due date, Martha befriended youngsters in the building, baking cookies for them, even making a pretty velvet dress for a lonely little girl whose mother worked all day. Observing all that activity, Florence Libin thought that ''Martha was a very nurturing person. She was like an auntie to all the children.''

Martha also had fallen in love with a cat she and Andy had picked up at a country auction. Martha named the feline Chigi (after the Chigi Palace in Rome) Toto, and the long-haired gray tiger kitten quickly became one of her ''best friends.'' She bestowed an extraordinary amount of affection on Chigi, so much that friends who felt she was somewhat cold and aloof at times wondered why she couldn't be as warm and loving with them. And Martha, they noted, rarely showed that kind of affection with Andy. As one member of the Stewarts' circle pointed out, ''Martha was always very connected to animals, very sympathetic toward them, very emotional about them. But that didn't carry over to people. She could be furious with you and then turn to the cat and treat it like an angel.''

Chigi was with Martha constantly—on her lap, on her shoulder, in her arms, on the kitchen table as she prepared meals, in bed. Like a proud mother, she once claimed the cat "even learned to answer the telephone—we found this out when the police arrived at the door alerted by a friend who had called our house to hear the plaintive squeals on the line. . . ." But one morning, reaching under the bed for his slippers, Andy discovered Chigi, who had become ill, in a state of rigor mortis.

Martha virtually fell apart, becoming highly emotional and agitated, in what her friends felt was an extreme response since she had owned the cat for only a short time. "But for some reason Martha loved that cat desperately," Florence Libin said. "Martha was *very* upset, and Martha was one who normally didn't show her emotions."

Shortly after Chigi died, Martha got another cat, which she also named Chigi.

But Martha wasn't to have a whole lot of time for pets, at least in the immediate future. Sometime in the early morning of September 27, 1965—a week beyond her due date—she went into labor, and a nervous Andy drove her to Manhattan's Roosevelt Hospital. By the time they got there, Martha's pains had subsided, and the expectant father was told he could go home and get some sleep. Several hours later, though, he got the call and raced back downtown because Martha had gone into advanced labor.

When he reached her room, he was shocked to find no doctors or nurses in evidence with Martha in the first stages of delivery. Panicked, Andy yelled for help as Martha began screaming in pain. After what seemed an eternity, a doctor came running in and personally pushed Martha in her bed to the delivery room, where moments later she gave birth to a chubby girl. The Stewarts named her Alexis Gilbert, in honor of her paternal grandmother's maiden name. They called her Lexi.

With help from a newly hired black housekeeper named Elsie and baby-sitting assistance from a budding young actress in the building named Valerie Harper, Martha didn't waste any time getting back into action. When Lexi was just three months old, Martha tried to put her to work as a model. At the time Paul Elfenbein, a highly regarded photographic illustrator, was doing a series of layouts of young mothers with babies for Johnson & Johnson. Searching agency books, Elfenbein's production stylist Kathy Tatlock came across Martha Stewart, with her "delightful-looking, all-American smile." Tatlock couldn't believe her good fortune when she learned that the model was a recent mother.

"We called Martha in, and she did a series of test shots," Tatlock said. "Martha loved the idea of the job because Johnson & Johnson was good pay." While the ad people at Johnson & Johnson loved Martha's looks, they hated Lexi's. "She had wonderfully exotic features, but she was odd-looking like one of those puppies with all the wrinkles," said Tatlock. "She just wasn't the prototypical Johnson & Johnson baby with blue eyes and blond hair." The job went to another mother-baby team, and Martha was extremely disappointed.

However, the Stewarts and the Tatlocks—Chris Tatlock, like Andy, was an attorney—quickly became close friends. Tatlock was the kind of woman to whom Martha had always been attracted: She was pretty, creative, and had a good pedigree. Her father was a prominent Chicago photographer. They also had similar interests: art, books, theater. And they cooked and sewed together. "Another common denominator was that we both wanted to find our own way in the world," Tatlock observed. But as with Norma Collier, Martha and Tatlock's relationship eventually exploded. As Tatlock put it years later, "Martha fucked me upside and downside and did the most pointedly cruel things to me." But all that was yet to come.

In the same month that Lexi was born, a much-hyped book on child raising was published, and it became Martha's bible for bringing up Lexi. Haim G. Ginott's *Between Parent and Child: New Solutions to Old Problems* put Dr. Spock's mid-forties *Baby and Child Care* manual to shame—mainly for its lack of sixties' hipness. The emerging women's liberation movement had begun attacking Spock for his sexist leanings. But beyond the jolly pediatrician's purported lack of political correctness, his ideas on child raising were deemed outdated and uncool.

A savvy Israeli-born child psychologist with a knack for getting lots of press, Ginott offered liberal parents like the Stewarts what conservative critics tended to view as far-out answers for raising the best and the brightest. His book, one social critic observed, was filled with "pat theories, avuncular anecdotes, quasi-psychiatric insights, and an air of false kindliness, all of which serves to mask the real message: You're doing it all wrong. *Here's* the way. [Ginott's book is] nearly irresistible reading for a certain type of mother, the college-educated, the self-improver, the one who has all her life been taught you can find the answer in a book." This description fit Martha like a glove.

Ginott's solutions involved the concept of mirror listening, long used by psychotherapists. He told parents to avoid judgment, criticism, and explanation. He also taught mothers—and millions of them read his book—a new way to talk to their children. After reading Ginott, Martha felt she had taken a crash course in child psychology and now had license to interpret for her daughter.

Norma Collier remembered that on the basis of Martha's recommendation, she started following Ginott's teachings with her first child, born two years after Lexi. "Martha wanted to raise *the* perfect child, and she talked about Ginott all the time," Collier said. "It was a joke. My husband and I laughed about it because it was really role reversal. You wanted your kid to think they were getting everything they wanted. There were key words like 'What do you want, darling?' Both Martha and Andy used to say that to Lexi all the time: 'What do you want, darling?' Using Ginott, you did everything to kiss your kid's ass—and you wound up creating a monster." Many years later Andy Stewart told a confidant: "I'm afraid what Ginott professed conforms to the way Lexi was raised."

Martha and Andy gave Lexi free rein, and the child acted out in ways that shocked friends. On a visit to New York, Gene Levy and his business partner accompanied Martha, Andy, and Lexi to an exhibit at the Whitney. "All of a sudden Lexi laid down on her stomach, beating the floor, screaming, and hollering," Levy recalled. "Martha and

Andy just stood there. They couldn't handle her. My wife
and I had two kids by that time and we would never let a
child get away with that. My partner was particularly appalled that a child would act that way and the parents would
not have any control over the child.''

Middlefield Life

About a month after Lexi's birth, Martha and Andy
plunked down virtually all their savings—about three thousand dollars—as a down payment on a dilapidated nine-
teenth-century schoolhouse without plumbing or running
water, near the village of Middlefield, in the Berkshire
Mountains of western Massachusetts. The Stewarts, who
wanted a weekend getaway place, gave the house a name,
Middlefield, in the proper WASP fashion.

"We were in ecstasy over our find," Martha declared
later. In a "Remembering" column called "The Good
Life," she claimed that the inspiration for buying Middlefield came from a book she had read in 1960 called *Living
the Good Life*, written by Helen and Scott Nearing, who
had fled the rat race for the country. The authors "were a
great inspiration to many of us early baby boomers," Martha stated. "They allowed us to dream about alternative
ways to live fulfilling productive lives. Although my husband [Martha's essay was published in April 1996, long
after her divorce] and I never managed to totally escape
from the city, we did attempt many of the Nearings' suggestions on our little property. . . . [W]e were thrilled with

the opportunity the house afforded us to experiment and set about learning to live the good life our way.'' Like Ginott on child rearing, the Nearings became Martha's gurus on alternative living.

Typically Martha painted a glowing and loving portrait of the Stewarts' life at Middlefield, which she discussed in at least two of her books and in her magazine. ''The gardens,'' she writes in *Martha Stewart's New Old House*, ''were my modest attempt to create a little 'Williamsburg' in front of the open porch.'' In a ''Remembering'' column she states, ''We took turns, Andy and I, lugging water in large pails from the stream to cook with, wash up with, and drink.'' In *Martha Stewart's Pies and Tarts*, she mentions the home-baked pies that won blue ribbons at the annual Middlefield country fair. In *Martha Stewart's Quick Cook* she writes immodestly that in Middlefield ''Andy learned carpentry, plumbing, ditch digging. . . . I became an excellent house painter, landscape architect, iron-stove chef, and basic jack-of-all-trades. . . . Every Sunday evening we lugged back bushels of fresh produce for ourselves and our friends in New York.''

Despite Martha's fairy-tale memories, the Stewarts' decision to buy Middlefield was in many ways a horrible mistake. The five years it took for the two of them to renovate the place were hellish, taking its toll physically and emotionally, and jeopardized their marriage.

Almost every weekend, except during the bitterest part of the winter, Andy, Martha, and Lexi stuffed themselves and their overnight gear into the old Mercedes for the four-hundred-mile round-trip drive. They left on Friday evening and returned late on Sunday night.

''Martha and Andy devoted a tremendous amount of energy and time to Middlefield,'' a longtime friend said. ''Andy did backbreaking work up there. He dug a cesspool. He turned a woodshed into an additional room, and then he built a wing behind the house. Both of them felt this enormous pressure to get it done, and get it done with perfection. It was all *very* stressful for both of them, and they fought like dogs. There were some very unpleasant times that were greatly upsetting.

"Martha would start arguments over the most trivial subjects, and they would go on and on, and on: 'You didn't load the car right! . . . How can you take so long to get the car unloaded? . . . Why are you so sloppy? How could you forget this or that?'

"Her manner with Andy became the source of much stress and anger. She was constantly accusing him of being 'dumb' or 'stupid' even though he was busting his ass doing laborer's work up there and then doing most of the driving both ways.

"There were times when there was utter and complete tension and long hostility-filled silences between them that you could cut with a knife. Suddenly Martha would start yelling at Andy, 'Why don't you have anything to say to me?' It sometimes reached a point where Andy saved up things to say to her to avoid that kind of confrontation.

"It was during the renovation of Middlefield that Martha started showing a dark side that many of us didn't know existed. Martha and Andy turned Middlefield into a lovely place, but the two of them were often at serious odds a lot of the time. That's the part Martha doesn't tell her readers and has probably never admitted to herself. Martha always felt she was in the right and Andy, or anyone else, was in the wrong."

Paul and Florence Libin, who often visited the Stewarts at Middlefield during the renovation period, remembered Andy as "a totally devoted husband, a Paul Bunyan who never seemed to be exhausted," and Martha as "very demanding. She would say to Andy, 'Go dig a well or a cesspool,' and he would go out and dig it. She'd say, 'Move this wood,' and he'd move it. He'd lug these big pieces of lumber around.

"When Martha said something, there was nothing tentative about it. She had very strong opinions about how things should be done. Martha pretty much made a lot of the decisions, and Andy seemed to go along with them."

Friends laughed behind her back when Martha went on about the minutiae of rural life, as if she were a pioneer woman. She'd spend hours fussing over the wood-burning stove, explaining how it worked, and constantly oiling it.

"It was *so* ritualistic," one visitor recalled. "We kind of got a big kick out of it."

The first Easter the Stewarts were at Middlefield Andy hid baskets of colored eggs and holiday candy behind trees for children to find. But whereas Andy could be childlike and fanciful, Martha was deliberate and finicky. She had kept a friend on the phone interminably the day before that Easter celebration giving her instructions, and checking them twice, on the things she was supposed to bring from the city to Middlefield: the precise number of straw baskets; the exact amount of eggs for boiling; the quantity of dye; and the number of jelly beans and coconut eggs for each basket. "Anal and controlling" was the way friends characterized her behavior.

"At first everything Martha and Andy did seemed to be a shared experience," an observer noted later. "They were like the perfectly matched couple. But then the control began to shift to Martha. She became the dominant one, Andy the submissive one. It was becoming—and it eventually became—a sadomasochistic type of relationship. Martha was the top, and Andy was the bottom."

Longtime friends, the McCullys—George was a university professor, Emily a children's book illustrator—were impressed initially with the work Martha and Andy had done on Middlefield. But their view soon changed.

"I thought Martha was really interested in fashioning a life, and when I first observed them, she and Andy were equally involved in things," Emily McCully said. "But then one day at Middlefield I was astonished to hear, after we examined all their handiwork, that they eventually planned to sell the place, and I realized that they were really entrepreneurs. And in the years that I still thought they were building this sort of aesthetic life and didn't think of it as an entrepreneurial enterprise, I assumed that the marriage was the center of it. But then I realized that this was *not* a great romantic relationship."

Mastering the Art

Like Ginott, whose advice Martha had followed to the letter for child raising, and the Nearings, whose manual for rural living she took as gospel, Martha also found a sixties guru for her budding interest in fancy cooking. With the publication in 1961 of *Mastering the Art of French Cooking*, Martha had become, like millions of others, a Julia Child devotee and wannabe.

In fact Martha so idolized Child that years later she was even accused by observant food critics of lifting some of her favorite chef's recipes for use in a book of her own. "At home, like all my contemporaries, I had Julia Child's *Mastering the Art of French Cooking* in hand, and worked my way through from cover to cover," Martha told readers of *Entertaining*. "Julia brought calm into the realm of haute cuisine and inspired confidence. I was determined to try everything."

In many ways Martha Stewart and Julia Child were mirror images. Both were tall and big-boned; both had gone to Seven Sisters schools (Child, née McWilliams, of Pasadena, California, was a Smithie); both had studied areas of history; neither woman had a master plan for her life (Child, six feet tall, had once even considered becoming a basketball player); both married erudite men; both had an interest in cooking and taught it; both had their phenomenal careers come to a boil when they were in their forties; both wrote best-selling books; both had highly rated television programs and had their TV premieres on the same station a quarter century apart; both were perfectionists; both could be martinets; both became overnight icons; and both were in the right place at the right time with the right product.

However, unlike Martha, who had no formal cooking training, Julia Child had studied at the Hillcliffe School of Cookery in Beverly Hills and later, while living in Paris with her Foreign Service officer husband, at the world-renowned Cordon Bleu, though only for six months. She also had studied privately with Master Chef Max Bugnard, formerly an assistant to Escoffier.

Despite working from Child's acclaimed cookbook, Martha remained something of a bumbler in the kitchen. Martha didn't realize, for example, that you couldn't leave egg whites in copper for any length of time without the eggs reacting and turning color. So her much ballyhooed Grand Marnier soufflé turned out to be as green as the copper roofs in New York. But Martha worked very hard on her dinners, and they *looked* beautiful. Many times guests would arrive and "ooh" and "ah" over the food, but Martha herself looked a wreck—her hair undone, her clothes sloppy because all her time and effort had gone into preparing the meal and not herself.

"Martha was always big on presentation," Norma Collier observed. "How the food looked was often more important than how it tasted. She'd come out of the kitchen with the platter and show it to each person and say, 'Isn't this the most *marvelous* rack of lamb?' She had to have each person at the dinner party look at it and say how *marvelous* it looked before she would serve it. As a result, she got the nickname Marvelous Martha among our friends because everything she did was always '*marvelous*'!

"Martha always had a need for admiration and attention, to be told that she was good. We all used to giggle about it, but it was kind of sweet in those days. It was the *germ* of what was going to happen with her."

Martha threw her first big party—ever—in December 1965. It was an enormous Christmas bash, a combination holiday, housewarming, and welcoming-of-Lexi-into-the-world party, at the Stewarts' Riverside Drive apartment.

(No one in Martha or Andy's circle could recall any special gathering of friends or family when Lexi had been born three months earlier.)

Martha had invited "absolutely everyone we knew"—the invitations said "Christmas Carols, Cocktails, and Desserts"—and she spent weeks planning the party, with Lexi "watching and 'helping' from her baby chair in the kitchen." Martha's spread consisted of baked ham, Polish sausages, biscuits and muffins, quiches, oysters, Brie, table wine, champagne, and an eggnog that she and Andy "invented on the spot" with bourbon and cognac.

She had invited a few old friends from Nutley, including her chum Lynn Sherwood Kaneps, who was someone Martha hoped to impress with her new chic lifestyle. "Out of the blue we got this invitation," Kaneps said. "What I saw was that Martha was not that comfortable, and she was a nervous hostess. I had hoped to see the baby, but we never got the opportunity, and Martha never once talked about her."

Other friends also noticed that Lexi was usually invisible at Martha's gatherings. "She never, ever brought her out like other young mothers in our circle did," said a close friend, writer Elizabeth Hawes, whose married name was Betsy Weinstock. "When we'd visit Martha and Andy, Lexi was always asleep on her parents' bed. We'd peek in on her or throw coats on her." Emily McCully, another member of Martha's salon, whose first child was born three years after Lexi, agreed. "Her relationship with little Alexis seemed odd. From the beginning Lexi was this sort of shadowy figure who was never in the forefront—*ever*—and that was certainly very strange."

Martha often threw theme parties, which were popular at the time. If friends had traveled to Spain, she'd have a paella party to celebrate their return; there would be Indian curry buffets and Moroccan pastilla dinners.

As she became more experienced with her cooking—and cooking was not something she had ever considered doing professionally during this period of her life—Martha began to have sit-down dinners for a dozen or more on a routine basis.

"I'd scurry around, borrowing tables, chairs, and dishes, run to Mother's in New Jersey for silver, and stay up late ironing napkins," she stated. "Then I'd squash everyone into our dining room, and Andy and I would serve, as efficiently as humanly possible, some complex entrée like parsleyed ham en croûte with Madeira sauce. Noise and a wonderful young confusion always reigned."

The Stewarts' friends were lively, bright, attractive young professionals, most of them Upper West Side liberals, politically and socially. There also was a small coterie of appealing young women—the Stewarts always surrounded themselves with good-looking people—whom Martha knew from Barnard or the modeling world.

For the most part the men were colleagues of Andy's at Webster, Sheffield, and the women were much like Martha. "They all wanted careers. They all wanted to be successful," said Alexander Cortesi, a lawyer who was a member of the circle.

Another friend, Roger Hooker, one of Andy's colleagues at Webster, Sheffield and later an assistant secretary of transportation in the Ford administration, said he was extremely impressed with Martha's drive. "She was strong, ambitious, and had her eye on some horizon, some goal, at all times. Whatever it was, Martha was indomitable and undaunted by things that daunt most people. She never had a lot of self-doubt."

Liz Hawes, who ghosted two of Martha's biggest-selling books, said, "My take on her back then was certainly *not:* 'Now there is the future style setter of the country and maybe the world.' She was just fun. She was ahead of us. I was very ambitious with food myself, but Martha was always a step ahead. In those days it was really ambitious to make spinach quiche, but Martha had already moved to miniature endive quiches. I didn't even *know* what an endive was; nobody knew what an endive was. So she was always a bit ahead.

"She knew about fabric. She knew much more about antiques. She had an eye for what was good, and what was fresh, and what was expressive of that particular moment. None of us had furniture, but you'd go into their apartment, and they would have eighteenth-century settles. Martha had an *eye*. It still wasn't conscious, but you knew that she had a consciousness of things beyond what the rest of us had.''

Her consciousness, however, was not focused on the turmoil that was tearing at the social fabric of the country during the mid-sixties, when Martha began her entertaining on a regular basis. At the Stewarts' dinner parties, Andy railed against the war in Vietnam, but Martha was indifferent to social issues, politics, and world affairs.

''She was smart and ambitious, but she was no intellectual,'' observed Roger Hooker. ''She didn't think her way through the larger world problems. Andy was doing that quite a lot.''

Emily McCully, who later won the prestigious Caldecott Medal for illustrating a children's book, recalled, ''It was a time of intense political activity, but that didn't figure in our relationship with Martha. She was still working as a model, and my impression of her was that she was kind of ditzy. Her interests were not very deep, but she was fun. The first time that Martha cooked a meal for us, it was already a kind of showy thing, and that became increasingly the case. Those dinners were all kind of pretentious and made us feel more adult. We were imitating a high style. It was sort of Ralph Laurenish.''

There were other parties at the Stewarts' involving a very small, select group of couples and singles, gatherings that would not be appropriate for inclusion in *Entertaining*.

''My husband and I were invited to a party once with this group when Andy was out of town,'' stated Norma Collier. ''My husband was sort of horrified at the behavior that he saw going on. Martha, for instance, was in ————————'s lap. She was acting pretty playful. My husband thought it was pretty terrible. My reaction was that Martha walked on the wild side. This is part of who she is.

''Later,'' Collier said, ''when they moved to Westport [in the early seventies], they had a pool put in, and I knew that they had nude pool parties. (It was the same black-bottomed pool that Martha would one day be seen lining with credit cards in a TV commercial.) Martha told me that these parties were happening, and she told me that she was not inviting my husband and me because she knew we were uptight Republicans, wet blankets.

"Martha was not embarrassed by any of this, said it was fun, and liked it. She's an experimental person and will do anything to get kicks or shock people. Andy would go along with anything Martha asked him to. Martha and Andy's relationship was typical back in the sixties of two young liberal people not clinging to each other only."

The man on whose lap Martha was ensconced at the party described by Collier was at the time a friend and colleague of Andy's at Webster, Sheffield. Like Martha, he was in his mid-twenties and, like Andy, was tall, very bright, and handsome, and he had been recently divorced.

"There was a lot of chemistry going both ways between Martha and me back then," he acknowledged years later, denying that they ever slept together.

"Martha was just great-looking. She had incredible sort of porcelainlike skin. It was remarkable the way she looked, *so* delicate, yet there was *nothing* delicate about her in terms of her personality. At that stage of my life I had a history of being involved with challenging women, so maybe that was part of our thing.

"Andy was a very close friend of mine, and so nothing beyond a flirtation was ever going to happen. Andy was a strong guy in those days. He could take care of himself. It wasn't like he was vulnerable or he was about to be cuckolded.

"I never had a sense that this thing between us was anything that was going to be acted on. But who the hell knows what would have happened? I don't remember having any feeling that Jesus, Martha's somebody I wouldn't want to get involved with. I don't remember what my fantasies were in those days, or whether I had any about her, or whether they would have stimulated a wet dream.

"It was odd, but Martha and Andy would make allusions about their physical relationship. Andy once made a curious remark, and I've thought about it over the years. He said that if he found out that some other guy had a better sex life than he did, he would really be bothered by that, that it would be troublesome for him if just the physical act of having sex was better for somebody else than it was for him. He said this in front of Martha, and I took it to mean that he was talking about his relationship in bed with her. I remember thinking 'Gee, what the hell does *that* mean?' I guess it would bother me too, but how would you even *think* about something like that? It was a weird thought." (Andy later told a confidant that he suspected that Martha and the man actually had had an affair.)

Other friends expressed surprise that Martha would have ever participated in such high jinks even though the country was in the midst of a sexual revolution. "Martha Stewart a swinger? No way," declared a close friend. "I can't believe in a million years that those kind of activities ever took place with Martha involved. But I could believe her *making up* that sort of thing just to get a rise out of someone or to show how hip or cool she was. Martha made up stuff all the time.

"I remember Martha going on a trip to the Caribbean and there was a nude beach and she wouldn't even take off her top. So the idea of Martha taking part in wild parties is pretty hard to swallow. But then again that was the era of sex, drugs, and rock and roll. If it did happen, I guess it shows she's more human, and less uptight, than I thought she was."

PART THREE

Making the

Richest Dough

The Stockbroker

Martha's dream of becoming a big-time model had faded: The girls who were now making it were younger, taller, skinnier, and more exotic. In the eyes of the fashion world Martha was over the hill. After Lexi was born, Martha's modeling assignments dropped off precipitously. Now, with Lexi in the terrible twos and old enough to be cared for by others, Martha began thinking about a job, a *serious* career, one that would pay *serious* money.

But Martha still hadn't entertained the idea of making a living from her knowledge of cooking, decorating, or gardening. As an associate at Webster, Sheffield, Andy was earning little more than fifteen thousand dollars a year. If the Stewarts wanted to continue to live in the style they were becoming accustomed to, Martha needed to find a high-paying job.

Another factor propelling her toward a new career was a long-held, overblown belief, now finally deflated, that the Stewart family had big money, and that Andy would one day inherit it, and that they would live happily ever after, without financial worries. For a girl who had come from poor roots, that kind of security was paramount. But now Martha was telling friends that one of the reasons she was looking for a big-money job was because the Stewart riches she had hoped to share and enjoy with Andy had been wiped out. In 1962, a year after Martha married Andy, the stock market took the sharpest dive since 1929, and George

Stewart, who had always invested heavily on margin, had lost his shirt. (At the time of his death, a quarter century later, his estate was valued at zero.)

"Martha told me that Andy's father was retired and went back into business on a deal where he risked a lot of his assets and lost the gamble," said Norma Collier. "So all of a sudden Martha felt like she was in a position where she had married money, and it was now all gone. She told me she said to Andy, 'I married you, and you had a lot of money, and now you have nothing. I'm going to go do it and make my own.' She said, 'Goddamn, I'm going to have to make myself rich and famous.' "

Over dinner one night with friends in early 1968 Martha brought up the subject of her job hunt. Did anyone have any ideas? Liz Hawes's husband, Davis Weinstock, said he knew a guy from the old neighborhood who had a hot little institutional boutique in the financial district. The next day Weinstock called Andy Monness, his childhood pal from Long Island, and said he had the perfect candidate for his firm, Monness, Williams & Sidel. Martha called Monness, and the two made a date to meet later that week at the company offices on the twenty-fourth floor at 120 Broadway.

Martha, however, has given a completely different account. She claimed that after Lexi's birth the idea of becoming a stockbroker like Andy's father had hit her. "It was either that or go to architecture school, and I would really have liked to be an architect, but I also really wanted to work. Andy's father was a stockbroker, and he encouraged me. We had wedding-present money we were investing in the stock market, and it was intriguing to me."

Still later she maintained that "the sole reason" she went to work on Wall Street was that George Stewart encouraged her "to sort of gamble. I liked that little bit of life too."

In any case, Martha met with Andy Monness, and she knocked his socks off with her one, two punch of beauty and brains. "She just made a terrific, winning impression right away," he said. "She looked good, and she was articulate." Like others in the business, Monness, then thirty, believed Martha Stewart could sell anything with that face and those legs.

The company was only three years old when Martha was hired, but as partner Kenny Sidel later boasted, "We were kicking the shit out of the staid, white-shoe, alcohol-drinking jackasses on Wall Street. The competition had become fat and stupid, and we went in and took the business away from them.

"These were not the wise guy years of the eighties. These were the years of hard work. These were the years when markets were difficult. These were the years when people were reluctant to do business with a newborn firm, with young people who didn't inherit their business, generation after generation. We watched them go bust, and we helped them go bust.

"And Martha was exactly like we were: *hungry, aggressive, intelligent, alert.* Andy Monness hired her right on the spot because she fit our mold, which was based on candor and hard work."

Sidel's scenario aside, it took no extraordinary expertise to peddle stocks in those days. The market was simmering, and the issues the firm chose to pitch were hot—at least in the beginning. Even an ex-model with a baby in one arm and a well-thumbed copy of Julia Child in the other could succeed without really trying too hard.

Monness was known for hiring people with offbeat interests, or from unrelated occupations. For instance, one of the firm's crackerjack salesmen at the time was a big, good-looking Irishman from the tough Red Hook section of Brooklyn, who had been driving a meat truck by day and producing amateur theatrical productions at synagogues on Long Island by night when Andy Monness discovered him directing Mrs. Monness in *Rashomon*.

"Andy watched me and said, 'You'd make a good salesman. You can make a lot of money. Come work for us.' I mean, that's the way they operated," recalled Brian Dennehy, who worked alongside Martha—and lusted after her—before heading for Hollywood to become an actor. Later Martha boasted, "I taught Brian Dennehy how to be a stock broker. . . . He was an absolutely terrible broker! And at 40, he became a movie star.''

All Martha needed to begin selling stock was to take a broker's exam, which she passed with flying colors in about three months. She was formally registered with the New York Stock Exchange as a broker in August 1968, right after she celebrated her twenty-seventh birthday.

Martha had started her second career at a frightening time in American history, a bizarre period when Martin Luther King and Bobby Kennedy were assassinated weeks apart; when police battled mobs of antiwar demonstrators at the Democratic National Convention in Chicago; when Haight-Ashbury became a hippie haven of Day-Glo–painted freaks mixing vats of Kool-Aid with LSD; when Andy Warhol was gunned down in his studio by a militant feminist; when Jackie married Ari; when fifty thousand poor people marched on Washington; when Nixon-Agnew won reelection. And Wall Street, as a result, was having its ups and downs.

Martha's starting salary was about $100 a week, plus her share of a commission pool. But within two years she would become one of the firm's star salespeople, with income ranging from a high of $250,000 a year, according to Andy Monness, down to a more realistic $125,000, according to Martha's mentor at the firm, Sandy Greene, a brilliant engineer turned financial analyst, who was a descendant of the Revolutionary War hero Nathanael Greene, and a first cousin of one of the firm's principals, Frank Williams.

On the other hand, Martha claimed, ''I was making about a hundred thirty-five thousand dollars, which was a lot more than even a medium lawyer's salary in those days,'' a pointed reference to the fact that she was bringing in bigger bucks than Andy at the time. ''We were basically really good hotshots. It was like the most enthusiastic and daring job I could have. It was very aggressive, and the money you made was amazing.''

Martha's dream had finally come true, at least for the time being: At Monness, Williams & Sidel, she made big money and rubbed shoulders with the rich and powerful.

She also was pursued by immensely wealthy men and had a generally high-flying, high-roller lifestyle, jetting from coast to coast, wining and dining in the finest restaurants with the likes of Ross Perot (whom she later supported for President) and financier Saul Steinberg. "Martha very much liked socializing with these guys who were really well known, the high-powered guys," said Sandy Greene. "We always had a slew of them around the office."

Martha's decision to venture into the go-go world of high finance disappointed close friends who, knowing her creativity, expected something else from her and felt she had sold out. "Martha was a vastly talented woman with the extreme ability to turn things into something wonderful, and that was and *is* her magic," Kathy Tatlock observed. "Martha had dreams, but she became impatient and abandoned those dreams because she saw she could make a lot of money fast as a stockbroker. Her ambition was so powerful. And that has continued to be her M.O. To Martha, the end has always justified the means."

A New Life

In order to accommodate the demands of her new job and lifestyle—days beginning at the office downtown before nine in the morning; late evening sales pitches, out-of-town jaunts—Martha had to make suitable arrangements for the care and feeding, and the early education, of her daughter.

By the time Lexi was two and a half, she was enrolled in a small Montessori nursery school in a brownstone a few doors from the Stewarts' Riverside Drive building. The child usually spent a half day there and the other half in the care of the Stewarts' housekeeper, Elsie, who also sat for other children in the building. In order to make the schedule work more efficiently, Martha sometimes left for work late or came home early. Andy meanwhile helped at the nursery in his spare time. Martha's brother Frank, bound for Vietnam where he would serve with distinction in combat as a helicopter pilot, assisted Andy building shelves and storage boxes for the school.

By the time Martha was ensconced at the Monness firm, the Stewarts had enrolled Lexi in the highly progressive, very expensive Rudolf Steiner School.

Founded in 1928 and located in a staid East Side Manhattan building, the school was based on the curious beliefs and teachings of Steiner, an Austrian scientist, philosopher, artist, and educator who had died in 1925. According to a biographer, Steiner "surveyed with clarity and intimacy the spiritual realities at work in the kingdoms of nature and in the cosmos, the inner nature of the human soul and spirit and their potential for further development, the nature and practice of meditation, the experiences of the soul before birth and after death, the spiritual history and evolution of humanity and the earth, and detailed studies of the workings of reincarnation and karma." Not surprisingly, many viewed Steiner at the time as a "radical scholar," if not a complete nutcase.

From the start Lexi seemed happy at the school, which she attended through kindergarten, and her parents had a good feeling about Steiner, especially because it was artsy and gave Lexi the freedom to express herself.

Martha had no qualms about being a working mother and sending her toddler to school at a time when many middle-class educated women were on hiatus from their careers until their children were of school age.

"Martha was an ambitious woman who just seemed to be able to handle it all," Florence Libin said. "Martha was exceptional among the young mothers I knew then who seemed to put aside their careers for their children. Martha decided she wanted a career as a stockbroker and she could send her child to day care and she could work and it would all work out.''

Years later Martha told an audience of fans, ''The only big mistake I ever made in my whole life was not having more children.'' But Florence Libin, who spent much time with Martha when their children were young, had a far different take: ''Martha felt that one was enough. She was happy with one. I have a feeling Andy would have liked more.''

In fact, as soon as Lexi was toddling around, Martha gave away her pram to Kathy Tatlock, who was pregnant with the first of her two daughters. To Tatlock the gift underscored Florence Libin's belief that there would be no more little Stewarts. ''Martha said they weren't going to have any more children,'' Tatlock said. ''When they had Lexi, they realized how much work it was and how much demand having a child would make on them. They both were very ambitious. They were a couple on the move, and they saw that having children cramped their style.''

With Lexi happily enrolled at Steiner, Martha turned her focus on learning the stock trade and building her commissions. Her world now revolved around hawking the stocks of small-growth companies that analysts such as Sandy Greene had picked as winners for sale to the firm's mostly institutional clients.

The woman who one day would sell style and elegance with charm and grace was now peddling the financial merits of Levitz Furniture, which sold velour sofas to the masses; a company called Bandag, which specialized in retreaded tires for drivers of clunkers; a hot little operation called Open Road, known for house trailers and recreational vehicles; and McDonald's, home of that gourmet delight the Big Mac.

''I learned how to be really competitive there,'' Martha later boasted. ''It [Monness, Williams & Sidel] was a tough environment with just a microcosm of Wall Street. The movie *Wall Street* had nothing on *this* firm.''

In several of her books, however, Martha painted a different picture of her life on the Street. She asserted that the job had made her a more organized wife and a better mother—rather than the brassy and ballsy businesswoman, which is the way colleagues and customers remembered her.

In *Entertaining* she says:

> [I]n New York, where I began working as a stockbroker, I had the opportunity for what A. J. Liebling once described as the requisites for writing well about food: a good appetite and an "apprenticeship as a feeder, when you have enough money to pay the check, but not enough to produce indifference to the size of the total." Meals in fine restaurants and conversations with some of the best New York chefs enhanced my knowledge of cooking. . . . I was a working woman then and had to be organized—sauce base on Tuesday, dessert Wednesday, entertain eight on Thursday. I always had bones in the refrigerator and stocks frozen in ice cube trays.

In *Martha Stewart's Quick Cook*, she states:

> When I was a stockbroker on Wall Street I was actually required to take clients out to fancy lunches and dinners as part of the job. It was in the dining rooms of New York's most famous restaurants that I was introduced to *haute cuisine*, and in the kitchens of those restaurants that I learned much about cooking. I would frequently eat something delicious at lunch, ask about the recipe or unusual ingredients, and rush home after work to re-create the recipe for my family.

In *Quick Cook* and the follow-up *Martha Stewart's Quick Cook Menus*, she boasted of the fine meals she ate with clients at New York's better restaurants. "When Pietro's ceased to exist," she noted, "I learned to cook shrimp their way." At Le Mistral it was the "excellent" fillet of sole with black butter that was her favorite and that also became a standard dish on the Stewart table at home.

She said she began *Martha Stewart's Quick Cook* as "a game" when she was a stockbroker, "several years ago." (In reality she had left the job a decade earlier.)

My daughter, Alexis, was very young and always hungry. My husband, Andy, was working as a lawyer then and was hungry for dinner the moment he got home from the office. When I returned home from work at five or six in the afternoon, I was faced with the daily challenge of feeding them interesting, varied meals. I lived as I envisioned a Parisian working woman lived, with an almost empty, but carefully inventive pantry and with an eye for what was fresh and inviting in the market.

"Martha," declared a friend after reading her words, "*puh-leeze!*"

Red Roses

While Martha claimed she had an eye out for the latest gourmet taste sensations to sate the Stewart palates, the men of Wall Street and the men-about-town were salivating over her. One morning, at the Monness office, a dozen long-stemmed red roses arrived at her desk with a romantic note attached that was signed simply "Andy." The problem now facing the flattered Martha was *which* Andy to thank for the surprise bouquet.

"Martha called me and told me about the flowers, and she said there were *three* Andys in her life at that moment," Norma Collier recollected. "There was her husband, Andy, and her boss, Andy [Monness], and there was this other Andy, who she said she wasn't having an affair with, a guy who she met and who *wanted* to have an affair with her.

"Martha said, 'Oh, my God, I don't know which Andy to thank. I have to find out whether it's Andy Monness or my husband.' She wasn't even thinking of the third Andy.

"I said, 'Well, I guess it's safest to ask Andy Monness first,' and she did, and he told her, 'No, I didn't send you any roses.' So then she thanked her husband—'How wonderful, Andy, thank you for the roses'—and Andy Stewart said, 'I didn't send you roses.' Then the third Andy finally called her and that's how she found out he'd sent them."

Martha was standing at a pay phone with Lexi at her side at one of the New York airports when Andrew J. Stein, making a call in the next booth, first spotted her and struck up a conversation.

Dubbed "Politics' Bad Boy" by *The New York Times*, Stein had, with the financial backing of Jerry Finkelstein, his politically connected millionaire father and publisher of the *New York Law Journal*, won election to the New York State Assembly at the tender age of twenty-three. Stein subsequently served for almost a decade in the powerful post of New York City Council president and later ran a costly but unsuccessful race for mayor of New York. He had a reputation for being brash, aggressive, and outspoken—and for wearing a *really* bad hairpiece, a tonsorial disaster the press often teased about. *The Times* once called it "a not-so-subtle toupee."

Smitten by Martha's shiksa looks, the Jewish Young Turk, who was a few years Martha's junior and had been married and divorced in his early twenties, introduced himself and then began his courtship, not only sending flowers to her office but taking her out for drinks and persistently calling her at home, presumably in hopes of winning a date, if not her heart, despite the fact that she was clearly married *and* a mother.

"Andy said that at first Martha was definitely flattered being pursued by a well-known guy, but that she quickly became bored," a confidante revealed. "Once, when Stein called, Andy lost his temper and told him, 'Keep the fuck away from my wife.' Andy said that Martha was lying in bed listening to the conversation and smiling. After that confrontation Stein stopped calling Martha at home. Martha told Andy that nothing had happened between her and Stein, and she said she was pleased that Andy had gotten rid of him for her. Andy never felt threatened by Stein; he thought the guy was a joke. Obviously there are other possibilities of what might have happened between the two of them because Andy never hired a private detective to follow Martha.''

Years later Andy Stein, who left politics to become a businessman, acknowledged having fallen for Martha, having pursued her, and having taken her out for drinks. ''In those days I was single and attracted to attractive girls, and Martha *was* attractive. She had a great look,'' Stein said. ''Her response to me was friendly enough. It was just a fleeting flirtation that lasted just a couple of weeks, or months, or something like that.

''We went out on three or four occasions, and all that was involved was three or four drinks. One of the places we went to was Raffles [a private club] at the Sherry Netherland Hotel. It was just sort of playful flirting, with no involvement. It never went anywhere. We didn't have sex or anything. It wasn't like I had an affair with her.''

Norma Collier said that on the basis of what Martha told her about Stein, ''it wasn't a big thing. But Martha could be flirty, and she liked men, and she liked affirmation.''

According to Wall Street colleagues, the fact that Martha was a sexy-looking woman in a horny man's world certainly helped get those long legs of hers in the doors of prospective clients. Coworkers agreed that Martha's sex appeal was the main reason Andy Monness had hired her in the first place; no one else on the Street had a hot-looking, classy blonde on its sales force in those days. In fact few women were working in Wall Street in the late sixties. At that time the New York Stock Exchange luncheon club still segregated women. So Martha became a featured attraction for Monness, Williams & Sidel.

As Andy Monness noted later, ''There was almost a novelty quality about her.''

''In truth, she was a little bit coquettish, and that was a little bit of her style,'' noted Sandy Greene, who sometimes accompanied Martha on client calls in New York and out of town. "Martha's [selling] style always gave me the impression of at least the beginning of leading a man on. She would smile and flirt, and a lot of individuals would respond to that. You never quite knew what was on her mind. She used her female wiles to open the door, to get somebody's attention."

Along with many of her clients, Martha's coworkers and employers, including Andy Monness, couldn't help being attracted to her. "Andy had distinct designs on Martha," asserted Greene, who became a partner in the firm. "He wanted her around. I suspect he never did succeed with her, but I'm sure he tried. I'm sure Martha wasn't interested in him. But he was in a position where she could have him do a lot for her, not *all* by any means, but a lot of what she wanted to do, like getting new accounts."

Greene believed that because Martha was aware of Monness's interest in her, she was able to manipulate and use him to her own advantage within the firm. "I think they both had a game going," he said.

Andy Stewart told a friend that he suspected that Monness had more than a professional interest in Martha. Monness, though, scoffed at such speculation, but he did acknowledge that "Martha was my dream girl. She just had *the* magic; she *definitely* had *the* magic. She just looked perfect for the part and acted perfect for the part. She was great-looking. She was articulate. She was bright. I said to myself, 'Oh, my God, this woman is really going to be a winner.' I said, 'I'll *definitely* take this prize.'"

Brian Dennehy also became close chums with Martha on the job, the two often hung out together, and he too had difficulty keeping his eyes off her. "In those days," Dennehy remarked, "she was skinny, and gorgeous, and extremely sexy. I would fantasize about being involved with her."

Martha was fascinated by the fact that Dennehy had grown up in a tough Brooklyn neighborhood. Although their childhoods were economically similar—hers poor Polish, his poor Irish—Dennehy's was on what he described as "the cutting edge of bad guys," and that intrigued Martha no end. "One time I took her to this big mob restaurant in Brooklyn, and she was engrossed by the characters.''

Dennehy, whom Martha tried to pursue romantically years later, after her split from Andy, said, ''I always thought she was incredibly sexy. But I never thought that I would be sharp enough, or smart enough, or successful enough then to have a personal relationship with her. That comes from what I consider to be my inadequacies, not hers.

''Martha was gorgeous, extremely classy and sophisticated. Just the fact that she would come in [as a saleswoman] and sit down for an hour and talk about things with guys or take them to lunch gave her a big advantage. I'm not talking about prostitution or anything like that. But just in the sense that these guys would be flattered that someone as attractive, and as smart, and as interesting as Martha would spend time with them.

''These guys would come in from Hartford or Chicago in their Brooks Brothers suits, and she'd whisk them off to Le Mistral or some other really fancy French restaurant, and they were pretty impressed. And these were sharp business guys who weren't pulling hay out of their asses. As a saleswoman she played the New York card, which was a much better card to play in those days.''

Dennehy, who was married to a costume designer, a woman he described as ''a hardworking, decent, terrific person,'' acknowledged that his wife was ''intimidated'' by Martha. ''There *is* an intimidation factor, and the easy way of dealing with that intimidation is to kind of laugh her off. But it ain't that easy.''

Martha also became quite friendly with Sandy Greene. Besides the stock market, the two had a strong mutual interest in gardening and cooking and spent considerable time together poring over seed catalogs and shopping together at nurseries on Long Island when they weren't talking shop, a fact that did not go unnoticed by Greene's new wife, a pretty Boston socialite who sported the colorful name of Blue Greene.

''I was the young wife meeting the glamorous colleague,'' recalled Blue Magruder, who left Sandy Greene after six years of marriage, not because of Martha but because her husband "was married to his career," of which Martha was an integral part at one point.

"Martha was beautiful, tall, extraordinary, an incredible cook," said Magruder, a Wellesley girl who was a descendant of the Lowells of Massachusetts. "It was impossible to compete with Martha because you simply couldn't, and you would end up feeling miserable. Sandy was close with Martha, and I was just the accompanying person. It was always Martha and Sandy having the conversations. I wasn't actually jealous because I knew Martha wasn't interested in Sandy romantically. She was interested in what Sandy *knew*. When we would get together socially, Martha's attention was always focused on Sandy. She just ignored Andy."

More Changes

By the end of 1969 Andy had decided to leave Webster, Sheffield, where he'd been an associate for almost six years. His decision to move on was highly worrisome and stressful for the security-conscious Martha, who had not yet started raking in the really big bucks on Wall Street. She thought that Andy shouldn't give up his secure position at a time when they were living fairly large and their joint income was still rather small.

But Andy had grown bored and disenchanted with his work, which mainly involved stuffy legal research and writing. If he had had his way, the Stewarts would have jumped out of the New York rat race for simple country living—

working the land, doing carpentry, baking bread, selling antiques, living in their little place in Middlefield. But Martha's increasingly glamorous life in the Wall Street fast lane—and the potential for rich rewards—had made all of that a pipe dream.

In early 1970 Andy did change jobs and negotiated a substantial salary increase in the process, much to Martha's relief. He went to work in the legal department of the Bangor Punta Corporation, a conglomerate named after an old New England railroad and a Cuban sugar company, that dabbled in everything from speedboat and private airplane companies to farming equipment and motor manufacturers.

Andy, who was to handle contracts, international deals, and antitrust work for the corporation, all of which he found more stimulating than what he had been doing, was often teased by his liberal antiwar friends because Smith & Wesson, the arms manufacturer, was one tentacle of the Bangor Punta octopus.

With their careers on track the Stewarts had a rigorous schedule. Andy was under the gun to learn a new area of legal work and impress his latest employers, while Martha "felt very pressured because she wanted to do well, and for the first year or two she was having a frustrating time of it," noted Sandy Greene. "She felt pressure to be right with the stocks she was recommending, and it was more important for her to be right than it was for her to make commissions or sell the last share of stock."

Meanwhile Martha had started bringing her personal problems to the office, and sharing them with Greene, who had become her confidant as well as mentor. "She was *always* complaining about Andy, about the house in Middlefield, about their apartment. She would bitch to me about those things. Some of it was just sort of venting frustration, and some of it was very legitimate, complaining that this, or that, or the other thing wasn't working right. But that was part of her competitiveness."

Just about every weekend the Stewarts were making the tiring round trip to Middlefield, where they were continuing to work hard restoring their little getaway house. They were also bickering constantly, friends said.

Late one Sunday night they returned to Riverside Drive drained from another grueling weekend, their new BMW sedan overflowing with boxes and bags of vegetables from their garden. Looking at their haul and suddenly realizing how exhausted they both felt, they burst into hysterical laughter and proceeded to toss all the food down the garbage chute. "What the hell are we doing? We must be nuts!"

The Stewarts decided to take a much-needed vacation. Their destination was Bogotá, Colombia, where Kathy and Chris Tatlock had moved. Tatlock had had a good position at the prestigious Wall Street firm of Winthrop, Stimson, Putnam & Roberts, which he gave up. An idealist, he wanted to go abroad for his government and do his part because he had not served in the military. A Hispanophile, who had spent much time in Spain and knew the Latin culture, he was able to secure a position in Bogotá negotiating contracts between the United States and the governments of Colombia and Ecuador for the Agency for International Development (AID), a Kennedy administration–era program offering economic and humanitarian assistance to developing countries.

For her part Kathy Tatlock left New York "all starry-eyed," but once in Colombia she quickly became disillusioned. "I loved the culture and the people but hated the autocracy and the American involvement."

After the Tatlocks left Manhattan, Martha and Kathy, who missed each other, corresponded regularly. As couples the Stewarts and the Tatlocks were extremely close and often had wonderfully wild times together. But Martha never let Kathy forget a seemingly innocent incident that occurred one night during a night on the town. After dinner and drinks the leggy Tatlock, who favored miniskirts and high heels, had gotten up on Andy's shoulders as they walked down Fifth Avenue. "My skirt was hiked up around my hips," she recalled. "Later Martha would bring that up on occasion, acting as if something were going on between Andy and me. There wasn't."

When Martha mentioned that she and Andy needed to get away from the daily grind and that it might be fun to see Colombia, the Tatlocks were overjoyed, and plans were immediately set in motion for the Stewarts, along with little Lexi, to make the trip.

The vacation became, in Tatlock's memory, the visit from hell. "To start with," Tatlock recounted, "their arrival in Bogotá was very hairy. They had a bad flight coming over, and they had to wait in the airport for a protracted period, and Andy became very sick when he got there and got even sicker very quickly. He had a horrendous systemic and local staph infection, and he developed horrible green pustules on his face, which Martha, who had a way with words and wonderful little terms, called the green meanies. Andy looked and felt horrible and ran a very high fever, and the doctor gave him what he called a horse shot of penicillin, which knocked him on his ass."

Instead of feeling sorry for Andy, Martha was angry, which shocked the Tatlocks. "Martha was *really* upset," Kathy Tatlock said, "because she was afraid Andy's illness was going to ruin *her* vacation."

One of the side trips that the Tatlocks had planned for the Stewarts' visit was to the lush coffee country. With Andy bedridden, the Tatlocks were all for canceling the five-day excursion. "Andy didn't think he should go, but Martha *insisted*. She was angry that he had gotten sick, actually angry at *him*, and was punishing him. It was shocking and disturbing."

Tatlock had witnessed some verbal abuse of Andy by Martha back in New York but had dismissed it as "just Martha being mad at the world. That's just Martha's modus operandi." But she had *never* seen anything like this.

In the end Martha won out, and the still-weak Andy made the trip.

"The first couple of days were just horrible," Tatlock said. "Andy was nauseated and feverish and weak and sleepy. We stayed in beautiful places, and Andy tried to take short outings with us, but then he'd go back to the hotel room and sleep. He spent most of the time in the hotel. And the three of us would go out and sightsee. That's how we did the whole coffee country trip."

The other curious sidelight of the trip was Martha's decision to leave her daughter behind in the care of the Tat-locks' two *muchachas*, who spoke only Spanish. "Lexi of course couldn't speak a word of Spanish, so it was up to my oldest daughter, who was only about three, to interpret for her. It raised my eyebrow that Martha was willing to leave Lexi, who didn't have the ability of communicating, with Spanish-speaking caregivers. That was a little beyond my understanding of parenting."

A Stepford Wife

In early 1972 the Stewarts, considered diehard New York-ers, startled friends with the sudden announcement that they were moving to the town of Westport, in Connecticut, where they had bought an old farmhouse that required extensive and costly renovations.

"We were very surprised because they always said they liked the city, and they had the place in Middlefield," said Florence Libin. "But Martha suddenly wanted to get out of New York, because they had fallen in love with that house."

However, Paul Libin had gotten a different take from Andy, who indicated the move to Westport was made as both a lifestyle choice and an investment. "There was no state income tax in Connecticut, and they were doing pretty well at the time, so it was a way of sheltering some of that income and getting a good piece of property."

Like the Libins, Liz Hawes was bewildered by the Ste-warts' flight to suburbia. "We had all been in an apartment sort of mindset and environment, and then suddenly Martha and Andy had just gone in a whole different direction by buying that house, which wasn't anything that any of us— or certainly anything that I—envied in any particular way,'' she said. ''We all had that primal longing for houses that you sometimes get hit by when you're living in New York. But other than that, the idea of actually moving to suburbia, which is what Martha did, was nothing of interest to any of us at the time.''

Over the years Martha has given various reasons for buying the house, ranging from her burning creative need to take something old and restore it to ''We thought we'd fix it up and sell it and move on.'' But the real reason was more prosaic: A year earlier Andy's company had moved its headquarters to Greenwich, he'd grown tired of the commute from Manhattan, and he wanted a home closer to his office.

The 1805 Federal farmhouse, which the Stewarts bought for sixty-three thousand dollars—a relatively hefty sum in 1970s dollars and barely affordable even with their earning power at the time—was at 48 South Turkey Hill Road, in the fancy Green Farms section of Westport. In order to buy the house and get some of the renovations started, Andy had to borrow money from his employers and Martha had to dig into her stockbroker nest egg.

The new old house—which was restored mainly by the Stewarts with their bare hands, a great deal of sweat equity, and angst—eventually became a showcase and part of the Martha Stewart myth. Called Turkey Hill Farm by Martha, the house became the headquarters for her catering and lifestyle enterprises, which she had still not conceived of when they bought the place.

In the spring of 1971, when the Stewarts took up residence, bucolic Westport, on Long Island Sound, was considered a unique place to live, an affluent bedroom community populated by commuting Manhattan professionals and creative types: lawyers, writers, advertising executives, artists.

As one longtime resident and keen observer of the town's social scene noted, ''Westport is and was in the center of

Yankee land, but with a bunch of liberals and very opin-
ionated, very active people. Around the time the Stewarts
moved here there was a review at a New York cabaret,
Julius Monk's Upstairs at the Downstairs, which portrayed
Westport as a key town. That meant at parties here couples
threw their house keys into the middle of the living-room
floor, and husbands and wives went home with someone
else's mate—you know, wife-swapping parties.''

Whatever the truth, Westport was an interesting community of highly intelligent, creative, well-to-do strivers
like the Stewarts, the perfect setting for a John Cheever
story. In fact, at about the time that Martha and Andy were
moving in, a highly entertaining new book, *The Stepford
Wives*, by Ira Levin, was published. It tells the story of a
fictional town in Connecticut—Stepford—a place much
like Westport, where the wives have been turned into chill-
ingly beautiful robots that have been programmed to please
their husbands with gourmet meals, enchanting parties, and
pristine homes, women who are experts in housewifery arts.
It was as if Levin, who also wrote the chilling *Rosemary's
Baby*, had somehow foreseen the Martha Stewart rage still
almost a decade away.

Even more eerie and ironic was the fact that a couple of
years after the Stewarts became Westporters, and around
the time Martha was getting her first catering business off
the ground, the town became the location for some of the
exterior shots used in William Goldman's film adaptation
of Levin's novel. Like other Westporters Martha went to
the location to watch the shooting.

When the film was released, the critic Pauline Kael observed that *The Stepford Wives* was ''about the encroaching
horror of suburban blandness . . . suburban women becoming overgroomed deadheads, obsessed with waxed, antisep-
tic households. . . .'' Some years later similar criticism was
heaped on Martha and her zealous followers.

The move to Westport, like Martha's decision to become a
stockbroker, was a milestone in the Stewarts' lives and did
not happen without bringing to the surface wrenching problems—some old and unresolved, others new and formida-

ble—that further weakened the fragile underpinnings of their already shaky eleven-year marriage.

One immediate concern was Lexi, whose emotional state drastically changed when the Stewarts relocated, a situation close friends felt was attributable not only to the move, and the disordered state of the house, but also to the unfettered drive of her young, upwardly mobile parents.

"When they lived in Manhattan, Lexi was fine because they were usually all together on the weekends at Middle-field, and Martha and Andy brought Lexi on vacations with them," a confidant observed. "Even though both of them were working hard, they tried their best to spend time with Lexi after school or after dinner. Sometimes Martha juggled her hours at the office or called in to say she was sick so she could spend a little more time with Lexi. Andy was a very loving and devoted father. And Lexi was very happy at Rudolf Steiner.

"But there was a visible change in her when they moved to Turkey Hill. They put her into first grade in the elementary school in Green Farms, and she was very unhappy there. For some odd reason Lexi became obsessed with disliking the school's principal, and she had difficulty making friends."

Norma Collier, whom Martha had designated as Lexi's guardian, also saw a change in Lexi's behavior. "She became a very pouty, irritable child. Lexi was also very controlling, very meticulous, just like Martha. My daughter, Kyra, used to play with Lexi at Turkey Hill, and they would color with Magic Markers, and Lexi would allow Kyra to take only one Magic Marker out of the box at a time. If she took more than one, Lexi would get very upset."

Because of Lexi's problems, the Stewarts took her out of Green Farms elementary school and enrolled her in a private school, Green Farms Academy, and her mood improved somewhat. But she remained unhappy.

"Something had started to go wrong, and Martha and Andy weren't sure what it was," the confidant said. "But Andy later thought it was a combination of the move, their jobs, and the great amount of energy he and Martha were putting into rebuilding the house that was causing Lexi's problems. The child definitely went inward, began to spend a lot of time in her room, and rarely enjoyed being with friends.

"And you couldn't blame her because the house was in a constant state of disarray. Rooms were being torn apart; plastic was hanging in doorways instead of doors because Andy and Martha were scraping the doors, and chipping the paint off the doors, and tearing the ceilings down. There was rat shit on the floors that had fallen from under the plaster in the ceilings. The floors were old and painted red. There were flimsy plywood closets in the hall nailed to the walls. It was a mess.

"Like Martha, Lexi was obsessed with tidiness. So her room was the first one in the house that the Stewarts got in shape, building bookcases for her and that sort of thing. Her room became her refuge from the mess in the rest of the house. Lexi escaped there."

The Stewarts spent all their free time trying to get the house at least into *livable* shape; the showplace it eventually became took years to complete. Martha's drive for perfection, and demand for more lavish improvements, made the project take forever.

Privately, Andy began comparing Martha's seemingly obsessive need for bigger, better, and more to the protagonist in the Brothers Grimm's German folk tale *The Fisherman and His Wife*, a story about an impoverished woman who also has an unquenchable drive that emerges after her humble husband catches a magical fish that grants wishes. Eventually the wife wishes to be like God.

In order to make Turkey Hill grander, the Stewarts, at Martha's behest, purchased two neighboring lots, one costing almost two hundred thousand dollars, that turned the original tract into a miniestate. They installed the black-bottomed swimming pool; constructed a livable barn and other outbuildings, including a chicken house (Martha preferred to call it a *palais du poulet*); and built a huge stone wall, among other improvements. Martha finally had the backyard that Eddie Kostyra had only dreamed about back on Elm Place.

"It was a major restoration, and we stupidly did it while

we were living in it, which I'll never do again, because it was very unfair to us," Martha said later. "I didn't entertain. I didn't have friends over for two years. We did everything ourselves except for the wiring."

Martha began to take out on Andy her many frustrations about the state of the house, the problems with Lexi, and the pressures of her job. In front of friends she declared, "Just look how beautiful *their* house looks. . . . I'm disgusted with the way *our* house looks . . . it's *too* messy . . . it's too small . . . it's not good enough." She also made personal attacks on Andy: "He's boring . . . disgusting . . . oafish . . . sloppy . . . he can't get *anything* right." She criticized Andy for not being like the high-powered businessmen she was meeting in her job. On more than one occasion she declared, "Why can't you be successful, like Ralph Lauren?" And there were times when she stated threateningly, "There are a lot of other men I could be with. . . ."

During one of those verbal assaults Martha declared in a fit of anger and irritation that she had slept with another man while on a business trip to Los Angeles. Andy was floored. But Martha dismissed the tryst as "a one-time thing . . . unimportant . . . uninteresting . . . unsatisfactory . . . merely an experiment."

"Andy wondered how he could stay with Martha after that," said an intimate. "He felt she was outrageous and terrible. He said, 'How do I handle this woman? She is just awful—even though I love her.' He was trying to struggle with this serious, unpleasant turn in their relationship. He was wondering, 'Can this marriage last? Can we turn it around? Can I make it better?' Actually it wasn't the claimed affair that really bothered Andy as much as Martha's constant unreasonable anger toward him, her total failure to look at herself, her inability to acknowledge error, to figure out *why* she was so angry, to apologize to him now and then. Martha's idea of an apology to Andy was to say something like 'It's my fault. I never should have asked someone as stupid as you to do this. . . .'

"Andy said he felt that Martha had two personalities: Martha A and Martha B. One was pleasant and fun; the other he referred to as the evil one. When he told her his theory, she just laughed, but she acknowledged she was consciously able to go from being the nice Martha to being the nasty Martha. "Andy urged Martha to see a therapist with him, which she did, but nothing changed. She always thought the therapist was stupid and was on Andy's side."

The Crash

Despite the intensifying conflict at home, Martha was at the top of her game on Wall Street. Much of 1972 and the early part of 1973 was strictly rock and roll in the market, at least for the stocks Monness, Williams & Sidel was peddling. Martha had become even more cocky and confident as her substantial commissions rolled in.

It was a heady time. There was even talk of Martha's becoming a partner. As Ken Sidel noted later, "She was working her butt off. Martha was hardworking, ambitious, and opportunistic."

And Martha knew how to sell like no one.

One afternoon she had a luncheon date with a client, the big cheese at a hedge fund, and they were to dine at a tony continental restaurant. But when they arrived at the appointed hour Martha discovered that her reservation had been lost.

Not the least bit flustered, she hustled her client around the corner to a hamburger joint where she breezed through her pitch and sold the client a whopping twenty thousand shares of Pamida, an Omaha-based retail chain on the order of a

Wal-Mart. Her commission for an hour's work was twenty thousand dollars, with a split to analyst Sandy Greene, who had researched, and recommended the company.

"For us," he said later, "it was a *huge* order."

Martha was raking in enough in commissions so that she was able to run out one lunchtime—presumably humming the ubiquitous "You'll Love It at Levitz" jingle—and buy a new Mercedes.

But Martha, poor all her life, mostly held on tight to the money she was earning. While she maintained a small investment account, it never amounted to very much. "She wasn't a gambler, she wasn't a player," a colleague observed.

With the bull market of the early seventies seeming to have an unlimited future, speculators and investors were buying like sharks in a feeding frenzy. Though Martha dealt mainly with institutional investors, she did convince some of her close friends—Norma Collier, Emily McCully, Roger Hooker, among others—to invest in the hot market and had acted as their broker, a decision a few would later regret having made.

Early each morning, chicly dressed and anxious to get to the office, Martha waited impatiently, tapping the toe of her Ferragamo shoe, at the Westport station, looking up the track for the New Haven Railroad's 8:05, along with a small cadre of other commuters headed for Grand Central. To her Brooks Brothers–suited fellow travelers, the slender, leggy blonde whom they eyed from behind their *Wall Street Journal*s and *New York Times*es was a welcome addition to their button-down routine.

Always charming and vivacious around interesting men, Martha quickly became acquainted with some of them, and through them she and Andy were introduced to their wives, expanding the Stewarts' social circle in Westport and environs.

Anatole Broyard, a writer and book critic for *The Times*, went home one evening raving to his own tall, gorgeous blond wife, Sandy, a dancer, about the "stunningly beautiful . . . very, very charming woman" named Martha Stewart whom he'd met on the train and how she and her husband had bought the old farmhouse on nearby Turkey Hill Road.

Soon the Stewarts and the Broyards were socializing. "Anatole used to say of Martha from talking with her on the train that she read a book more closely practically than anybody else he knew," recalled Sandy Broyard, who was widowed in 1990.

Through Sandy Broyard, Martha met and became friendly with the writer Jill Robinson, daughter of MGM studio boss Dore Schary. A self-described former "speed addict," Robinson was in the process of finishing a gritty autobiography called *Bed/Time/Story*. Published in 1974, the book, which became a best-seller, was billed as "a devastating odyssey of a couple who experiment with every contemporary idea and experience of love, every kind of encounter with sex. . . ."

After Robinson's husband, a mathematician, abandoned her, which is what the book is mainly about, she moved to Westport on the advice of Sandy Broyard, "who really rescued me," and another friend, the literary agent Lynn Nesbitt, who became part of Martha's circle and represented her for a brief time.

While Martha and Robinson were from different worlds, the two women easily bonded. "Martha was everything I wanted to be at a certain point in my life," Robinson said. "I wanted to be really stylish and good at things and to make my house wonderful. And I wanted to be independent, and successful. It seemed to me Martha was doing all those things."

Another commuter like Broyard who befriended Martha was a young entertainment lawyer named Alan Bomser, who was married and the father of two. "I found her attractive physically," he said. "She was enormously charming, animated, and interesting. I was flirtatious, and she was flirtatious to a point."

In short order the Stewarts and the Bomsers—Jill Bomser, Alan's wife, had worked in the production end of TV soap operas—became "great friends." The Bomsers' little girl, Jennifer, was the same age as Lexi, and the youngsters became playmates. Like Martha, Jill Bomser had an interest in cooking and food. And the Stewarts and the Bomsers had a mutual interest in communal living, which they discussed at great length.

"Andy and Martha and Alan and I spent a lot of time talking about the possibility of living communally somewhere, buying land, gardening together, baking bread together," Jill Bomser said. "I know that was one of Alan's and my fantasies, and Andy and Martha took part in those discussions. Andy was the one who was probably more interested, but Martha was *so* talented at the types of things that one would have to do to live on a commune or on a farm—the gardening, caring for the animals, making everything from scratch. That side of her would have been valuable.

"We were probably smoking some dope at the time, but this wasn't going to be a hippie thing. We would have separate family dwellings, as opposed to everybody living on top of each other, but we'd have a communal garden and maybe a communal kitchen. Our idea was a little bit classier."

Despite their utopian vision, the dream was never realized. Like the Stewarts, the Bomsers had a rocky marriage and were eventually divorced.

When they met, both couples were in the process of fixing up their houses, but the Bomsers were far ahead of the Stewarts. They owned an enormous eight-bedroom place in neighboring Weston that had once belonged to ABC news anchor Harry Reasoner. "We had a fifty-five-foot living room with three sort of undefined areas: a pool table at the back that I put in, and a place where you could sit and hang out, and then a big fieldstone fireplace in front of which was this king-size water bed," Alan Bomser said. "And after dinner we would all kind of hang out in the water bed in front of the fireplace. We were relatively young, and it was fun."

For Martha, the good times were about to come to a crashing halt. The beginning of the end began with a shift in the fortunes of Levitz Furniture. The Florida-headquartered national company had been virtually minting money selling schlocky furniture in high volume, having made its reputation on Wall Street as a pioneer in the concept of the warehouse superstore. But the company's rapid growth suddenly skidded to a stop, leaving a huge amount of inventory. A downturn in the economy in late 1972 and early 1973, along with the growing Watergate scandal, were having an impact on the markets, and money was becoming expensive. Those factors all combined to leave Levitz in dire straits.

But that didn't stop Monness, Williams & Sidel and its sales force from continuing to push the company's stock.

"One afternoon Martha saw Frank Williams basically berating one of her customers because he hadn't bought any Levitz yet," recalled Sandy Greene. "Levitz was around seventy, and Frank said it's obvious it's going to a hundred twenty or some number like that. The next morning Levitz put out a press release saying its next quarter's earnings were going to be disappointing, and so of course the stock took an instant collapse.

"Martha was not as much hurt as she felt betrayed and embarrassed for her customer because Frank had been so aggressive, and he was exactly wrong. His timing couldn't have been worse. That was probably the single event in my mind that really got Martha thinking about whether she wanted to be in this business anymore. She was really disturbed.

"A few months later Martha and I were on the shuttle going to Boston to see clients, and Levitz had laid another egg, and it was in the *Wall Street Journal*, and we read the story as we were sitting on the plane, and she said, 'Oh, my God, I don't believe it!' She was absolutely disgusted because selling Levitz was the reason why we were going to Boston. She was quite disturbed because this product she was selling wasn't what we had made it out to be."

In early 1973 Martha had also begun communicating her concerns to Andy about the goings-on at Monness, Williams & Sidel. He wasn't surprised.

Almost from the start Andy had expressed his opinion that the firm was unstable, that the stock market was precarious, and that this was not the way Martha should be earning a living. Knowing that she was prone to exaggeration, he had especially warned her not to hype any of the stocks that she was selling, fearing that if the firm went under, Martha might face some liability. He believed too the job was having a devastating impact on their marriage. He strongly advised her to quit.

Martha also commiserated with her colleagues at the office. "When the business started going south," Brian Dennehy recalled, "we'd talk to each other each day and say, 'Goddammit, I *hate* coming in here.' All of a sudden it wasn't fun anymore. And it was at that time when we realized that the success, and the money, and the fun that we had actually hid the fact that we were not doing essentially what we really wanted to do. I'm sure that was as true for her as it was for me. We were never obviously seriously professional Wall Street people."

Still more anxiety was in store for Martha when close friends to whom she'd recommended stock began taking financial baths. Norma Collier, for one, claimed that Martha "lost a lot of my money—five to six thousand dollars—in over-the-counter stuff.

"They were all wild men at that firm," Collier said. "They were rough and tough, but Martha was *not* rough and tough, and I think she got swept along with it. My account with the firm was probably typical in that Martha went along with what they told her to put me into. Unfortunately she kept me in, got herself out, and I rode the whole thing down. Martha had gone on vacation, and I called Andy Monness, and I said, 'Andy, I'm really uncomfortable being in these stocks.' And he said, 'I can't believe you're still in them.' And I said, 'Martha says she's still in them.' And he said, 'She's been out for months.' And that was the first jolt that my friend could do something like that to me. I confronted her. I said, 'You lost me a chunk of change.' But she refused to take the blame."

Another friend, Emily McCully, had invested fifteen to twenty thousand dollars—all the money her mother had left her—in stocks recommended by Martha and lost it all. "We gave a bunch of it to Martha, and we didn't pay any attention, and the market fell. I was resentful of Martha. I was pretty upset, and I was ashamed that I hadn't been paying attention to the stocks. I was told that she felt really bad about it and took it hard."

Sometime in the spring of 1973 a disillusioned and depressed Martha, her commissions having dried up, her faith gone in the product she was selling and in the firm she was working for, handed in her resignation to Andy Monness.

"Martha felt the pressure of being wrong," he observed later. "I think what caused Martha a *great* deal of trouble was realizing that she didn't necessarily get an A just because she did her homework, just because she was intelligent, and just because she worked her ass off.

"When you bought someone a stock at sixty and suddenly it was thirty-seven, they hated you. She had trouble dealing with that. But in this business you can't be a perfectionist because you're going to be wrong forty percent of the time. What happened had an emotional impact on her. It upset her because she was so much of a perfectionist. So she said, 'This is it. I have to go try my fortunes doing something else.' "

Like the prices of the stocks she had been peddling, Martha's world had come tumbling down, leaving her shattered.

Floundering

For the first time since before she started modeling in high school, Martha, at thirty-two, was without an identity or a career. Having been brought up by her father to succeed and never to quit, Martha took the Wall Street crash as a personal defeat, a new and frightening feeling for her. For the first time in her life, Martha had not been in absolute control of her fate, and that had a devastating emotional impact on her.

''I was a nervous wreck at the end'' was all she has ever said about that terrible period in her life. ''I woke up with hives. I could have gone maybe more into research. But I liked the sales part of it, the human contact. But I wanted to sell things that were fun to sell. And stocks weren't anymore.''

But Martha's reaction was far more severe than the skin disorder she described. ''Martha had a nervous breakdown basically, and she had to go into therapy,'' stated George McCully, who visited her at the time. ''She was struggling with who she was. She had a real identity crisis, a personal identity crisis, the big one, or at least the *first* big one. I remember a couple of conversations—one with Martha and Andy and one with Martha alone—when she told me that she was going through this terrible period of self-doubt and that she felt she was *nothing* after having been on an extraordinarily productive onward and upward track that began in Nutley.

''It was explained to me that Martha was deeply depressed, that she was seeing a therapist or had seen a couple of them, several of them, and that she was really searching for who she was and what she should do. She felt not like a parasite exactly but kind of like a fifth wheel. She felt *useless*, felt she wasn't pulling her weight, was out there in nowhereland, in Westport, without anything to do.

''We were talking in the kitchen at Turkey Hill, and she said that she was just terribly depressed, that she felt useless and empty and just needed to find something to do with herself. I knew that she was miserable. I know it was serious, but it wasn't treated as a clinical thing. It was treated as a shrink kind of thing.''

Slowly Martha began to emerge from under the dark cloud that had enveloped her, and she began seriously searching for the third career of her life. For a time she considered becoming a real estate agent. She knew houses, had proved herself a supersaleswoman, and had the perfect Waspy look to sell property in the gentrified Westport area. She took the required test and got her license.

At the time Anatole and Sandy Broyard were buying and

selling beautiful old houses that were on the weekend house tours. Sandy thought it curious that Martha, who was still in the process of fixing up Turkey Hill, was showing up at every one of the Broyards' open houses, poking around and asking questions. But Broyard was unaware of the crisis Martha had been through, or that she was considering real estate sales as a line of work. In the end Martha concluded that selling houses didn't push any of her buttons.

Instead she retreated to Turkey Hill, where she played full-time housewife and mother for the first time since the early days of her marriage and the birth of Lexi. She was frenetic around the house, like a woman possessed, like a woman controlled by some perverse outside force, like a real-life Stepford wife. Driven to keep herself occupied, Martha once got up on a ladder and painted the entire house by herself. Neighbors saw her in the early-morning hours maniacally mowing the enormous lawn with an old-fashioned hand mower, or they'd see her down in the dirt planting seeds or weeding as the sun rose in the east. If she wasn't in the garden, she was hand-washing linens she had bought the day before at a tag sale, pouring lemon juice through the stains to remove them.

She'd stay up until 2:00 A.M., stenciling her floors, a project that caused much contention with houseguests, who were ordered by Martha to remove their shoes before they entered the house, so as not to mar her handiwork, or face never being invited back. "That took on such an importance that everybody had to conform to it with the 'shoes off,' with the 'careful where you walk.' There was an enormous focus on not messing that up, and it got to be *grotesque*," noted Alan Bomser.

"I'd go over there, and she'd be ironing sheets with a big sheet ironing machine like in professional Laundromats," recalled one close pal and neighbor, Janet Horowitz. "It would boggle my mind, and my eyes would bug out of my head. I couldn't believe it. Martha refused to have help. She was willing to work on her own and wanted to get the things done and didn't want to spend the money. It was important for her to be frugal."

Martha later acknowledged that "for many years I re-

sisted hiring a housekeeper.'' She ''finally broke down''
and hired one, Necy Fernandes, ''an expert in cleaning and
organizing,'' to come in ''one day a week.''

Friends watched her, noted her quirky and curious ways,
shook their heads either in awe or sympathy, and decided,
''Well, that's Martha. *Martha's Martha.*''

Despite long days packed with feverish housework, Martha remained extremely unhappy. Her emotional state manifested itself in physical problems: severe migraine
headaches, insomnia.

''I once went over there at four in the morning, and she
was a mess, so sick,'' said a close friend, Ann Brody. ''The
intensity of her personality was mind-boggling.''

Martha had gone into a period of soul-searching about
what to do with her life. ''We would sit in her kitchen, and
she was at her wit's end and depressed, and had no direction at that point, and was lost,'' said Janet Horowitz, who
for more than two decades was among Martha's closest
friends. They had become acquainted in New York because
Andy and Janet's husband, Len Horowitz, were fellow lawyers at Bangor Punta. They became friends when the Stewarts moved to Westport, where the Horowitzes had settled
a couple of years earlier.

Martha and Janet were completely different types, both
physically and emotionally: Horowitz was petite, with dark,
curly hair, a warm, sensitive Jewish Mutt to Martha's cool,
detached Waspy Jeff. While she didn't find Martha a warm
person, Horowitz was drawn to her archetype, ''the driven,
perfectionistic woman,'' and found her fascinating to be
around.

''Martha wouldn't have been the person I would have
gone to if I needed help with something because she
doesn't have that kind of warm personality that I need,''
Horowitz said later. ''But I saw the positive side of her.''

Like others who were or who became members of Martha's circle in Westport, Horowitz was in a helping profession, in the field of psychology and education. Some of the
others, such as Sandy Broyard, too were or became coun-
selors and therapists, and all of them appeared to have one

thing in common: They found Martha's focused, driven persona an interesting study.

"But when I first got to know her in Westport," Horowitz recalled, "she certainly wasn't an aggressive type of person. She was struggling and questioning. She was lost. I didn't see the side that was there when she was a stockbroker."

Mommie Dearest

For the first time since Lexi was an infant, mother and daughter were constantly together now that Martha was without a career. In her books and magazine Martha has portrayed a perfect relationship. She described Lexi as "a very thoughtful child." She wrote of how Lexi remembered "the first basket-weave heart cake I ever made . . . adorned with pink royal-icing roses [that] was very well received by her friends at her sixth-birthday party . . . she also recalls the very plain Bundt cake I made at the last minute for her seventh birthday. She says I stuck a fat candle in the center and didn't make frosting because I was too busy shingling the garage roof."

She has told readers that Lexi loved potato chips and described how she took her to a town in Massachusetts where chip potatoes were grown. She has reminisced fondly about Lexi's childhood camp days in Vermont and how Lexi was "genuinely surprised" that her mother "had taken the time every day to write her a one-page letter." She has written of the "many hours" she and Lexi spent together milking and petting goats owned by a friend.

Martha dedicated *Pies & Tarts* to Lexi, "who makes pies and tarts but never eats them," and she told readers that Lexi was the inspiration for *Martha Stewart's Quick Cook Menus*. She also lovingly described a Mother's Day scene where she "waited serenely in bed" while Lexi "brought her breakfast on a tray decorated with roses."

But the warm and fuzzy relationship that Martha has depicted was more fiction than fact, according to friends and family members. Indeed it was precisely Martha's treatment of Lexi that concerned Janet Horowitz after she became close to Martha.

"Martha was *not* one of those warm, nurturing mothers," asserted Horowitz, whose two daughters were younger than Lexi. "Lexi was a nice sweet girl but a difficult and unhappy child. She always seemed lonely and very isolated. I got very close to her because she was the kind of kid who I felt needed contact, and so I would pull her in with some warmth and caring, and she responded.

"One thing that was very upsetting to me was how Lexi would change if I was with her and Martha walked into the room. She suddenly became another child. I had never seen anything like it. I would be with Lexi and she'd be warm and smiling and talking and free, and it was a nice interchange. Then Martha would walk through the room, and Lexi would freeze. I mean literally. That child changed in front of my eyes every single time Martha came near. She actually got tight and couldn't talk. You could see anger moving in on her, and she almost had to flee the room. It was just unbelievable."

Horowitz believed that the problem was related in part to Martha's own chilly childhood. "She never really felt loved or cared about as a child, and that's probably why she had problems growing emotionally," she contended. "I felt Martha was shut off emotionally."

Because of the close friendship that developed between Lexi and Jennifer Bomser, Jill Bomser also had an opportunity to observe Martha in the role of a mother. "I like to think that I can see the good side to most people in most situations," Bomser noted. "I'm sure that I was looking for Martha's good side, and because I was so impressed with her talent and creativity, I tended to disregard the negative side. But I don't even want to use the word 'good' in describing Martha as a mother because that would be a lie. She was really *hard* with Lexi, and with my kid too. Jennifer reminds me today when I jump to Martha's defense, as I occasionally do, when I'll say, 'God, she's so incredible. Look at what she's accomplished. Maybe she's not totally happy, but you know, who is—because you can't have it all?' Well, Jennifer reminds me what Martha was *really* like as a mother.

"Jennifer has told me stories of when I wasn't there at Martha's house, or I was somewhere else in the house, or outside, or whatever, and Martha would come down really hard on them for doing something or not doing something. Jennifer remembers Martha as being a real slave driver, saying things like 'You and Lexi *have* to go down and clean the chicken house!' And do this, and do that. These were *little* kids, and she was ordering them around. Martha was a *real* slave driver. She didn't let Lexi and Jennifer play a lot or be free. There was constantly something that had to be done, and she made these little kids do it. It was as if her magazine or her television show were rolling right then, and these little kids were part of the crew. There was always *something*. She had this philosophy that the kids always had to be working."

When Lexi was nine, Martha said, "She likes housework. She can clean a bathroom faster than anyone. The gardens don't interest her that much—probably because they interest me so much."

Jill Bomser noted, "There wasn't a lot of love and warmth from Martha toward Lexi. When it came to love and warmth, that's where Andy came in. He was an incredibly warm and loving father and absolutely crazy about Lexi, and that's where Lexi was getting love."

Sandy Greene's wife had the impression that Lexi's "moodiness" was one of the reasons why Martha left Monness, Williams & Sidel, so that she could stay home and devote more time to her daughter. "She was asking whether the job was worth it if Lexi wasn't happy,'' Blue Magruder recalled. ''Lexi was a quiet, sort of resentful child who was fairly dutiful. You know, setting the table right. Martha was always telling her to stay out of the way because the grown-ups were talking, which Lexi wouldn't tolerate, so she kept zooming around. That child was being ignored and obviously needed a great deal more attention from her mother.''

Through Jill Bomser, Martha met Ann Brody, an extremely bright and determined woman, who also had a strong interest in cooking. Like the other women in Martha's circle, Brody, the wife of an orthopedist, had two daughters and a son, so she also was in a position to judge Martha and Lexi's relationship.

''When Lexi was the star of a school show or was getting an A, Martha was the proudest mother in the world, but I got the feeling that Martha felt Lexi interfered with her direction and distracted her,'' she observed. ''If Lexi was sick, if the kid was in pain, and Martha had something to do, she'd get angry at *Lexi*. Martha had a hell of a temper, and she'd voice her frustration, her anger: 'Why does Lexi have to be sick *now*?'

''Lexi was a very unhappy kid. And Martha demanded— the way her father probably demanded of her—that Lexi had to achieve. She had to be number one in the class. She had to look gorgeous. She had to have her dress hemmed a certain way. There was always something.

''What really pissed me off was that Lexi would come home from school and Martha and I would be working in the kitchen and the kid would be hungry and Martha would scream at her to get out of the kitchen. I was always concerned about Lexi because she was so miserable and unhappy. I tried to be as compassionate and loving as I could to her. I couldn't really talk to Martha about that kind of stuff—you know, 'Martha, why are you treating her so badly?' Martha wouldn't acknowledge it. After a while, having witnessed things like that, I found it became uncomfortable to be around Martha a lot.''

One afternoon Lexi and Amanda Brody's playing got on Martha's nerves. '' 'Amanda,' '' Martha declared, '' 'I'm going to come to your house while you're asleep tonight and cut off all your long fingernails.' Amanda is in her thirties now, and she's not forgotten that,'' Brody asserted.

Another former friend and colleague of Martha's, Gail Leichtman-Macht, recalled how Martha refused to pick up Lexi at school when she became ill. ''Martha said, 'Well, I'm *not* going to get her.' So I went to pick up Lexi,'' Leichtman-Macht said. ''And that kind of thing happened a few times. Martha thought either Lexi was playing sick, or she didn't have time to go get her, or it wasn't her *priority* to pick up Lexi. If I had a child who had a history of hypochondriacal behavior and she called from school, I might be more likely to say, 'Oh, that's just her, you know. Her thing acting up again; I'm going to ignore it.' That's very different from when the school calls and says your kid is sick and the mother says, 'I'm not picking her up, I'm too busy.' When I picked up Lexi that day, it seemed to me like she had the flu. It was clear that the child was not a priority in Martha's life.''

One afternoon Andy and Martha were in the kitchen at Turkey Hill when they heard a thump and Lexi screaming at the top of her lungs. They went running and found the child, then about nine, in a great deal of pain after having slipped and fallen down the stairs. ''Martha's reaction,'' according to a family confidant, ''was to start screaming at Lexi, telling her how stupid she was for falling and hurting herself. Andy was trying to comfort Lexi, which was impossible because he was in the middle of this screaming argument between his irate wife and his injured daughter. They didn't know for a week that Lexi had fractured her arm.''

The Uncatered Affair

Martha has professed that the idea for going into the catering business—her first formal step to becoming America's "Diva of Domesticity"—was not part of any master plan but rather a "chance" happening that occurred while she was giving cooking lessons in her kitchen to Lexi and her playmates.

From there, she writes in *Entertaining*, she "tentatively" placed an ad in a local newspaper, offering her services "only to find myself preparing blindly for a wedding for three hundred. The menu was a novice's—extravagant, demanding and unprofitable . . . I stood by the buffet table and watched the aspic melt off the oeufs en gelée. . . ."

For Martha, catering was *the* perfect occupation: She was a good cook, she presented food creatively, and she was a tough, proven saleswoman, and a great pitch artist, and self-promoter. As her Wall Street pal Brian Dennehy, observed, "Martha retired to a world that she knew every aspect of, and could control, and could make into a commodity that she could sell."

However, in a number of respects Martha's version of becoming a caterer differs markedly from the accounts of partners or employees who saw her business develop. "Martha taught kids when we were together, that's true, she'd have a little cooking class for Lexi's friends, but it was like *Mommie Dearest*. Martha was gritting her teeth, saying, 'Sweetheart, you have to do it *this way*.' They were

171

not happy, bright faces at all,'' maintained Norma Collier, who became Martha's first fifty-fifty catering partner, a key fact Martha has chosen to ignore in her published works. ''The kids were looking at her like they didn't like her, and she was going on with her cookies or whatever. The minute Martha finished, the kids were gone like a shot. There was clearly no relating to them on her part.''

Ann Brody, who also was there at the launch of Martha's professional catering career, agreed. ''If Martha thought Lexi was supposed to learn about cooking, she'd give her three cookies to decorate, *maybe*, and *that* was a big deal.''

Jill Bomser, who like Martha was an excellent cook and went on to operate two restaurants of her own, said Martha's idea to go into catering ''was born under my nose, and what happened was that she, in her own aggressive way, went out and got her first job.''

Bomser recalled that the first affair she and Martha catered together was, in fact, the same one mentioned in *Entertaining,* a wedding held, as Martha writes, ''on a sweltering August afternoon in an unsheltered beach club in Darien.''

''Martha and I worked on it together,'' said Bomser, who received no credit in Martha's book. ''It was your typical first catering job, where almost everything went wrong— even for Martha. It was in the middle of the summer. It was easily ninety-five degrees, and we had done a lot of cold food, things that could melt. And the bride or somebody in the wedding party fainted in the middle of the wedding. But everybody thought Martha was *fabulous*.''

Despite the problems that had occurred that day, Martha was hooked. She saw she could make money from something she knew well and loved to do and could control completely. ''She definitely had her head turned around that this was going to be a career for her,'' Bomser said.

But Bomser never worked with her again. ''She was a total perfectionist, and everything had to be done her way. She was extremely critical, judgmental, and *very* intimidating. There was a time when I idolized her, was in awe of her. I saw Martha as my alter ego. But I didn't have her great drive. There was a side to her where she would walk over people who got in her way. Her priorities were very different from mine.''

Bomser saw the dark side of Martha one sunny afternoon, and the incident all but ended their close friendship and left her thinking years later that Martha was "a very schizophrenic kind of person.'' The Bomsers and the Stewarts had made plans for a picnic at the beach, and Martha had baked pies with fresh blueberries that she had ordered picked from her garden by Lexi and Jennifer Bomser. Martha had choreographed the whole event, packing several of her beautiful Shaker baskets with a variety of foods, all covered with picture-perfect checkered tea cloths, which Martha had hand-washed and freshly ironed.

"There were always a lot of cars in Martha's driveway, and somehow or other one of the baskets got placed under my car, and I didn't know it, and I got in to back out, and the car rolled over the basket,'' said Jill Bomser, whose recollection of what happened next is engraved in her mind.

"Martha started to shriek, absolutely shriek, at me at the top of her lungs. She just turned into another person and just started screaming obscenities, calling me horrible names: 'You stupid fucking idiot!' 'You dumb fucking bitch!' It was horrible and frightening.

"Finally I pulled out of the driveway, leaving my family behind, and I just took off and didn't come back. I was terribly upset, and I drove around and cried for a couple of hours. It seems really silly as I look back on it, but it was a pretty traumatic experience. But that was basically it for me and Martha. She never stopped by to say she was sorry.''

Now that Martha was taking her first tentative steps toward starting a full-time catering business, she and Ann Brody got together on a few projects. Brody, who already was active in the food world, working as an assistant to a food photographer in New York, asked Martha to help her with a shoot that involved the cooking of suckling pigs. The two women had great fun working together, and the first shoot resulted in subsequent jobs for the two of them for *Cuisine* and *Family Circle*. The photo sessions were held in Martha's country kitchen. With hanging brass pots, beautiful appliances, and other accoutrements, it was a natural setting for a food story.

At first Brody was incredibly impressed with Martha. "She *worked* at being unpretentious, was sort of aloof in her own way, but basically was friendly and very positive. Martha was driven, which for me was very positive, because I was a working woman too, and I didn't see a lot of that in Westport in the seventies. I saw a lot of very bright, well-educated women who were *not* driven at all, who were *not* working, who had *no* desire to work, and Martha was clearly different. She had always worked. She had earned her own way. I had a lot of respect for her."

Soon Martha and Brody were doing catering jobs together and had even started teaching cooking classes in the adult education division of the Westport public school system. Because of good word of mouth, they also were getting invitations to teach cooking to women's organizations, such as the Fairfield Organic Gardeners, of which Martha, an enthusiastic organic gardener, had become a member.

One afternoon some sixty members of the club held their monthly meeting in Martha's Turkey Hill kitchen that, according to a local reporter who was invited by Martha to write about the class, "contained every modern convenience imaginable, yet retained all the charm a 170-year-old room had to offer."

It was one of the earliest newspaper stories about Martha Stewart, who had learned the value of self-promotion from her father. When it came to getting publicity about herself, Martha was always indomitable. "I would sell my mother to get my name in the newspapers or get my face on television," she unabashedly told Norma Collier.

According to the local newspaper account, the crowd watched in awe as Ann Brody whipped up homemade mayonnaise in an expensive blender called a Dessaux Fils and listened transfixed when Martha said, "You spend seventy percent of your time in the kitchen. You should have the right tools." The story noted that Martha had been devoting weekends to her catering business, mainly a one-person operation, although it said she occasionally collaborated with others, such as Ann Brody, whom Martha described as "an excellent cook who's fast and competent."

The reporter noted that "Martha's reputation has spread literally, as well as figuratively, by word of mouth. That is how she gets the clients the likes of Sophie Gimbel, of Greenwich, who has commissioned her to cater her grand-daughter's wedding."

While it all sounded perfect on paper, Ann Brody's relationship with Martha was about to come to a quick boil. Like Jill Bomser, Brody quickly discovered that cooking with Martha Stewart was no piece of cake.

"We were investigating whether we could become partners," Brody explained later. "Martha was starting to get a lot of business. She was working like a bandit, and even Andy was helping make deliveries. But she needed to be the boss. We had disagreements. It could be over anything, like the way I put an eggplant on a table. Martha's dictatorial, and there wasn't a lot of room for other people's ideas—unless of course she could *use* them.

"Martha had a way of antagonizing people. She'd lose her patience. She'd yell a lot at everybody: me, Andy, whoever was around. I would walk out. Finally you'd get to the point where you'd say, 'Martha, shut up!' Her temper was often caused by exhaustion. She never slept. She'd get up at four o'clock in the morning and clean things. She 'didn't need sleep' is the way she described it, which of course is bullshit. The poor thing has a lot of need to be in constant control, and when you go to sleep, you're *not* in control. It's very simple.

"She felt that nobody could do anything good enough for her. None of us was competent. She was the only competent one, so she made people feel bad. She made so many people unhappy that a negative cult started up. But Martha was determined to succeed, and anything she perceived that would slow her down was unacceptable to her. From the start, she wanted to be a nationally recognized, exceedingly successful person. To her credit she never lost focus."

For Norma Collier, going into the catering business with Martha seemed like a good idea. They'd been friends for more than a decade and spent so much time together that people had started taking them for sisters. "We'd go shopping separately and come home with the same things. We wore the same glasses."

Despite her stock market loss, Collier still thought of Martha as a good and loyal friend, a fact that was underscored one afternoon when Martha dropped by unexpectedly, only to find that Norma was out. While she waited for her to return, Martha busied herself in Norma's kitchen, polishing every single one of her copper pots, a couple of double boilers, and a big mixing bowl. When Norma walked in the door, Martha wagged a finger at her. "I can't believe you let your copper get so tarnished," she admonished.

Collier was as good a cook as Martha, if not better, having studied the art of French cooking, not from Julia Child's book, but from chefs in France when she worked there as a model. And the two friends often cooked together. To all intents and purposes, Martha and Norma seemed like a natural team, at least on paper.

But Collier did have some reservations. She knew Martha could be a difficult person, was aware of her drive and ambition and her propensity to intimidate and step on people. "But I went into business with her anyway," Collier declared ruefully years later. "Now, how dumb can you be?"

They decided to call their venture the Uncatered Affair, a name they conceived at Collier's dining-room table. Two shrewd cookies, they also decided as part of their business plan that they wouldn't do any serving, just cooking—and in their own kitchens. Their selling point was that the client's guests would never know the meal had been made by someone else—thus the name, an *Uncatered* Affair. Another marketing strategy was that they would use only natural ingredients in their concoctions. Business soon boomed.

Recalling her early catering period in *Entertaining,* but never once mentioning Norma Collier's role, Martha says:

Suddenly food had a new national importance. Fashion magazines created lavish food and entertaining departments; all newspapers hired restaurant critics, who became public figures. Innovative French chefs became heroes.

Men began to cook. And each year . . . hundreds of cook-books appeared, extolling undiscovered and rediscovered cuisines, reminding us of the epicurean philosopher Brillat-Savarin's aphorism, "Tell me what you eat, and I will tell you what you are."

Martha and Collier each went out and bought restaurant-strength Garland stoves, so enormous and gleaming they looked like Orient Expresses in their kitchens. The partners sent out classy advertising flyers to homes in Westport and neighboring affluent communities. They catered parties. They gave cooking classes. For more than a year the busi-ness steadily grew, and the two women worked as smoothly together as imported pâté on toast points. But suddenly their partnership started to turn sour, like month-old milk.

Out of the blue Martha began to criticize, belittle, and contradict Collier in front of clients and cooking class stu-dents. "Oh, no, that's not the way to do it. *I* do it better. Do it *this* way," Martha would say as Collier's jaw dropped. Collier recalled one session where she was dem-onstrating how to knead dough when Martha, in one of her moods, "literally hip-checked me in front of the class and said, 'Don't do it that way, do it *this* way.' I was really annoyed. The students' eyebrows were disappearing into their hairlines. They couldn't believe it."

When the breads came out of the oven, Martha scooped the loaves into a big basket that she had brought with her and said, 'Must run now,' leaving Collier to handle the cleanup. "Everyone said, 'Are you going to let her get away with that?' " Collier recalled. "I said, 'I don't think I'm going to be working with her much longer.' Martha was becoming someone I didn't know anymore. She was getting *really* mean."

The final straw was Norma Collier's discovery that Mar-tha Stewart was ripping her off. "Our arrangement was she was going to get clients in Westport, and I was going to get clients in New Canaan, and we both would do the work and share the proceeds," Collier explained. "I would call her up and say, 'We have this client,' and we'd do the job together. That's what I did. But that's *not* what she did.

"I eventually discovered that Martha was getting catering jobs and doing them herself and keeping the money and never telling me. I felt betrayed. The day I went to confront her I walked into the house, and I heard her in the kitchen saying to Andy, 'But *I'm* more creative . . . *I'm* more talented . . . I work harder . . . *I'm* much better than she is. . . . Of course I should get more money out of this business . . .'

"She was going on and on to Andy, and Andy, as the kind husband he was to Martha, was saying, 'Yes, dear, well, then you'll have to tell Norma.' I walked into the kitchen and said, 'I can't believe you're saying that! We're either partners, or we're not, and if you're out to screw me, I don't want to ever talk to you again. I'll walk out, and we'll divvy up whatever's left.' Martha said, 'It's no big deal . . . these are small jobs . . . I can handle them myself. . . .' I told her that our agreement was fifty-fifty and that she was sharing in money from the jobs that I was generating. She said what she did was her business. I told her it was totally unfair. Martha and I didn't speak to each other for years.''

Martha's intense need to succeed was tied in part to her father's failure as a salesman, according to former colleagues. "Martha told me she had a mission to redeem him, and she wasn't about to let anyone"—Norma Collier, Jill Bomser, Ann Brody, *anyone*—"stand in her way," one asserted. "Martha firmly believed that her father, whom she described as a genius, had been discriminated against because he was Polish and had never been able to reach his full potential. This discrimination thing was almost a paranoia with her. So Martha's mission was to become successful come hell or high water, to prove to the world that a poor Polish Catholic girl could make it, and through *her* success she felt she was somehow going to redeem her father. At the same time I never got the impression that she was real happy about her Polish heritage. It was all very strange and psychologically complex.''

The Market Basket

The Common Market, in Westport, was far ahead of its time in the mid to late seventies. A chic minimall, housed in a ten-thousand-square-foot barnlike structure overlooking one of the little tributaries of the serene Saugatuck River, it was home to a new wave of upscale boutiques aimed at the area's very affluent residents. The complex had been influenced by Harrods and another London retailing operation called Browns, a grouping of unique shops on South Moulton Street, selling trendy clothing and other fashionable goods.

The Common Market's centerpiece was the Ralph Lauren-Polo shop, an elegant and hip setting, where customers could try on clothing in dressing rooms that had once been church confessionals. The exclusive Lauren franchise was operated by the owners and founders of the Common Market: John Macht, a former Macy's executive, his then-wife, Gail Leichtman-Macht, who had a background in food and art, and Dick Goldman, a veteran retailer, and his wife, Pat. Their setting drew an affluent clientele. On any day shoppers might find themselves next to the Paul Newmans or the Robert Redfords, among other celebrities who lived in the area.

Besides selling chic apparel, the mall also had a small, charming food court where products from Great Britain's Fortnum & Mason and Crabtree & Evelyn were sold, and every afternoon, at four o'clock, shoppers were served tea and crumpets. "It was a nice little touch," John Macht said. "Very English, slightly affected, but not bad."

A couple of times a week his wife drove to a wholesale market in the Bronx for fresh fruit, and she also made arrangements to sell brownies and other goodies from Zabar's and fresh breads and éclair croissants from Orwasher's, both highly regarded Manhattan purveyors of food. Despite the creative effort, though, the Common Market's food area took in no more than a few hundred dollars a day.

Enter Martha Stewart.

A free agent now that she and Norma Collier had gone their separate ways, Martha had become intrigued with the potential of the Common Market, nosing around, asking questions, staking out the food area. "One day she came in and approached us with the idea of taking over the shop, managing it, infusing it with much more interest, and creating a real food presence in the store," Gail Leichtman-Macht said.

The key to Martha's proposal was to sell freshly prepared food, the kind she was known for making. "At the time," Leichtman-Macht noted, "there were a couple of prepared food stores in New York that were just starting to take off and were getting good word of mouth. It coincided with more women going to work and with people wanting high-quality food that wasn't a frozen dinner."

The Common Market partners heard Martha's pitch, liked her vision, and decided she was the one to put their retail food business on the map. All that was required was one final get-together that would allow the owners to see how Martha handled herself in her own environment, Turkey Hill. An intimate lunch was arranged by Martha for Leichtman-Macht.

"The kitchen was warm and welcoming and wonderful," she recalled. "There were no service people; it was *all* Martha. I sat down, and she served up a fines herbes omelet, which she had prepared. She served some rolls, which she said she made, but which I knew she didn't because I knew Eli Zabar's stuff, and I knew they were from Zabar's.

"Nevertheless it was all very nice. But I felt immediately

that she was very intimidating, and very appealing, and very attractive, all at the same time—and I didn't believe her. She didn't feel *real* to me. I felt that she was almost *too* good to be true and that it was really important for her to present perfection as opposed to a vulnerable self or a natural self. And beneath that there was a kind of urgency that I felt uneasy about.

"I found her to be very supercompetent in the way she did things. For example, chefs chop onions and look at you at the same time, and I'm always saying, 'You're going to cut your fingers off.' And there was some of that in Martha. There was a kind of practiced, skillful approach to doing things, and it went from the way she prepared the food, to the way she spoke, to the way she kind of engineered things.

"At that lunch I knew she had a plan that she was following, a script of her own making, *definitely* of her own making. She did not write an outline. I didn't see her that way at all. She had it all in her head, and the wheels were always turning. She knew what she wanted to accomplish and how she wanted to accomplish it, and she pulled it off. She made a lovely lunch. And we hired her."

They offered Martha a salary of $250 a week to manage the food area, which she immediately named the Market Basket, which the owners thought had a nice ring: "The Market Basket at the Common Market." Her agreement with the Machts and Goldmans was that she would be in the store five days a week; manage and improve the business; prepare the foods, such as pâtés, that were to be sold; create a new look for the shop; and share with the owners a percentage of any catering jobs she generated by way of the Common Market.

"In the beginning we were really comfortable that Martha was going to do all these things," Leichtman-Macht said. "She was going to have a daily menu, which was going to be printed in the local newspaper, and people could come in the morning and order what they wanted for dinner from the menu, or they'd come in late in the day after the train ride home and pick up dinner."

Without the owners' knowledge, however, Martha ran an

ad in the local newspaper seeking women who wanted to make extra money cooking at home and selling their dishes to her. Those women, not Martha, would become the actual cooks—"independent contractors," Martha called them—whose food would be resold at the Market Basket at a considerable markup. The women were paid for their time and ingredients.

"What Martha did was both clever and in some ways dishonest," asserted Leichtman-Macht. "It wasn't how she had presented it to us. On the other hand, it worked very well."

While Martha has touched on her catering career in interviews and in her books and magazine, she has said little about her role in the retail food business. In *Entertaining*, though, she did mention the Market Basket, putting her own special spin on it. She said she had "organized" what she described as "a guild of local women" to cook foods for sale at "a small gourmet shop."

In the beginning things went smoothly. Virtually overnight Martha had transformed the look and feel of the shop, much to the owners' delight and satisfaction. The space was filled with pretty decorations and charming antiques. Colorful *objets* were scattered throughout the space or hung from the ceiling. The artifacts—jugs, pots, quilts, baskets—some of which were for sale, belonged to a friend of Martha's, an elderly woman who ran a folk art business in Westport. Martha often crowed about her friend's energy and youthfulness. "Can you believe it?" she once declared to Gail Leichtman-Macht. "She's in her sixties—and she's still menstruating!" All of which was more information than anyone needed to know.

Meanwhile, Martha's call for cooks was met with an enthusiastic response. Interestingly a number of the respondents were coming from troubled situations: Some were in rocky marriages or had been recently separated or divorced and were searching for something to occupy their time. Still others had psychological or emotional problems, and most of those chosen by Martha shared a trait: They were non-confrontational and submissive.

As one former close associate of Martha's observed years

later, "Martha often got involved with highly creative women whom she could dominate, manipulate, use, and abuse, women who wouldn't fight back. They'd be mistreated and come back for more. They'd have a love-hate relationship with Martha. It was very weird."

On a bitterly cold, snowy day after reading Martha's advertisement, twenty-three-year-old Vicky Negrin placed a little basket on the doorstep at Turkey Hill, an offering that she hoped would win her a job and secure for her a bit of validation and recognition. The contents included samples of her workmanship: a swatch of fabric imprinted with leaves, a few small watercolor paintings, baked goods, and some writings.

With long, curly hair, doe eyes, and a childlike voice, Negrin had an ethereal quality. She had studied art and dance at Bennington, had hoped to transfer to Martha's alma mater, Barnard, and eventually got a degree in literature from Columbia. For a time she had worked as an assistant to a New York artist-writer and his wife and had helped them produce a book. At the time she answered Martha's ad, the five-foot-six Negrin, a victim of the eating disorder anorexia nervosa, weighed between ninety and one hundred pounds.

After interviewing her in the cozy kitchen at Turkey Hill, Martha immediately hired Negrin essentially to manage the Market Basket, which Martha was supposed to do.

"Vicky was like Martha's personal slave," recalled John Macht. "Martha worked her all kinds of hours. She used to chastise her, and she used to take credit for what she did, and she was very domineering and dominating over her. Vicky was a lost soul."

Gail Leichtman-Macht agreed. "Martha was like Simon Legree to Vicky's Topsy," she observed. "Martha was an absolute taskmaster. It was a very symbiotic relationship. Vicky needed to be abused, and Martha abused her. Vicky was the first anorexic I ever met. I didn't even know what the disorder was. I just knew she was painfully thin, and she was inordinately connected to food, and she was at Martha's beck and call—an absolute doormat—which was kind of disturbing."

Years later, healthy, married, and the mother of five children, Negrin candidly and painfully recalled that period of time—about four years in all—that she and Martha were linked in what Negrin agreed was a dominant-submissive relationship of sorts. "I was like the little waif who trotted after her and did everything that I was supposed to do and picked up the crumbs," she said. "I didn't quite idolize her, but I admired her. I was a little afraid of her, because I was fearful anyway, so she had a grip on me. I was always scared and wanted to please. Martha can be a tyrant, very critical and unscrupulous, and make people feel bad enough so that they'll do better."

Negrin could not recall any specific details of Martha's treatment of her. "When things are painful, you blot them out," she pointed out. "I blotted it all out. It did happen. And that's why I ended it with her. That's why I didn't go back for more."

Martha had led Negrin, who was paid "very little" and worked "very long hours," to believe that the Market Basket was her brainchild and that she was a partner in the business. She also recalled that there was constant "friction" among Martha, the Machts, and the Goldmans: "I could feel the friction. I could feel that Martha wasn't happy being there. I could feel that the Machts and the Goldmans weren't really happy about Martha being so independent and strong."

Negrin said that some of the arguments had to do with Martha's not sharing with the owners their cut from catering jobs she generated through the store. "There would usually be these flare-ups after she had catered a party," Negrin recalled. "Martha would get really angry and leave. There was a lot of tension, stress, and smoke."

"The *Gnomes* Cookbook"

Around the time Martha left the world of high finance for the cosmos of food, Andy, at thirty-five, had abandoned his staid position at Bangor Punta for the far more glamorous and creative universe of publishing.

When Bangor Punta's general counsel moved to the Times Mirror Company in 1973 as the publishing conglomerate's general counsel, he hired Andy as his assistant general counsel. Martha was pleased. The new job had cachet and prestige and paid more money than Andy had ever made before. She also saw Andy's position as an opportunity for her. Thinking that one day she might want to write a cookbook, she now had the perfect entrée into publishing. It couldn't hurt. After all, Times Mirror was at the time a media giant, owning nine book companies, a slew of popular magazines, and a number of influential newspapers.

In 1976 Andy's boss, Martin Levin, vice-president in charge of book publishing, was faced with a major problem: what to do about eighty-year-old Harry Abrams, the feisty founder and driving force behind Harry N. Abrams, Inc., publisher of lavish coffee table books. Because Abrams was in poor health and extremely difficult to deal with, Levin had quietly started looking for a successor.

Andy thought Levin had gone off the deep end when he offered him the job. But the timing couldn't have been better. Andy had grown to love publishing and had tired of the law. In early 1976, after several months of negotiations, he was appointed executive vice-president of Abrams.

Not long after Andy took office, Harry Abrams and Martin Levin got into an enormous fight that ended with Abrams storming out of the company, taking with him a number of the best book projects scheduled for the next few years, which he used to start a new company, Abbeville Press. At that point Andy was immediately promoted to president and chief executive officer of Abrams, with an enormous salary and fabulous perks. Overnight he had become a publishing mogul. He felt as if he had died and gone to heaven.

In 1977, when Martha had started working at the Market Basket, Andy's career at Abrams was soaring, launched with a giant best-seller about little people entitled *Gnomes*. The beautifully illustrated and imaginatively written book, describing the enchanting habits and life of mythical gnomes, had been published successfully a year earlier in the Netherlands and was being peddled unsuccessfully in this country until Andy picked up the U.S. rights for a song, even though he was practically laughed out of the editorial board meeting at which he proposed the acquisition.

The book, including the beautiful calligraphy, had to be translated into English. However, instead of securing the services of a professional calligrapher, who would expect to be paid well and receive acknowledgment and possibly even royalties, Andy talked to Martha, who talked to her talented worker Vicky Negrin. Overjoyed to get recognition for her artistry, the acquiescent and dutiful young woman agreed to do the calligraphy on a wink and a nod.

"Vicky had this beautiful, spidery writing, but she told me she never got any real credit," said Ujala Hsu, one of the women Martha had hired to cook for the Market Basket. "She was as upset as someone like Vicky, this soft, gentle sort of person, could get, and I said to her, 'Listen, ask them to give it to you in writing next time.'"

After *Gnomes* was published, Negrin received a pittance for her work, one hundred dollars, and no written acknowledgment in the first edition. "I just figured there would be acknowledgment because I'd always gotten it on books I'd worked on with others before,'' Negrin said. "I must have mentioned that to Martha, and Martha said, 'I'll fix it.' They put my name in the second printing, but it was never in again because I guess they just didn't think it was that important.'' When the book became a best-seller, Negrin wasn't invited to any of the publishing soirees thrown by Abrams or the Stewarts.

A shrewd publisher and promoter, Andy told the people at *The New York Times Book Review* that *Gnomes* was nonfiction. He wasn't really lying, only following the author's point of view. The book had been written as if gnomes actually existed, and since no one had come forward to disprove the thesis, Andy felt comfortable with his pitch, though he was surprised and amused that the paper went for it. *Gnomes* became a *New York Times* nonfiction bestseller, quite a feat since the book's subject clearly had nothing to do with reality.

Along with the book's phenomenal sales, more than a million copies, there were enormous profits from licensing agreements for spin-off products: *Gnomes* towels, *Gnomes* canvas book bags, *Gnomes* miniature ceramic figures, *Gnomes* datebooks, *Gnomes* posters, even a *Gnomes* sleeping bag, among other items. Hollywood cashed in on the act too, with a *Gnomes* video and a made-for-TV *Gnomes* movie. Because of Andy's vision, royalties and residuals rolled into Abrams's coffers, along with the giant profits from the ongoing sale of the book.

Witnessing this success and the potential for lucrative spin-offs, Martha, who was still juggling management of the Market Basket with her catering, wanted a piece of the action too. One of her ideas was a chain of fast-food healthfood restaurants called Gnome Huts, a concept she bounced off the ever-accommodating Vicky Negrin.

"Martha's idea was that you could drive up and get yourself carrot juice and get your tabbouleh or your hummus sandwich with garden vegetables,'' she recalled. "Martha said it would be a franchise just like McDonald's.''

The imaginative Negrin, however, had a more realistic idea that grabbed Martha's attention. Negrin had been working on a little recipe book that would "celebrate life and nature, the way that *Gnomes* would have done it." The book, which she had tentatively entitled "The True Book of Gnome Cookery," later changed by Martha to "The *Gnomes* Cookbook," contained recipes for meals such as "Day Dream Sandwiches," "Full Moon Pancakes," and "Spring Pea Salad." There was a section on "Principles, Practices and Methods of the Gnome Kitchen" and a chapter on how "Omens, Talismans, Chants and Charms," played an important role in gnome cooking.

Martha saw the commercial potential immediately. "She said, 'This is a *great* idea!' " Negrin recalled. "She told me she would help me market the book, and Andy was going to publish it. It was my idea. I made up the recipes and stories, and it had my drawings and paintings. I even matched the watercolors to the ones in the *Gnomes* book. My soul was in that book."

But Martha appeared to have a different agenda from the one she communicated to Negrin. She immediately proposed "The *Gnomes* Cookbook" to Andy, who also saw its moneymaking potential. He put together a draft of a publishing agreement that called for an advance of at least several thousand dollars for *Martha's,* not Negrin's, first book.

But Martin Levin hit the ceiling when he heard about the project. He believed a book written by the publisher's wife—apparently no mention was *ever* made of Vicky Negrin's role—was a conflict of interest, and he ordered Andy to drop the project posthaste.

Martha was furious and called Levin's decision stupid. "Who else could do a book like this better than me? I can do it better than *anybody*!" she declared.

Martha then told the innocent Negrin that Abrams had decided against publishing because the authors of the original *Gnomes* book wouldn't give their approval. In the end Negrin said, "I felt used by Martha."

Dark Clouds

The enormous success that Andy was savoring in his first year as a publisher was overshadowed by a dark cloud that appeared from nowhere, leaving him terrorized and bewildered and Martha in a state of high anxiety about her future.

It began routinely on a bitterly cold day in early March 1977, when Martha's youngest brother, George Christiansen, went canoeing on the rapids of the Housatonic River, in rural Connecticut.

Of Martha's three brothers, Andy had always been closest to George, a frail, sad youngster, who often was the target of his father's verbal abuse. Andy had witnessed George, between the ages of eight and fifteen, sometimes reduced to tears by Eddie Kostyra's sharp tongue. Unlike his strapping brothers, Eric and Frank, George didn't fight back. (Later George abandoned the name Kostyra and adopted his wife's maiden name, some say to spite his father.)

Because of George's problems at home, Andy and Martha had taken him under their wing, and he often spent extended periods with the Stewarts at Turkey Hill and at Middlefield. "We were extremely close," Christiansen acknowledged. "It was just like Andy and Martha were my surrogate parents."

On that fateful day on the Housatonic, Christiansen was twenty-five, three years out of Rutgers University, and a Sears, Roebuck executive training program dropout; he couldn't take "the corporate inbreeding and the cutthroatness," as he put it, and discovered he was allergic to certain odors in the stores. He then moved in with the Stewarts in Westport, became a carpenter's apprentice, and found his calling working with his hands. With Martha's help—and her controlling influence—he eventually started a contracting business. Though indebted and staunchly loyal to her, they would have their share of battles.

The river was extremely rough the day Andy and Christiansen went out, and as they were negotiating the rapids, their canoe suddenly overturned. Andy slammed into a rock, hitting it hard with his hip, which was bruised and painful, but the injury quickly healed and soon was forgotten.

Two months later, in early May—the same month Andy announced the September publication of *Gnomes* at the American Booksellers Association Convention in San Francisco—he discovered a lump where he had been injured. His doctor told him not to worry, but Andy sought a second opinion and was advised to have the mass removed. Surgery was scheduled at Roosevelt Hospital, where Lexi had been born a dozen years earlier.

On the day of Andy's operation Martha shocked coworkers by reporting to work at the Market Basket. "He was in the hospital, and she was at the store," recalled Eva Wiener. "I said, 'What in the world are you doing here?' And Martha said, 'I have a business to run.' She's a tough person, and it didn't seem to faze her."

The biopsy showed that Andy's tumor was cancerous, caused, the doctors speculated, by the trauma of the blow he had received in the river. At Sloan-Kettering, the famed Manhattan cancer hospital, Andy was bluntly told by a surgeon that he had three options: radiation, amputation of his leg, or death. Andy was overcome with fear; Martha didn't know what had hit her.

The next day at the Market Basket she recounted the terrible news to Gail Leichtman-Macht. "This is sort of so typical of Martha," Leichtman-Macht recalled. "She told me that she had dropped Andy at his office after visiting the doctor so he could pick up some papers, and she was waiting double-parked in the car for him, and a policeman wanted to give her a ticket. She said it was more than she could take, and she broke down and started to cry and said, 'Please, please, don't give me a ticket,' and he didn't. When she related the story, it was more like 'Look what I accomplished. He didn't give me the ticket' rather than 'My husband has cancer, it's so awful.' She was talking about how overwhelmed she felt, but it really became about the parking ticket and *not* about Andy's cancer, and that's kind of how she did things mostly. You lost track of the fact that the reason she was in the car in the first place was that poor Andy had cancer.''

Within days of the publication of *Gnomes,* Andy began the first of more than two dozen debilitating radiation treatments, the outcome of which was uncertain. At the office he kept his cancer a secret.

Meanwhile Martha had gone into what some viewed as a terrible depression. ''Martha collapsed, basically,'' stated George McCully. ''I went down there right after his surgery, and it was the first time I'd seen them since Andy was diagnosed. I found Martha in the darkened bedroom. She was totally destroyed, *abject*. I sat on the bed next to her holding her hand while she cried. She said she was *nothing* without Andy, that she was *totally* dependent on him, that she just didn't know what she'd do if she lost him.''

Ann Brody believed that Martha had begun to take a long, hard look at what the future held for her now that Andy's life was in jeopardy. ''Prior to his illness they were not happy as a couple, and I thought that marriage was going to break up,'' she said. ''But when Andy got sick, their cross dependencies went back into place, and I felt they got close again. But his illness might have given Martha a little more impetus to push harder and faster. I think Martha was thinking about her future even before Andy got sick. She wondered what would happen to that perfect little world she tried to create with her house, and barn, and chickens, that edifice that she felt would give her some dimension. Martha cried. Martha hurt.''

It struck members of the Stewarts' inner circle as strange to see Martha showing compassion for Andy after years of witnessing her treating him "like shit," as Jill Bomser noted bluntly. "I've never seen anybody treat a husband, or a maid, the way she treated Andy," Bomser declared. "She was verbally abusive, unbelievably critical, constantly belittling. Andy would kind of laugh it off or be embarrassed or squirmy about it. But he never said, 'Fuck you, Martha.' He would just have this embarrassed look on his face, as if to say, 'Can you imagine that my wife is really talking to me like this?' "

One Mother's Day Andy had a special surprise for Martha. He had gotten up early, gone to the kitchen, and fixed a tray for her, with freshly cut roses in a vase. But Martha had awakened in a bad mood, complained that something on the tray wasn't right, and threw it at him. While she bathed, he was forced to get down on his hands and knees and clean up the breakfast he had lovingly prepared for her.

Andy had become a busboy for Martha at catering events, too. When he arrived to help clean up after one such party, she was furious because he was a few minutes late. Going down in the elevator, Martha pointed at him and told several of her young female assistants, "Don't *ever* get married. Men are *so* stupid and disgusting." Outside, Andy asked Martha for the keys to the car, but instead of handing them to him, she threw them in a puddle, forcing him to stoop down and pick them up.

Martha's public abuse of Andy seemed unrelenting and had become widely known to friends and colleagues, who whispered among themselves about her latest outrage. For example, as the Stewarts drove home on a cold, rainy late-November night after an evening at the theater in New York City with their friends Bart and Mariana Pasternack, their Suburban blew a tire. Andy managed to maneuver the big vehicle to the side of a dangerous stretch of I-95, but when he got outside in the driving rain to change the tire, he had difficulty finding the jack, which was out of view in the darkened engine compartment. Meanwhile Martha had started screaming at him, blaming him for the blowout, accusing him of not watching the road so as to avoid hitting the piece of metal that had caused the flat, denouncing him as a moron for not knowing where the jack was stored.

Adding insult to injury, she made him take off the new raincoat that she had bought him because she didn't want it to get dirty while he fixed the tire, forcing him to get drenched in his tuxedo.

"She treated him like a dog," declared Martha's brother Frank Kostyra. "I remember one instance when Martha threw a Christmas party and there were guests like Patty Hearst there, and she huffed and screamed at Andy and snarled, 'Get that out of here! How dare you bring that in here!' because he had placed a trash can near the table and had forgotten to put a liner in it.

"We all were together in New Orleans at a book convention and Martha had to leave early because one of the gardeners had burned up a tractor in the barn at Westport. I stayed on with Andy because he wanted to take a trip down the Mississippi River. But she wouldn't let him enjoy it. She kept calling him, saying, 'Get back up here this minute!' I listened in on the telephone conversation because we were in the same hotel room and she was just bitching and bitching at him: 'You need to be up here. You don't need to be down there. Come right back here. Now!' She couldn't accept the fact that he was going to take a day off and be with a family member and not be doing something for her."

George McCully, a frequent guest at Turkey Hill, particularly after his divorce from Emily McCully in the late seventies, witnessed Martha's treatment of Andy firsthand. During one visit Martha had asked Andy and McCully to move a pile of lumber that was being used in the construction of the barn, and the two men had worked from morning until late afternoon in the heat. When they finished, Martha arrived to inspect their work.

"Of course, she wasn't happy and threw a scene," McCully said. " 'Oh, you are so stupid! You put the wood over there, and I wanted it over here.' She just gave us hell and wanted us to move all the wood again. Andy, looking sheepish, said, 'Oh, Martha.' And I said, 'Martha, why don't you go fuck yourself?'

"Now I don't think anybody ever talked to her that way, certainly not Andy. She was stunned. Her jaw dropped. Her eyes opened wide. She stormed out of there. But I was angry. I thought, 'Well, *screw* her. I don't need this.' Andy whispered, 'Don't talk to her like that,' and I said, 'Andy, if you're not afraid to throw a bigger scene than Martha, she's going to run all over you.' ''

On another occasion, Martha had dispatched Andy and his one-time UVA roommate and longtime friend Gene Levy, who was visiting Turkey Hill from Little Rock, to Middlefield to clean the grounds and plant some trees. But they soon hit rock, making the site unusable. ''I said, 'Andy, let's move away from the rock and plant over there' and he said, 'Oh, no! Martha would *not* be happy unless these trees are in a *perfectly* straight line. She'd be *furious* at me.' Here we were two hundred miles away from Martha and she's controlling everything that Andy and I were doing. It was crazy!''

Some years later, a journalist writing a magazine profile of Martha contacted Levy, who recounted the tree-planting incident, which became part of the published piece. ''I told the reporter, 'Martha's a brilliant person, but she's very controlling.' That's a true fact. After the article ran, I got a message from Martha on my answering machine: 'Gene, how could you insult me the way you did? Why don't you wait until I'm dead to say bad things about me? Call me back. I want to discuss this.' I called her and got her machine. I just said, 'Martha, I never said anything derogatory about you. I just told the truth—that you are a controlling person.' But it made her very mad, infuriated her. She never talked to me again.''

George McCully was also present when Martha made embarrassing remarks about Andy's abilities in bed, which she described as ''inadequacies.'' One time Andy became so infuriated, according to McCully, that he told Martha, '' 'Well, the only reason we didn't have more children is that you didn't want any more stretch marks.' She was just putting him down sexually—not that he couldn't get it up but that he didn't want to make love enough, or whatever. And from what I understand of Andy, that's *not* true.''

In direct contradiction of her put-downs, Martha frequently bragged to women friends about Andy's prowess, even offering him to them like one of her Market Basket desserts, according to Norma Collier. "One day, when we had the Uncatered Affair, Martha and I were driving to the apple orchard in her truck, and I was unburdening myself to her because it was the end of my marriage. I had no relationship with my husband at that time, and Martha said to me, much to my amazement, 'If you can't sleep with your husband, you can sleep with Andy. He's *really* good. He'll do *anything* you tell him to. Andy has *always* been in love with you. You can have him.' Can you imagine her offering her husband? I laughed. I said, 'Martha, you've got to be kidding,' and she said, 'No, he's really very good in bed.' I said, 'I'm not going to share your husband. It is bizarre.' "

At the same time that Martha was curiously offering Andy's sexual services, she was also extremely possessive of him. Martha's college chum Wendy Supovitz Reilly, who had lived for a time with her first husband in Greenwich, not far from Westport, recalled an odd conversation she had with Martha that left her feeling a bit shaken. "Martha said something strange like 'Oh, I've got to watch out for you, Wendy. We can't have you around here too much because Andy has an eye for pretty girls.' I said, 'Phooey. Why would you say something like that?' Since Martha was so much prettier than I was, I just took what she said to be meaningless. I felt, 'Why would he look at me?' I never once thought Andy played around. He was very charming, very polite, very pleasant—just what one would expect."

Once Martha arranged for another extremely attractive former Barnard friend to stay the night at Turkey Hill with Andy while she was out of town. Later Martha savored speculating about whether Andy and the friend had slept together.

As for her own sexuality, Martha once boasted while trading war stories with a girlfriend in a Chinese restaurant, "I can will an orgasm whenever I want. I have the power. Having an orgasm is like anything else in life. It's about power." At the same time, she lamented the fact that she didn't have an opportunity to have a lot of sexual experiences before she met and married Andy.

When Martha's catering business took off and the kitchen was jumping with attractive young assistants, Martha put out the word that none of them was to have any communication with her husband. Even magazine editors doing shoots at the house were given similar warnings. "We were told, 'Don't talk to Andy. Don't look at Andy. Martha gets bitterly jealous, and if you do, you'll never be back here,' " recalled Mary Emmerling, decorating and food editor at *Mademoiselle* at the time. "So of course we obeyed the rules. But I never got the impression that Andy was a flirt. He was always a perfect gentleman."

Despite their marital history, Andy hoped some good would come from his brush with cancer, that Martha would soften toward him, that the tragedy would bring them closer together. Instead, according to a confidant, Martha aimed more anger at him: "She told him many times that he was 'stupid' for going canoeing, that he was to blame for his cancer. She was in a constant state of irritation and anger. She also told Andy that she had to look at him as being dispensable. Later she even claimed to some people that he didn't have cancer, that he was pretending—just to get her sympathy."

The Proprietor

While the Market Basket under Martha's mostly absentee management was a glowing success, the operation she was running wasn't strictly kosher. By hiring free-lance cooks who worked out of their home kitchens and by buying their tasty concoctions for resale in the shop, Martha was circumventing local and state regulations. Those laws required that catering kitchens be separate from normal kitchens, meet certain health and sanitary standards, and be certified by government inspectors.

The statutes were adopted by jurisdictions to protect consumers, but in those days the practice of selling foods made in unlicensed kitchens was not uncommon, and Martha wasn't alone. In New York City, where the gourmet takeout shop concept was coming into vogue, sale of foods made in uncertified kitchens was the rule rather than the exception. Inspections were hit-and-miss, and overworked enforcement officers were busy cracking down on restaurant kitchens littered with mouse droppings, rather than targeting housewives baking chocolate chip cookies in their unlicensed Calorics.

But someone apparently had dropped a dime on Martha's operation because the authorities started staking out her shop. "I don't know how they found out, but inspectors were parking in the parking lot of the Common Market," said a former employee of Martha's. "If we got caught, she told us to lie and say we were bringing the goods from her house, where I think she had a certified kitchen. But I was never stopped, and I was never questioned."

Gail Leichtman-Macht confirmed that questions were raised about the legality of the precooked foods sold in the Market Basket and that ultimately "a full working kitchen that *was* licensed" was installed on the premises.

Meanwhile the Machts and the Goldmans had other problems with Martha. Their initial sunny-side-up relationship had begun to sour.

Martha's personality, for one thing, started to get on Dick Goldman's nerves. "She always had to be number one, always in the limelight, and she was a bully to the people who worked for her, who were indentured slaves," he said. "Vicky Negrin was working in the store all the time and doing a wonderful job, but Martha was taking credit for it. Toward the end Martha couldn't cope with all the different things that were required to run the shop and do the things that *she* wanted to do—which was to promote Martha Stewart."

Another problem involved the financial split from Martha's catering jobs, according to Pat Goldman. "Any catering jobs that she got through anyone who came into the store or that was related to the store were supposed to be credited to us or billed through us. But that wasn't exactly happening. After a while we couldn't quite figure out who brought in the business for whom."

John Macht, who handled all the Common Market's merchandising, also began to stew quietly over the fact that Martha was rarely on the premises as she had promised. "In the end," he said, "egos got involved. It got to be very complicated."

The coup de grace occurred sometime in the second year of Martha's employment when a *New York Times* reporter, Florence Fabricant, whose brother was a friend of Gail Leichtman-Macht's, wrote a glowing feature about the Market Basket based on an interview she had with Martha at the shop. When the story ran on the front page of the Sunday *Times'* Connecticut section, the owners were furious. They felt Martha had taken undue credit for all of the store's success. Especially annoying to them was the fact that she had referred to herself as the "proprietor" of the Market Basket.

A few days after the story ran the outraged Machts and Goldmans, having already decided to give Martha the heave-ho, called her into their office. "We thought the story Florence wrote was gorgeous, wonderful, everything you would want," Gail Leichtman-Macht said. "And as we're reading it, we see 'Martha Stewart, the *proprietor* of the Market Basket at the Common Market,' and like the floor fell through. We were all aghast seeing that word 'proprietor.' The guys were enraged."

Suspecting she was about to be canned, Martha came into her bosses' office fully prepared to fight to keep her job.

"This is how smart Martha is," said Leichtman-Macht, still amazed at her chutzpah years later. "She came in with a *dictionary* in her hand. And the dictionary was open to the word 'proprietor.' And she said that the third definition of the word 'proprietor' was 'manager,' which is what she had been hired as. And she said *her* definition of the word 'proprietor' was 'manager.'

''We said, 'Too bad, Charlie,' and that was it. We fired her, and she walked out.''

Keeping her dismissal a secret, Martha left friends and her free-lance cooks with the impression that she had departed the Market Basket to devote more hands-on time to her catering business.

Family Affair

In the spring of 1979, when Martha lost her job, her personal life was in a state of chaos. While Andy had completed his radiation treatments, it would be another five years before doctors would know for certain whether he was out of the woods, and that added enormous anxiety to the Stewarts' already stressful lives.

Meanwhile their marriage continued on its downward spiral. Privately friends told Andy that if he rid himself of Martha, he would rid himself of his cancer. They saw the two linked in some metaphysical way.

But a reader picking up *People* magazine around that time would have thought the Stewarts were the neatest, sweetest, hippest, healthiest, happiest couple to come down the pike since Mike and Carol Brady. The story, headlined MARTHA STEWART CATERS FOR THE NEWMANS AND RED-FORDS, WHILE ANDY COOKS UP ''GNOMES,'' was the first to introduce the superwoman and her hubby to the masses. At that point Martha didn't have a national reputation. But *People* got the popular media ball rolling, and soon the name Martha Stewart was in the mind's eyes, and the Rolodexes, of editors and TV show producers across the country—under *L* for "lifestyle."

The *People* article was generated by Martha through a friend of a friend who worked at the magazine. *People* photographed the Stewarts standing outside their "Connecticut barnyard," Martha holding a basket of eggs laid by her chickens and Andy with a black Cochin in his arms. There were shots of the photogenic couple sprinkled between the blocks of puff-piece text. One showed Martha chatting up her writer pal Jill Robinson in the Stewarts' glorious kitchen, while all around them sophisticated-looking guests munched on smoked trout and almond dates wrapped in bacon. But what *People* readers didn't know was that the folks in the photograph were merely props, according to Barry O'Rourke, a well-known food photographer, who had begun working with Martha on *Mademoiselle* and *House Beautiful* assignments in the late seventies. On the day *People* visited Turkey Hill, O'Rourke received a telephone call from a harried Martha. "She asked us to dress up and come over right away because she needed some attractive people in the photograph," he chuckled. "It wasn't like 'Gee, come on over because we'd love to have you for cocktails.' It was 'Come over and be a prop.' "

People compared the Stewarts with "the Swiss Family Robinson" and described Martha's growing catering business. And Martha revealed gossipy tidbits about her clients: "Redford likes zucchini and banana bread, [Beverly] Sills the chocolate Victoria tartlets, and the [Paul] Newmans order up teriyaki for his racing crew."

Out of the blue, at the end of what had been a routinely upbeat profile, Martha was quoted as saying, "We have never even come close to getting divorced," while Andy added, "There are difficulties between us, things that grate. She is more practical. I am more theoretical. I'm forgetful and a bit sloppy. If I leave something where it's not supposed to be, she will say, 'What is this x-y-z doing here?' My carelessness annoys Martha and her reaction to it annoys me." *People* readers waiting to hop into their dentists' chairs must have been left wondering, "What's this all about?'' But her friends knew: The Stewarts' marriage was in deep trouble.

Martha suffered additional anxiety and stress over her relationship with Lexi, who, by the time she turned thirteen, had gone from being a sad and sullen child and adolescent to a sad and sullen *and* angry teenager, feeling real resentment toward her mother.

A *House Beautiful* staffer on a shoot at Turkey Hill told her boss, Mary Emmerling, that she once witnessed Lexi seated in the kitchen with a knife stuck in the table, saying, ''I'm going to kill her someday.'' Emmerling wasn't surprised. ''Lexi hated—I mean, *despised*—all these people in her house shooting and photographing. She just *hated* it. She wasn't getting any attention. You could see it on her face. Here was this lonely teenager getting zero attention.''

Even Martha's loyal brother George had begun siding with Lexi because he didn't think she got enough attention from her mother. Martha arrived at the Market Basket one morning, expressing concern about Lexi's emotional state and their relationship. It was Lexi's birthday, and Martha said Lexi was crying and complaining because her mother was never at home, never there for her. But when Martha did make an attempt to bond with her daughter, Lexi found fault with her methods, as did Martha's friends. One activity that drew criticism, and smirks all around, was Martha's decision to make Lexi a member of Martha's ladies-who-lunch crowd. She began showing up with Lexi in tow at fancy Fairfield Hunt Club lunches, with Martha's girlfriends present. Lexi found the whole scene repugnant.

''There was a lot of tension between Martha and Alexis,'' observed Naiad Einsel, an illustrator who was a friend and neighbor of the Stewarts'. ''Whatever Martha said, Alexis disagreed with. Martha would tell me something, and say it in a sweet voice, talking about Alexis, and then Alexis would say, 'It wasn't like that at all,' or, 'No, you didn't do it that way. That wasn't the way it happened at all.' That kind of response may be typical teenager. But Martha and Alexis *weren't* close.''

At school Lexi complained of various physical ailments, which Martha suspected were imagined. By the end of eighth grade Lexi had come to despise Green Farms Academy and told her parents she wanted to go elsewhere. Martha and Andy took her to several boarding schools and found one that Lexi seemed to like. For ninth grade she transferred to the very exclusive Choate Rosemary Hall school, in Wallingford, Connecticut. While it was little more than an hour's ride northeast of Westport, Lexi rarely came home, even on weekends, so alienated had she become from her parents.

After a year she became dissatisfied with Choate too, and Andy had to make last-minute arrangements to get her admitted to his alma mater, the Putney School, in Vermont, from which Lexi got her high school diploma.

Martha was also faced with serious problems involving her youngest sister, Laura, and her aging father, Eddie Kostyra. By 1979, when she was twenty-two, Laura, the baby of the Kostyra family, had blossomed into a beautiful but troubled young woman who suffered from a drinking problem and bouts of depression. Her difficulties, family members said, stemmed from her relationship with the Kostyra patriarch, who made life difficult for the last and unplanned member of the brood.

As one family observer asserted, ''Laura's relationship with her father was horrible. He was a monster. Not often was he physically brutal, but he was an offensive, unpleasant person to be around, and it was very hard for Laura as a young girl growing up.'' Frank Kostyra recalled how when his father once offered Laura some money for something, she angrily responded, ''I don't want money. I want love.''

The situation had become so intolerable for Laura when she was a student at Nutley High that Martha moved her out of dysfunctional Elm Place and into Turkey Hill, which was dysfunctional in its own way. For about a year Laura attended high school in Westport, but she ran into the same problems that had existed at home. Like Eddie Kostyra, Martha tried to dominate and control everything Laura did. At the end of the school year Martha suggested that Laura go live at the Stewarts' Middlefield place. But Laura found rural life lonely and isolated. One day she took the car out and ran it off the road. The Stewarts surmised she had been drinking, which she had started doing as a teenager.

Laura returned to New Jersey to finish school and was graduated in the Nutley High class of '73. Unlike her high-achieving sister Martha, who appeared on virtually every page of her 1959 yearbook, Laura seemed lost in the crowd. But her yearbook picture showed a smiling, pretty, self-confident graduate. The notation underneath was lyrical, joyous, and optimistic: "A field of tall hay. Crowns of wild flowers. Songs of birds. A whistle of wind. A deep-blue sky, Hand in hand. Such a fine day." Like all the Kostyras, Laura had learned to display a happy face in public.

Of the Kostyra children, only Laura failed to get a college degree, which angered and disappointed her father, who had always stressed education and ambition. Instead of going to Northeastern, where she'd been accepted, Laura went off with a pleasant young man whom she hoped to marry. The couple lived for a time in Florida, where they were involved in hot-air ballooning. Their relationship ended, however, and Laura returned home. By the late seventies she had become a very unhappy young woman. As one observer noted, "She had come from a fucked-up family. She didn't have a job. She didn't have a career. She'd been in and out of relationships."

Like George, Laura moved to Westport to be close to Martha, even though the sisters had a difficult relationship. A creative cook and baker like Martha, Laura worked on and off in her sister's catering business—on and off because Martha frequently became enraged at something Laura did and fired her on the spot. The two fought constantly. "They'd go back and forth, back and forth," said a friend of Laura's who also worked for Martha. "Martha treated Laura the same way she treated Andy—like dog shit. I can't count the times I saw Martha bring Laura to tears with her criticism, with her meanspiritedness."

Not long after Andy had become president of Abrams, a new editor in chief, Digby Diehl—good-looking, personable, bright, and single—was brought on board. He had held the prestigious post of book editor of the Los Angeles *Times*.

Martha took it upon herself, against Andy's wishes, to

throw a party to introduce Laura to Diehl, who was eight years her senior. Andy was adamantly against Martha's playing Cupid because he thought it would be awkward to have one of his key people dating his sister-in-law. In any case, Laura and Diehl seemed to be a match, began seeing each other regularly, and Laura quickly grew emotionally and romantically attached to Diehl.

"We had a very pleasant but intense relationship," Diehl said later. "While I felt that Laura was a really sweet young woman, she wanted very much to have a relationship. That was certainly something that she sought and I think that she needed. I didn't think that I was it, and I was letting the relationship trail off essentially. She was a sweet young woman who didn't need any more troubles in her life, and I was certainly not trying to add to them."

When it became clear to Laura that Diehl was distancing himself, she became depressed and agitated. "I came to understand partially through Martha and Andy after the relationship between Laura and myself was over that there were more serious problems than I had realized," Diehl said. "Those problems related to Laura and her family, particularly her father. But it is hard to imagine our relationship being *that* fundamental an issue in her life."

Frank Kostyra said, "Laura did have a breakdown. She had been the underdog in the family since childhood. She started to drink a little bit and got heavy with the wine, and there was drinking on the job while she worked for Martha, and everybody was talking about it in the family: that Laura was imbibing too much, trying to drink her sorrows away, and feeling sorry for herself, and that just led to more depression. There were times when Martha had to let her go. They would spit venom back and forth at each other. They yelled a lot. Yelling is the way the Kostyras talked, and Laura and Martha got into that."

About Martha, Laura declared: "Our relationship has been a complicated one at times, because of the roles Martha assumed as a big sister, mother, employer, teacher, critic, and friend. Be that as it may, Martha has always been there for me when I needed her, and I will always love that devotion."

Like all Kostyra family members, Laura has been mentioned a number of times in Martha's published reminiscences, and Laura, like the rest, has been portrayed as having the perfect, happy life. However, there was one curious mention in the June–July 1992 issue of *Martha Stewart Living*, which deviated somewhat from the norm. In an essay entitled "On Honesty," Martha complained—some thought ironically—about how dishonest public figures, a category that she certainly fell into, had become. Martha noted that a number of them—she pointed her finger specifically at politicians and sports personalities, "are daily revealed to be masters of deception. . . ."

She continued: "As a child, I was encouraged to tell the truth, and I did. My sister Laura remembers that I was a good child and never did anything very wrong, while she 'did everything wrong, and told lies to escape punishment.' " Martha concluded by telling her readers that "dishonesty is a thief of time, of energy, of pride. We must remember—and teach our children (and perhaps our political figures)—one essential: the truth shall make you free."

By the mid- seventies Eddie Kostyra's health had begun to fail, and he had started drinking heavily. Before boarding the bus to his office at Herculite Protective Fabrics in Manhattan, where his job involved selling plastic-coated, bacteria-free mattress covers, he started the day in the now-famous kitchen on Elm Place with a bizarre concoction of orange juice, stale coffee, and red wine—and his drinking went downhill from there. "Ed was killing the pain with vodka," his son Eric Scott, the dentist, acknowledged. "At the end I'm sure he was a heavy drinker, and that was strictly to kill the pain."

The pain Kostyra was experiencing was angina, one of the many symptoms of a serious heart condition that had developed some years earlier. Kostyra, who always had viewed himself as a doctor without portfolio, decided to treat himself, mostly by ignoring the problem or by imbibing. What he needed was open-heart surgery, but he kept putting off the inevitable.

Martha had become aware of her father's drinking and

was irritated with him and nasty toward him because of it. While she loved him—he was the only man she ever truly idolized—she also felt disgust, frustration, and anger when she saw his erratic alcohol-induced behavior. When, during his infrequent trips to Westport, he made boozy suggestions about how she could improve her beautiful gardens, Martha exploded with annoyance and irritation.

But Martha was extremely concerned about her father's declining health and during the spring and early summer of 1979 made several trips to Nutley, where she pushed, prodded, and finally pleaded with him to get double-bypass surgery, which the doctors had recommended. On August 31, 1979, Eddie Kostyra was in a bed at New York Hospital, gaining strength for the operation scheduled for the next day, when he suddenly died. His death came just ten days after his sixty-eighth birthday and twenty-eight days after Martha's thirty-eighth.

Eddie Kostyra's funeral mass, held at Our Lady of Mount Carmel Roman Catholic Church, four days after his death, became one of the most embarrassing events in contemporary Kostyra family history. Years later, Father Edward A. Haber, who presided, revealed, ''I've never experienced anything like that in the thirty-eight years I've been a priest.''

Martha was in the front row next to her mother, who was wearing a veil and playing nervously with a ball of tissues. Andy, who had been at Martha's side when she learned of her father's death, had gone to Russia on long-scheduled publishing business, with Martha's consent. The other Kostyra children—Laura, Kathy, George, Eric, and Frank— along with the dead man's sister, Estelle Burke; his brother, Hank Kostyra; and assorted in-laws, cousins, and children, all sat quietly through Father Haber's mass.

When it came time for the eulogies, only Frank Kostyra stood and strode to the pulpit. For the next ten minutes, reading from a prepared letter that he had intended to mail to his father before his demise, the third-born child proceeded to vent years of built-up anger and hostility. He spoke mostly in biblical terms, quoting from Scripture, using words like ''rebuke'' and ''admonish,'' which he'd picked up during a troubled post-Vietnam marriage to the daughter of a southern preacher.

Everyone in the church, whether he agreed with Frank or not, was shocked. Kathy's husband, Mark Evans, a lawyer, leaped to his feet, as did Kostyra's brothers, Eric and George, who moved swiftly toward the pulpit, determined to silence Frank.

"It was really embarrassing," recalled a cousin. "But Aunt Martha said, 'No. Let him be. Let him say what he wants.' And Frank continued. It was very embarrassing—truthful, I must say—but embarrassing to the family, to my aunt, to himself. It was terrible. I couldn't believe what I was hearing in the church."

Remembering the moment, Eddie Kostyra's sister, Estelle Burke, who was sitting with her daughter, said, "I was ready to go up and try to stop him myself. I was just seething because after a person dies, you don't talk about him that way. My brother was very critical, yes, but he did it for the kids' good. Frank just kept going on and on and on and talking about my brother and our mother, and he knew things that he shouldn't have. But his mother said to let him go. I guess she wanted him to get it off his chest. The priest almost had a fit."

Chuckling about the incident later, Father Haber said, "I was shocked. Usually at a funeral service you get up and say what a great guy the deceased was. But all of a sudden he began to harangue his father, saying that he wasn't too happy with the way he was as a father." The priest said he had learned a very good lesson from the Kostyra funeral. "Now I ask people to write out and show me in advance what they are going to say. I was caught off guard that day, and I decided I'd never let it happen again."

Years after the event Frank Kostyra said, "I think in some respects Martha was jubilant because what I said were her own words also. She didn't like Dad in many respects. As far as I can see, she doesn't like men. She tries to use them and abuse them, and she didn't like Dad because Dad was a very hard, stern, strict person when it came to things that we were doing. Martha got with me later and said that every single word I said at Dad's funeral was the truth. Her words were 'It was the whole truth, Frank, the whole truth. Everything you said was true.' ''

After the embarrassing mass, the laying to rest in the Kostyra family plot at Holy Cross Cemetery, and a delightful Martha Stewart–prepared luncheon at Elm Place, the saddened daughter returned to Westport. The most important and influential man in her life, or so she has said, was gone forever.

Loehmann's, the discount women's clothing store, in Norwalk, was best known for its designer label bargains, not as a place to mourn the dead. But that's where Sandy Broyard ran into Martha a few days after the funeral. Martha looked chic in a fringed suede jacket, jeans, and boots as she roamed the aisles, rummaging through the schmattes.

"Martha didn't look downtrodden at all," Broyard recalled. "She looked great. Martha loves bargains. She prides herself on spotting something inexpensive that has a designer label. So she was wandering around shopping, but she said she was kind of devastated and felt very lost with her father being gone."

Cookie Cutters

After her ouster from the Market Basket, Martha wasted no time opening a new version of the store, named Martha Stewart's Market Basket, which operated out of a little shop, a short walk from Turkey Hill. Martha had tried to generate the interest of investors, hoping to run her business with other people's money. She felt she had a lot of experience and expertise and a good track record with her catering business, which had been helped along by the name recognition she had developed at the Common Market, by good word of mouth from satisfied clients, and from the publicity she was continuing to get for herself.

So Martha had quite a formidable little prospectus in hand when she approached potential investors. One such angel was Eva Wiener, who had been hired by Dick Goldman to work in the food area at the Common Market. Wiener had once mentioned to Martha in passing that her well-to-do husband, Sam, might be willing to back his wife in a small food business.

"Martha wanted a deal, but it wouldn't be a fifty-fifty proposition," Wiener said. "The way Martha wanted it, Sam was supposed to put up half of the money, but I was not going to get fifty percent out because Martha said she had all the customers. We said, 'No way.' Martha probably approached me because she knew my husband had the money and she wanted to use me because I'm a hard worker."

In the end Wiener was relieved that she didn't go into partnership with Martha. "I saw her take advantage of too many people at the Market Basket," she declared. "I saw that nothing is important to Martha other than Martha. She's shrewd at business, and she's a smart person. But I could never say that Martha's a nice person."

Others also turned down Martha's offer. They felt she was "too greedy, too abusive, and too egomaniacal," as one put it, "to want to get involved with her."

Without investors Martha was forced to fund the shop with her and Andy's money, about five thousand dollars. She ran the store with the help of her sister Laura and a few other women. But the shop generated very little business, forcing Martha to close the retail outlet in under a year.

Meanwhile Martha was creating other opportunities for herself. She was continually pitching stories about her activities to the editors of the Westport *News*. She was always doing one thing or another with the Westport Historical Society, for instance, that got her photo in the paper one week, a story about her latest project the next. She also was starting to penetrate national publications, such as *Mademoiselle*, *House Beautiful*, and *Bon Appétit*, among others.

Through the good graces of well-placed friends in the women's magazine world, like Mary Emmerling, Martha was being asked to contribute occasional articles about food, gardening, and decorating. *Good Housekeeping*'s furniture and decorating editor, Joanne Barwick, who lived in Westport, had become aware of Martha's growing reputation through all the local publicity. In early 1978 Barwick was working on a prototype of a new monthly to be called *Country Living*. Having heard so much about Turkey Hill Farm, she made a date to meet Martha and came away smitten with the house and the lady of the manor. In July 1978, when the premiere issue of *Country Living* hit the stands, Martha Stewart's kitchen, in all its copper-potted, butcher-blocked, Garland-stoved glory, graced the cover.

"Inside was a layout of a wonderful holiday dinner that Martha had cooked, and we're all in the picture having this marvelous dinner in Martha's ideal kitchen," Barwick said. The first issue of *Country Living* was an immediate and enormous success—a half million copies sold out in a few weeks—and it propelled a number of careers, among them Martha's. Seeing the interest in the "country movement" as exemplified by the *Country Living* sellout, Barwick was named editor in chief of *House Beautiful*. A year later, in 1979, Barwick recruited Mary Emmerling away from *Mademoiselle* and made her decorating editor. On Emmerling's recommendation, Barwick hired Martha as *House Beautiful*'s free-lance food editor, putting her name on the masthead, which gave Martha a national magazine identity, a major credential, and real credibility.

Barwick found Martha to be "a creative, driven, ambitious and focused dynamo." Or, as another former *House Beautiful* female editor put it less diplomatically, "A royal bitch on wheels who would have gone after Joanne's job in a minute if she had had an opportunity." That thought had in fact passed through Barwick's mind on occasion, she acknowledged, during the time Martha was affiliated with the magazine. As it turned out, though, Martha was a better cook than a facile writer or editor. She found writing arduous and boring, and she usually waited until the last minute to complete and turn in her assignments. Her pieces, according to Barwick, were often heavily edited and slickly rewritten by *House Beautiful* staff people. But readers never knew the difference. Martha, who always believed her own publicity, loved seeing her name in print and had already begun to think of herself as a writer and journalist. She was even telling friends that one day she'd have a magazine of her own. Knowing Martha, they had no reason to scoff.

Martha was always looking for creative ways to make a buck, such as her aborted attempt to cash in on Vicky Negrin's "*Gnomes* Cookbook." She knew a number of artistic people like Negrin, people with inventive minds that she could pick for ideas. Among them were the Einsels: Naiad was a talented illustrator, and her husband, Walter, a prominent sculptor.

Martha had met Naiad Einsel in 1974, when she was overseeing the design and sewing of an enormous quilt that the town of Westport, like other communities across the country, planned to enter in a contest, one of the many events set for the nation's 1976 bicentennial celebration. Einsel was looking for sewers, and Martha applied and quickly won a spot alongside thirty-three other local women. Her assignment was to sew the Green Farms Congregational Church portion of the quilt, which portrayed different scenes in Westport history.

Martha and Naiad found they had many common interests—art, cooking, old houses, antiques—and they became friends. The only fly in the ointment was the way Martha treated Andy, which shocked and upset the Einsels, an older couple who had a very close and loving relationship.

"They came off *publicly* as a very handsome, happy, nice couple," Einsel observed. "But Andy was always saying, 'Oh, Martha's mad at me.' When he was complaining about her, he acted like a little boy. He'd say things to us like 'Oh, I can't do that. Martha would be mad at me.' There was a party when she opened her little shop, and afterwards there was a lot of cleaning up to do, and I heard her yelling at him: 'Andy, get that!' 'Andy, pick that up!'— really *very* unpleasant. Friends who lived close to them used to hear her screaming out the window at Andy loud enough for all the neighbors to hear: 'Andy, get in here right this minute and pick up the . . .' whatever, using a bossy tone of voice.''

One evening the Einsels accompanied the Stewarts to the ballet in New York, and on the ride home they stopped for ice cream. Martha became furious when Andy accidentally dropped his cone. ''Martha was sitting in the backseat yelling at him, 'How can you be so sloppy?' '' Einsel recalled. ''Andy usually didn't say anything when Martha belittled him, but this time he said, 'Gee, Martha, you just treat me like a piece of shit! If something happened to you, if you spilled something, I'd be concerned about it. But when it happens to me, you don't give a damn.' It really surprised us that he talked back, and it was a very tense drive home. We were glad when the journey ended.''

The Stewarts' marital problems aside, Naiad Einsel still enjoyed Martha, and they remained friends. Every Christmas Einsel made cookies for her chums, using cardboard cookie cutters she had designed in the shape of animals. Martha loved Naiad's work and had borrowed the cutters supposedly for some of her own baking, eventually returning all but one. Walter Einsel then started making the cookie cutters out of copper, which truly impressed Martha. She mentioned them to Andy, who engaged Einsel to make a cookie cutter in the shape of a gnome so there could be gnome cookies at the *Gnomes* book party. The Einsels were paid seventy-five dollars for their efforts.

When Martha opened Martha Stewart's Market Basket, she approached Einsel once again, this time with a proposition to sell the cookie cutters in the shop. When Einsel, busy with other projects, said the design and manufacture would be too time-consuming, Martha proposed a second option: The Einsels could just design the cookie cutters, and Martha would find a way to have them made, a proposition the Einsels found acceptable.

Martha agreed to pay the Einsels a royalty on each cookie cutter that she sold. That was the last the Einsels heard about the deal—until several months later, when Naiad picked up *The New York Times* and saw a photograph of Martha in her kitchen putting together holiday baskets for a prominent client, Ralph Lauren. In the foreground was a big copper pig cookie cutter, a replica of the cardboard one Martha had borrowed from Einsel but had never returned. "It upset me, but I'm one of those people who cannot bear confrontation, and I sort of let it go. I didn't want to make a big issue out of it. I just complained to my husband."

Not long after, Einsel heard from a friend that Martha was doing a land office business selling the cookie cutters mail order from her home and over the counter at her shop. The Einsels had received not a copper penny of the royalties Martha had agreed to pay them, nor had she told them that she was marketing the item.

Finally Einsel confronted Martha. "Martha said, 'Oh, I told Andy I thought you were being cool about something, and I thought it might be the cookie cutters.' She said, 'Well, that's a whole long story, and I really wasn't happy with the way they were manufacturing them, and I really would like to get together with you again and really work together on some good stuff, and we'll get together next week and talk.' So then I waited for that call from Martha that never came. She never called to discuss the cookie cutters or the royalties or the other projects. Nothing.

"Different people said I should have sued her. We had a friend in town who owned a bookshop and he also was a lawyer and he kept saying to me that I had a case against Martha. But I said, 'I just can't sue a friend.' "

Martha, on the other hand, was extremely litigious and wouldn't miss an opportunity to sue if she thought she had been ripped off. That fact was underscored by an incident involving a Connecticut couple, Tony and Carolyn Halsy, whom Martha took to court after the couple delayed paying her for a catering job. The Halsys refused to pay after Martha doubled her cost estimate just two weeks before their planned party. Later Carolyn Halsy said, "She just had us trapped. It seemed very egregious. It seemed pretty blatant what was going on."

The Halsys—he was a well-to-do young businessman— entertained frequently in their beautiful Connecticut home and had never before had a bad experience with a caterer. For the Christmas of 1979 Carolyn Halsy decided to throw a party for friends and family. Always planning their social calendar far in advance, she began looking for a caterer in early September and decided to call Martha, having heard good things about her.

Martha came to the Halsys' home, discussed the menu—hors d'oeuvres followed by a buffet dinner—and then quoted a price that Halsy found acceptable. The two shook hands, and Martha said that she would put a contract in the mail. Halsy felt "confident" that Martha would serve her well. "It sounded good," she said later. "I didn't have any insecure feelings about her." But September passed without a contract from Martha, and then October. By the end of November Halsy had grown concerned since the invitations had been sent out, and the RSVPs returned. She expressed her concern to her husband and then telephoned Martha, who said she was sorry about the delay and promised to get the contract in the mail right away. When Halsy opened the envelope a few days later, she was floored.

"The price was about double what she quoted me when she was at the house," she said. "I felt like I had been slapped in the face." Halsy immediately telephoned Martha and said there must have been some mistake, that the contract price was far more than their verbal agreement. "Martha said, 'Well, I had a migraine headache that day. I couldn't possibly do it for that amount. This is what the price is.' I couldn't believe it. It was two weeks before the party, and you can't go out and find new caterers then. She knew she had us. And this excuse about the headache, well, I remember clearly when she was here and she didn't seem to be having a migraine headache. She was fine."

Having no other choice, the Halsys allowed Martha to fulfill their arrangement. "I was pretty pissed off at Martha Stewart, and so was my wife," Tony Halsy said. "I wanted her apology. This for me was a matter of principle. I don't like to be taken advantage of by people. So I just said to my wife, 'I'm not paying her. This woman is arrogant. I'll wait until she sues me,' and she did." Halsy contacted his attorney, "who found some ridiculous section of Connecticut law that deals with door-to-door salesmen, and we mounted a defense based on that."

Prior to the trial date Andy called Halsy. "He said, 'What are you doing?' And I said, 'Look, your wife was dishonest about this, and deceived us, and tricked us— whatever you want to call it.' He said, 'Well, then why did you go forward with her?' I said we felt we didn't have any choice since it was so close to the time of the party. Then he said, 'We don't need your money. I'm president of my own publishing company.' The guy was really obnoxious to me, and I probably said something vulgar to him, and I slammed down the phone."

On the day of the trial an angry Halsy and a livid Martha showed up to do battle. But the case never got to court. The judge, in conference with Halsy's attorney, told them to settle, that he didn't want to take up the busy court's time with such a trivial matter. In the end Halsy paid Martha what was due her. "But it took her eighteen months to collect," he declared, still savoring his ploy. "She was *so* irritated by the nerve of these people not paying her. She had to spend money. She had to hire a lawyer."

During Martha's years as a caterer the Halsys weren't the only customers who felt as if they had been served a raw deal on a silver platter. There was a constant stream of complaints about Martha's ethics and tactics that never went to court. At one Martha Stewart–catered cocktail party, for instance, people complained about how terrible the food tasted. A friend of Martha's, who had recommended her to the party givers, said later that she had checked with a trusted servant who was present and been told, "This is the food we served last night. It's been redone and made into hors d'oeuvres." The same clients later received a bill to cover separate taxi rides for Martha's employees from the train station to the party site. The clients had actually witnessed the employees getting out of one cab, and they were furious.

Other clients were shocked to discover that Martha had taken off with leftover food and drink. "The next day people would say, 'Where's the liquor? Where's the ham?' " a catering friend of Martha's asserted. "And Martha would say, 'Well, you ate it all,' and they'd say, 'No, we didn't. It was on the table when you were packing up.' Martha would recycle it and use it at another party.''

Besides customers who felt duped by her, and friends who were bamboozled by her, Martha surprised magazine and catering colleagues who, after watching her in action, thought she was venal and unprincipled.

''We had *such* problems with her,'' Mary Emmerling recalled of Martha's period as food editor at *House Beautiful*. ''Whenever we would photograph somewhere, we would leave all the food and say to the people on location, 'Look, have a party tonight.' But when Martha was on the scene, that changed. All of a sudden the food was packed up and ready to go. I said to Martha, 'Wait a minute, this lady's having a party, what are you doing?' And Martha said, 'Oh, no, I need this food for a catering thing tomorrow.' That became a real problem for us at the magazine. That sort of thing was typical of Martha. No matter what we were doing she would start packing it up and taking it home.

''I once had a beautiful all-white party, a country picnic, at my loft downtown, and I saw the kids packing up the hams and the turkeys, and I said, 'What are you doing?' And they said, 'Oh, Martha said to take it unless you ask for it.' And they winked and said, 'Just ask us to leave it,' which I did, and they left it. But if you didn't ask, they were under strict orders from Martha to take it for her own personal use at parties she catered.''

In one instance, Martha got into a postphotographic shoot battle over food with Joe Ruggiero, who was the director of advertising for Ethan Allen Galleries. Ruggiero had hired Martha to star in a twenty-minute sound and slide presentation called ''Christmas in Connecticut'' that was shown in the furniture chain's 250 stores across the country to lure in customers. Martha recorded the voice-over and was photographed by Barry O'Rourke, a pal of Emmerling's, during a week of intensive production. All went well until the very end.

''To me,'' said O'Rourke, ''it was so bizarre because Joe packed up the food and said, 'I'll take it home,' and Martha said, 'No, I'm going to use this smoked turkey for a catering job tonight.' So they got into a big argument over this *food*. They were well close to screaming at each other.''

Ruggiero said he didn't want to give up the centerpiece, a

big turkey. "But Martha wanted to use the food for a party that night," Ruggiero declared. "I felt the food should stay because Ethan Allen paid for it, and I felt the crew should share it, and that's the way it ended. Martha didn't get it."

Helpers in Martha's catering business, such as Clare McCully, were shocked when they discovered that Martha was actually recycling wine to use in the fancy Ralph Lauren gift baskets she had been contracted to prepare and distribute for the clothing mogul. McCully, the second wife of the Stewarts' longtime friend George McCully, had been invited by Martha to spend time with her learning the tricks of the catering trade and was flabbergasted by what she witnessed.

"At parties she catered, Martha loved to get the bottles of wine that were sort of half full or a quarter full and bring them back to the catering kitchen in Westport to make homemade vinegar, which would end up in Ralph Lauren's gift baskets," McCully asserted. "There was a whole period when we were kind of snickering about it because if there was even wine in people's glasses, she would kind of dump it in a bottle to take home. When I asked Martha, 'Well, what about germs?' she said, 'No, it's alcohol, and that kills all the germs.'"

Continued McCully, "Nothing went to waste. Hors d'oeuvres that she served the night before and that weren't wilted, she'd serve at another party. She told me, 'You know, Clare, that's how you make your profits.' Martha's philosophy was like someone at a restaurant who had eaten half his steak and tells the waiter, 'Oh, wrap it up, and I'll take it home.'

"Other times, if there was wine or liquor left over, she would take the bottles and give one or two to her favorite person on the crew, and they would giggle about it. But it was stealing."

Martha also openly boasted that she refused to pay debts if she wasn't satisfied with the product or service provided to her. "I know she stiffed a lot of people," asserted Naiad Einsel. "She would say, 'I refused to pay for that. I'm just not going to give him a cent.' She even mentioned that she had seen a therapist and that she didn't pay him because she felt he didn't help her."

Martha continued such practices long after she had become rich and famous as America's doyenne of taste and style. In June 1995 she was sued by her loyal and longtime gardener Renaldo Abreau, a Brazilian immigrant, for allegedly failing to pay him thousands of dollars in overtime.

Abreau charged in a lawsuit that along with trenching the Martha Stewart asparagus and trimming the Martha Stewart shrubs, he handled the Martha Stewart security, did the Martha Stewart repairs, looked after the Martha Stewart pets, and washed the Martha Stewart cars. As evidence that she made him work overtime for her he produced notes he said Martha left for him that showed he did routine caretaker work. One said: "Basement smells BAD look for cat poops, change litter. Happy Valentines Day." Another declared: "Apartment: Prepare all the woodwork. In the entire apartment—scrape all the windows and sand any chipped paint on door frames, etc." For all that, he claimed, Martha paid him fifteen dollars an hour, which she increased to sixteen dollars, but never "appropriate compensation" when he worked more than forty hours a week.

Everyone thought Martha would quietly settle out of court with the gardener to avoid the adverse publicity. Instead she aggressively defended herself at the trial in October 1996. She contended that Turkey Hill was an actual farm, and Abreau was "an agricultural worker" and not entitled to overtime pay under the 1939 U.S. Fair Labor Standards Act.

The news media, which had fawned for so long over Martha and helped in large part to make her the icon she had become, now began to turn on her. With news writers salivating over the fact that someone had nailed her publicly—Abreau was David to Martha's Goliath—gloating stories about the lawsuit appeared from coast to coast.

But in this case Goliath won. In March 1997 a Connecticut trial referee ruled in her favor. "It's like O.J.," said a court observer. "Martha naturally had a high-priced 'dream team' lawyer to defend her." And that's a good thing, as the lifestyle guru often intoned.

But in 1979 all that Sturm und Drang was in the far-distant future. Martha was still little more than a hustling Westport caterer waiting for her main chance.

PART FOUR

*The Fine Art
of Entertaining*

Entertaining

$\sim$

Whatever Martha's business practices, she continued to generate lucrative jobs with fancy clients, parties ranging from a dozen or so, for an intimate dinner, to hundreds for a corporate bash, raking in big bucks in the process. Friends helped her along the way. A neighbor, who was director of the American Institute of Graphic Arts, for instance, hired her for an event, which resulted in a lucrative contract with the Cooper-Hewitt Museum.

Another such affair turned out for Martha much like that legendary Hollywood story about Lana Turner's discovery by a producer at Schwab's drugstore on Sunset Boulevard. In Martha's case she was catering a party for an Abrams book when a powerful publishing colleague of Andy's discovered her making omelets and thought, "Honey, I'm going to make you a star."

Following the enormous success of *Gnomes*, Andy published another beautiful fantasy book called *Faeries*, by Brian Froud. In order to launch it properly, he hired Martha to plan and throw a party that the publishing world would not soon forget. While Andy's boss at Times Mirror wouldn't allow him to publish a book by Martha, he saw no conflict of interest in her making a buck catering parties for the house.

Martha surpassed even herself with the *Faeries* soiree, which was thrown in December 1978, a party so memorable that four years later *The New York Times* was still raving about it as "the most unusual Stewart-catered Christmas party." The setting was the U.S. Customhouse, in lower Manhattan, which Martha and her crew transformed into a magical fairy-tale forest, with hundreds of evergreen trees sparkling with tiny lights and with the pretty young women on Martha's staff dressed as fairies. At the witching hour a thousand guests—including the heads of all the major publishing houses, senior editors, publicists, and executives from the major book chains—were served omelets filled with red caviar, or cheese, or vegetables. Andy, the book's publisher, was as usual pressed into service by Martha to help; he was with the group whipping up the eggs.

Alan Mirken, president of the Crown Publishing Group, which encompassed a number of publishing imprints, was duly impressed. Mirken had known Andy for several years and considered him a colleague and friend. But Mirken had never socialized with the Stewarts and didn't know Martha from Betty Crocker.

"I was lucky to be there that night," Mirken noted years later. "It was an extraordinary party, and I was smitten by what I saw. When I was talking to Andy during the evening, I said, 'Who's your caterer? This is terrific!' Martha came over, and she had all these cornrows in her hair, and she looked great, and Andy said, 'You have to meet my wife; *she's* the caterer.' I said to her, 'I think you should do a book.' Martha said she wasn't quite ready, but she thought she would be soon. I thought here we obviously had somebody who was very talented. The food was very good, very different-looking, and the whole package of the party was incredible. So I felt she had book potential in her. I was lucky that I was in the right place and made the right suggestion."

Mirken also felt confident that Martha could produce a publishable manuscript because Andy, whose business savvy and artistic creativity he trusted implicitly, would be heavily involved in the project. That fact, combined with Martha's promotable talents, good looks, and articulate and bright personal style, made him believe that he'd have another best-selling author in his stable.

Meanwhile Martha's friend Mary Emmerling *was* ready to do a book. Emmerling had already researched and written an outline for a book about "American country style" that had become so popular, as underscored by the enormous success of Joanne Barwick's *Country Living* magazine. Because of her friendship with Martha, Emmerling first pitched the book to Andy on the sand at Bridgehampton one weekend when the Stewarts were houseguests. But Andy rejected the idea out of hand. "He said, 'We don't do those kind of books. You'd be better off at Potter,' " Emmerling recalled.

Potter was the publishing house of Clarkson N. Potter, a division of Crown, which was headed by Mirken. Potter had just published the best-selling style book *High-Tech* by Joan Kron and Suzanne Slesin. "Because *High-Tech* was so high-tech," said Emmerling later, "Potter was looking for a book on 'country,' something soft to counteract *High-Tech*. I had my tearsheets from *Country Living*. I had all the business cards from every antiques show I'd ever been to. I put together a quick outline. So I had the book."

In 1980 Potter published Emmerling's *American Country: A Style and Source Book*, which became an overnight sensation, the first of an enormously successful series of books by Emmerling, who earned the sobriquet "The high priestess of country."

"Martha was really, really pissed," a mutual friend of theirs said. "She was jealous that Mary was doing something Martha desperately wanted to do."

Around the time Emmerling got her first book deal, Martha catered a party for another of Andy's coffee table books, *Broadway Musicals*. Once again Mirken was on the guest list for the event and was knocked out by Martha's work, even though the bash was held in Macy's basement, The Cellar. "We should really talk seriously about doing that book," he told her. This time Martha said she was ready.

During intense negotiations Andy secured an advance for Martha on the order of thirty-five thousand dollars, a royalty of about 7 percent, a photography budget, and other benefits usually offered to a published author. Andy naturally knew all the ins and outs of the book game, and being a pal of Mirken's, he was able to secure a good deal for Martha's highly speculative first book. Martha never would have become *Martha* without Andy's help.

But when Martha presented her first outline for *Entertaining* to the editors at Clarkson Potter, they were appalled. "It was *so* daunting," recalled Carol Southern, the publisher. "She had omelets for two hundred and cocktail parties for a hundred. It was all so *huge*. We said, 'Martha, we'd love to do this, but we need to try to make it a book for the *home* cook.' And so with *great* difficulty we sort of managed to persuade her to alter some of the quantities because she really was thinking *big* parties."

If Andy couldn't publish Martha's books, the Crown Publishing Group was next best. It was an aggressive company founded in 1933, in the midst of the Depression, by Alan Mirken's uncle Nat Wartels, who had built a reputation as a master merchandiser, with a simple, but successful philosophy: Offer your customers good value for their money.

At Turkey Hill Martha and Andy began planning the book, which they agreed would contain a great many photographs and lots of recipes—all gathered, cataloged, and documented over the past couple of years during catering jobs. The book would be called *Entertaining*, even though the Stewarts weren't certain at that point whether the title accurately reflected what Martha wanted to convey to readers. She wasn't sure whether to the public, entertaining meant going out to see a Broadway show or having a magician come to the house. Martha, however, believed it meant entertaining people in one's home with good food and in style. But her vision wasn't immediately obvious to everyone involved in the project.

Its title notwithstanding, *Entertaining* would be, to all intents and purposes, a cookbook, albeit one more sumptuously produced than any other in the past, with gorgeous color photographs of food printed on expensive paper. Still, it would follow the tradition of a genre that dated back to *Deipnosophistai* (The Learned Banquet), a treatise on food

Martha had a love-hate relationship with her father, Eddie Kostyra, who was a "crazy force" in her family. His parents wanted him to become a doctor, but he became a gym teacher after graduating from the Panzer College of Physical Education and Hygiene. For most of his life he worked as a pharmeceuticals salesman.

In her many books and in her magazine, Martha has painted a happy portrait of life in the Kostyra homestead at 86 Elm Place in Nutley, New Jersey. But friends and relatives remember a gloomy and austere atmosphere. Today Martha has almost as many houses as her childhood home had rooms. Courtesy of *National Enquirer*

Front and center and already in the fast lane, cute little Martha Kostyra was the third-grade pet of Yantacaw Elementary School teacher Irene Weyer *(standing in rear)*, with whom Martha developed a lifelong bond.

Courtesy of Judy Stothoff

Martha *(back row, second from left)* strikes a pose in an elementary school Christmas play. The outfit was sewn by her mother, Martha Sr., who as a young girl learned to sew and passed that talent on to her daughter.

Courtesy of Judy Stothoff

After an active academic career at Nutley High School, Martha *(second from right)* prepares in June 1959 to go off to Barnard College with a partial four-hundred-dollar-a-year Rotary Club scholarship. High school beau Mark Hallam is on Martha's right.

Courtesy of Orecchio Publications and TV

Bridesmaid Martha *(second from right)* played cupid for high school chum Nancy Teischman *(center)* by arranging for her to meet her future husband, Norm DeGrote, at a Nutley bowling alley.

Martha at Nutley High's 1958 "Miss Gauntlet" dance with her "one hot high school romance," Peter Farabaugh, an obstetrician-gynecologist's son, who some say Martha stole from her best friend.

Martha's big debut appearance in the press was this 1958 photograph in the New York *Journal-American*. The pretty seventeen-year-old high school senior enters City Hall to invite New York Mayor Robert Wagner to a military ball, where she was crowned Sweetheart of Xavier High School's Regiment. She's escorted by her date, Second Lieutenant William Carey, who later married Martha's first cousin Diane.

Martha's the queen of the hop at Xavier High School's military ball. Martha, already a model, made her gown with her mother's help.

Martha's college years at Barnard were hectic, requiring her to work as a maid and model to support herself before she met and married Yale Law School student Andy Stewart. Martha dropped out for a year to be with Andy in New Haven. She graduated in June 1964.

Martha had been modeling since high school, but her career got a major boost when she was chosen by *Glamour* from thousands of entries as one of the ten best-dressed college girls in America. Because she was so poor, her entry photographs pictured her wearing outfits borrowed from a wealthy Barnard classmate.

Courtesy of Frank Horvat

In the mid-seventies, Martha started her first catering business—The Uncatered Affair—with longtime friend and former model Norma Collier *(holding her youngest child)*, but their partnership was a disaster. Martha's daughter, Lexi, is standing with arms folded.

Considered by friends to be the warmer and more loving of Lexi's parents, Andy Stewart juggles apples for kids at a weekend event near the Stewarts' home in Westport , Connecticut.

Martha, in the beach chair, already was a best-selling author in August 1984, when she threw a small party at Turkey Hill. Her marriage to Andy Stewart *(far right)* was on the rocks, and Martha would come to suspect inaccurately that he was having an affair with her flower arranger, Robyn Fairclough *(third from left)*. Marinda Freeman *(fourth from left)*, who ran the catering operation, asserted Martha sent her "bizarre" letters.

Martha Stewart's famed Turkey Hill home, in Westport, Connecticut. It is here that she earned the reputation as America's doyenne of domesticity for her taste in cooking, gardening, decorating, and entertaining. Later, to avoid paying a gardener overtime under a federal law governing agricultural workers, she claimed in court that Turkey Hill was actually a farm.

A seemingly happy Stewart family gathering at New York's Sherry Netherland Hotel, less than a year before Andy left Martha. *Standing, from left to right:* Andy's sister, Diane Love; George and Ethel Stewart; Lexi; Victoria Love; and Andy. Kneeling are Martha, in the mink, and Diane's son, William Love.

Four months after Andy left Martha in April 1987, she poses in her Turkey Hill kitchen with flower consultant Robyn Fairclough. The Stewarts were divorced in 1990, and Andy married Fairclough in 1993.

Courtesy of Judith Pszenica/NYT Pictures

This seemingly cheerful pose of Martha with her longtime friend director-writer Kathy Tatlock, on the *Secrets of Entertaining* set in late June 1987, masks the hell the lifestyle queen was putting Tatlock through. Five months later, Martha fired Tatlock, who had to take legal action to get thousands of dollars in fees owed to her.

Courtesy of Kathy Tatlock

Lexi and Martha both dated Dr. Sam Waksal, a New York immunologist, businessman, and investor.
Courtesy of Robin Platzer—Twin Images

Martha scored big when Time Warner put its vast resources behind her magazine. Here she is accompanied by Time Warner chief Gerald Levin. But by early 1997, Martha went solo when she paid millions of dollars to take control of her own destiny.
Courtesy of Photoreporters

In 1996, happily married Andy and Robyn adopted a baby boy they named Hudson. Here, Andy holds his son at the couple's farm in Vermont.
Courtesy of Kevin Wisniewski/Rex USA

and food preparation written in the second century B.C. by Athenaeus, a Greek gourmet. The treatise was presented in the form of a dialogue between two banqueters, who talked for days and related recipes for such dishes as stuffed vine leaves and several varieties of cheesecake.

Medieval Europe also produced cookbooks. Among the earliest in English was *The Form of Cury* (the word "cury" meant "cooked food"), compiled in the twelfth century. It consisted of 196 recipes, many of which revealed their French origin in names such as "Blank Manng" and "Payn Fondewe." One of the first French cookbooks, called *La Ménagier de Paris*, was published in 1394 and contained recipes for such delicacies as frogs and snails.

The printing press revolutionized the culinary arts by making cookbooks widely available. The first known to have been printed, in 1485, was produced by an Italian, Bartolema Scappi, who mainly recorded recipes for marzipans and other sweets.

Cookbooks proliferated as the rising middle classes gained interest in better food preparation. The first cookbook written by a woman was Hannah Wooley's *The Queen-like Closet*, or *Rich Cabinet*, published in 1670. The secrets of French cuisine were made available to a wide public by the cookbooks of great chefs like Alexis Soyer (1809–1858), whose *Shilling Cookery for the People* sold more than a hundred thousand copies.

One of the most successful and popular cookbooks of all time was produced in the United States in 1896, when Fannie Merritt Farmer took on the editorship of *The Boston Cooking School Cook Book*, Farmer was the first to standardize the methods of measurements of her recipes, assuring reliable results to her readers.

The twentieth century saw a prodigious burst of interest in cooking. In the early 1920s, for example, the Washburn Crosby Company, which was in the flour-milling business, invented Betty Crocker, a fictitious homemaker and cook, to answer consumer letters. In the late twenties, through a corporate merger, Crocker became a logo of General Mills, and her name and face quickly became synonymous with cookbooks and cake mixes. For decades Crocker was one of America's most widely known food advisers.

By the late seventies a cookbook revolution was abroad in the land, and Martha saw herself as an *über*–Betty Crocker, who wanted to reach the masses, not just the sophisticated wealthy. She saw herself as a presence in supermarkets and was thinking about eventually doing something on a very broad multiple-volume scale, such as the how-to books that Time-Life produced. Martha, who felt strongly that she could be a tastemaker, had chosen a perfect time in history to produce *Entertaining*. As the prominent food writer and critic Richard Sax, who played a key role in a literary scandal surrounding *Entertaining* after its publication, observed later, ''Martha did *Entertaining* at the exact epicenter, the exact moment, when things were bursting out all over the place in the food world. Everybody and his brother were publishing a cookbook. There were suddenly four food magazines instead of one or two. There were cooking classes. There were cooking trips. The food revolution was happening in terms of people being exposed to new and different kinds of cooking. This really was the beginning of the height of a golden age of food, so Martha was in the right place at the right time with the right idea.''

Though the Stewarts' marriage continued to be on shaky ground, and Andy continued to be the dough that Martha loved to pound, he generously acted as her agent, editorial director, lawyer, chief negotiator, and majordomo—all with the hope that success from the book might finally exorcise whatever demons had possessed her through their years together and make life happier for both of them.

The Ghost and Mrs. Stewart

With Martha's deal signed, the most important issue still to be resolved before work could proceed was finding someone to write *Entertaining*. Alan Mirken had greenlighted a project with a first-time author who could never have turned in a publishable manuscript on her own.

Andy felt strongly that Martha needed a professional writer, and she readily agreed. She hated writing. Besides, she had her booming catering business to oversee. But as one longtime pal asserted, "Martha paints her own landscape and walks in it." With a book contract in hand, Martha presented herself as a writer to the world. "Mrs. Stewart carries her I.B.M. typewriter from room to room and from her home to an adjacent studio building, depending on her mood," *The New York Times* reported in a profile. Described by the *Times* reporter as an "energetic writer," Martha was quoted as saying, "If it's cold, I work in the house before 8 in the morning or late at night. Sometimes I start at 11 P.M. and write until I drop, or I get up at 3 or 4 A.M. When it's light out, I type a first and final draft straight out of my head and hate revision. It's a painful experience. I'm not a born writer."

For *Entertaining*, Martha had to find a writer she could work with and control—another in that long line of bright, creative, nonconfrontational people whom she seemed to draw to her. Enter her old friend Elizabeth Hawes.

After the Stewarts had moved to Westport, Martha and

Hawes lost touch. However, around the time Martha was thinking about *Entertaining*, Hawes fortunately reentered her life. "We were actually broke, and we had all these babies, and we decided to leave the city, and Martha found us a house to rent in Westport—a very nice house right around the corner from her—and that is how we hooked up again."

In early spring 1979 Martha approached Hawes with the book-writing proposition. By then Hawes had left the editorial staff of *The New Yorker* and was free-lancing, mostly writing food pieces for magazines like *Gourmet*. Like Martha, she had never tackled a book before, but she was thrilled at the prospect and agreed to collaborate. Hawes called her literary agent, Roberta Pryor, at International Creative Management (ICM) to negotiate a contract with Martha. Her thinking was "This is going to be a fifty-fifty deal."

"I called Martha Stewart, and she was *appalled* that I would want royalties for my client," Pryor disclosed years later. "I said, 'Elizabeth is a good writer. She works very hard, and if you are going to sign a book contract and *you're* not going to write the book yourself, then you have to be prepared to pay somebody to write it, and they have to share in the proceeds.' Martha said, 'Talk to Andy.'

"He complained and whined to me that Martha only got a seven percent royalty on the book, and because of that, he and Martha wanted to pay Elizabeth a flat fee. I said, 'That's no reason why you should try to get an excellent *New Yorker* writer for a cheap amount of money.' He wasn't very pleased. I told him that I couldn't tell my client to go ahead and write the book without sharing in the royalties, and he said, 'Forget it. It's not going to happen.' "

Pryor was suddenly out. Acting as his wife's agent, Davis Weinstock then spent weeks trying to hammer out an acceptable contract with Andy, who had a reputation in the publishing world as a hard-nosed negotiator and businessman, despite his mild-mannered personal style. As Pryor put it later, "Davis Weinstock found himself agreeing to things he shouldn't have agreed to, and they fucked themselves." In the end the Weinstocks agreed to a deal nowhere near the fifty-fifty arrangement that Liz Hawes had anticipated.

While Martha made hundreds of thousands of dollars in royalties on *Entertaining*—and the book would catapult her career as America's "Diva of Domesticity"—Hawes earned only a few pennies on each book sold. "As I recall, I got one-half of a percent of Martha's royalties and a writer's fee of something like three thousand dollars—part up front and part on completion of the book," she said. "And then I got a bonus of about a thousand dollars when we finished because I ended up doing a lot more work at the end because Martha wasn't around. Andy looks like a big teddy bear and has the physical presence of one too. He's somebody you feel extremely warm towards. But Andy is, for all his teddy bearishness, a very tough negotiator, a very tough soul, equally skilled as Martha at manipulation."

Once the contract was signed, though, Hawes, who described herself as being "by no means savvy, not aggressive by nature, and rather trusting," took an optimistic approach to the project. "I was sure everything would work out fine. Martha was my friend. We were doing this together. We were creating it together. There wasn't anything threatening about it. I didn't think that we were playing hardball."

The two novice authors began to meet almost every day, either in Martha's kitchen or in Hawes's. "Martha was excited," said Hawes. "But she didn't seem to have any idea what the book would be about. We had no idea what we were doing. Really, truly, we were operating by the seats of our pants in the beginning."

After floundering for a time, Martha began to reminisce about the Kostyras and growing up in Nutley, describing how her mother cooked and entertained. Hawes's ears pricked up, and she furiously scribbled detailed notes, never even considering using a tape recorder. Martha used the family stories as a jumping-off point to discuss her own experiences as a hostess, caterer, and cook. She had found her story line. And it would become the leit motif of almost all her future publishing endeavors.

At the typewriter Hawes wrote Martha's stories in a simple-to-read, easy-to-understand, chummy first-person style. *Entertaining*'s first paragraph, for instance, begins: "I grew up in a large family that *always* had guests. I loved the ease with which my mother added extra places, a big platter of vegetables, a special pie. . . ."

Whether Martha was telling the truth about her family and her formative years in Nutley or whether she was fantasizing, creating a myth, was not Hawes's concern. "I did no research," the writer revealed. "I didn't check the accuracy or truthfulness of any of the things Martha told me. She was totally in control of the story. To me, it all seemed rather folkloric: this big family and their Polish kitchen, and the father's fruit trees outside, and all those kids. Martha always put a good spin on things."

In late 1981 Martha turned in the manuscript, which, besides Hawes's text, included hundreds of color photographs, practically all taken by Andy, captions, and dozens of recipes.

Carolyn Hart, the editor, had never done a cookbook before, and that fact had initially concerned Martha, who had never written one. Martha had told Hart that she didn't want *Entertaining* to "intimidate" readers, and Hart had responded by telling Martha, "If you can make me understand it, you'll accomplish your goal." And Hart *got* *Entertaining* with her first read of the manuscript.

Hart's boss, Carol Southern, was equally overjoyed, attributing much of her acceptance of Martha's manuscript to Liz Hawes's writing skills. "We were just relieved when Liz's manuscript came in to have something that we didn't have to rewrite, that was literate, that had sentences that were well constructed," Southern said. "It was simple but eloquent. We didn't often see manuscripts that well written."

At the top Alan Mirken was elated too. "Liz did a great writing job," he declared.

Despite all the kudos, Hawes, who was still recovering from the royalties' mugging she had received at the hands of the Stewarts, was in for still another shock. When the galley proofs arrived, she saw for the first time that her

name was not on the jacket. The cover was dominated by
Martha Stewart—her byline and a picture of the smiling
hostess standing in front of a beautifully decorated dining-
room table. Equally disturbing to Hawes was the credit line
on the first inside page that read: "By Martha Stewart, Text
with Elizabeth Hawes." Many cowriters, in fact, don't receive a writing credit. But Hawes, who had poured her heart
and soul into the project and had always viewed Martha as
a loyal friend, felt betrayed. "Martha did *no* writing for
Entertaining," Hawes declared. "She wasn't the author of
Entertaining. It was certainly her book, but it was my prose.
But Martha didn't want to take any chances that she would
be identified as other than the author. She wanted it to be
her book."

Confronting Martha, Hawes demanded that the credit
"text with" should have said "text by." But Martha was
immovable. "She said, 'That's the way it is.' She argued
that the use of the word 'by' sounded like she didn't have
anything to do with the text. She said the ideas were hers,
and that she would look like the *co*author if the word 'by'
was used. She said she was insecure about having people
think the book was ghostwritten. We argued. We went
around and around. But by then it was too late. It was
beyond disappointing for me to get up to publication and
get a 'thanks for your help' kind of thing when I considered
myself a full collaborator.

"I was incredibly annoyed and was stomping around
talking to my husband and saying, 'I can't believe what's
happened.' " Hawes said she didn't take legal action because "Martha was a friend and we'd had a wonderful time
doing this book. I sincerely expected we'd have our arms
around each other, walking in the limelight together. But
in the end I was left hurt and disbelieving that I was getting
so little credit."

Hawes took her complaints to Carol Southern and Carolyn Hart but was told that Martha was adamant and would
accept no other wording than "text with." Southern advised Hawes, "You'd better give in."

Later Southern, who was given her own imprint at
Crown, which had become a division of Random House,

said, "Liz was the writer, no question. I remember thinking at the time, 'How clever of Martha to get a *New Yorker* writer.' Nobody had ever done that for a cookbook. That was a very original idea. In the end Liz was sort of astonished at Martha's ambition. Martha has a way with people where she makes them feel important and that they're making a contribution. She can be very comfortable to be with, and I can imagine Liz going over there to work with her like pals together. And then suddenly Martha has walked off with the star billing. I can see how Liz would feel."

Author! Author!

Entertaining had an initial press run of twenty-five thousand copies and a cover price of thirty-five dollars, both extraordinarily big numbers for a cookbook at that time. "They were very cautious about the number of books printed," Martha noted. "The first printing, I think it was 25,000 copies, and I was sort of disappointed, and my husband thought I was nuts. He said, 'That is an enormous amount for a first book.' " Martha had been asking for a first printing of thirty-five to forty thousand copies. In the end she was on the mark because the demand was bigger than the initial supply.

As Carol Southern remembered, "Martha was *always* pushing us, pushing us to a point where we were a little nervous. She just would persist and persist and say, 'I really want this . . . I really want that.' *Entertaining* was a first in that it was a really expensive color book. We were terribly worried that it was *too* expensive and that no one would pay that kind of money for it. Everybody was very nervous about it because nobody knew who Martha Stewart was. We went out on a limb with Martha.''

The Stewarts *both* were perfectionists, and they wanted a *perfect* first book for Martha, so they demanded quality. ''One of the things that Andy noticed was that a tablecloth wasn't colored exactly in the book as it was at home,'' Alan Mirken pointed out as an example of the Stewarts' vigilance. ''But nobody else knew that. It looked very nice in the book, but Andy knew it wasn't the right color. It wasn't like we were printing a Monet art piece that had to match exactly. It was just a tablecloth that was very pretty either way. He gave us his input—they both did—and that was fine. But we did what we felt we had to do.''

About a month before *Entertaining*'s publication date, Martha began pestering Andy to help her plan and produce the enormous launch party, which would be held at Turkey Hill and catered of course by Martha and paid for by her publisher.

But Andy was resisting Martha's nagging. After a phenomenal five-year run as president and CEO of Harry Abrams, he had decided to give up his prestigious, powerful, and well-paid position to start his own high-quality illustrated book publishing house, Stewart, Tabori & Chang. Martha was vehemently against Andy's decision, seeing it as a big gamble, which she didn't believe he could handle. Andy had to borrow about a million dollars to start the company. Martha saw wings on the money.

Andy was now working even longer hours than before, trying to get his first small list of books published. Curiously, his lead title was an elegant, sumptuously photographed food book much like *Entertaining*, called *Glorious Foods*, by Christopher Idone, a prominent Manhattan caterer, who had a roster, like Martha, of rich and famous clients. Like Martha's, Idone's book was scheduled for fall 1982. Andy was not only guiding Martha's book but also overseeing one that would be in direct competition with hers. Martha had mixed feelings about the conflict. On the one hand, she hoped *Glorious Foods* would do well, giving

Andy's new venture a shot in the arm and enriching the Stewarts' bank account. On the other hand, she was worried that Idone's work would cut into *Entertaining*'s sales and her glory and fame. Martha and Andy, it appeared, wanted it both ways.

As the publication date for *Entertaining* drew near, Martha became more stressed, anxious, and on edge. Her future, she accurately felt, was riding on what would happen in the coming weeks. She continued to beseech Andy to take time off to help her with last-minute preparations for her big book party.

One evening, about a week and a half before the bash, Martha's appeals went over the edge. Andy and Martha, along with the young son of a colleague of Andy's, were returning to Westport after having had dinner in Manhattan. It was about midnight, and they were heading outbound on the Bruckner Expressway, passing through the South Bronx. "Martha wanted Andy to take a week off to assist with the preparations for the garden party for *Entertaining*, and Andy told her he could only spare a couple of days because he had important business at Stewart, Tabori & Chang," a confidant stated.

"Martha can get really livid if you don't do what she wants. And she got really livid. She said, 'If you don't promise you'll do it, I'm opening this car door, and I'm jumping out.' Andy said, 'I just can't.' And Martha opened the car door.

"They were at a ramp, and Andy grabbed Martha's arm and braked, but she jumped out while the car was still slowly rolling and ran down the ramp into this horrible neighborhood, which was like *Bonfire of the Vanities* territory.

"It was a very dangerous spot, and it was late at night, and it was a very, very unpleasant situation. Andy had to get out of the car and chase Martha and plead with her to get hold of herself and get back in the car and out of the street, which she eventually did after much coaxing.

"Later I said to Andy, 'That's why Martha is the way she is today. You should have just let her run into the Bronx.' And he said, 'She would have gotten hurt.' I said,

'But you never allow her to suffer the consequences of one single thing she ever does.' Martha does whatever it takes to get what she wants, and that can involve pretty strange behavior. She could have gotten killed that night.''

Martha's actions didn't come as a complete surprise to Andy, and to the friends he later told about the incident. During the years of the Stewarts' marriage, Martha occasionally threatened suicide if she didn't get her way, and Andy always gave in.

Martha's tantrum in the Bronx worked. Andy gave her the time she required, and her book party came off as planned.

It was a glorious and glittering affair, in the inimitable Martha Stewart fashion. Tables were filled with beautiful food; there was a barbecue; bottles of the dessert wine Dubonnet Blanc were everywhere because earlier in the year Martha had become the U.S. spokesperson for the company, her first product endorsement, which was short-lived.

Crown's publicity department had sent out the invitations, and top editors and business executives were on hand from Crown, Clarkson Potter, and other major houses, congratulating Martha on her fine writing job and her creativity. Key executives from Dalton, Walden, and the book clubs also were in attendance to celebrate *Entertaining*'s publication.

Martha Stewart smiled and sparkled and looked like the happiest and proudest woman in the world that night. She was the star, the center of attention, the newly crowned lifestyle queen, at her coronation. At least for that brief joyous moment she appeared content.

Everywhere there were piles of her dazzling book, which was dedicated to Lexi, to Eddie Kostyra, and to Andy ''for his encouragement, good nature, and support.''

But there was something surreal about the evening, according to Norma Collier, whose on again, off again friendship with Martha was briefly on again. ''Andy and I were walking the paths of the garden and people were coming up to him and saying, 'Oh, Andy, congratulations, the book is so wonderful, you must be very proud of Martha.' And he was smiling and saying, 'Oh, thank you. I am proud of her.' And then we'd walk on and he'd whisper to me, 'I've got to get out of here. I've got to leave her. I can't live like this anymore.' And I thought, 'Oh, God, this is like a Fellini movie.' ''

Stop, Thief!

A born saleswoman, Martha hit the road to pitch *Entertaining*, determined to make it a best-seller. For a month she spearheaded a publicity blitz that took her from coast to coast, border to border, giving interviews, cooking demonstrations, autographs, and winning legions of loyal followers, the charter members of what became an enormous cult of Martha Stewart worshipers and wannabes. But her book and her philosophy also infuriated others, many of them feminists who thought she was turning back the clock on the many advances made by women by telling them to return to the kitchen. They became charter members in an enormous cult of Martha Stewart detractors. Eventually Martha became one of those celebrities whom people loved to hate.

In Los Angeles she made a hysterically funny appearance on Merv Griffin's nationally syndicated talk show when she locked claws with the South American spitfire Charo. Earlier in the greenroom the two women had gotten off to a bad start, and by the time both appeared on camera they were hissing at each other.

Looking like a Pilgrim in a Laura Ashley dress buttoned to her throat—''that's what my public expects me to wear," she once told a colleague—Martha asked Charo, wrapped in something skintight and revealing, to help her make hors d'oeuvres. The mischievous Griffin, convinced that the wild singer-dancer didn't like Martha's lofty manner, waited for the fireworks with a straight face.

As Martha was demonstrating how boursin cheese stuffed into snow peas could make for a delightful dish, the last of Xavier Cugat's five wives suddenly blurted, "But, dear, your food gives me gas. I'm not coming to your party." Taking Charo seriously, Martha wagged her finger at the butt-wiggling Vegas cutie, proclaiming, "Well, *you'd* never be invited. . . . Here, Charo, stuff a snow pea." Griffin, standing between the two women like a referee, said, "Ladies! *Ladies!*"

Watching at home, friends of Martha's chuckled at her performance. "It was *so* funny. Charo made mincemeat out of Martha," recalled Sandy Broyard. Nevertheless Martha ate up the publicity—good or bad. As far as she was concerned, some of those Merv Griffin viewers were going to go out and buy *Entertaining*, and that was all that mattered. As one friend noted, "Martha's underlying philosophy has always been 'Who cares what people think?' "

On the road promoting *Entertaining* and her subsequent books, Martha quickly gained a reputation as a shrew among the media escorts assigned to take her to bookstore signings and TV and radio appearances. "She's a real screamer," asserted a West Coast book publicist. "Martha will yell at anyone—the limo driver, her staff. Anything you do, it's never good enough for her. She wants bookstore displays rearranged at the last minute. The signs are never big enough for her. And then she's ready to skip out before she's finished autographing books. [Such an incident occurred in Buffalo, New York, in 1996, and received wide press coverage.] She pretends she's taking a bathroom break, but she's out the door, and furious women are left standing around with unsigned books. And Martha says, 'Oh, who cares?' I never heard her say thank you, and she never gives anyone credit. She takes all the credit herself. 'Oh, it worked out well,' she'll say. 'Wasn't that a good idea of *mine*.' "

As a result Martha eventually was given the book escorts' "Golden Dartboard Award," a secret dishonor bestowed upon the "agreed-upon biggest asshole of the year," according to one account.

Liz Hawes, who had already been knocked to the mat by Martha over the money and by-line issues, was in for yet another low blow to her bruised ego. When a big book party was thrown for *Entertaining* at the Remarkable Bookstore, in Westport, Martha basked in the spotlight but didn't invite the writer.

"Somebody mentioned the party to me. I didn't know anything about it," Hawes said. "I was stunned. This was my *hometown*, and it was Connecticut, where many of my writer friends live. A friend who knew the bookstore owner called her and said, 'Do you realize what Martha Stewart's done? Do you know there's a coauthor?' The owner called me and apologized and said she hadn't realized."

Five years earlier Martha's onetime cooking partner Ann Brody had moved to Washington, D.C., where she went to work as an executive with Giant Food, a supermarket chain. By the time *Entertaining* was published, Brody had made a name for herself as an innovator: She had developed the concept of a gourmet supermarket for Giant and was in the process of opening the first store in the affluent Washington suburb of McLean, Virginia, near the Hickory Hill estate of Ethel Kennedy. Brody thought it would be wonderful if Martha would make an appearance to sign books, which would promote *Entertaining* and Brody's store at the same time.

But Martha brushed her off by telling her to call her publisher. "I was sort of dumbfounded because I thought she was a friend," Brody said. She got a similar response when she talked to Martha's publicist, whose first question was "How many books can you sell?" "I said, 'I don't know. The store's not open yet.' And she said, 'Well, Martha has no time for that. When you know how many books you can sell, call me back.' "

Shortly after the store had its grand opening, Brody received an unexpected call from Martha, due in Washington to hawk *Entertaining*. "She said, 'I'd love to see you while

I'm here, and I have to go to this store before my TV appearance to get ingredients to demonstrate a recipe. Are you anywhere near there?' I said, 'Martha, that *is* my store.' So this limousine entourage arrived, and Martha hopped out and walked in, and I said, 'How are you?' She nodded, looked at the produce section, and said, 'What, no flowering kale?' As she was leaving, she said, 'You know, I could have sold a lot of books here. Why didn't you let me know?' I said, 'Martha, because I should never have had to make a second call. You know, that's where we differ. I take care of my friends.' And that was that.''

Not long after, Martha made a return trip to the nation's capital, once again to plug *Entertaining* and to speak at a benefit luncheon for the Washington Home, a nursing facility and hospice. Now in great demand as a speaker, Martha charged and received thousands of dollars per engagement. Her appearance at the Washington function, called ''Entertaining People,'' had been suggested to the event's chairman by a former Westport friend, Diane Sappenfield, whose husband had become a part owner of the Watergate complex. ''Martha was great,'' Sappenfield recalled. ''She put on a slide show and told the packed audience how she went to estate auctions and tag sales, picking up bargain dishes and linens.'' But when the Martha wannabes went home, the event's sponsors were left to deal with their honored guest's bill. ''They didn't get everything in writing from Martha regarding the costs for her visit, and with Martha, you have to get *everything* in writing,'' Sappenfield observed. ''So when they got Martha's bill, it was more than they anticipated because she added in what she considered her expenses: the limousine and the fancy dinner at Jean Louis, in Georgetown—that sort of thing. Because it was a charity event, it left a bad taste in everyone's mouth. They said, 'This got way out of control. Why did she do this to us?' Martha was a huge success—until they got their bill.''

On the West Coast Martha was guest of honor at a dinner thrown by her publisher and attended by stars of the food world. Sitting at her table was the grand food eminence

Craig Claiborne, revered for his books and articles and for his knowledge of the art and enjoyment of cooking. While Martha was honored by his presence, Claiborne had told colleagues that he thought she was a ''mere amateur, an interloper,'' and he seriously questioned the origin and ownership of a number of the recipes he saw in her book. When she got home from the trip, Martha confided to Dorian Leigh Parker, one of her cooks, how upsetting her confrontation with Claiborne had been.

''Martha told me that Craig turned to her and said, 'You know, I have a bone to pick with you.' And she said, 'What is that?' And Claiborne said, 'Well, I'm the *only* person at this table whose recipes you *didn't* steal.' I must say, Martha was *very* indignant.''

In her acknowledgments in *Entertaining*, Martha had credited Parker—a former high fashion model and the sister of cover girl Suzy Parker—along with two other valued workers, Brooke Dojny and Charlotte Turgeon, ''for their help in cooking and testing *my* [italics added] recipes.'' But were they really Martha's? Or had they been lifted, as Claiborne had suggested?

''Very few of the recipes *were* Martha's,'' Parker asserted. ''One third of the recipes were ones that Liz Wheeler [another member of Martha's kitchen staff], and I, and other people, gave her.''

From the day that *Entertaining* was published, allegations of plagiarism—the stealing or passing off of ideas or words as one's own without crediting the source—stalked and haunted Martha for some years to come. Norma Collier, for one, said she called Martha after reading *Entertaining* to complain that many of her personal recipes and ideas, such as the basket weaving on a wedding cake, which Collier had gotten from a picture in *Larousse Gastronomique*, had appeared as Martha's own. Andy responded by saying, '' 'Well, you know what, Norma, we checked, and you can't copyright a recipe, and just for insurance we changed four tablespoons to a quarter of a cup or vice versa.' They did things very deliberately.''

In the late seventies Barbara Tropp, fresh from a graduate program in Chinese studies at Princeton, had written two articles for the Cuisinart magazine *The Pleasures of Cooking* that included ''classic'' recipes and recipes that were ''idiosyncratic'' to Tropp's Chinese cooking mentors. By 1982 Tropp's first book, *The Modern Art of Chinese Cooking*, was appearing in bookstores across the country, simultaneously with *Entertaining*. Tropp was close to, or known by, a number of highly respected food writers, including such luminaries as James Beard, Paula Wolfert, and Barbara Kafka.

''One day I got a note from one of my old buddies saying 'Barb, you might be interested in taking a look at this new book called *Entertaining*. I think the author stole a bunch of your recipes,' '' said Tropp, breaking years of what she termed ''a no comment attitude on the subject of Martha Stewart.''

Leafing through the big, glossy volume, Tropp came to a chapter entitled ''A Chinese Banquet for Ten to Twelve,'' which began, ''My daughter, Alexis, introduced me to the pleasures of preparing Chinese food at home. She loves to browse in old cookbooks and new food magazines, and, like many young people, is particularly attuned to the fresh combinations of flavors and textures in Chinese food. . . .''

Then Tropp froze. The recipes she saw were straight out of her published magazine articles. ''I was shocked because it was just so clearly plagiarism,'' she asserted. ''And what equally shocked me was that it was virtually verbatim. Some of these dishes were names I even had made up. It was so blatant. It was clear to me that Martha Stewart had lifted my work without attribution.''

Tropp went home and dashed off an irate note to Martha's publisher. ''I got a letter back that was a non sequitur. It said something like 'Dear Miss Tropp, we're delighted that you liked Martha's book. We will send you an advance copy of her second.' It angered me, and I called up a bunch of friends to tell them what was going on. I felt very injured and wrote postcards to some of the people in the business who were very influential, people I regarded as my mentors. I explained to each of them what had happened and asked for suggestions about what I should do. And in telling them what Martha had done to me, they told other people.''

Soon Martha's actions were a cause célèbre in the very insular and often bitchy food world. One of those who heard about the scandal was an old high school friend of Tropp's, Richard Sax, a chef and prolific food writer who was then writing a book review column for *Cuisine*. He was, as he acknowledged later, ''the first to expose Martha Stewart for recipe plagiarism. I had known about what she had done for over a year, but *Cuisine* didn't want to handle it. They felt it was too hot and too finger pointing. They finally decided to do something when recipe plagiarism had become a problem in the industry.''

After Sax's ''not nasty, but sort of juicy,'' article appeared, Martha telephoned him and ''was very kind of hands-on-hip indignant, very kind of high horse. She was saying, 'How could Barbara be making such a big deal of this thing?' She called me to chew me out.'' Martha wasn't through. She followed the call with a written point-by-point rebuttal of Sax's claims.

''But she never really addressed the issue,'' he asserted. ''She came back by saying there was *supposed* to be attribution but never explained why there *wasn't*. Martha's recipes were *verbatim* Barbara Tropp's—I mean, *ingredient* by *ingredient*. She used exact phrases. I checked them side by side in researching my piece. Then Martha set out to prove that terms used by Barbara were not terms that only Barbara knew but were used more widely. Martha claimed she had citations from Chinese cookbooks. It was almost like the O. J. Simpson trial: She was fighting on the merits of very small points.'' (It also was shades of how Martha had handled her dispute with the owners of the Market Basket over her use of the word ''proprietor.'')

Furious at Tropp for causing the brouhaha Martha told the Chicago *Sun-Times*, ''Maybe Barbara Tropp is jealous that my book has sold 120,000 copies and hers has only sold 5,000.'' The paper checked Martha's assertion with Tropp's publisher, who said, in fact, Tropp's book had actually sold 15,000 copies and was in its second printing.

"Martha's saying that about Barbara was one of the least gracious things she could have done," Sax said.

As the scandal escalated, Tropp received another letter from Martha's publisher saying that she would receive credit in the next printing. In fact Martha had changed the Lexi-Chinese banquet sentence to read: *"With several of the recipes inspired by the Chinese scholar and chef Barbara Tropp* [italics added], *Lexi executed her first Chinese banquet at thirteen as an anniversary surprise for Andy and me."*

Chinese scholar Barbara Tropp really saw red this time. "These weren't recipes that were *inspired* by me. They were recipes that were *stolen* from my writing. It was an *affront*, and it had nothing to do with my career and cooking. It had to do with the realm of writing. This was strictly intellectual. It wasn't economic. In my own books, when I use recipes of other people, I credit them. I don't say it was *inspired* by them. There's creative plagiarism, and there's blatant plagiarism—and this was blatant."

Like others who have had their problems with Martha, Tropp described herself as a nonaggressive person and decided to drop the issue and move on with her life. "I don't like conflict. I don't like to be embroiled. I'm a small, dark-haired Jewish girl, and there's no way I'm going to get embroiled with my psychic opposite. When I meet tall, lanky blondes like Martha Stewart who are into their power, I step aside."

(Besides having food writing in common, Tropp, like Martha, had grown up in New Jersey and graduated from Barnard. Some years after their contretemps had blown over, Tropp learned that the now very rich and powerful Martha Stewart was to be appointed to Barnard's board of trustees. "Now *that* upset me," Tropp declared. "I felt that was an affront. I believe that people who serve on the boards of colleges should have honorable professional lives. I learned at Barnard what plagiarism was and how one properly gives attribution. So the fact that someone like Martha Stewart who flouted what I learned there would be on Barnard's board struck me as a terrible, horrible affront.")

Although Tropp and others declined to take action, allegations of plagiarism continued to surface, and stories about Martha's questionable methods had begun to spread from food journals into the mainstream press. In its December 1, 1986, issue, *Newsweek*, for example, charged that Martha's "debt to other cooks seems clear. The crusty mustard chicken in 'Quick Cook' [Martha's second book] appears in Julia Child's *Mastering the Art of French Cooking*, as do the orange-almond cake and a sister to the raisin-cherry pound cake in *Entertaining*.... [A]t her November [1986] seminar Stewart distributed recipes on her letterhead for a *chaud-froid* sauce and a chocolate jellyroll that came straight from Child and *The Joy of Cooking* respectively."

Each time a new charge was lodged, Martha asserted that her recipes had been developed over the years in her catering business. "Sweet-and-hot cabbage pickles and lionshead meatballs are not Barbara Tropp's inventions," she said. "They've been around for years. And Julia Child acknowledges that orange almond cake was being made a couple of hundred years before her books were published. Recipes are in the public domain. Some of my recipes have been picked up by others, and I've never complained. I see it as a form of flattery." In fact, recipe ownership is difficult to prove, and cookbook writers often build upon earlier recipes.

Another of Martha's victims was Richard Jeffery, a respected still-life photographer. Their relationship dated back to 1978, when Jeffery was assigned to shoot a feature story about Thanksgiving at Turkey Hill for *Cuisine*. In 1980, around the time Martha began gathering material for *Entertaining*, she asked to borrow Jeffery's pictures, saying she needed them to make a presentation to a client. He was happy to help her out.

Shortly thereafter Andy retained Jeffery to work on *Glorious Foods*, and his impressive work on that book led to a long series of assignments for *Home Entertaining*, a special supplement of *The New York Times*. Because of his busy schedule, Jeffery forgot about the photographs that he had lent Martha, and a decade passed before they once again came to his attention. In 1990 a cookbook publisher wanted to use one of them, and the editor informed Jeffery that it had appeared in *Entertaining*. Jeffery was puzzled because he didn't recall ever selling photographs to Martha for the book. In fact he hadn't. She'd just gone ahead and used them without his permission and without compensation, in violation of U.S. copyright law.

"I telephoned her and confronted her, and she denied doing *any* of those things," Jeffery said. "She said, 'I sent you a copy of the book,' and I said, 'Oh, come on, Martha, that's not true.' She said, 'You signed over the rights to me,' and I said that wasn't so. She said, 'I bought the rights from you.' And I said, 'If you can send me a copy of a check from you to me with my endorsement, I'll drop the whole thing.' And she couldn't."

Jeffery hired an attorney who specialized in copyright infringement, and he began preparing a case against Martha that he intended to file in federal court unless a satisfactory out-of-court settlement could be reached. To avoid a lawsuit, Martha offered Jeffery a thousand dollars through a lawyer. Jeffery felt this was an insult. The offers kept escalating, and finally his attorney saw a settlement in sight. "He said, 'Why don't we settle for fifteen thousand dollars?' I said, 'Why don't we try for twenty?' and Martha's side—Random House, which had bought the Crown Publishing Group—agreed. We settled in May 1993. And that was the end of it. But I had to pay half to cover my legal costs."

Around the same time, Martha had one of her assistants call Jeffery, requesting to borrow even more pictures. "She's got *big* balls," he declared later. "Nothing she does shocks me."

All the News That Fits

Besides the stew over plagiarism, Martha found herself in the soup when readers discovered that a number of recipes in *Entertaining* simply didn't work. The phones started ringing off the hook at Turkey Hill—Martha's number was still listed—with complaints from hysterical and irate cooks voicing their displeasure. And poison-pen letters from outraged Martha wannabes began overflowing her publisher's in box.

"We spent a lot of time on the telephone talking to people who would call and say, 'Well, I'm having a dinner party for twenty-three people and I just made the lemon curry, and it didn't work.' Of course it didn't. Following the recipe was their first big mistake," said John Hilts, a bright young graduate of the New York Restaurant School who worked in Martha's catering kitchen. "We knew there were some glaring errors in the book, and that blew a lot of people away."

Marinda Freeman, who served as executive director of Martha's catering business, Martha Stewart, Inc., during the two years following the publication of *Entertaining*, said, "I'd report the calls to Martha, and her comment was 'Well, *they* must be doing something wrong because *I* know the recipe is right. *They* just aren't doing it right.' She dismissed the complaints out of hand. She never acknowledged that she might have made a mistake."

As far as Martha was concerned, *Entertaining* was *the*

best cookbook ever produced, despite all the hullaballoo about where and how she got her recipes and whether or not they worked. From the moment Elizabeth Hawes started writing, Martha predicted it would be a monster best-seller. And she believed book critics would share her view. Many did. Ruth Diebold's comments in *Library Journal* typified those of many reviewers. She announced that Martha had a "fine eye, a sense of theater, and a respect for both physical beauty and the taste of food. . . . Recipes are excellent, well explained, and usually practical, though occasionally flair overcomes common sense. A rich-kid book but never a snobbish one, this is a treat for eye and palate."

Publishers Weekly, whose prepublication reviews are closely watched by other critics and booksellers, gave legs to *Entertaining* with a rave. "One of the most sumptuous books of the season, replete with gorgeous color photos and meticulously detailed recipes, this knockout volume well justifies its price."

But Martha's main concern was what *The New York Times* would say. She even asked Anatole Broyard to use his influence to have the review assigned to a friendly critic. He didn't. For Martha, Wednesday, December 15, 1982, was a day that would live in infamy. *The Times'* food editor Marian Burros came in low and hit hard, pounding *Entertaining* like a piece of tough veal.

While she praised Martha's book for being one of "the year's most beautiful," she wrote that it belonged "in the living room rather than the kitchen. One would no more dream of cooking from [it], spattering it with olive oil as you work, than one would think of thumbing through an expensive art book while eating fried chicken." She said it was a book "for browsing to glean ideas for table settings or menus, for looking at the beautiful photographs, or for enjoying vicariously what is eaten at parties" when a caterer is in charge.

Burros observed:

Mrs. Stewart is a woman of many talents who lives and works in a beautiful country house in Connecticut. She is seen throughout the book gardening, beekeeping, picking

248 *Martha Stewart*

sunflowers, feeding chickens, cooking, posing with her kitchen staff. She can describe how to put together a party with style but one is better off not using her recipes, which are fraught with errors.

A recipe for tomato fettucine with snow peas Alfredo, a strange combination, calls for four pounds of pasta and about three and a half cups of sauce. Instructions for preparing tortellini, broccoli and pesto call for eight pounds of tortellini, three bunches of broccoli and two cups of sauce. The result in both cases is, as might be expected, pasta that is virtually unsauced.

A recipe for gingered flank steak saté calls for a two-pound flank steak and a marinade containing two tablespoons of salt and two tablespoons of soy sauce. The saltiness makes the dish inedible. The directions say to reserve the marinade to pour over the steak but there is no marinade left. In several recipes, ingredients are listed out of order, and in one appear to be part of the stuffing but turn out to be a garnish.

Martha was livid. *"That Marian Burros is a bitch!"* she declared to her pal Clare McCully.

McCully said Martha began making "paranoid" statements, such as " *'They're* after me. *They* don't want me to be successful. But I'm going to be more successful than all of them put together.' She said, 'I'm going to *get* them.' Martha became defensive that the food people were making light of her because she was just a caterer. She ranted on and on about how hard she had worked all of her life, how she had worked for everything that she had gotten."

Martha angrily telephoned Burros at *The Times,* the food writer disclosed. "She was horrified about my review. She was very upset. She told me that she had told some friends that she was going to call me, and they had told her that she was very courageous. She asked me if I had tested the recipes, and when I essentially told her that I had—I personally didn't, but they were tested for me by a tester whom we've used for some twenty years—it was as if she didn't believe me." Burros wasn't surprised by Martha's call. "We get all kinds of phone calls from people who suggest we've done things we haven't done. I defended myself.''

Later someone sent Burros a clipping of an interview in another newspaper that quoted Martha as suggesting that "I had not told the truth, that I had not tested the recipes. But the bottom line to all this was the recipes that we tested didn't work.''

Burros's review became the talk of *The Times,* recalled Bryan Miller, who had just come aboard as the newspaper's restaurant critic and was a neighbor of Martha's in Westport. "It was the first time I'd seen a cookbook really taken to task. There was a big brouhaha about it, and Marian had to defend herself quite vigorously. Anytime there's a backlash from something you write, *The Times* usually checks with you to make sure you are on steady ground, and maybe Marian had to go in and back up accusations.''

Four days after Burros's devastating review a glowing feature about Martha appeared in *The Times'* Connecticut section. Written by Patricia Brooks, it gushed about Martha's bustling holiday catering business and actually raved about *Entertaining*, which Brooks effusively described as "lavishly oversized" and "full of inviting color-plates that show Bosc pears in red wine with crystallized violets crowning the top of each pear. On another page one sees tomato fettucine with snow peas that also looks good." It was the same recipe that Brooks's colleague Marian Burros had sliced and diced a few days earlier as "a strange combination.''

The lengthy feature also showed the smiling author-caterer making up Ralph Lauren's Christmas baskets in her Westport kitchen, with one of Naiad Einsel's copper cookie cutters in the foreground.

While Martha's publisher was disappointed over *The Times'* stinging review, everyone was overjoyed by the sales figures: The first printing of twenty-five thousand copies had quickly sold out. As Martha noted, "We had to reprint it immediately, so we went up to 50,000.''

To avoid future problems with defective recipes, Clarkson Potter hired a free-lance food editor, Anne de Ravel, to check all of Martha's recipes in her next two books, which were already on the burner: *Martha Stewart's Quick*

Cook, set for 1983, and *Martha Stewart's Hors d'Oeuvres*, scheduled for 1984.

"I was hired right after the whole thing about plagiarism and the review Burros did. They felt the recipes needed to be checked," said de Ravel, a former food columnist for the Hartford *Courant* who at the time was a food tester for *The New York Times'* twice-yearly *Entertaining* magazine supplement and was married to Bryan Miller. "I wasn't testing the recipes but checking on the accuracy of the ingredients and making sure that no steps were missing." De Ravel recalled that when she worked on *Martha Stewart's Hors d'Oeuvres*, she thought "the recipes were *very* sketchy. I don't think Martha really tested the recipes herself. I had to fill a lot of holes because Martha's recipes were not consistent. I warned Carolyn Hart, her editor, that while they might be accurate on paper, they might not be accurate in a kitchen. My impression was that that was all fine with Martha. All she cared about was that at the end everything was done, and it *looked* good."

Family Secrets

As a consequence of the hectic and stressful pace that accompanied her growing celebrity, Martha began suffering from more frequent and debilitating migraine headaches and long, painful menstrual periods that often caused her to take to her bed. Feeling debilitated, Martha passed on her misery to friends and coworkers who frequently bore the brunt of her wrath. Later, one described her as "the PMS poster girl from hell."

For a woman who survived on three or four hours of sleep a night and wasn't one to linger under the covers because she had too much to accomplish each day, Martha was infuriated by her monthly problems, and she wanted them eliminated.

In early 1983, with another book deadline looming, with her catering business exploding, with growing demands for her presence at cooking seminars, with speaking engagements around the country—and with more and bigger plans for the future—Martha, at the age of forty-one, decided after consulting with her doctor to have a hysterectomy, which she was convinced would make her feel better.

Dorian Parker heard about the planned surgery from Martha's mother while the two were gossiping in the catering kitchen at Turkey Hill. "She said Martha had been having terrible headaches and excessive menstruation. I'll never forget it because Martha Kostyra said, 'A hysterectomy is a marvelous thing. Oh, you can't imagine how different Martha will be afterwards. When I had mine, I can't tell you how full of energy I was afterward.' I said, 'Full of *energy*? I quit! Martha already has more energy than Superman.' "

Vicky Negrin, who had remained on talking terms with Martha despite the abuse to which she had been subjected, wasn't surprised that Martha had decided to submit to such major surgery at a relatively young age. "I always felt Martha had a terrible time with being female, with her cycle," Negrin observed. "She'd complain a lot about headaches and pain. She thought the headaches had something to do with her period. So she said, 'I'm going to get rid of the whole thing.' The feeling she gave me was that she was happy to have a hysterectomy. She didn't mind. She wasn't scared. She just wanted to get it over with so she wouldn't have those awful periods anymore and could get on with her career. She certainly didn't want to have any more children."

Martha told Clare McCully, " 'My breeding days are over. I'm not going to have any more children. I'll let them take my plumbing.' Martha told me that she had a very, very difficult pregnancy, and I was never sure whether that was true. But I don't think she liked being pregnant from what she told me. She certainly didn't like having menstrual periods. She felt it was an intrusion of nature, and so, when she had the operation, she felt she now had command over nature. I thought it was amazing the way she acted. I've had friends who have gone through that and felt like their foot was cut off, but Martha said, 'Well, *that's* done. Turn the page.' ''

Looking back years later, Dorian Parker had a different view of why Martha had decided to have the operation. "She just didn't want to be a woman anymore. She had many masculine characteristics. She was extremely aggressive about personal relationships with people. She felt, for instance, that people working for her would work better if they were competing with each other. So she would tell one person what so-and-so said about her. She set people against each other. And that's a masculine managerial characteristic. She did that with me. There were two other women working in the kitchen, and Martha would say to me, 'You know what they said about you. . . . Why don't you defend yourself?' I said, 'I don't have to defend myself from anybody.' But that was the kind of situation that Martha enjoyed because she felt that we would work harder and better if we thought we had to excel over the other person. So that made the atmosphere in her catering kitchen horrible.''

According to Norma Collier, Martha had decided to have her uterus removed but not her ovaries so she wouldn't be thrown into an early menopause.

Meanwhile, Martha's hysterectomy actually caused more dissension between the Stewarts because she had deliberately scheduled the surgery at a time when she knew Andy would be out of the country on publishing business. Upon his return she continually embarrassed and harassed him in front of others by claiming he had left her in her hour of need. "We were in the car with Martha and Andy, and she brought up the fact that he wasn't there for her when she had the operation, and he went berserk,'' revealed Janet

Horowitz. "Andy was driving, and I thought we were going to be killed because he drove off the road. He was beside himself. He *wanted* to be there for the operation, and she arranged it, manipulated it, and changed the dates so that he was out of town at the time, and that's when she went into the hospital. She kept bringing it up, and I thought Andy would go out of his mind with frustration. But the time he went off the road—that was a terrible, *terrible* experience."

When she got out of Roosevelt Hospital, Martha also vehemently complained to members of her staff because none of them came to visit her. "But no one went because no one felt close enough or intimate enough with her," Dorian Parker asserted.

Actually Martha *did* have guests during her weeklong hospitalization. Instead of relaxing, she held interviews from her bed with applicants for the newly created post of executive director of Martha Stewart, Inc. "We connected by phone, and she set a time for me to be interviewed in her hospital room," said Marinda Freeman, who got the job. "She was in bed, and that's how I was interviewed. That was *pretty* trippy. Martha *never* stops for a moment."

Observers of the Stewarts' marriage—Martha and Andy's twentieth anniversary had come and gone shortly before *Entertaining* was published—had begun wagering in private on when it would end. Andy was miserably unhappy, and Martha was interested only in becoming more famous, powerful, and rich.

During Christmas 1982 Andy fled to the wilds of Tierra del Fuego, off the southern tip of South America, to study the habits of a native animal, the guarco, leaving Martha to spend the holiday season with a sullen Lexi. Putting on a happy face for a visiting *New York Times* reporter, Martha said, "We're pouting because he's away. That's why we're having a party." The bash for "fourteen friends" included a menu of Beluga caviar—"It's Alexis's passion and my special Christmas splurge for her"—and iced vodka.

With her writing, catering, and lecturing career jumping, Martha had even less time for Andy or Lexi. Andy usually had to go begging for something to eat because Martha was too busy overseeing elegant catered meals for others. He often found himself boiling an egg for dinner at ten o'clock before going to bed alone. Because the catering business demanded so much of her time in the evenings, Martha often got home well after midnight. But instead of joining Andy, she stayed up doing paperwork, washing dishes, preparing her schedule for the next day, reading. Though she was tired, she was too wired, too stressed, and too much of an insomniac to sleep, which resulted in embarrassing moments during the day: She sometimes dozed off in the middle of a conversation or at a social engagement. Her lack of sleep also made her cranky and argumentative, which made life difficult for her employees, friends, and family members.

Like her father, Lexi was not a happy camper. Despite the fact that Martha plied her seventeen-year-old with caviar or maybe because of such coddling, the teenager acted petulent, insolent, and moody—at least in the company of her parents.

A close friend of the Stewarts' recalled watching with astonishment over lunch one day as Andy spoke "practically baby-talk" to Lexi—"Does little Lexi want a big glass of milk?"—while Martha treated her daughter like an equal, "trading sarcastic remarks, which Martha would try to laugh off."

On another occasion Martha was seated at the dining-room table boasting to dinner guests that she and Lexi were about to spend a week together at a health spa. "Not health spa; it's *fat* farm, Martha," Lexi interjected, calling her mother by her first name.

"No, no, no," Martha said. "We're going to a wonderful spa, and we're going to have massages."

"Fat farm, it's a *fat farm*," Lexi reiterated to the other guests, who were visibly embarrassed by the crossfire. "*She's* ten pounds overweight, and she looks *fat*," declared Lexi. "But *she* won't admit it."

"You're not fat, dear," the diplomatic Andy said to Martha, who glared knives back at him.

Martha's employees also observed the interaction between mother and daughter and gossiped among themselves about what a brat Lexi was, and what a failure Martha was as her mother.

"From my vantage point Martha was trying to be the dutiful textbook mother—attempting it but not getting the results," observed Rafael Rosario, who worked in the catering end. "I could see competitiveness and anger in Martha's relationship with Lexi. I could see it in both of them. Martha always was subtly implying that Lexi was *so* wonderful, and had *such* a wonderful life—and Lexi *hated* to be put on a pedestal by Martha.

"I saw Lexi's eyes glaring at Martha. I kept thinking of Ann Blythe as Vida, Joan Crawford's ungrateful and resentful daughter in *Mildred Pierce*"—which ironically also is about a housewife who becomes a driven success in the food business—the restaurant game, in Mildred's case.

"Lexi looked at Martha as the controlling mother," continued Rosario, "who plays the dutiful mother and icon around people, but isn't like that in real life. And if anyone knew what life was like at home, they'd think differently. And that's exactly the way it was."

"As successful as Martha and Andy were," observed Clare McCully, "they were totally inept as parents. Lexi was always sort of like an apostrophe in their lives. They didn't focus in on her problems at the right time in her life, and when they did give her attention, it was not the kind of attention that she probably needed or wanted."

At Putney Lexi was considered a loner, extremely shy, uncommunicative, and socially inept. "Basically," as one high school pal recalled, "Lexi didn't talk." But she excelled academically and was health conscious; she jogged and played field hockey. "But she wasn't considered cool," another classmate noted, "mainly because she didn't smoke pot, which in those days was something that was socially important."

In many ways, the classmates observed, Lexi was much like her mother. "She always worked incredibly hard, and her room was beautifully done," one of them remarked. "Lexi didn't have extravagant things, but it was obvious she had a very sophisticated sense of style. Her room was pretty hip for a seventeen-year-old kid in those days. She cooked. She did a lot of beautiful weaving. I felt she was multitalented.''

In the spring of her junior year Lexi came out of her shell a bit and started dating a classmate, Nick Dine, son of the prominent pop and expressionist artist Jim Dine. They had become friends while living in the progressive school's only coed dorm, which housed four boys and four girls, all ninth and tenth graders.

During vacations and holidays Dine usually visited Turkey Hill and stayed with Lexi in a little apartment above the garage, where she had moved after abandoning her bedroom in the hectic and still-under-renovation main house. It was during those visits that Lexi and Dine fell in love and started sleeping together.

"Martha and Andy were very good about it," Dine said later. "They were *very* hands-off parents. They let Lexi do whatever she wanted. The Stewarts were very hip, so it was really fun there. They treated me like an adult.''

The arrangement, however, shocked members of the Stewarts' inner circle. "I was there when they were both shacked up in the garage and would kind of come down, I guess between couplings, to eat a little food," George McCully said. "From what I knew, Martha and Andy never expressed any feelings of regret that Lexi was sexually active. They [Lexi and Dine] both were children of superproductive adults who basically ignored them, and they probably found a lot of mutual comfort in putting down their parents. Martha or Andy introduced me to them like this was perfectly normal as what you do in Westport, Connecticut. None of my kids would do that. But to Martha and Andy it was perfectly routine.''

Dorian Parker, who was aware of Lexi's sexual activity, said, "She did exactly as she pleased. While Martha allowed it, Lexi's grandmother—Martha Senior—was very upset about the fact that Lexi was as free as she was. It freaked her grandmother out. Lexi lived over the garage, and she had *many* boyfriends, and her grandmother didn't approve of that.''

Dine said that while he loved Lexi at the time, he found

her to be "a troubled person," which he attributed to her life growing up at Turkey Hill. "Andy was the sweetest guy, and Martha was always wonderful to me, but they both were pretty crazy, and Lexi definitely had her quirks. Andy was a very weird, obtuse kind of guy who was supershy. Lexi's personality was much closer to his; she was *very* quiet, while Martha was *so* demonstrative. She was very flamboyant and loud, and she was always the one doing the talking. Lexi would cringe when her mother talked. I felt Martha's business at home affected Lexi. Martha was just incredibly focused on her work, and that was it. When I stayed at the house, I felt like I was part of this Martha Stewart, Incorporated world.

"The most curious thing was that they were living this incredible sort of *über*-life. Everything was *so done*. But at the same time their house was uninhabitable. The kitchen was unbelievably beautiful, but the rest of the house was always being worked on. It was a mess."

Among Lexi's boyfriends after Dine was a handsome black basketball player from Columbia University, who also was accepted by Martha and Andy. "They were pretty relaxed about enforcing old-fashioned moral restraints on Lexi," explained a family intimate. "They didn't think that anything she was doing was immoral, but they did feel discomfort and concern over health issues and the possibility of pregnancy, and they didn't always like the guy.

"Martha did view many of Lexi's activities as a form of rebellion. When Lexi was dating the black guy, who was very nice and good-looking, there was some talk that she was tossing the race card in their faces. There also was a lingering concern that it could develop into a long-term relationship and end in marriage. Martha and Andy's only worry was about the problems Lexi would bring on herself by marrying someone of another race. Otherwise they didn't think of it as a problem."

When Lexi began her senior year at Putney—the same year that *Entertaining* was published—she began applying to colleges. Martha and Andy thought that George Mc-Cully, who had earned his undergraduate degree at Brown University, might be of help in getting Lexi admitted there.

"I wrote her a three-page single-spaced letter of recommendation, and I told the truth about Lexi, and she
didn't get into Brown," McCully acknowledged. "I saw a
lot of Lexi while she was growing up. I said basically that
she was intelligent, talented, and accomplished and had *survived super*talented, *super*accomplished, *super*perfectionist
parents, who were in many ways distracted from parenting
by their professional lives, and that therefore, she would be
an interesting and valuable member of the university community. But I noted that they had to realize that Lexi was
coming from an extremely attenuated atmosphere at home
and was a complicated person."

In June 1983 Lexi graduated from Putney and, according
to Nick Dine, was among the top five in a class of fifty.
That summer, at Martha's behest and against Andy's better
judgment, Lexi went to work in the photo department at
Stewart, Tabori & Chang. She showed up at the office
wearing sexy, revealing clothing, which offended the strait-
laced sensibilities of her father's elderly English secretary,
who lectured the young woman about workplace apparel.
Lexi was angered and offended and complained to Martha,
who wrongly blamed Andy for putting his secretary up to
it. Things went downhill from there, and the job was
quickly aborted.

Following in her mother's footsteps, Lexi applied to and
was admitted to Barnard, where she began classes in September 1983, just as Martha's second book was about to
roll off the presses.

A Marketable Commodity

After entertaining, Clarkson Potter put out a book a year with Martha's name and face gracing the jackets. To publishing insiders, the first few books were known in the trade as "quick and dirty"—done fast and inexpensively. Nevertheless, they became best-sellers.

Martha's second book, aptly titled *Martha Stewart's Quick Cook: Two Hundred Easy and Elegant Recipes from the Author of* Entertaining, was especially easy to get into the bookstores. If Martha's fans thought she was holed up in her studio pounding away on her IBM, as she claimed, they were dead wrong.

"We made a deal with *House Beautiful* for Martha's *Quick Cook* columns, and that book, which we felt very comfortable with because it was inexpensive to produce, sold well," publisher Carol Southern disclosed. "So the sales of *Entertaining* continued, and Martha's success just built, and we just kept going."

Using the word "entertaining" in *Quick Cook*'s subtitle was part of the promotional strategy to sell more copies of *Entertaining*. Putting Martha's face on the cover again and adding her name to the title were done to increase her recognition factor. Clarkson Potter's goal was to make her as recognizable as Betty Crocker.

"We knew we had something very special in Martha Stewart," Alan Mirken said. "She was beginning to get a reputation."

Quick Cook was written in the chatty style that Elizabeth Hawes had established in *Entertaining* and that was the model for all of Martha's subsequent books and her magazine. For instance, a brief description of Martha and Andy's experience with their weekend home in Middlefield was used as a jumping-off point in *Quick Cook* for a recipe called Salade Niçoise à la Middlefield.

To make Martha appear more down-to-earth, *Quick Cook*'s promotional copy declared: "Martha is like thousands of busy American women. She has a career and a family, and there never seems to be enough time to cook at the end of the day. . . . Martha Stewart proves that dinner in a hurry doesn't have to mean a frozen casserole heated up in the microwave. . . ."

To make it appear Martha had the wonderful marriage she had been writing about, she dedicated the book in part to Andy ". . . for tasting all the *Quick Cook* recipes."

In 1984 Potter brought out her third book, *Martha Stewart's Hors d'Oeuvres: The Creation and Presentation of Fabulous Finger Foods*. Added to the cover was a small box with the words "A Martha Stewart Food & Entertaining Book."

Her fourth book, *Martha Stewart's Pies & Tarts*, was published in 1985; by then *Entertaining* was in its fourteenth printing, with a whopping 270,000 copies sold, a phenomenal success. To show she was the loving mother she portrayed herself to be in her books, Martha dedicated her latest tome to Lexi, "who loves to make pies and tarts but never eats them." The book's jacket noted that Martha was "at work on other books in her Food & Entertaining series as well as a book on weddings."

Like the *Cherry Ames* books she had devoured in her youth, Martha now had her own scrumptious series—a goldmine for the author and her publisher. "The people at Crown and Clarkson Potter became Martha's grateful slaves," observed Dorian Parker, who also wrote a cookbook published by Potter. "I was there one day talking to my editor, and another editor rushed into the room and said, 'Martha's coming! Martha's coming!' It was as though she said God was descending."

*   *   *

With the publication of *Entertaining*, Martha overnight became the country's premier expert on "lifestyle." She had her books, her catering business, but she wanted more.

When she learned that a prestigious consulting job was open at *The New York Times*, she let her publisher and her pal at *The Times*, Anatole Broyard, know that she was interested and told them to pass the word. Martha was no stranger to *The Times,* which had done a number of feature stories about her. So when news of her interest reached the right people, Martha was invited to Forty-third Street by Carrie Donovan, the style editor of *The New York Times Magazine*. The job in question was "consultant" for a twice-yearly Sunday supplement called *Home Entertaining*. In the parlance of *The Times*, it was known as a Part Two, one in a series of special magazines that included the popular fashion issues.

The term "consultant," however, was a misnomer. While it was a free-lance position, the job called for the talents of an experienced reporter and editor who could develop story ideas; assign writers, photographers, and stylists; field-produce complex assignments; and be politically savvy enough to keep the *Times* managing editor Abe Rosenthal and the *Times Magazine* editor Ed Klein happy believers.

"It was a big job for which we paid peanuts, but Martha wanted it *badly*," recalled Donovan, who also served as senior editor in charge of the supplements. "Martha came in to see me, and I was enchanted with her. So this very beautiful and very creative person came into our lives."

But almost from the beginning Martha put *The Times* on the back burner. Once she had gotten the job and her craving for instant gratification had been sated, she turned her attention to more pressing and lucrative projects: her books and her catering company, among others.

"Martha was hard to find, wasn't there when they needed her, and she'd come breezing in and try to get everything done in a day, and they were just having heart attacks trying to meet deadlines," asserted Bryan Miller, who wrote a number of pieces for the supplement during

Martha's three-issue tenure. "For some reason they thought she was gonna roll up her sleeves and sit down like all the other minions. No way. Not Martha. So the work wasn't getting done."

Martha brought in at least one trusted friend and writer, Liz Hawes, on a free-lance basis. "Martha basically used *Times* money to try to make up for the little she paid Liz for her work on *Entertaining*," a pal stated. "And of course Liz did top-notch work, so that made Martha look good to Carrie [Donovan] and Abe [Rosenthal]."

Initially Donovan thought that Martha "produced, and what she produced was good. She seemed efficient. Her ideas were great. I can't say it was all sloppily handled." But Donovan acknowledged that difficulties began to arise. "The copy person was always hanging by the straps, waiting for copy at the very last minute. We were closing copy on an edition, and one of the assistants came to me with a list of names of women and asked me if I knew who any of them were. I didn't. And she said these women had called and said that Martha had promised that they would get credit for styling. I'd never heard of them, and I said it was too late to get their names in. How Martha resolved that was none of my business.

"And Martha wasn't liked by certain people at *The Times*. Marian Burros didn't like her. Marian and [food writer] Mimi Sheraton were always stewing around and saying that Martha's recipes didn't stand up." However, a piece by Burros, "A Taste of Summer," appeared in Martha's first issue, and Sheraton's "Cool Green Tastes for Warm Days" ran in the second. "Martha loved it, just loved it," a *Times*man recalled. "Here were members of the food Mafia whom Martha despised, and who despised Martha, and now in essence they were turning in *Home Entertaining* assignments to her. Martha was gloating."

Privately, though, Martha was telling friends how much she resented the food people at *The Times* and how difficult they were making her life there. "She felt that she had been blackballed by Marian Burros and that Marian was after her, and that Marian and her friends were putting Martha down behind her back and complaining about her because she wasn't really a trained chef but a mere caterer," Clare McCully said. "That *really* got to Martha. She said she was having just terrible fights with *The New York Times* staff, that she found it very difficult to work with them."

One cover story that Carrie Donovan desperately wanted for the magazine involved a dinner of the St. Andrew's Society, dedicated to Scotland's patron saint. Donovan arranged for someone to lend *The Times* a grand home with an enormous paneled dining room so that twenty kilt-wearing members of the club could be photographed having an elegant dinner. That assignment, according to photographer Richard Jeffery, who shot the dinner, was about to spell thirty—the end, in reporter jargon—for Martha's career at *The Times*.

"Martha was there overseeing the story, and we were busy shooting, and when we finished, she had disappeared," Jeffery recalled. "Part of her job was to make sure the house was left as we had found it but Martha split, and there was no one left to clean up, so myself, my assistant, the free-lance art director, and a girl who worked for Martha stayed until three or four in the morning cleaning the place. There was no excuse for her to leave like that, and she never gave anyone an explanation. Carrie found out about it."

After discussions with Rosenthal and Klein, Donovan said she was forced to let Martha go. "I just thought she was going so crazy with all the things she had to do. I even had to track her down and call her in some place like Denver, where she was doing a book promotion or something. I said, 'Martha, it's too crazy. I think we can pull this off somehow a little more easily using someone else.' She was disappointed, but that was it."

Martha never disclosed that she had been sacked by *The Times* but told everyone she had left because of her books and catering commitments. *The Times* people also remained mum. For Martha, though, her short stay at the paper of record was extremely beneficial: The job gave her enormous credibility in the publishing world, new and invaluable journalistic contacts—and a hot book idea.

*   *   *

While on location for *The Times* in New Orleans overseeing a feature on the outdoor cooking of Paul Prudhomme, chef and owner of K-Paul's, a popular local restaurant, Martha decided that a book on the pleasures of outdoor entertaining could be a winner. Returning from bayou country, she excitedly pitched the idea to Andy, rather than to her own publisher, with whom she had an exclusive contract. Visions of a best-seller for Stewart, Tabori & Chang danced in Andy's head. As an aggressive publisher he had watched enviously as Clarkson Potter and the Crown Publishing Group raked in big bucks from the sale of his wife's books, and he coveted a piece of her publishing action. But Crown's contract had Martha sealed up tighter than a tin of caviar.

With nothing to lose, Andy approached Alan Mirken and asked for permission to publish an outdoor entertaining book with Martha. Mirken said he'd allow "*input* from Martha" but would not permit her to be identified as the author, nor would he allow the use of the word "entertaining" in the title.

Andy was delighted. Elizabeth Sahatjian, who wrote for *Cuisine*, was quickly contracted to write the manuscript in collaboration with Martha, an arrangement similar to the one Martha had had with Elizabeth Hawes. "We would sit in her kitchen or talk by telephone, and she would tell me stories and anecdotes and supply the recipes," said Sahatjian. "The book and concept were her idea, but she told me that she couldn't actually do the book because of a contractual problem."

For Andy, the project ran into a roadblock when Richard Jeffery, the photographer who had shot most of the pictures on assignment for *The Times* and owned the copyrights, demanded fair compensation for his work. Andy had hoped to get the pictures for little or no cost. "Andy told me that Martha was getting half the royalties," Jeffery said. "I told him *I* wanted half and he said, 'Well, we're not going to do the book.' I said, 'Well, you can't because I own the film. If you don't give me half the royalties, I'm not going to let you use my film.' That took care of that, and he agreed. He knew he didn't have a book without my photos.''

Meanwhile several additional scenes had to be shot, including the cover photo. "When we got to San Francisco for the shoot, Martha settled us into a very nice hotel," Jeffery recalled. "But the next day she made us move to a cheaper hotel because she thought it was too much money for Andy to spend. Both of them were *very* funny about money.''

In 1985, Stewart, Tabori & Chang published *Outdoor Pleasures: Picnics, Parties and Portable Feasts*, by Elizabeth Sahatjian. But the book had Martha Stewart's imprint all over it. Andy had put Martha's name on the cover as "consultant," and the book opened with a signed introduction by her. There was even a photograph of the smokehouse at Turkey Hill, which was becoming a familiar location to readers of Martha's books.

"*Outdoor Pleasures* clearly was a Martha Stewart book— even without her face on the jacket," a publishing executive involved in the project later observed. "Andy had stretched Martha's involvement for name recognition purposes as far as he could without pissing off Alan Mirken.''

But Mirken liked *Outdoor Pleasures* so much that he subsequently reprinted it at Abbeville Press, changing the title to *Outdoor Entertaining* to "take advantage of the fact that Martha had done the introduction.''

Because Martha was making herself into such a marketable commodity, everyone seemed to want a piece of her, including the old-line British foodstuffs firm of Crabtree & Evelyn, whose executives believed that having Martha's name on the cover of the company's first cookbook would mean a classy best-seller. But their decision to get involved with her turned out to be yet another "very unpleasant, difficult, and complex situation," as a key participant in the book project described it years later.

In 1985, Crabtree & Evelyn sponsored an exhibition of modern illustration at the Cooper-Hewitt Museum in Manhattan. Martha's company had been contracted to cater the opening night's gala "black and white" theme party.

As usual, Martha's team of cooks, stylists, and servers turned in a stellar performance. Elizabeth Kent, Crabtree & Evelyn's advertising and public relations director, and Peter Windett, the firm's designer, were awestruck by the presentation. "It just took our breath away," Kent said.

For more than a year the Crabtree & Evelyn people had been discussing doing a cookbook that would highlight the company's reputation and style. During those meetings Martha Stewart's name had constantly come up, and the consensus was that she, more than anyone in the food world, could produce the kind of exquisite book to which the company would give its imprimatur. The Crabtree people soon would learn Martha's secret: She did little, if any, of the actual work.

On the evening of the black and white party, Kent found herself standing next to Martha and took advantage of the situation to broach the cookbook idea. Martha's ears pricked up instantly, and she indicated that she would be interested. In fact she even suggested the perfect publisher for such a project. Kent, who knew Clarkson Potter published Martha, was surprised when Martha named Stewart, Tabori & Chang.

A meeting followed shortly thereafter at Andy's office. Martha agreed to all the stipulations, and not long after a deal was cut for the *Crabtree & Evelyn Cookbook*. The contract called for Martha to write it and Stewart, Tabori & Chang to publish it. "We were very smitten by Martha," Kent stated. "Her books were gorgeous, and we just thought she was the perfect person to do it, and we were just all so enthusiastic about the project."

After the Crabtree & Evelyn people went on their merry way—having agreed to pay Martha a sizable royalty in exchange for her writing and creative expertise—she picked up the phone and called Brooke Dojny, a talented food writer, who had worked for Martha Stewart, Inc., some five years earlier. Without Crabtree & Evelyn's knowledge, Martha was about to farm out the writing job to Dojny and a colleague, Melanie Barnard, neither of whom had ever written a book before, and pay them a modest writing fee for work Martha was under contract to perform.

As Dojny explained later, "Martha's contract with Crown precluded her from authoring the book, so she hired Melanie and me to do the recipes, and then she just kind of turned the whole thing over to us, and we just checked in periodically with her. Her involvement in the book was really quite minimal."

While Dojny and Barnard were hard at work, *Newsweek* did a feature on the amazing Martha Stewart success story. In it, she boasted that *she* was in the process of writing the *Crabtree & Evelyn Cookbook*. The story noted critically that Martha also was associated with Perrier-Jouët champagne, Sterling Vineyards, and Aga stoves and went on to quote an unnamed food writer as saying, "If you have any editorial credibility, you don't go near a product. If you ask a good chef during a demonstration what knife sharpener he's using, he'll say, 'See me afterward, I don't endorse.' "

Headlined THE ART OF SHOWING OFF—WHAT MAKES MARTHA STEWART COOK? IT ISN'T HER APPETITE, IT'S HER AMBITION, reporter Laura Shapiro's article charged that Martha's "quick domination over a crowded [cookbook] field" had "little to do with good eating" and that her elaborate recipes were conceived "to impress an audience that wants to admire food . . . it's what one food writer calls 'competitive entertaining. . . .' " Martha called the *Newsweek* story "horrible."

The Crabtree & Evelyn people meanwhile were in for quite a surprise when they got their hands on the first draft of Martha's manuscript. "It was incredible," Elizabeth Kent stated, still annoyed years later. "Right at the top of the page it said, 'From the Kitchen of Brooke Dojny and Melanie Barnard.' After reading it, we immediately had a meeting with Martha and Andy to say, 'Look, we think this is all too complicated, and nobody's ever going to cook these recipes, and if they do, they're never going to cook them again.' We realized that if Martha had seen the manuscript, it had been only briefly because she didn't know what was in the book. She just looked at us blankly.

"The one thing that Martha never dreamed we would do

was go off and try all the recipes. All of a sudden we were hearing that they were taking forever to shop for and cook. I spent a long time with the book, and thought it would be a dinosaur before it was even published. One recipe required you to cook several pounds of tortellini and put it in a bowl, so you had wet tortellini when you were done. And then you were supposed to fill them with egg salad. Well, you can imagine what happened: The guests picked up these wet and clammy tortellinis and took a bite, and the egg salad shot out the other side!''

Back at Crabtree & Evelyn's American headquarters, in Woodstock, Connecticut, the company's owner, Cyrus Harvey, was having a conniption, furious that Martha had pulled a fast one. ''I called Andy, and I said, 'I want Martha's name taken off the book; we're going to do it ourselves.' I tried to get out of the contract. I offered Andy Stewart money to let us out of the contract, and he said, 'No, it's going to be our book of the year.' We finally wound up doing the book ourselves, and it was a sensation. Stewart, Tabori and Chang hardly lifted a finger. We did all the marketing. The whole book ended up being Crabtree and Evelyn's work. It was totally ours. Martha Stewart's name was purposefully left off, but she got a substantial royalty and continues to get one because the book still sells.'' After all the problems had been resolved, the cookbook was published in 1989 and eventually sold more than a hundred thousand copies.

''The last thing in the world we anticipated when we got into this project was that we would have trouble with Martha Stewart,'' declared Elizabeth Kent. ''At that point we were thrilled to have a contract with her. Later, we felt it was very unprofessional of her to undertake a project and not really care about the outcome. And it's really amoral that she would accept royalties on a book that she virtually had nothing to do with.''

Turkey Hell

At Turkey Hill revenues from Martha's catering business were fast approaching seven figures annually, much of it attributable to her growing fame, the attendant publicity, and the indisputable fact that she was running a tight ship with a hardworking, creative crew. However, a number of people associated with Martha during the mid-eighties before she scuttled the business altogether for bigger and better ventures often compared that ship with the USS *Caine*.

While there was never an inquiry about missing strawberries, Martha did conduct a probe to find the perpetrator who had marred the stainless steel on one of her stoves by cleaning it with Brillo. "Martha wanted all her equipment cosmetically mint," a former colleague stated. "And if it wasn't, it was wacko time. One time she came marching into the kitchen in her safari jacket, conducted an inspection, and discovered a couple of scratches and some marring on the stainless steel. She was furious, and everyone was scared to death. She came up to each of us. 'Who did this? I'm going to get to the bottom of this! Someone's going to pay.' No one would admit anything. She was absolutely livid. After she left, we all nervously laughed. It was a scene right out of *The Caine Mutiny*. She was like Captain Queeg in drag."

Martha was overseeing a crew of about thirty who were filling twig baskets with various kinds of breads for a party when she noticed that one young woman hadn't placed a slice of rye in precisely the right spot. "She had a shit fit," a former employee remembered. "She screamed at the girl, 'You have *ruined* this party!' And then she proceeded to dress down this girl in front of everybody until the young woman was in tears."

When a new assistant cook snapped a knife blade while boning a leg of lamb, fear gripped the rest of the kitchen crew, who knew how violently Martha reacted when one of her implements was broken or damaged and had to be replaced. The kitchen supervisor turned ashen and told the frightened offender, "Just take the blade and bury it in the trash. Don't mention this to anyone. For your sake, forget it ever happened."

No one, not even her mother, escaped Martha's wrath. Martha Sr., who sometimes helped out in the catering kitchen, was chopping vegetables when Martha strutted in for a surprise inspection. "*Mother!*" Martha bellowed, scaring the elderly woman half to death. "Look what you're doing!" Martha was infuriated because Mrs. Kostyra had accidentally dropped a few pieces of the carrot she was slicing on the cement floor that Martha had had covered with deck paint so that it always looked immaculate.

On a catering job one of Martha's chefs and Martha's mother were working side by side wrapping prosciutto around figs. The chef, a young woman, was asking the stolid matriarch about the hearty Eastern European cooking for which she was known. But their pleasant conversation was interrupted when Martha swooped down on them, examined their work, declared it sloppy and unacceptable, and demanded that they start over. "And don't ask my mother about any of this," Martha barked at the chef. "All she knows how to cook is peasant food." After Martha exited, the chef looked over at a hurt and embarrassed Martha Sr. "Oh, it's okay, dear," she said. "Martha's just Martha." The impression the cook came away with was that the mother was used to being verbally abused by the daughter.

Martha knew precisely how to get to her mother. When they bickered in front of the staff, Martha often attacked the Kostyra family roots that she has reminisced about and mythologized for her public. "Nutley was a stupid place," she'd say in a fit of anger. "I hated Nutley, and that stupid little house, and that little kitchen."

If Martha wasn't picking on her mother, she was bickering with siblings. One Thanksgiving she threw a tantrum when she learned her sister Kathy Evans was having a competing turkey dinner at her house in Greenwich. "Martha was very angry and she left a message on the machine at Kathy's using truly foul language like the f-word," a relative disclosed. "Kathy heard the message and then asked all of us to listen to it. Kathy said, 'I just can't believe this girl.' She thought Martha's message was repulsive and uncalled for. As I recall, Martha said, 'If you and your son-of-a-bitch husband want to have dinner *there,* that's just fine and dandy with me. I don't care. You're all just jealous of what I've done with myself, jealous of my success.' My mouth just dropped open. I thought, 'This is Miss Martha?' It was a shocker."

One of Martha's more bizarre relationships was with Marinda Freeman, an attractive blonde in her early thirties, who had been running a lucrative business selling gourmet desserts to restaurants, stores, and caterers when she was brought on board as the forty-thousand-dollar-a-year executive director of Martha Stewart, Inc. The job entailed overseeing the business end of the catering operation, along with arranging Martha's exploding travel and lecture schedules.

"My initial take on Martha was, 'Oh, here's somebody I can work with and I can relate to,' " Freeman stated years later. However, she was aware of Martha's quirky side, the staff morale problems, Martha's marital difficulties, and her terrible relationship with Lexi. And there were things about Martha that upset her. For instance, she heard from staffers that Martha sometimes kept the tips that satisfied clients gave to her to distribute to the catering staff.

"Martha would try to hedge by saying that the client had never given her tip money," asserted Rafael Rosario, Martha's party coordinator at the time. "But I challenged Martha. I said I spoke to Mrs. So-and-So, and she was so effusive about how the party worked out and how the staff was wonderful and that she was certainly going to call Martha and okay tips for us. But Martha denied it. This happened a number of times.'' Freeman claimed that on occasion Martha pocketed the money and instead gave the staff leftover food.

But Freeman was a professional who tried to look beyond all that. She believed she had found a creative, entrepreneurial environment to work in and figured that if she kept her nose clean, she and Martha would have a fruitful relationship.

Then the letters began arriving. ''Within the first six months after I started working there, Martha began writing me these two- and three-page single-spaced typed letters that were raving, belittling, saying just awful, nasty, off-the-wall things about me personally,'' Freeman asserted. ''The letters contained wicked attacks, some of which involved criticism of my job, but most of which were on a personal level and had nothing to do with my professionalism. I would be reduced to tears.

''Her modus operandi was always to attack after the fact, never to inform before. I never knew if I was supposed to be doing something or not doing something. It was only after the fact that she'd write these letters and say I was 'stupid' and 'a jerk.' I thought, 'Excuse me? Where did this come from? Business is booming right along, and then it's like this wham-o from outer space.' It was like a Jekyll and Hyde thing.''

Freeman showed the letters to a colleague who had been affiliated with Martha since the Market Basket days in the late seventies. ''The letters *were* upsetting,'' the woman, who read them, acknowledged. ''Knowing Martha,'' she observed later, ''it looked like she had a plan in writing them. In my opinion, it looked like she was trying to force Marinda to leave and was driving her out of there.''

For almost two years from the time she got Martha's first missive, Freeman rode an emotional roller coaster of good and bad times. ''There were periods I would think Martha was really normal, and I would laugh and carry on with her and have conversations and have meetings,'' Freeman said. ''And then she would turn and be nasty and leave me more letters. I was always left wondering what was going on until

I finally got it: A snake is a snake. It took the longest time for me to get that message.''

Just as the colleague had predicted, Martha gave Freeman the heave-ho, and her firing came in an appropriately off-the-wall manner. Martha and Freeman were sitting at desks at opposite ends of the business office of Martha Stewart, Inc., so that their backs were facing. Freeman was on the phone booking a flight for her boss with the woman at Martha's travel agency. ''All of a sudden Martha picked up the extension and started screaming into the phone at me at the top of her lungs, saying that I wasn't handling the reservation correctly. The woman on the other end must have thought we were all nuts. So I just hung up the phone, stood up, turned to Martha, who looked like a madwoman, a crazy person, a woman who was not rational, and said, 'I am not going to put up with your behavior anymore,' and I walked out the door.'' Martha promised to pay her two weeks' severance, but when Freeman asked for the money, Martha put her off and then sent her a check for only one week's salary. That didn't surprise Freeman, who claimed Martha had alienated many of her vendors by not paying them or by mistreating them.

Meanwhile, when Freeman applied for unemployment compensation, Martha tried to block her from getting benefits. ''She started a stink. She harassed me. It was a real hassle. I had to get a lawyer. She didn't win because she didn't show up for the final hearing. In my whole life I've never come across anyone who was this lousy to people.''

In the half dozen years since she had started catering, Martha had developed a magic formula that quickly turned her operation into a cash cow. Martha was quite willing to share her secrets for success with Clare McCully, who was starting her own catering business and was serving an informal apprenticeship at Turkey Hill. Among Martha's tips was to charge clients an enormous markup. When McCully said she didn't think she could get away with that, Martha boasted, ''Well, people are dying to have Martha Stewart cater their affairs. They'll pay anything I ask.''

Another of Martha's pointers had to do with the type of

personnel hired to staff the parties. Her criteria for selecting
waiters, which Martha spelled out in great detail, came as
a shock to McCully. "Martha had a lot of unemployed
actors working for her, good-looking, gorgeous guys,"
McCully said. "It was a hoot for them because they would
play different roles. One would play Eduard for the night,
and he'd take on that particular persona. They were hoping
that while working at the fancy events Martha was catering,
they might run into a director or producer and get an acting
job."

McCully thought the waiters were fun and interesting
and indeed perfect for the role. Martha explained that there
was a very simple reason why a number of young men she
hired worked out so well. " 'They're my little gay boys,' "
Martha told McCully. " 'I have a crew of faggots—didn't
you know?—and that's one of the keys to my success.'
Martha would watch them and laugh and say, 'Clare, when
you start your business you have got to hire them. They're
the best. They make such wonderful waiters.'

"It was clear to me from things she said that Martha had
a real hang-up about gays, a real vindictive, vicious side to
her about them. She'd watch them carrying trays out of the
kitchen, and when they were gone, she'd pick up a tray and
imitate them, sort of mincing and saying, 'My, look how
my little gay boys primp and preen.' They were like toys
and amusements to her. I really came to believe that Martha
was a man hater. *Big time*."

Staffers too thought there was a streak of homophobia
in Martha. As former party coordinator Rafael Rosario,
who was gay, noted, "Martha's a bright woman, a successful businessperson, but she's also *very* provincial. She
wouldn't have made the same comments to me that she
made to Clare, but she was *always* condescending."

He recalled how Martha became upset if particular waiters were what she described as "overly effeminate." She
would instruct Rosario to have them "tone it down" because she believed their appearance made her clients "feel
ill at ease and put them off," he said. "I just laughed and
said, 'Well, we may be gay, but we're doing the job.' "
On one occasion Rosario arrived at a catering event wear-

ing a white dinner jacket and a powder blue antique tuxedo shirt. "Martha said, 'Your outfit looks so gay.' I said I thought it was coordinated. She glared at me and said, 'Oh.' But she wouldn't step over a line with me."

On a number of occasions Martha had locked horns with Rosario's predecessor, Guy Alexander, who was eventually fired after a big blowout. He subsequently died of AIDS. "I don't know if AIDS was an issue with Martha and Guy," said Rosario. "But Martha *was* concerned about it. She wondered whether her waiters should wear gloves or shouldn't be handling food. She threw it out to see what I'd say. It was in the back of her mind.

"Guy was adamant about how things should be done. They had shouting matches, and Guy was very angry at Martha and was trying to make Martha see reason. They butted heads once too often, and she fired him. When Martha hired me, Guy told me, 'You're going to have to swallow a lot and bend with her.' I found that if you let Martha initially walk over you without speaking up, she'll eventually screw you."

Martha's remarks about gays had surprised Clare McCully, who had never thought of her as having prejudices. After all, she was a Polish American who had overcome the kind of supposed discrimination her father had blamed for his own failures. So McCully was taken aback even more when she also heard Martha making disparaging comments about her South American household help.

In 1979 Martha had hired her first housekeeper, Necy Fernandes, a bright, competent, and efficient Brazilian immigrant, who came in to clean and run errands one or two days a week. Martha treated Fernandes relatively well, and the mistress of the house and her servant developed a good working relationship. Over the years Fernandes became a loyal assistant.

When Martha mentioned that she needed help in her garden, Fernandes recommended a young man named Selso, who had recently arrived from Brazil and spoke little, if any, English. Because he didn't have a place to live, Martha let him stay in a tiny room under the barn. "He was en-

thusiastic but uneducated, a sweet fellow,'' said a friend of
the Stewarts', ''and Martha treated him like dog shit. She
was constantly abusing him verbally, talking down to him,
treating him miserably, almost like a slave on a plantation.
She would insult him to his face. She underpaid him. It was
pretty horrifying and heartbreaking.

''But he did what Martha told him to do. He tried very
hard and was very dedicated and very proud when he did
something good. But she was *so* mean to him that he was
having a virtual breakdown. Selso finally left in tears one
day after about three years. He just couldn't stand working
for her anymore. He said Martha was killing him.''

After he left, Fernandes introduced Martha to the Abreau
brothers, Renato and Renaldo, also Brazilians. ''They were
all very conscientious workers, but Martha used to make
fun of them behind their backs,'' McCully recalled. ''Once
we were standing in the closed-in porch, looking out toward
the pool area where they were working, and she said, 'Look
at them. Those are my little gringos.' She said it as if they
were her 'darkies.' I cringed. I knew they were grateful for
the work, and it was a lovely place to work at, but I wondered if they knew how she really felt about them.''

Morale was low too because of the way Martha treated
Andy. Staff members felt it was difficult to maintain any
kind of respect or decorum when they'd see her treating
her husband, as one ex-staffer put it, ''like a dog turd. We
were all bystanders, and it was truly disgusting.''

''Andy was sort of this dreamboat figure,'' a chef said.
''He was very sweet and kind of bumbling, and Martha
was always shrieking at him. This one day she was hollering for him to do something for her, and we watched out
the window. She came tearing out of the house. Andy was
down on his knees working in the garden with his Walkman
on, and Martha was standing at the top of the slope with
her hands on her hips, shrieking, 'Andy! Andy! Get your
ass up here this minute! I have other work for you to do.'

''Another time Martha was standing at the stove, and
Andy came up and put his hands on her shoulders in a very
affectionate gesture, and she just sort of turned into an ici-

cle. He dropped his hands to his sides and walked away. It was really awful. I remember thinking, 'Oh, my God, I shouldn't be here. This is not a pretty sight.' She busted his chops continually, and she didn't care who saw it.''

At times like that, when Martha didn't want to be bothered by her husband, she'd tell him to "go talk to Robyn," Robyn Fairclough, Martha's trusted young flower consultant and all-around helper. ''Martha encouraged Andy to spend time with Robyn,'' a close associate stated. ''Martha kept pushing them together, saying, 'Andy, talk to Robyn. You two have so much in common.' '' Another colleague recalled Martha's saying on a number of occasions, ''You two would be just *perfect* together.'' Martha, who had acknowledged Robyn's work in *Martha Stewart's Hors d'Oeuvres* and in *Martha Stewart's Pies & Tarts*, later charged that Fairclough was the woman who stole her honey.

During the summer of 1985 the people from Aga, for whom Martha acted as a spokesperson, came to Turkey Hill with a crew to shoot a promotional film of the domesticity diva extolling the virtues of their stoves. To make it appear for the cameras that there was a party going on, Martha pulled together a group of friends, neighbors, and her kitchen crew, had them all dress up, and posed them sitting near the pool. But while the cameras rolled, Martha got into a fight with Andy.

''She was really going after him, and they were going back and forth at each other, and the director had to stop the cameras several times until Martha cooled down,'' a member of the kitchen staff recalled. ''Everyone on the set wanted to fade in the background. The members of the film crew, who had no idea what in hell was going, were laughing their asses off. They thought it was some sort of joke.''

One summer weekend George and Clare McCully accepted an invitation from the Stewarts to spend a relaxing weekend at Turkey Hill. As usual, though, Martha expected Andy to perform all his chores before he could have any fun. George McCully joined Andy in his labors in the garden, working under the boiling sun for several hours, with plans to play tennis afterward. Around one o'clock they cleaned up, got in Andy's car, and left for the courts.

In the house Martha was stewing. She groused to Clare McCully that Andy would take more than the hour she had allotted to him for his play time, thus avoiding other chores and errands she had scheduled for him for the remainder of the day. "Within five minutes of their leaving, Martha said, 'They're going to take advantage of the situation. I know it. And we won't see them again until five o'clock.' "

McCully, who had been witness to a number of Martha's tirades against Andy, tried to calm her. But Martha, who was compulsively scrubbing pans in the kitchen, was growing increasingly agitated. Finally she couldn't stand it any longer. " 'Come on, we're going to get them.' I said, 'Martha, don't be ridiculous. This is silly. They've been gone only fifteen minutes.' I thought she was being crazy, but I started to go and get the car seat for my son, Philip, because I didn't want to argue with her. But she said, 'We don't have time for that. We have to find them right now.' "

Seeing Martha's fury building, McCully was concerned about riding with her, particularly since little Philip wouldn't be safely secured in a car seat. "Just get in," Martha demanded, and then tore out of the driveway. "I didn't feel safe. She was driving like a crazy woman. I felt my personal safety, and my son's, were in jeopardy. We sped down the street, and Martha pulled into a driveway. I saw this gray-haired man mowing his lawn, and I thought he looked familiar. He turned around, and it was Paul Newman. Martha rolled down the window and yelled, 'Have you seen Andy?' Because of the way Martha was acting, he must have thought there was an emergency. He looked concerned, and he said, 'No, Martha, I haven't seen him. What's up? Is there something wrong?' And Martha said, 'Well, Andy and this woman's husband have gone off to play tennis, and I've got to find them because I know they're going to play all afternoon, and I have things for Andy to do.' Paul gave Martha a look like he'd heard the stories about her, and started backing away from the car, saying, 'No. Sorry. Haven't seen him. Hope you find them.' "

Martha raced out of Newman's driveway on two wheels

and flew down to the next neighbor, who had a tennis court, but Andy and George weren't there either. Furious, Martha began running stop signs and finally screeched to a halt in the parking lot of the country club. She went from court to court, with no luck.

"She came back to the car and she said, like some detective, 'But they *were* here, I *know* it. . . . We'll find them even if it takes all day.' It was like she was on a mission to ruin Andy's afternoon. I thought, 'This woman's a true control freak, and she's *real* crazed.'

"We flew back to the Stewarts' and pulled into the driveway, and she was *really* angry. She slammed the door and I got Philip out and I'm walking up to the house behind Martha—and there are Andy and George on the veranda having a beer. As soon as Andy saw Martha, he popped up like a piece of toast because he'd been caught red-handed relaxing, and he started apologizing to her. And George, who is probably the only person on earth who has ever told Martha to go fuck herself, was sitting there with a defiant look on his face as if to say, 'What? We played tennis, and we're having a beer. What are you going to do about it?' Then Martha started in on Andy. 'Where the hell have you been?' And Andy was apologizing to her. 'Right, Martha, I'll change my clothes, and I'll get back to work.' He walked into the house, and Martha said, 'See, they spent more time than they should have.' And I looked at my watch and it was one minute after two o'clock. They'd been gone the allotted hour. Martha followed Andy into the house, and she started screaming at him. I said to George, 'Can we go home? This is not fun.' The whole scene was very scary."

While the interpersonal activities within the confines of Turkey Hill played like a bizarre soap opera, the business side of Martha's catering operation was under intense scrutiny by local authorities who for a number of reasons were not smitten with the queen of domesticity's commercial style.

Officials of the town of Westport, who had been keeping an eye on the goings-on at the Stewart place for some time, had decided that the madame of Turkey Hill and her husband were running an illegal house of catering.

On a Thursday evening in late February 1985 Martha arrived home from Houston, where she had given a two-day fifteen-hundred-dollar-a-pop-plus-expenses seminar on home entertaining, to find a summons ordering her to appear in the Bridgeport, Connecticut, Superior Court on the following Monday. Martha claimed that the sheriff was a "horribly rude" man who had "pushed his way" through the door. "It was a nice homecoming," she said angrily. "I couldn't sleep all night."

Martha wasn't surprised by the legal action, claiming she had suffered "harassment" for several years from zoning officials making unannounced visits to her home. But she was shocked that she was being charged with operating an illegal home catering service because a few months earlier she had moved her operation out of the house into space at 10 Saugatuck Avenue, in Westport. But the town attorney, G. Kenneth Bernhard, still maintained that Martha didn't have the required zoning permits to operate a "full-scale" catering business in her home. Martha denounced the whole action as "a grave assault on cottage industry . . . an unconstitutional move on the part of the town and an invasion of my privacy."

She claimed that Westport officials were going after her because she was famous, and that they were attempting to deprive her of the joy of cooking. She maintained she needed the many stoves in her house to photograph pictures for her books, and what's more, she felt she had the right to have as many stoves as she wanted. "If I wanted ten kitchens, I should be able to have them," she proclaimed. "Stoves are part of my art."

And if the town didn't like it, well, Martha threatened to sue all of Westport.

Through the spring both sides engaged in legal combat. To counter public opinion, Martha turned on the charm and gave a press conference. "It seems once you've made *The New York Times*, they seem to watch you a lot closer," she declared. "But I don't think this will hurt my reputation." Then she took local reporters on a tour of Turkey Hill to show them that nothing illegal was going on. The local papers had a field day. Headlines blared: AUTHOR DISPUTES TOWN CHARGES; LEGAL ACTION UPSETS WESTPORT CATERER; KITCHEN CONTROVERSY SIMMERING; HEARING IS DELAYED AGAIN FOR STEWART; CATERER'S SUIT HEADED FOR THE BACK BURNER?

The battle, which at one point seemed headed for a trial, was settled out of court in June 1985. Andy drafted an agreement acceptable to town officials and the court. The Stewarts agreed not to do any more catering work at the house. Furthermore, they promised not to use the studio garage (which Lexi had used as an apartment) as a separate residence; the town claimed the apartment constituted a violation of zoning laws. They also agreed to disconnect the gas line to the upstairs stove, and Andy promised to connect the garage permanently to the main house so that it could not be considered a separate structure. Finally, the town won the right to inspect the Stewarts' estate after giving reasonable notice. The Stewarts were allowed to keep their basement kitchen in the main house and use the studio as their main kitchen. All seemed peaceful, at least for the moment, at what friends and associates had dubbed "Turkey Hell."

I Ought to Be in Pictures

From the beginning Martha's goal was to be on television. "I'd trade my mother to be on the tube" was a constant refrain.

The *Today* show gave her early national exposure when Willard Scott, the goofy weather guy, was assigned to Turkey Hill a couple of times to do features on the lifestyle lady. For example, bleary-eyed viewers across the country were treated to live coverage of the seemingly happy Stewarts having their morning coffee together, views of their exotic gardens, and the lady of the house prepping the Thanksgiving holiday bird.

But what Martha desperately wanted was her *own* show. With a generous introduction from Norma Collier, who'd been put through the Veg-O-Matic over the years by her friend, Martha met a Washington, D.C., television executive, Peter Murray, who thought he could successfully package her. "I told Peter, 'I'll introduce you to her, but be careful that she doesn't screw you,' " Collier recalled. "Peter said, 'Oh, Norma, I never thought you were the type to be so jealous. Why would you say that?' And I said, 'Peter, if she screws you because you haven't been careful, I'm just going to say I told you so.' And within six months Peter called me up and said, 'That bitch!' And I said, 'Ah, told you so.' "

At the time Murray was president of Wetacom, the production arm of WETA-TV, the public broadcasting station in the nation's capital. While Wetacom was generating a lot of production business, none of it was very visible. Murray and his boss, Ward Chamberlain, president of WETA, chairman of Wetacom, and a big gun in public television, had been searching for the kind of original programming that was coming out of the production units of the stations in New York and Boston. Both thought Martha was the answer to their problem.

"When *Entertaining* came out, Martha seemed like a natural for television," Murray observed later. "The momentum had taken over. The country's interest in Martha Stewart had come alive because she was so well produced by herself and by Andy. The production values in *Entertaining* were *enormous*. It was a very attractive package. The Stewarts really knew what they were doing in terms of product, and the product *wasn't* entertaining: It was Martha Stewart herself. And they had that in mind from the beginning. Certainly Martha Stewart had that in mind."

After Murray met Martha, he came to the conclusion that "she was a crazy, extremely focused, extremely driven, hardworking person who was just single-minded about becoming a big success. Martha was extremely aware of what she had created with *Entertaining* and who she created it for. She saw herself as a *personality*, so television is what it had to be for her. Getting on television is what drove her. She had TV on her mind all along. *That* I know. She sure as hell didn't see herself as a caterer."

Murray, who'd heard lots of horror stories about Martha over the years, had an informal meeting or two with her and came away actually liking the woman. "She was charming and fun," he said.

In fact, during the time they were talking about getting together on a possible TV project, he escorted her to a fancy black-tie benefit in Washington attended by George Bush, then Ronald Reagan's vice-president. It was at that event that Murray saw Martha, the operator, in action for the first time.

"Every countess in the place, Martha knew who they were, and was up next to them every second," he recalled. "She has enormous confidence and terrific skills in being charming to whom she wants to be charming. When George Bush walked in, she made a beeline to him, immediately got the photographer, and said, 'Excuse me, Mr. Vice-President, but would you have your picture taken with me?' Obviously at an event like that Martha's all business.''

During one of their initial get-togethers at Turkey Hill, Martha told Murray enthusiastically, ''If you want to see what's going on, come with me.'' A few days later the two flew to Boston, where Martha had a speaking engagement. Already a true believer, Murray was left staggered by what he had witnessed in Beantown. ''She was promoting her book in a museum and there were a couple of hundred women there and these women all *looked* like her,'' he said, still amazed years later. ''It was *incredible*. If there were such a thing as middle-aged, upscale women groupies, Martha had them as followers. And that was an *amazing* target audience. I watched her play to those women, and I watched the audience, and it was as if they were undergoing a religious experience.''

Murray returned to Wetacom headquarters, briefed Ward Chamberlain, and got the green light to cut a development deal with their newfound messiah. ''Peter had what was a hell of a good idea, which was to involve Martha in a program with us,'' Chamberlain said.

Shortly before *Quick Cook* was published, a series of meetings was held between Murray and the Stewarts, with Andy acting as Martha's agent. Wetacom wanted exclusive television rights to Martha, with the objective of producing a lifestyle program and selling it to a national sponsor. ''Martha didn't approach TV like 'Gee, maybe I'll get lucky and get a TV show,' '' Murray gathered from his conversations with her. ''It was: 'I *am* going to have a television show, and it's a matter of how best to do it.' Andy was advising her on the contract we put together, but it was very clear that Martha was the one in charge. While he was a tough negotiator, it was *all* Martha.''

After they had hammered out an agreement in principle, Chamberlain asked to meet Wetacom's new golden girl in person before the contract was formally signed. Martha, who wanted to get a take on him too, threw a seal-the-deal meal, knocking the Waspy Chamberlain's argyle socks off by cooking duck in the fireplace, something he'd never seen done before. Chamberlain was sold, and the deal was signed. One key clause demanded by Andy permitted Martha to walk with a chunk of change if Wetacom didn't deliver an acceptable project in a specified amount of time.

The next step was to put together a pilot, which Murray planned to use as a selling tool. He hired a producer from a glitzy New York ad agency, who spent what Wetacom managing producer Geoffrey Miller recalled was "a shit-load of money" to assemble "a bad slide show." But those problems were nothing compared with the star herself, who drove Miller up the wall during visits to Wetacom's Arlington, Virginia, studios.

"It was," he proclaimed, "one of the worst experiences I ever had in production." At WETA-TV, which produced *MacNeil/Lehrer* and other inside-the-Beltway programming, Miller had rubbed shoulders with some of the best and the brightest. "As a producer I trained George Shultz to handle hostile reporters. [Then–]Secretary of Defense McNamara was always around. I was used to government figures of fairly high stature. Even though they might show up in limousines and certainly were powerful people, they weren't prima donnas. Martha Stewart *was* a prima donna. She felt a sense of entitlement that was incredible. She just kind of flowed through the WETA studios in a floor-length mink, acting incredibly arrogant and starlike. She didn't want to record at particular times, and she wouldn't do retakes. She was particularly difficult. She was cold and aloof. She insisted on being waited on. She was very impatient. 'When can we do this? Why can't we do this right away? Why do I have to sit here? What are we waiting for? I want to get out of here.' I found her terribly affected in terms of her intonation, her delivery. But she was *very* good at performing."

The pilot used existing videotapes of Martha's appearances on various talk shows, plus a new voice-over. But the final cut was dull. Peter Murray thought the tape needed some juice, so he arranged to have a film crew present at Turkey Hill for one of Martha's parties. As it turned out, the bash was an event staged by Richard Jeffery, who was shooting a feature for one of Martha's *New York Times Home Entertaining* issues. Jeffery had thought the party might be dull and had arranged for a mariachi band to be present.

But Martha and Lexi livened things up when they got into a shouting match reportedly over Lexi's outfit, a pair of bib overalls with no shirt on underneath, leaving her ample breasts essentially exposed.

With the tape finally completed and edited, Peter Murray hit the road to find a sponsor and a syndicator. Through a colleague he got a meeting with one of the biggest television syndicators in the business at the time. It was a session he would not soon forget. "This guy went berserk. He said to my colleague and myself, 'You're a fucking idiot. How dare you bring in this Connecticut snob's book and that tape and put it on my desk? No one's interested in Martha Stewart. No one will ever be!' It was the first time I'd ever been thrown out of an office in my life."

In short order, though, Murray did find a potential sponsor for Martha after talking to a number of advertising agency people in charge of television production for corporate clients. At Compton Advertising, then one of the top ten on Madison Avenue, the key man in the program development group adored Martha and thought her taped presentation was fabulous. He took the idea to the account people who also signed off on it for Procter & Gamble and its product Dawn, a dishwashing detergent. The Compton people wanted either a syndicated program or a show for the burgeoning cable market. The program's concept still needed to be developed.

Under a tentative agreement Martha was to do thirteen shows out of Washington in return for a talent fee of fifty thousand dollars. The Wetacom executives thought they'd gotten a bargain.

But not long after Murray struck the deal with Compton, he left Wetacom, after reportedly losing a power struggle with another executive for Chamberlain's favor. "I turned the project over to Ward and the group at Wetacom and said, 'Here you go.' Ward was very much interested in the

Martha project. He was in lockstep with me all along the way."

Six months later though, Murray heard from his man at Compton that Martha had "reneged on the whole deal, had opted out. She abided by the conditions of the contract. But the show never happened."

Michael Cunningham, the chief financial officer for WETA at the time, said that Wetacom's agreement with Martha included "a window during which time she would not entertain other offers and be exclusively ours. It ran its course, and that window expired. We paid her something in order to keep that window."

Geoffrey Miller said the show was never developed because "Peter Murray was really the driving force behind it, and there was nobody to follow up."

Years later Ward Chamberlain, who had become vice-president and managing director of WNET-TV, in New York, exclaimed, "Christ, I wish we had put that show through in some way. Martha was a terrific talent."

From the moment she signed to write *Entertaining*, Martha had been nudging Alan Mirken and Carol Southern to let her do television and home videos tied to the themes of her books. "She was determined to get into video," Mirken acknowledged. "She was anticipating what later became her successful television program. Martha wanted to do video. We respected Martha. We did video. Simple as that."

Martha tied both her first television special, produced by Boston's WGBH-TV, and her first mail-order video, distributed by Crown Video, together in a big red bow in 1986 and called it *Holiday Entertaining with Martha Stewart*. The production, underwritten by Pepperidge Farms, Swift-Eckrich Butterball turkeys, and Sterling Vineyards, was shot months before the show actually aired at Thanksgiving. Martha had the drive to move forward with the complex project despite an already full plate. Crown had hoped to bring out her weddings book at the end of the year, and the Clarkson Potter people were screaming for the manuscript, but Martha was far, far behind schedule.

At the same time her personal life was in shambles. Andy had already brought up the subject of a separation, and Lexi, finishing Barnard, was more alienated than ever.

Also, another horrific tragedy had struck Martha's sister Laura, and its impact had a devastating effect on everyone in the Kostyra and Stewart families.

After a long, troubling period Laura Kostyra had finally found happiness with Kim Herbert, a handsome, budding actor, whom she met while working for Martha's catering company, which supplied boxed lunches for the cast and crew of the Stratford American Shakespeare Festival Theater, in Stratford, Connecticut. "Laura and Kimmy were a perfect match," his stepmother, Janice Herbert, declared. The two fell in love and after a quick courtship were married at Turkey Hill—an old-fashioned wedding that Martha naturally produced and featured in a chapter of *Entertaining* entitled "Afternoon Cocktail Reception for Fifty."

A likable young man, described by one friend as an Adonis, Herbert was the son of Leo Herbert, who for decades had been Broadway producer David Merrick's property manager and, in that capacity, was a beloved member of the Broadway theater community, having been involved in more than 120 shows on the Great White Way over the years.

Laura and Kim moved into his one-bedroom apartment near Times Square, and not long after, Laura gave birth to the first of their two children, a son, Christopher. To support his small family, Herbert, who "wasn't a very good actor," according to his stepmother, worked as a propman with his father and bought a small company that manufactured mirrored disco balls.

Because the apartment became too small, Kim, Laura, and the baby moved into the Kostyra homestead, in Nutley, where the widowed matriarch was living by herself. "She was very able and was having an enjoyable life and really didn't need to have them move in at that point," Janice Herbert observed. "It was difficult because she's a hard lady and a tough lady, who wants to take over, and Laura and she didn't seem to get along too well." Not long after the move, Laura had another baby, Sophie.

In early May 1986, around the time Martha was in pre-production for her first TV special, on which Laura was scheduled to make an appearance, Kim Herbert complained of stomach pains. His doctor sent him to the hospital, where appendicitis was misdiagnosed. Herbert, in fact, had a very aggressive form of lymphomic cancer. Herbert was thirty-two, about to turn thirty-three later in the month. He didn't know it at the time, but he had five months left to live.

Like Ethel Stewart, Herbert's birth mother was a staunch Christian Scientist. At first, though, Herbert sought medical treatment at Sloan-Kettering, where Andy had undergone treatment for his cancer. "They thought they could save Kimmy, but it was such an aggressive cancer," Janice Herbert said. "They were trying everything. They were drilling holes in his head to treat him with chemotherapy. They were using him as a guinea pig almost."

Finally Herbert gave up on the treatments and got deeply involved in the Christian Science Church because, as his stepmother noted, "He was trying desperately to live." In October 1986, a month before Martha's show was aired, he died.

As Martha's holiday special got into production, Herbert's fatal illness and Laura's panicked and depressed state hung like a pall over everyone except, it seemed, Martha, who believed in the adage "The show must go on." Acting as if nothing untoward was happening, she performed like a seasoned trouper.

At least that's how it appeared to viewers, who saw Martha at her charming best: happily touring a cranberry bog in thigh-high rubber boots, cheerfully making puff pastry for the outside of the turkey (an idea she had lifted from a family friend); gleefully selecting the table settings from her antique cupboard, and grandly picking from her garden a huge pumpkin that she magically turned into a soup tureen. The final dinner scene showed what appeared to be all the members of Martha's family, the folks all of Martha's readers had become familiar with from her books, *pretending* to be happy and enjoying themselves.

To viewers, especially Martha's growing legion of fans, it looked perfect. It wasn't. For one thing, the two most important people in Martha's life, her husband and her daughter, were missing from the picture. Andy and Lexi refused to participate as human props in still another of Martha's commercial ventures. Behind the scenes a variety of weird and wacky events also occurred, one of which would have shocked Martha's fans. In one broadcast sequence Martha was shown taking scrumptious-looking game hens out of the Turkey Hill smokehouse. But before that scene had been shot, the smokehouse actually caught fire, causing what one crew member later described as "a hysterically funny Keystone Kops scene." Flames shooting out of the little structure had alerted Martha to the emergency, and she had frantically raced to the scene of the blaze, dragging a garden hose, followed by various blasé crew people, faux concerned family members, smirking kitchen assistants, and a macho Brazilian groundskeeper. When they reached the blaze, Martha discovered that the hose was too short. Hightailing it back to the main house, with everyone in her wake, she got a hose extension and returned to the scene, where someone aimed a weak stream of water at the roof to put out the fire, which had been touched off by melting fat from the little dinner birds. "Martha was jumping up and down," a crew member recalled. "She was just totally freaked, hysterical. The birds were pretty crispy critters by that point but still usable for the scene."

Meanwhile, Martha had gotten into a shouting match with the groundskeeper, whom she fired on the spot in front of everyone after he talked back to her. "Leave my property this minute," Martha snarled. Infuriated, he got into his car and drove off.

Ten minutes later Martha realized that she had forgotten to retrieve the big ring he had in his possession that held the key to every lock at Turkey Hill. Said an eyewitness, "Martha really freaked out. She's saying, 'Oh, shit, I just fired that Latino, and he's got my keys. What if he comes back and cuts my throat in my sleep?' " Worried, Martha telephoned an off-duty Westport cop and hired him to stand guard over the property to prevent the fired groundskeeper from returning.

When the TV crew was setting up its lights and other equipment in the house and the barn, Martha followed them around like a bloodhound, constantly reminding them that if there was any damage to her property, there would be hell to pay. At one point Martha spotted some dents in the floor and became enraged. "Suddenly she's going around checking the women's shoes to see who's wearing heels that might have dented the floor," a crew member recounted. Martha also berated her grieving sister Laura, who then quit the kitchen detail, and she had a tiff with Robyn Fairclough, whom crew members saw crying.

Also present in Martha's entourage were several pretty Scandinavian girls, who were helpers and whom she "treated like her whipping girls," a crew member recalled. "She humiliated them. She ridiculed them. They were very attractive, and she seemed to be threatened by them, and so she treated them terribly. She'd talk to them in a low, cutting voice as if to say, 'You don't deserve to exist if you don't do this right.' She was constantly correcting them."

The program's taciturn producer-director, Christopher Gilbert, also had his hands full with the diva. "He was having problems communicating with her," a crew member recalled. "He would give her instructions in a very polite way about content, but if she didn't like his criticisms or suggestions, she would turn and twist things around and make it appear that he wasn't being appreciative of her or that he wasn't being polite to her. She was very manipulative in that way. The problem was Martha could brook no criticism whatsoever, so for Chris it was a course in 'Walking on Eggshells 101.' In fact everyone was walking on eggshells because we had heard what a bitch she was."

At the same time, Martha continually flirted with all the young men on the crew. Her favorite, though, was a sound technician who had been directed to install a wireless microphone on her body—"a truly weird experience because she was extremely sexually aggressive with me," he disclosed.

A decision had been made to place the mike on the inside of Martha's thigh rather than under her blouse or in the area of her waist, the usual places for such devices. The reason for the lower torso location was that she was going to be walking and talking and would be entirely in the camera frame, and the director didn't want the mike to show.

"The mike had already been taped around Martha's thigh, and I was asked to adjust it, and Martha was being very aggressively accommodating," the audio guy said. "She opened up her skirt and was looking down at me with this very come-hither kind of expression, and she said to me, 'Go higher with it if you want. Go ahead, it's okay with me.' There were a few people about six feet behind us, but only known to both of us was this little exchange going on. I didn't respond to her. I'm a professional. And I was offended by what she was saying because it was such an obvious sexual comment. It was just so ridiculously flirtatious. I could tell she loved me being beneath her and that she was into real sexual game playing. It was like a power thing with her. I didn't raise the ante. I didn't return the flirtation. Her advice on going higher with the mike would have put it past her garter belt to within an inch, to be clinical, of Martha Stewart's vagina."

In any event, the aptly titled *Holiday Entertaining with Martha Stewart* was a complete success. It was shown on a number of public television stations across the country and got good reviews. *Newsweek,* however, pointed out that Martha had "cheerfully used the sponsors' products— though she was careful not to name them—and even roasted a shortening-injected Butterball instead of a fresh turkey. A serious cook would have been mortified."

Nevertheless the tapes of the program sold well enough that Crown made a deal with Martha for more. WGBH-TV also signed to do another holiday special with her the following year, while Martha announced she had plans for a daily half hour program of her own.

Housewife-humorist Erma Bombeck, in her nationally syndicated "At Wit's End" column, said she'd seen the show and acknowledged that Martha Stewart had "absolutely knocked me out." But she pointed out that "the Norman Rockwell" scene of Martha's family sitting down to an elegant meal served by a hostess who resembled "Loretta Young coming through a door" wasn't the way it was in real life.

"I said to myself, 'What's wrong with this picture?' Then it hit me. There was no television set. . . . [S]he didn't have to lug 14 folding chairs . . . she didn't have to time the mashed potatoes because Minnesota was on the three-yard line with a third down and the score tied. . . . I could do a Martha Stewart, too, if I didn't have a husband in front of the TV set looking so lifeless I once outlined him in chalk!"

Martha scoffed at Bombeck's glibness. Good or bad, she viewed the column as more publicity for herself. She was about to conquer the world, as she declared to a newspaper interviewer at the time. "The object now is to get as many people as I can [as viewers and book buyers]. They want to improve their lives. They want to make things a little nicer. They want to look at a dish and say, 'Oh, that's a great dish; I'm going to remember to use that next time.' "

Asked if she thought it incredible that she'd become an arbiter of taste, Martha declared emphatically, "No. Somebody has to."

Weddings

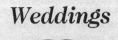

Martha's publisher was overjoyed with the TV show and all of the star author's other high-visibility activities because the bottom line was it sold more books: Almost a million of her first four books were in print by mid-1986, and the first, *Entertaining*, had sold well over three hundred thousand copies, with more printings being ordered.

Still, Alan Mirken was daily asking Carol Southern, "So, where's *Weddings*?"

A recently inked deal for a syndicated column got Martha's name and pitch in more than sixty newspapers across the country, increasing her following by millions.

Still, Carol Southern, under pressure from Alan Mirken, kept asking Martha's editor, Carolyn Hart, "So, where's *Weddings*?"

There was a waiting list to attend Martha's three-day entertaining seminars, at a thousand to fifteen hundred dollars a pop, in Westport, and in towns and cities around the country.

Still, Carolyn Hart, who needed the manuscript *yesterday*, kept leaving messages on Martha's machine, asking, "So, where's *Weddings*?"

But Martha was just *so* busy. She had what she described as "a backbreaking schedule"—to wit:

> Like this week, I had my teaching seminar Tuesday, Wednesday, Thursday—people come to these from all over the country. Then Friday morning I had two columns to do, so I had to get up at 5 o'clock and write them, and at noon we had to catch a plane for a meeting in San Francisco Friday night. Saturday—it's like this all the time, it's really *stupid*—Saturday we drive to Monterey and had a book-signing and party in Carmel. Then on Saturday night I was the judge of the gourmet gala for the March of Dimes and had to give out the prizes and stand next to Clint Eastwood—*Mayor* Eastwood. Then on Sunday morning I had a meeting with the people from Sterling Vineyards where I'm doing another seminar, and then lunch at the Pebble Beach Club, then back to San Francisco. I got home at 3:30 yesterday morning, then had a full day of meetings and went to the New York Antiques Show last night. That's the way it is. It's crazy.

Martha agreed that yes, she was becoming a star. And with a straight face, she declared, "I'd much rather be anonymous. Because you go and you dress up and people think you're showing off. When I'm writing a book like *Weddings*, I'm certainly not showing off; I'm writing a real serious book there.''

Knowing she couldn't actually write *Weddings*, Martha *and* Carol Southern had put pressure on Liz Hawes to forget all her past bad experiences and take on Martha's latest book. "I wanted Liz to write *Weddings*, and she was *very* reluctant," Southern said. "She felt she got *really* screwed by Martha on *Entertaining*. And I said, 'But, Liz, it's such a good subject. If nothing else, you'll have royalties for the rest of your life. This book will be a bible.' "

Hawes was torn. Aside from her past difficulties, she had done considerable research for a book she later wrote about New York City apartment buildings. But her interest was piqued because *Weddings* would involve actual reporting *and* writing and would deal with culture and style.

Martha turned on the charm and claimed everything would be different this time. Hawes reluctantly agreed after she demanded and got a contract that was more in her favor. "I wanted to be sure I got cover credit," she said. Later, though, Martha again attempted to slither out of that part of the deal.

"We knew *Weddings* would be a big book," Southern said. "We knew we would sell a lot of copies, and we also knew that it was a narrower book than *Entertaining*. So, again, there was nervousness because we were going to price it at fifty dollars. And anyway, Martha *always* made us nervous. She was *always* making us stretch. There was tremendous pressure to get *Weddings* in. It was horrible. We wanted to get the book out for Christmas 1986, but we couldn't make it. By that time Martha's availability was less, and it was just hard to get a manuscript written, hard to get Martha to sit down. It was really, *really* difficult. We would have weekly status meetings where Carolyn Hart and I would meet with Alan Mirken and the production crew. It was: 'When are we getting captions? We're missing pictures.' I mean, it was *agony*.''

Having catered hundreds of weddings, Martha had conceived the book knowing that the wedding industry was extremely lucrative, generating billions of dollars annually. Brides, grooms, and their families needed advice. One of the most popular chapters in *Entertaining*, in fact, was the last one: "The At-Home Wedding." In her files Martha had socked away hundreds of photographs that had been taken by Andy and others of nuptials she had catered, along with detailed notes about them. Much of the raw material already was in the can.

Liz Hawes got to work. "In some cases I went back and interviewed those people, and I talked to the bride and groom about how they reached their decisions. I interviewed lots of tent people and lighting people and got their stories.

"Lots of the weddings, though, Martha hadn't catered, and she would do a real convincing number on the families. She'd tell them, 'Oh, it's going to be *the* most beautiful book that's ever been done, and everybody's going to have it, and we're doing *the* most beautiful job, and we're using *the* world's most wonderful photographers, and we're recording it as a social chronicle, and you'll want to be a part of this, and it won't take anything away from your privacy.' People were flattered because she told them they were planning such beautiful and special weddings. But some said, 'Absolutely not. This is my wedding, and it's private.' " But not too many.

"Typical Martha. We were on our way to cover a wedding on Martha's Vineyard, and on the way we saw somebody else setting up a tent. 'Oh, let's go find out who they are,' Martha said. 'Look at that beautiful horse. It'll be a beautiful picture.' So Martha jumped out of the car and charmed this young couple, and sure enough, we came back four hours later and were at their wedding and photographed it, and it's in the book."

One wedding that Martha desperately wanted included because of the glitz and glamour was that of Sophie Desmarais, the beautiful daughter of a rich and powerful Kennedyesque Canadian family, to a young man named Michael Kaine. The dramatic ceremony was held in Montreal's seventeenth-century Notre Dame Church, and the celebration at the Museum of Fine Art. "To get that one,

Martha really had all lines open," Hawes said. "She finally got in through the help of Jean-François Daigreand, who designed the wedding."

Most of the time Hawes worked alone with a photographer. "Martha was extremely busy with other projects and was getting even busier. She was working on several other books. She was moving forward with her TV deals and the videotapes. There were periods when we'd go months without talking, and certainly there were times when we needed to get together and couldn't because she just wasn't available."

Attention, Kmart Shoppers

During the fall and winter of 1986, as *Weddings* was marching slowly down the aisle toward consummation, a seemingly unrelated series of events was transpiring in a Detroit suburb. These events, unbeknownst to Martha, would have a profound impact on her future. At the Troy, Michigan, corporate headquarters of the giant Kmart Corporation, president and chief executive officer Joe Antonini had formed an ad hoc committee with the mandate of finding the retail chain's weak or broken links and fixing them. The group of four also was asked to develop ideas for the future of the company, which at that point was riding high. That year posted sales of $23.8 billion, making it second only to Sears as America's largest retailer. Kmart counted *half* of all Americans among its shoppers.

The committee, which insiders dubbed Joe's kitchen cabinet, consisted of Kmart's vice-president of corporate planning, Mike Wellman; a professor at Wayne State University named Pat Kelly; a lawyer and merchandising expert from New York, who was a close associate of Antonini's, Marjorie Alfus; and Barbara Loren-Snyder, a former Detroit advertising executive turned consultant.

The group quickly got into action, targeting the city of Nashville, Tennessee, which had one of the highest concentrations of blue-collar retail outlets that were competitive with Kmart's demographics. Kmart's stores there were found to be drab and dirty, and its image in the eyes of consumers was actually *sub*-blue collar. One department, home and kitchen products, was underproductive in terms of sales; its lines of merchandise were completely out of kilter with the competition, and it was horrendously disorganized. The bottom line was that everything appeared wrong, and nothing seemed too right. Antonini's team had to come up with a plan—fast—to keep Kmart shoppers from going to Wal-Mart and Target.

As a veteran advertising executive, Barbara Loren-Snyder always firmly believed in research, and her research had told her that the home was going to be the center of American family life in the late eighties, into the nineties, and probably into the twenty-first century. It was called cocooning, a word coined by the corporate trend spotter and guru named Faith Popcorn.

One of the reasons that Joe Antonini had reached the pinnacle at Kmart was because during his watch Jaclyn Smith had become a spokeswoman for the company. The former star of *Charlie's Angels* had lent her name and face to a highly successful line of clothing, the Jaclyn Smith Signature Collection, sold exclusively by Kmart. The collaboration had been a financial success for all concerned and had made a tremendous impact on Kmart's presentation in its apparel departments. Moreover, the likable, personable, and photogenic Smith had done wonders for Kmart's public image.

Loren-Snyder had come to the conclusion that Kmart needed another Jaclyn Smith, and the focus had to be on the home area of the company. Her first stop was the library and then the bookstores, and that's where she stumbled across Martha Stewart, whose four books were prominently displayed. "I'm not a cook, so I'd never heard of her," Loren-Snyder acknowledged later. "I said to myself, 'Maybe she's the woman. She'd know how to put together not only food but centerpieces, and she might eventually be able to develop a product line of tablecloths, linens, dinnerware.' I looked at the book, and I thought, 'She's extremely attractive, the right age, a wife, a mother.' Just seeing her picture, I thought, 'She's *America*.'" On a scrap of paper she wrote down Martha's name and "Westport," which was on one of the book's jacket flaps, and left the store, thinking, "I'm going to go for her."

In her office she dialed Connecticut information and was surprised to learn that Martha had a listed number and even picked up the phone after a couple of rings. "I said, 'Martha, you don't know who I am, but I have outstanding credentials, which I will send to you if you're interested in my offer, which is to make you a multimillionaire. I represent a company I'm not at liberty to identify at this time. I would like to get together with you and show you why you should consider becoming a major personality for this company.' She seemed suspicious, which is why I offered to send her my résumé."

But Martha agreed to meet with the mysterious woman on the phone. Loren-Snyder scheduled their get-together for the day *after* the next ad hoc committee meeting. "I had to have the meeting with Martha scheduled in case they liked the idea," said the shrewd strategist. "If they didn't like the idea, I could call her up and say I had to cancel. She didn't know who I was anyway."

Between getting off the phone with Martha and her meeting at Kmart headquarters, Loren-Snyder put together a campaign that made Martha the cameo for the company's home and kitchen department. The plan called for Martha's books to be sold throughout the chain. It called for an original product line, such as designer tablecloths, to be put under her name. "We'll make her Ralph Lauren for the masses," she thought. She envisioned a Martha Stewart television show for Kmart and a magazine that would contain Martha's recipes and household tips, to be given away at Kmart stores. Martha would also be a major part of the Kmart Sunday newspaper supplement, which at that time was seen in about 50 percent of all the homes in America.

At the kitchen cabinet meeting Loren-Snyder stood up and gave her pitch. On the conference table she piled a stack of Martha's books and laid out photographs, magazine, and newspaper stories about her. No one present other than Mike Wellman had ever heard of this Martha Stewart woman. "Wellman was a gourmet cook, one of those yuppies," Loren-Snyder explained, "so he was very familiar with her." In fact, Wellman told the gathering that he had overseen a Kmart stockholders' dinner the previous February and the caterer had used recipes from *Entertaining* to prepare the dinner at Wellman's instruction.

Antonini was definitely interested. A visionary, he told Loren-Snyder, "Go for it!"

Back at her office she decided that she'd rather not have an informal meeting with Martha at her home in Westport. So she telephoned, reconfirmed their meeting for the next day, and suggested that they hold it at her lawyer's office in New York, which Martha vehemently opposed. Loren-Snyder was unaware that Martha's lawyer was also Martha's unhappy husband and that the couple was in the throes of horrible marital problems. But Loren-Snyder prevailed.

On the flight to New York, the consummate strategist had decided that she wasn't going to make a fancy presentation with storyboards. From everything she had read about the woman, she knew she would be dealing with "an enormous ego," and the best way to win that ego over was to focus on her company's desire to make Martha millions, to make Martha a star.

In order to stay focused, Loren-Snyder had written a cheat sheet in ink on the inside of her right wrist, below her gold watch, so that no one could see it. It consisted of three words, one right under the other, which read, from top to bottom, "Me," "Star," "KM."

The "me" on the list represented Loren-Snyder's credentials, which she felt she had to reiterate because she wasn't positive that Martha had understood their significance. "Star" represented what Martha would become if she agreed to the pitch. Loren-Snyder would tell her: " 'I will make you the Betty Crocker of the 1990s. You will be a multimillionaire. You will gain national recognition. You will be in every newspaper. You will be on television. You will be in magazines.' I had to convince her, knowing that she had this ego thing, that she would become a star. Once I convinced her of that, I didn't think it would be as bad when I told her that the company was Kmart. I wasn't going to mention Kmart until I got her so hot to trot that I wouldn't lose her. I knew that if I said Bloomingdale's or Saks Fifth Avenue, it would be a different story. But, if I said Kmart right away, it would be 'uh-oh,' and of course that's exactly what happened."

Loren-Snyder met Martha in the lobby of Stewart, Tabori & Chang's building, and from the moment she introduced herself, she could tell that this was the last place in the world Martha wanted to be. Once the initial introductions were made in Andy's office, the hostility between wife and husband was palpable. But Loren-Snyder proceeded with her laundry list of how she was going to make Martha rich and famous while the unsmiling Stewarts listened intently.

"I got to the end, and I told her that the company that I represented was offering to give her a substantial fixed annual salary, plus expenses for 'personality days' at stores throughout the country. And then I said, 'Kmart.' Martha sighed and looked *very* disappointed.

"I told her that there were twenty-three hundred Kmart stores in the country. I told her that Martha Stewart products would be in every one of those stores. By the time I finished I could see that the impact of Kmart had softened on her. She could see the dollar signs. Suddenly her mood had changed. She was as high as she could possibly be. They both were."

Loren-Snyder had saved discussion of compensation for last. Now she informed Martha that those millions she'd mentioned would actually be made in royalties on products that were sold, not from straight salary. "I have been advised that I can offer you fifty thousand dollars a year," she told Martha.

" 'Fifty thousand dollars?' " declared Martha incredulously. " 'You've got to be crazy!' Martha went absolutely berserk," Loren-Snyder recalled. "She said it was horrible. She demanded to know why I was wasting her time."

Loren-Snyder, who had withheld the real number she'd been authorized to offer, sighed, stood up, and said, "Well, Martha, what did you expect?"

"Two hundred thousand," Martha responded.

Loren-Snyder thought, *"Bingo!"*

Thanking the Stewarts for their time, she said, "You'll be hearing from our lawyer because we're going to be able to work this out. And, Martha, you *will* be a star."

Outside Loren-Snyder grabbed a cab, laughing all the way to La Guardia, where she raced to the first available pay phone and placed a call to Marg Alfus. "We got her!" she whispered into the phone. "Start the negotiations."

What Martha and Andy had no way of knowing was that an annual fee of $250,000 had been authorized by Antonini. Kmart had gotten its new spokeswoman for fifty thousand dollars a year less than it had budgeted.

But what would have happened had the deal fallen through? To cover all possibilities, Loren-Snyder had a backup spokesperson in the wings, a woman named Jenifer Lang, a personable cookbook author and chef, whose husband owned Manhattan's Café des Artistes.

At Kmart headquarters Joe Antonini was happy about the deal Loren-Snyder had cut with Martha, but he wasn't breaking out the Dom Pérignon. Two hundred thousand dollars a year were still two hundred thousand dollars a year for somebody he'd never heard of.

Several weeks after Loren-Snyder met with Martha she arranged for her to visit Kmart headquarters to have lunch with Antonini and the Kmart chairman, Ben Fauber. "It was really odd because Martha showed up with sores all over her hands, and Joe looked at her and said, 'Martha, what's wrong? What's the problem there?' And she said, 'Well, I worked all day yesterday in the rose garden.' She actually came in there with no nail polish on and with her hands totally messed up from thorns. But that's the side of her that I wanted to present to the public, to the consumers who were Kmart's target. But as it turned out, they were *not* Martha's target.'' Loren-Synder and the honchos at Kmart didn't realize it at the time, but Martha would become a major aggravation, and her products would be only modestly successful, while the PR and publicity would be enormous.

In the end Martha agreed to two hundred thousand dollars a year for five years, plus three thousand dollars for each in-store visit she made—she was required by contract to make thirty a year—which added another ninety thousand dollars annually to her fee, plus expenses, and sundry perks, along with royalties. Looking down the road, she hoped to make a fortune.

When news of the deal broke in early 1987, Martha spread the word that the contract was worth five million dollars, a misleading and erroneous amount widely reported by the press. As Loren-Snyder saw it, ''Martha wanted everybody to think she was getting *millions* up front, which was part of her own strategy to further enhance the Martha Stewart image.''

The deal made headlines across the country, but many observers saw it as a freaky marriage. *The New York Times* pointed out:

> Many strange combinations have come out of American kitchens in the 80's, but Kmart may have served up the pièce de résistance with its recent announcement that entertainment guru Martha Stewart has signed a five-year contract to be its national spokeswoman and a consultant for home fashions. . . . Martha Stewart's link with the nation's second largest retailer might have seemed an odd combination—but then, people once laughed at goat cheese pizza, too.

Kmart launched Martha Stewart with a series of spot television and magazine ads. Its objective was to get her face in front of the public and tie her upscale image to the company as quickly as possible. But it actually took two years for the first Martha Stewart signature brands to hit the shelves.

PART FIVE

A Bittersweet

Concoction

The Split

Beginning in the mid-seventies, when Martha was working as a stockbroker, Andy wondered whether their marriage could survive. By 1982, when her first book was published, the idea of leaving her had become a reality for him.

Several times in the early to mid-eighties Martha also had voiced *her* unhappiness, sometimes in vitriolic notes in which she expressed her disgust with Andy and said she wished *he'd* leave. Martha had left one such note on the top of a cupboard. Upset after reading it, Andy had dropped it where he found it, and Martha Sr. happened to come upon it. Shocked by its content, she confronted her daughter, who then berated Andy for embarrassing her by leaving the note in plain sight.

By the fall of 1986, as the final edits were being made on *Weddings* and on Martha's TV special, Andy had started keeping a mental record of good times versus bad, and the bad times far outweighed the good. He decided he finally had had it with Martha.

Once again, though, he suggested they seek counseling, but this time he told her that if they couldn't resolve their problems, he'd have no other choice but to leave her.

"Martha just went nuts because she knew Andy was serious this time," a confidant said.

One afternoon, while the Stewarts were bickering in the checkout line at Stew Leonard's, a popular supermarket where an autographed eight-by-ten glossy of Martha hung on the wall next to other celebrities like Paul Newman, Robert Vaughn, and Gene Wilder, Martha exploded in a screaming fit as other shoppers blanched behind their carts. "She lost it," an eyewitness recalled, "and was screaming at him because he told her he was leaving. She was *so* angry. It seemed like she didn't care who recognized her or who heard what she was saying. I remember her yelling at one point, 'Now that you have money of your own, you're leaving me, after all these years.' " Other shoppers giggled as they watched the furious, the self-proclaimed housewife extraordinaire marching out of the store spitting fire, with her red-faced husband in tow. However, Martha did agree, once again at Andy's behest, to see a therapist.

"Andy couldn't believe what Martha was saying because *she* was the one becoming richer by the day, but was claiming to the shrink that Andy no longer needed her because of *his* financial successes," a confidant noted. "Andy was so frustrated and angry. He said, 'Can you believe her? What a grotesque, crazy, ridiculous, misplaced accusation.' "

In early January 1987 Andy secretly began looking for an apartment in Manhattan. A few weeks later at dinner with the Stewarts, a friend in whom Andy had confided let his secret slip by asking how the apartment hunting was going. It was not the way Andy had wanted Martha or Lexi, who was present that night, to learn about his plan to move out. The disclosure touched off an emotional avalanche that engulfed the entire family. "It was a disaster," revealed a friend. "Martha had known nothing about Andy's plans. She went absolutely nuts. Lexi became furious at her father. Andy felt guilty and horrible. They all were suffering."

In the subsequent confrontation, Andy admitted to Martha that he had been unfaithful during their marriage, a revelation similar to the one Martha had made years earlier when she was working as a stockbroker. "They were having a huge argument," a friend said later, "and the subject of affairs came up in the context that it had been a two-way thing. Martha asked Andy for details, but he was reluctant to tell her anything other than to say yes, he had done that, and so had she."

Still, Martha pleaded with Andy not to leave, telling him she loved him, a feeling she rarely declared. "With *Weddings* about to come out, the last thing in the world Martha needed was a marriage scandal," a close friend observed. "And she didn't want to tarnish her image with the Kmart people. It was clear she was manipulating Andy to stay because of her career. And that's what he came to believe too."

Martha suggested to Andy that if he really wanted to distance himself from her, he should move into the barn, and he did for a short time. The quid pro quo was that they try therapy one more time. Martha agreed, but their sessions were a repeat of past unsuccessful visits.

On April 1, 1987, with a shaky marital truce in effect, Martha put on her confident, successful, happy author's face for the much-ballyhooed publication of *Martha Stewart Weddings*, the dedication of which read: "To my husband Andy: Our wedding will always remain my favorite and to my daughter Alexis whose wedding I look forward to with pleasure."

Martha boasted to an interviewer, "The hard work is about to begin on this book; they're sending me on a back-breaking book tour."

A full-page photo in the book's Introduction showed Martha, her hand clasped in Andy's, happily leaving the Episcopal chapel at Columbia under a shower of rice a quarter century earlier after being joined in holy matrimony. Later Frank Kostyra claimed credit for having taken the photo and asserted that his sister never gave him timely acknowledgment or payment. At one point he considered suing her for copyright infringement.

Among those listed in the acknowledgments was Elizabeth Hawes, who, Martha wrote, "worked with me on the text of *Entertaining*, and has again lent her beautiful prose to this work." Later Hawes said, "Even though cover credit was written into the contract this time, there was a question raised by Martha about whether my name could go on the cover because it would somehow interfere with the frosting on the wedding cake. I said, 'Too bad—it's in the contract.' "

But none of that was known to Martha's readers, who snapped up the seventy-five thousand first printing of the beautifully designed and illustrated fifty-dollar book.

Despite their growing marital difficulties, Andy and Martha had double-teamed the executives at Crown and the editors at Clarkson Potter to get everything they wanted in *Weddings*. "Together they were very insistent about the quality of the pictures and the typeface and the way it was laid out because they wanted it to look a very special way," Hawes said. "They were very demanding. Martha would go into these layout meetings when they were putting things together—with my text in hand—fussing about the style. Martha and Andy saw it as a breakthrough book that nobody had ever done before. There were certainly bride books out there and bride magazines, but Martha and Andy and the publishers thought this would be huge, and it was."

Andy, who had produced a number of his company's books in Japan, had discovered a paper stock there that he thought would be appropriate for *Weddings* and recommended it be used. "At the last minute," Carol Southern said, "Martha came rushing in and said she liked the Japanese paper better than the paper we were using. 'I want you to use *this* paper,' she said. We said, 'Oh, God, Martha, we're already over budget.' And she said, 'Well, let's investigate it.' In the end we used it."

Alan Mirken said, "She was a perfectionist, and she wanted everything to be right, and she would fight to get it right." Privately he had been fuming because Martha had not delivered *Weddings* early enough for Clarkson Potter's scheduled pub date. Her lateness in turning in manuscripts was a constant problem. As Mirken noted, "She was always so busy with so many other things." But for once Martha's tardiness worked in everyone's favor. "We discovered that the wedding season really started in February. Because of Martha's lateness, we had lucked into a better time to launch a wedding book."

As with most of Martha's previous books, *Weddings* was well received by the critics. *The New York Times* called it "a fifty-dollar, five-pound ode to perfect . . . [the] luxuriously photographed, romantically written tome is a wedding voyeur's dream.''

The Times quoted Martha as calling her latest work ''a social document of life in the 1980's,'' describing the brides depicted as ''icons for the 80's,'' and declaring that the documented weddings were ''fabulous,'' and some ''very, very fabulous.''

The Times noted that the book ''features the photogenic Ms. Stewart herself,'' and the photogenic Ms. Stewart declared, ''I am a commitment to a kind of life style, that's what I am,'' which she asserted was the reason for her enormous popularity. Nowhere in the article was the real writer, Elizabeth Hawes, mentioned.

Patricia Leigh Brown, of *The Times*, proclaimed: ''Martha Stewart has a perfect life. The exotic Araucana chickens she raises at her Westport, Connecticut, 'farmette' are perfect. The azalea bushes she planted in the garden for her husband, Andy, for Father's Day are perfect.'' (Andy wouldn't be around to see them. He was in the process of packing his bags the day *The Times* story appeared.)

Martha told *The Times* she was already hard at work on her sixth book, *The Wedding Planner*, and her seventh, *Cooking from the Garden*. She said that for another future book, she had purchased an 1838 Federal house nearby and planned to write about its restoration and do a video on the project. She also boasted that she had started production on a series of hour-long videos called *Martha Stewart's Secrets for Entertaining*, and she discussed plans for a syndicated TV show. But her books would always be first, she declared. ''I try to write about subjects nobody has treated in the personal way I do,'' she told *The Times*. ''What I'm writing about is a lifestyle and a catalogue of material I've paid attention to for a long time. I want my books to be a standard—a standard of perfection from which people can pull ideas. It's an idea I got from an American Poultry Association book called, 'A Standard of Perfection.' ''

Nothing was reported about the wedding expert's marital difficulties. The key people at Crown and Clarkson Potter had become painfully aware that their best-selling author's marriage was falling apart on the eve of the launch of what they hoped would be her biggest book ever. The publisher had big plans for *Weddings*, including a massive promotional tour for Martha and a launch party in New Orleans that would cost a hundred thousand dollars. Martha also got her first booking on *The Oprah Show*, with the famous host telling her millions of viewers, "If you're planning a wedding, it is *the* book to have." Sales of course shot through the roof.

But as one Crown Publishing Group wag put it later, "The irony was too much. Here was Martha promoting this beautiful book about weddings, and her marriage was exploding in front of her eyes. We figured the press was going to have a field day. The joke around the office was that we should change the title to *Martha Stewart Divorces*."

At one point Martha met with Alan Mirken to fill him in on what was transpiring back at Turkey Hill. "It was a troubling thing to her because they were very close, and at some point I guess that just went away," he said. "It was a very difficult thing for her to come to grips with because she had always done everything *she* wanted to do, and I think she would have wanted at that point to stay married. And Andy was probably just a little bit lonely because Martha was so dedicated to her career."

In early April 1987, just three months before the Stewarts' twenty-seventh wedding anniversary, and while Martha was on the road hawking *Weddings*, Andy split. It was not an easy thing for him to do, and he later told friends that he cried the day he did it.

Only two people were at Turkey Hill that day: Kathy Tatlock, who was doing preproduction for the *Secrets of Entertaining* video project, and Martha's loyal housekeeper, Necy Fernandes.

Fernandes had tears in her eyes too when Andy told her, "Look, Necy, I just want you to know I don't want to leave, but I can't stand this anymore." She said she understood. Andy packed several bags and wrote a "Dear Martha" letter, which he left on the kitchen table.

Kathy Tatlock had been hired by Martha a few months earlier as a "fifty-fifty partner" to direct the video series, but Martha kept watering down her deal without Tatlock's knowledge. On the day Andy split he handed Tatlock the contract for the first time, which had her down for a surprising 10 percent. "I was walking Andy out to his car, still in a state of shock over the contract, when he suddenly turned to me and said, 'Kathy, I'm through with Martha. I'm moving out. I won't be coming back.' And that was the exact moment that he left."

Andy drove into Manhattan, where he took up temporary residence at the University Club. Several weeks later he moved into a small apartment off Central Park West. "I left her," he later told a close friend, "because she became gradually an awful person. She was selfish beyond any imagination. She was untruthful, unpleasant, rude, and angry all the time. Martha was never able to accept responsibility, never able to apologize, never able to look inward, never able to look at herself. Every attempt she's ever made to talk to a shrink has been a total failure. With her, it's a contest with the shrink. She just won't look inside. She won't look for a minute about why she is the way she is. It's the kind of guiltlessness that a wild creature has, that a predator has, because it has nothing in its nature to detect its own cruelty."

When Martha stopped home on a short breather to change wardrobes before resuming her pitch stops around the country, she found Andy's note and was told he had flown the coop. She was devastated. For Martha, the best of times had become the worst of times.

Not long after he left, Andy paid a visit to his friends George and Clare McCully. "The breakup happened when the book came out, and Martha thought that was deliberate on Andy's part," Clare McCully said. "She was very angry because she felt there was probably the potential for some adverse publicity. But Andy had reached his breaking point. He said, 'I don't want film crews in the kitchen in the morning. I want to be able to come down and make myself a cup of coffee. It's my house. And our house has become a studio. We need a home.' While he was here, Martha called and said Andy was going through a crisis, was being ridiculous. She said his leaving had nothing to do with her.

She said, 'Men get like this.' She thought he'd come back.''

Meanwhile, someone who knew what was going on behind the seemingly cheerful facade of Turkey Hill dropped a dime and telephoned the tabloids. On April 24, 1987, under the gossipy headline IS 'DIVORCES' NEXT? the New York *Daily News* gloatingly reported:

> Andrew Stewart, whose wife, Martha, wrote the lavish coffee table book, *Weddings*, has been apartment-hunting in New York. Insiders say that the Stewarts' marriage of 26 years has hit rocky waters . . . the move comes at a rather awkward time, since Martha, the wedding authority and syndicated columnist, is on a national tour pushing sales of the new book. . . . Both Stewarts vehemently deny any marital strife. "It's completely and absolutely false," said Andrew. . . . "We are happily married," Martha said.

Getting Even

What really shocked Martha about Andy's departure was that for the first time in their marriage *he* was in complete control, *he* had had the last word. As a result, she required constant attention and reinforcement from her friends.

"After Andy left, she was calling me every day," said Janet Horowitz. "If it wasn't once a day, it was two or three times a day. I was a crutch, and she needed to talk, and it was getting very heavy for me. It was so upsetting. She was *very* needy, *very* vulnerable. That was the worst time for her. It was a real shock to her that he had left. It was a shock because *she* wasn't in control anymore. She made comments like 'How could he do this at this time?' She was shocked that she didn't have a say in it. It was a control issue."

Horowitz had become aware of the bizarre incident in which Martha had confronted Andy and had torn a patch of hair out of her scalp. That frightful act, Horowitz believed, underscored the "rage" Martha was feeling at the time and continued to feel for a long time to come.

"Martha's need to control was *so* dominating that she would do almost anything to get what she wanted, and she wanted Andy back," Horowitz observed. "I think she felt 'If he sees how badly I'm suffering, he'll come back.' She was desperate at that point. Her reaction to Andy's cancer some years earlier wasn't as extreme as when Andy left her. That was the most emotional I had ever seen Martha."

But Horowitz and other friends thought that Andy was long past the point of showing any sympathy for Martha. "He had been thinking of leaving for many, many years," she affirmed. "My feeling was that he finally left for health reasons. He was having constant bodily problems that were related to the stress of the marriage. His back was so bad that they were going to operate. He was miserable. He was dying in that relationship."

Aside from the loss of control, Martha was infuriated by the timing of Andy's departure, during her book tour.

"It was the worst," she acknowledged several years later. "It was a very horrible thing. [It's] very hard to feel nice about a person after he does something like that, knowing that that's exactly what you're on [the book promotion tour], with his picture in the wedding book. He got me where it hurt the most. Paying me back for whatever I did to him all those years that made him be so mean to me."

Martha had put together a soupçon of her own personality traits that she believed had sparked Andy's decision to leave. "He . . . thought that I was a very selfish person," she said. "I think that was a total misunderstanding of me. 'Cause I think I'm personally very unselfish. And yet that was one of his complaints. I'm sure he was tired of helping me. He helped me a lot; I admit it. I helped him a lot, also, and he forgets that. Well, I did, a lot. I think he got tired of my drive and my desire to do lots of things."

In the days and weeks after Andy left, Martha bounced between one extreme mood and another. In the hopes of winning him back, she first tried the attention- and sympathy-getting act of pulling out a patch of her hair, which only served to frighten and alienate Andy even more. When that didn't work, she tried to be nice to him.

A couple of weeks after he had fled, she invited him back to a Turkey Hill Easter party attended by friends and Kostyra family members. To the surprise of many, Andy accepted. But he had no intention of staying. His only reason was to remain friends with Martha and especially Lexi. Andy made several visits through that spring and summer, during which Martha was on her best behavior. On one occasion, he specifically returned home to make a cameo appearance playing "the daddy" in "The Buffet Party for Family and Friends," one of the episodes in the three-part *Martha Stewart's Secrets of Entertaining* series.

"Martha went back and forth between trying to cajole and seduce Andy, by making it more attractive for him to come back," observed Tatlock, who, at Martha's urging, had moved temporarily into the little apartment above the garage because Martha wanted her to be closer to the ongoing production. At the same time Martha required the shoulder of an old and loyal friend to lean on as her emotional state worsened. Tatlock, who witnessed and experienced many of the weird goings-on at Turkey Hill during that period, described as "bizarre" Andy's decision to appear in the *Secrets of Entertaining* buffet sequence at a time when he was trying to escape from Martha. When she questioned him about it, Andy threw up his hands. "I don't know how I could have tolerated Martha's behavior and then come back and done her bidding," he told her. "But that just speaks to the kind of power that she has."

But every effort Martha made to lure Andy back permanently failed miserably, and by September he had stopped his visits to Turkey Hill. At that point a furious and distraught Martha began a campaign of harassment against Andy that started slowly but intensified when he actually filed for divorce and after she learned that he had become romantically involved with Robyn Fairclough.

"When Martha realized she couldn't win Andy back, that's when the vitriol began," Tatlock noted. "Martha was very angry. She felt very betrayed. She felt that she had really helped Andy through that whole period of his cancer. She said she was instrumental in nursing him back to health and that he had repaid her by cheating on her. She told me that when she was a stockbroker, there were opportunities to have dalliances, but she said she had remained faithful."

According to a number of the Stewarts' friends, Clare McCully among them, Martha began stalking Andy not long after he left her. "Andy visited us quite often that first fall, and strange things were happening," she asserted. "Andy suspected Martha was having him tailed. His mailbox in New York was broken into. He constantly had to change his telephone number because even though it was private, she'd get it and call him. He'd call us with a new number and say, 'Don't write it down. Memorize it, and swallow it.'

"He was out of town meeting with another publisher, and she called his office and told his secretary that something terrible had happened to Lexi. So Andy called Martha, who must have had the call traced because the next thing we knew she was on the phone to us, and we hadn't heard from her for months. In the course of the conversation she asked whether we'd seen Andy. George lied and said, 'No, how's he doing?' And then she didn't want to talk to us anymore. She said, 'Well, have a nice day,' and hung up. Of course nothing was wrong with Lexi. Martha was just playing one of her games. She has those sadistic, crazed ways."

Another time Andy attended a meeting with Martha at the office of her attorney. After a difficult and stressful couple of hours of hassling over financial issues, Martha said to Andy, "Well, you haven't even asked about Max," his favorite of the Stewarts' two chows. A week or so earlier Martha had mentioned in passing to Andy on the phone that the dog had been hit by a car but was okay. But when

Andy now inquired about the dog's health, Martha told him, "Well, he's dead."

Andy was shocked speechless. Even Martha's lawyer was taken aback by the manner in which she blurted out the news. "Jesus, Martha," he said, "you didn't have to tell him like that." Beside himself with grief, Andy ended the meeting and returned to New York. Sadly he telephoned a Turkey Hill neighbor to ask why he hadn't called him about the dog's demise. "What do you mean?" asked the uncomprehending friend. "I saw Max this morning. He's fine."

At Turkey Hill, meanwhile, Kathy Tatlock witnessed firsthand Martha's often curious and sometimes frightening behavior and became concerned about her emotional and physical well-being. On a number of occasions, particularly after the hair-pulling incident, Tatlock recommended that Martha seek help to deal with her anguish, anger, and frustration, but she rejected the advice.

Everyone in Martha's circle was concerned about her emotional state. Another friend, for example, gave Martha some marijuana, hoping it would help her relax, but it didn't.

"Martha was not sleeping at all," Tatlock noted. "She had *horrible* insomnia. She sometimes would barge into my room in the middle of the night to confront me with one thing or another." On one such occasion a highly emotional Martha demanded that Tatlock attend a predawn screening of decades-old photographic slides she had found among Andy's possessions. "She flipped the covers off me and said, 'I have to show you something.' She was frantic. She had already set up the slide projector in her office, which was adjacent to my bedroom, and she wanted to show me slides of Andy as a teenager with his girlfriends at the time. "I said, 'Martha, why do you care about these? You didn't even know Andy then.' But she was furious that he had kept those photographs all those years. I told her I felt that she was being silly, that there *were* issues she had with Andy, but those pictures weren't among them. But she told me that I didn't understand.

"By the end of the slide show she said that maybe she

would make an album of the pictures for Andy. I said, 'Oh, Martha, you are a very confused person. You start out by saying you're going to destroy these things, and you end up by saying you're going to make a photo album and present them to him. Why would you do a thing like that? Just give him back his damn slides. They have no interest to anybody but him. It's his past.' But she said, 'No. I think I'll make an album. In the meantime I'm going to hide these things. Don't you dare tell him that I have them.' ''

When Tatlock first moved into the compound to direct and produce the *Secrets* video project, Martha treated her royally, installing her in the small, sunny, modern suite that Lexi had used when she was home from boarding school. The bedroom contained a lovely four-poster bed that had belonged to Andy, and there was a small, fully equipped kitchen and bathroom. The lower level, once the garage, was now being used as Martha's TV kitchen, where Tatlock was directing the cooking sequences for the videos.

Initially, Martha was a gracious hostess and gave Tatlock every amenity: a pile of crisp, white, ironed sheets; a half dozen fluffy down pillows, and an eiderdown comforter for her bed. Every day the room had fresh flowers from the garden that Martha personally cut. In the bathroom there was an enormous wicker basket overflowing with soft towels of every size, in Martha's favorite color, white. Tatlock was given an open invitation to anything in the enormous restaurant refrigerators downstairs: the Perrier-Jouët champagne; wine from Sterling Vineyards, one of the sponsors of the *Secrets* series; and the mouthwatering leftovers from Martha's various cooking projects. ''Sometimes she would cook for me herself,'' Tatlock pointed out. ''She took good care of me. The treatment was exceptional, and it made me feel very special and very wanted.'' Martha introduced Tatlock to everyone, including Kmart executives. ''This is my director,'' she'd say. ''She's brilliant and very creative.''

But when Tatlock went home during a break in the production, the good life at Turkey Hill changed, and Martha suddenly turned against her. While Tatlock was away, Andy returned to the house and reclaimed some of his personal possessions, including the bed that Tatlock had been sleeping on.

"That was one of the landmarks in the separation," in Tatlock's view. "The point when Martha fully realized that Andy was making a new life for himself, that he never was coming back, that he had even taken his bed."

Martha was furious, and Tatlock, because of her proximity, became a target of her rage. "At first," Tatlock said, "I was allowed to leave the new sofabed open. But then she told me she needed to have the bed closed during the day. I was required to take all my notebooks, papers, reference materials, and supplies of one kind or another and put them away every morning, so there was almost no evidence of a human being living in that place. I had to unmake my bed every morning and make it up again every night.

"That was the beginning of control, a power play. Gradually all the services to me stopped. She told me very tersely one day that I'd have to clean out the little refrigerator that was in the apartment. She said, 'It's stupid for me to be paying the electrical bill for just you.' I had to empty and unplug the refrigerator. She also made the kitchen downstairs off limits to me, so I had to go to the Chinese takeout place to get my meal for the evening.

"She painted the bathroom sill and left the window stuck open. It was starting to get cold. I told her on one visit that I couldn't put the window down because I was afraid that I'd chip the paint if I forced it. She said she would look into it right away but never did. She also told me I could not turn on the heat, and I was freezing to death. Because it was so cold, I started to stuff towels in the open window. But when I'd come back to my room at the end of the day, the towels would be gone and the window would still be open, and she would say, 'Oh, you're tougher than that.'

"She even eliminated the bathmat. She left me with one washcloth and a small towel. I had to step on the cold tile floor in my bare feet or else stand on my washcloth after getting out of the bath. Whenever I would ask, 'Martha, what's going on?' she'd say, 'Nothing. Whatever do you mean?' "

Because Tatlock was so heavily invested in the ongoing video project, and because of their long, close friendship—''I knew she was hurting''—she continued to endure Martha's treatment. ''I was forced to get up at five in the morning several times a week because she wanted me to exercise with her. She said, 'It'll be good for you, and it'll be fun for me because I'm so depressed.' Because she was an insomniac, and because she also had such a crazy schedule, she would have the trainer come at five-thirty A.M. I would get up and open the gate for the trainer, and get the water, and prepare the barn, which she was using as a gym. The trainer would come, but sometimes Martha wouldn't appear. Sometimes the trainer wouldn't come because Martha had canceled the appointment but didn't tell me, and I would be waiting there at five-thirty in the morning. Martha never apologized but would say, 'I'm sure I told you she wasn't coming. I guess you just didn't remember.'

''I'd even get up and exercise with her mother when Martha was away on vacation. Martha would say, 'Please, please, I'm paying for all this. Would you just go exercise with her? It'll be good for her.' Later I got a bill from Martha's office for all my exercise classes. The whole thing was like a sick joke. You'd think an evil witch was at work.''

Hell Hath No Fury

In March 1988 Andy filed for divorce in Bridgeport Superior Court, claiming that his marriage to Martha Kostyra Stewart had "irretrievably broken down," and he requested that the court grant "equitable distribution of property."

Under Connecticut law at the time a sheriff was required to serve complaints, summonses, and subpoenas on the defendants in divorce cases. But whenever the sheriff arrived at Turkey Hill with pertinent papers, Martha did her best to duck him.

"Andy knew it would be difficult and unpleasant, but he thought the divorce could be resolved in six months by settlement," said a confidant later. "But whenever a sheriff set foot on that property to serve her, Martha was hell on wheels. She would just make it very unpleasant for him. They attempted to make service a number of times and were unable to, even though she was there. Martha fought Andy tooth and nail. What he thought would take six months to settle went on for years. Martha's position was that since Andy had left the house, *everything* belonged to her."

When Martha finally accepted service of the divorce complaint, she immediately filed a motion, which was granted by the court, that put a seal on all hearings and records in the case of *Andrew Stewart* (plaintiff) v. *Martha Stewart* (defendant). "Defendant requests that, as a Kmart spokesperson and prominent food consultant, records be closed," Martha's motion said. "National media exposure of the above records could be detrimental to the defendant's reputation and occupation, as well as the interests of parties not involved in this action such as Kmart."

By the time he filed for divorce, Andy had fallen in love with Robyn Whitney Fairclough, who was two decades his junior. Fairclough, daughter of a J. C. Penney executive and a schoolteacher, had grown up in the affluent Westchester County community of Briarcliff. In Robyn's senior year of high school the Faircloughs moved to Westport. Fairclough eventually went West to study art at the University of California at Santa Cruz and returned to Westport after graduation to pursue a career as a painter.

In the mid-eighties she joined the horde of young women working in Martha's catering operation. When the Stewarts were away, Fairclough often house-sat, taking care of the pets, feeding the chickens, and running errands. Because she was frequently around, sometimes even living in one of the spare rooms outside the main house, she and Lexi, close in age, became friends.

In time Martha herself grew quite fond of Fairclough, respecting her artistic abilities and creativity, and began utilizing her talents. Robyn became Martha's regular consultant on flower arranging and styling and was acknowledged for her work in the *Weddings* book. When *The New York Times* did a feature story on Martha's Kmart deal in late August 1987, several months after Andy had left, a beaming Martha and a smiling Robyn were photographed looking chummy in the Turkey Hill kitchen.

"What Robyn found sort of weird was that Martha would always say, 'You and Andy would be just perfect together,' " Clare McCully said. "Martha used to push them together, laughing about it in her way, which was more of a put-down of the two of them. It was sadistic. She really didn't mean it, and it was a warped thing to say. But their relationship did not happen until after Andy left Martha."

After the Stewarts' breakup, published reports suggested that Andy had actually run off with Fairclough, but that was not the case. In fact, Robyn continued to work on and off for Martha for months after Andy's departure. In one instance Robyn sought Martha's advice on a flower-arranging book idea and gave the proposal to Martha to read. Robyn also did the flower arranging for a big Christmas party that Martha threw in December 1987, eight months after Andy had left.

However, once Martha learned that Andy and Robyn were together, she refused to pay Fairclough the five hundred dollars she owed her for the party, and Fairclough was forced to sue Martha in small claims court in Norwalk in 1988. Martha eventually paid Fairclough a portion of the money due her. But Martha never returned Fairclough's book proposal.

Martha began alleging to certain friends that Andy and Robyn had been having an affair while Andy was *still* living at Turkey Hill, an accusation that Andy vehemently denied. Martha claimed she had evidence. She said she had discovered Fairclough's sweater in Andy's car, which she felt buttressed her suspicions. Andy contended Martha fabricated the story. He asserted that nothing of a romantic nature occurred between Robyn and him until almost a year after he left Martha.

"I learned about Robyn from Martha," Kathy Tatlock stated. "She told me about the sweater, and she felt that had tipped Andy's hand. She said Andy was a liar and a cheat and that Robyn had betrayed her friendship and generosity and also had betrayed Lexi, who was Robyn's friend."

In a counterclaim to Andy's divorce action, Martha charged that her husband "has on repeated occasions and continues to commit adultery. Plaintiff willfully deserted defendant more than one year prior to date of this Answer with total neglect of his duty to the defendant."

Whatever the truth, when Martha discovered that Andy and Fairclough were an item, her rage intensified. At four-thirty on the afternoon of March 16, 1988, Martha stormed into Andy's office, at 740 Broadway, in Manhattan, and "created a scene and disturbed the conduct of the plaintiff's business by, among other things, ripping up the complaint she was served with and refused to leave when so requested by plaintiff,'' according to a motion to restrain filed by Andy.

> The defendant threatened to break a window in the plaintiff's office which is located on the 11th floor of an office building. This was the second time in the last three months that the defendant had engaged in such conduct. The plaintiff requests that the defendant be restrained from entering upon the plaintiff's personal residence [at] 25 West 76th Street, or office, unless by written consent.

According to Stewart friends and former employees familiar with the incident, Martha burst into Andy's quiet offices, screaming at him and threatening him. "She was so goddamned angry and outraged," said an observer. "She threatened to throw things out the window—or rather through the window. She was ranting and raving, and Andy was going crazy trying to stop her, trying to calm her down, and trying to get her out of there before someone got hurt. She picked up stuff from his desk and went to the window and held it back in her hand as if she were going to throw it through the window. She was threatening him with, 'If you don't do this, or that, I'm throwing your shit out the window.' She was having a temper tantrum like a five-year-old. It was scary. At one point Martha actually reached across Andy's desk and slapped him in the face."

Several years later Martha denied that such an assault had ever happened. "I didn't slap him. We had an argument," she claimed. "That's the kind of stuff any divorced people go through, and it's nothing relevant to my life."

Meanwhile, Martha filed a motion with the court that requested that Andy "cease harassment, telephone calls and insults." She further charged that Andy "has taken girlfriend on vacations and holidays and physically abused defendant." Andy denied all of Martha's allegations.

On March 21, 1988, Martha and Andy signed a stipulation that said: "Neither party is to go to the other's business or home. Neither party shall harass or abuse the other party." The judge hoped that the order would put a halt to their angry bickering.

"[H]e did a lot of strange things which are very hard to forget," Martha claimed. "He was a weak man during this time, very weak. He didn't want me to talk to him; he had to make a clean break. It was a very childish, weak thing to do."

Despite the court-ordered attempt to keep Martha and Andy apart, he subsequently alleged that she had violated its terms, and, in a motion for contempt, claimed that she had gone to his "residence without invitation and refused to leave." On July 20, 1988, in a motion to cease harassment, which the court granted, Andy alleged that Martha "physically grabbed him and screamed at him in public, sent letters to individuals known to the plaintiff in which she has made derogatory remarks and has made numerous telephone calls to plaintiff vilifying him."

Five years later, in a *Martha Stewart Living* "Remembering" column aptly titled "Writing Letters," Martha noted that there was a tradition of letter writing in the Kostyra family that had been encouraged by Martha Sr. For the first time Martha mentioned her divorce to her magazine readers and described a curious one-way correspondence she had had with Andy. "During my separation and divorce from my husband, I wrote many, many letters to him and kept copies of all of them. I did this not from a sense of morbidness, but from a sense that in years to come I might understand better how we both felt and thought during that terrible time, when understanding was elusive and, for me, almost impossible."

Friends of the Stewarts, who either saw the letters or were told about them by Andy, described them as "mostly terrifying . . . not very nice . . . very upsetting." One friend said, "A number of times Martha wrote, 'This is the last letter I will ever write to you,' but they just kept coming."

Andy and Robyn had already fastened their seat belts aboard the Alitalia flight bound from Kennedy Airport for Rome, where Andy had business to conduct, when suddenly he was paged by a stewardess. Only Andy's secretary was aware of his itinerary, and she would have paged him only in case of extreme emergency. Andy nervously strode to the front of the plane, where he was told someone was at the entrance to the ramp with a message for him. It was Martha, highly agitated, holding yet another letter in her hand.

"Andy told me that when he saw her standing there, his heart flew to his throat, he was so frightened," a friend recounted. "He said, 'What the hell are you doing here?' And she said she had a letter for him, the *last* letter she would ever write to him. But when she saw the look on Andy's face, she shoved the envelope through an opening in the ramp, and the letter fell to the tarmac. Then Martha turned and walked away. Andy said he never could figure out how Martha had found him, but she had an eerie way of popping up at various places."

Meanwhile other strange and frightening incidents caused anxious moments for Andy and Robyn Fairclough. Andy discovered that the engine oil in his car, which Fairclough had been using, had been drained after someone had unscrewed the stopper on the oil pan. One evening Robyn walked out of her Westport art studio and just missed stepping in a huge pile of fresh dog dirt that someone had seemingly placed there. Getting into her car on another occasion, she was shocked to find that someone had used a knife or a key to scratch the paint. Robyn's parents, who lived in Westport, began receiving disturbing telephone calls from a man, and then a letter arrived containing scurrilous remarks about their daughter. Andy confronted Martha about the various incidents, but she denied any involvement.

Frank Kostyra, who had gone through a nasty divorce himself, visited Martha around the time of the split to offer his moral support. He found Martha belligerent and unresponsive. "She looked at me and said, 'You are all *happy* that I'm going through a divorce. You're *glad* that I'm suffering. You all [Martha's siblings] *hate* me because *I'm* the successful one.' And I looked at her, and my heart was just cut open, and I said, 'Martha, you're my sister. I love you, I don't feel that way. We are flesh and blood.' I went to give her a hug to console her, and she pushed me away, turned around, and stomped off."

He also said that Martha boasted to him at the time about

having a confrontation with Fairclough. Martha said she was driving in her black Mercedes on Turkey Hill Road when she spotted Robyn jogging. "Martha told me she rolled down her window and said to Robyn, 'Of all the streets in Westport, you have to jog in front of my house? If I catch you here again, I'll run you over.' "

Friends, such as Clare McCully, recalled that such incidents made Fairclough a nervous wreck. "It was very disturbing for Robyn. She felt that Martha was trying to make her life miserable. For a long time Robyn was afraid of Martha. She suspected Martha had keyed her car, and Robyn felt she was being stalked by Martha. Robyn had a studio in Westport, and she said she thought she saw Martha sitting in her Suburban, with the interior light on, staring up at her window. At one point Robyn had to get an unlisted telephone number because Martha was calling her at two and three in the morning. After a time Robyn felt she had to close her Westport studio because she just couldn't take it anymore."

As McCully's husband, George, declared, "If Andy had any doubts that he was doing the right thing by divorcing Martha, she certainly confirmed it in spades when he saw how she behaved. She destroyed any affection he could have for her, and there *was* a residue of affection there."

Fear of Erica

In her 1994 "mid-life memoir," *Fear of Fifty*, Erica Jong, a classmate of Martha's at Barnard, described an unnamed "blonde," a married friend, who lived in "Greenwich," a woman who spent her days "antiquing furniture" and "restoring antique quilts." Jong noted that her pal had kept a "creative house à la Martha Stewart—the woman who earned her freedom by glorifying the slavery of Home."

Jong, whose slap at Martha seemed to come out of left field, added that the woman in question was the wife of "a chilly surgeon" who "was never home." As a consequence, she spent a great deal of her spare time, Jong told her readers, "in a hotel room in Stamford with a variety of swains half her age. . . . She always brought her own vintage champagne, Beluga caviar, home-baked pumpernickel, home-cured capers, homegrown shallots and onions—chopped. The napkins were linen, the flowers fresh from her cutting garden." Taking another swipe, Jong noted that "Ms. Stewart would have approved."

The anonymous character Jong was describing in her "real-life novel" sounded remarkably like Martha herself—except of course for the hotel room shenanigans. Known for mixing fact with fiction and never delineating the two, Jong went on to describe the woman as "the high priestess of adultery," who supplied recent divorcées with résumés of men who were expert at "cunnilingus, fucking, hugging and backrub."

In 1982, the period Jong described in *Fear of Fifty*, Martha's *Entertaining* had just been published, and her views on subjects ranging from cooking to linen napkins and fresh flowers were made known to an enormous audience for the first time. *Entertaining* also resulted in Martha's gaining the same sort of literary celebrity that Jong had savored since 1973, when her "zipless fuck" novel, *Fear of Flying*, was published to critical acclaim and enormous sales, all of which established a rivalry between the two.

In the acknowledgments of *Entertaining*, Martha had cited Jong—along with E. L. Doctorow, Jill Robinson, and Anatole Broyard—as "writer friends . . . whose dedication to their art inspired and encouraged me." Oddly, though, none of them had been involved in any direct or even indirect way with the book, and Jong, for one, had not even been made aware of Martha's generous credit. Later Jong said, "I didn't know she viewed me as a role model," emphasizing, "I never would have seen the acknowledgment because *Entertaining*'s not the sort of book I would ever read."

While Martha credited Jong as a literary mentor, Jong and Martha—now the *two* shining stars of Barnard's class of '63—had had, in reality, a stormy relationship. And by 1988, with the breakup of her marriage, Martha was shocking confidants by naming Erica Jong as one of Andy's lovers.

"After the split, Martha told me Andy had slept with Erica," stated Wendy Supovitz Reilly, who was also an acquaintance and classmate of Jong's at Barnard. "I was visiting Martha, and she kept saying, 'He betrayed me. He slept with the kitchen help. He had an affair with Erica Jong.'

"She was ranting on about her anger and being upset. There was a small group of us from Barnard who had come to New York for a class reunion, and we were invited to Martha's house. We were all listening to her and saying, 'Oh, *that* bastard. He's *really* terrible,' the typical thing you say to a friend when you're being supportive. Martha was just very upset, very hyperverbal, spilling everything out. After I heard that there was something with the kitchen help, and Erica, and everyone else, I figured Andy was screaming out in one way or another. By doing it right under Martha's nose, it's obvious he was trying to get her attention.''

After college Martha and Jong had lost touch. But in the mid-seventies they became reacquainted when Jong settled in Weston, near Westport, with her third husband, Jonathan Fast, a budding writer and the son of the best-selling novelist Howard Fast, of Beverly Hills. At the time Jong was thirty-two, and Fast was twenty-six.

The Fasts and their baby, Molly, had moved to Connecticut from Hollywood, where Jong had unsuccessfully tried to turn *Fear of Flying* into a film. Happy to escape Los Angeles, Jong quickly settled into Connecticut's gentrified lifestyle—''writing, yoga, dogs and cooking,'' as she put it.

She became a regular customer at the Common Market, where she and Martha reunited. When Martha held a brownie-baking contest as a promotional gimmick, Jong served on the panel of celebrity judges. Nevertheless Jong never really liked Martha, as she made plainly evident in her comments in *Fear of Fifty*.

After settling into their new suburban lifestyle, the Fasts began throwing Malibu-style parties in their sprawling house that featured a hot tub outside their bedroom. For a time the Stewarts were part of their social set. Occasionally they brought George McCully, then between marriages, along to Erica's parties, thinking he might meet a fun woman there.

''People were cavorting naked,'' McCully recalled. ''It was fun. I remember Martha saying, 'Oh, you ought to go over and spend some time with Erica. She really likes you.' When it came to Erica, Martha adopted a kind of arch, amused air. The dynamic between Erica and Martha was mutually wary, like two prize cats circling each other.''

Clare McCully said that Martha later ''tortured me'' with stories of those wild parties at the Fasts'. ''She said that Erica thought George was 'well-hung,' and I said to Martha, 'Yeah, he is.' She took some delight in saying, 'He could've been with Erica Jong, but now he's with you.' ''

At a party at the Stewarts', "Martha spent the whole evening flirting with a very good-looking and very successful married banker," Jonathan Fast recalled. "He and his wife were our best friends in Weston. The flirtation was extremely blatant and aggressive. I think they knew each other casually. I felt left out because Martha wasn't flirting with me. Martha was very good-looking, but she just always seemed very cold and manipulative and cutthroat. She usually ignored me at these parties because there were other more important people for her to talk to."

And what was Erica's take on Martha? "Erica thought Martha was a bitch," Fast asserted, "and Erica was *very* sympathetic and attracted to Andy."

After Andy published *Gnomes,* he decided to produce a series of similar books in the same fantasy genre, including one on witches. His thinking coincided with Jong's completion of her seventh book, *Fanny,* for which she had done an enormous amount of research on witches and witchcraft. "We were at a dinner party, and Andy told me *Witches* would be a big illustrated book," Jong recalled, "and I said, 'You have to understand that if you're going to write about witches, you have to deal with the feminist issue.' I started to explain to him where the witch cult came from, and he said, 'Oh, my God, you've got to write this book!' "

But Jong, who received large advances, didn't think the twenty-five thousand dollars Andy was offering were enough. "I had a little baby," she said. "I was the breadwinner for my family. And he started being impossible. He said, 'You have to write this book. You *must* write this book. You're the *only* one to write this book. You're the *only* one who understands the subject.' And Martha wanted me to do this book, posing on her husband's side, totally wanting his success, totally trying to get him to sign me. Both of them wooed me with dinners at their house and at our house. There was substantial couple wooing. They played on my interest in the subject because there was no real money being offered to me."

Jong recalled having a number of meetings with Andy, just the two of them, during which Andy made light of Martha. "He used to do these comic riffs about all the chores Martha made him do. He told me about picking up the eggs from the chickens, weeding the garden, and we'd laugh. It was *his* retaliation. It was clear that he was like the farm boy—or so he presented himself.''

Eventually, Jong said, she caved in to the Stewarts' concerted efforts. "They were," she said, "very good at seducing me. I did the book for a pittance. It was a labor of love. Andy was very smart, very clever. He was good at reading people because he saw that I was passionate about the subject, so he was able to get me to do a book for very little money.''

But Jong emphatically denied, as Martha had alleged to friends, that she had had an affair with Andy. "Andy was *very* flirtatious," she claimed. "But it was party flirtation of the Updikean suburban sort. There was no ass grabbing. He wasn't *shtupping* me. I never sleep with publishers because you always get screwed financially when you do that.

"But the fact that Martha would be jealous of me—*that* I can understand. I'm a symbol of her opposite, and people are always irked by their opposites. Her marriage wasn't in good shape. People have seen me, because of my absurd public persona, as the sexual liberator, as sexually threatening. On my gravestone it will say, 'She first said, "zipless fuck." ' So to Martha, I would have been seen as freewheeling and sexual, and so I would have been seen as threatening. It doesn't surprise me to have my name bandied about when a marriage is coming apart. I'm used as a symbol, so maybe that's how the rumor got started.''

On the other hand, Jong claimed that she had heard that *Martha* was the one playing around, like the woman she had written about in *Fear of Fifty*. "I always heard that *she* was involved with people, that *she* was having a lot of affairs. But every powerful woman who's exposed to the public eye gets a lot of flak. There's been no woman who's been in the public eye who hasn't received slurs and attacks. Any woman who stands out there—whether it's Hillary Rodham Clinton, or me, or Martha Stewart—gets an unfair shake, and it has to do with misogyny, pure and simple, and hasn't anything to do with reality.''

But Jonathan Fast had a different take on the relationship

between his wife and Andy Stewart: "I heard that Erica *did* have an affair with Andy. Erica played a guessing game with me at that point. She said, 'I've been having an affair with somebody. Who do you think it is?' Then I saw Andy at Janet Horowitz's house, and he seemed really embarrassed and sheepish to see me, so I made the decision on that basis, which certainly isn't enough to take a person into court. But he was the only person I could think of who met the specifications. I have no difficulty believing that Erica went to bed with Andy. She would go to bed with anybody. She had affairs after her marriage, during her marriage, before her marriage. I don't think Erica was a difficult woman to seduce."

Meanwhile Andy told friends, who had also heard the stories about his alleged fling with Jong, that there was no truth to them. While Andy had in fact acknowledged to Martha past indiscretions, he firmly maintained that Erica Jong was not among them.

"Andy was really upset," said a Stewart confidant. "He said that Erica had called *him* and asked *him* to come to her house and that *she* was flirtatious and may have even been kind of physical. When I asked him for details, he said, 'We didn't make love.' But he said he felt that Erica 'was pretty direct' with him. He said he found her bright but not physically attractive. At some point Andy said he talked to Martha about the rumors. I know he hoped the rumors would go away. At first he thought they were being spread by Erica. But then he began to suspect Martha because she was making conflicting comments about him. To some women she would say he was great in bed and that he was sleeping around, and to others she'd say he was a dud. One thing about Martha, she never has to be consistent."

In any event, by the time *Witches* was published, Andy had left Abrams to start Stewart, Tabori & Chang. At that point Jong and the Stewarts had little, if any, contact. In the end it came down to Andy's and Erica's word against Martha's.

*   *   *

In May 1988, Barnard's class of '63 held its twenty-fifth reunion. Erica Jong didn't attend—she was to be the lead speaker at the class's thirtieth—but Martha, on a panel with several other distinguished class members, did give a talk, one everybody in attendance would never forget. (Although Martha graduated in 1964, she considered herself a member of the '63 class.)

"All of a sudden Martha said that all the assumptions she had made about her life had been turned upside down and shattered because her husband had left her. It was extremely naked," recalled classmate Caroline Birenbaum. "Maybe Martha had already talked about her marital problems on talk shows, or maybe she was rehearsing for something that she was going to do somewhere else, which would be the cynical way of looking at it, but that's not the way I felt. What she had to say was extremely intimate, as if it came out unexpectedly, because she was back among the people where it had all started. She met Andy while she was going to Barnard, and they courted there, and here she was back at Barnard. It was a very, very intense experience.

"The general reaction from everyone there was very sympathetic. She was in tremendous pain, and she was very open about it and was probably quite astonished at what she had done. It was very emotional. On the other hand, there *are* other things to talk about at a reunion. But what was so funny was that suddenly she stopped talking about her marital problems and started talking about her baby chickens and how she felt it necessary to wipe their bottoms every day. Obviously it was very humorous to all of us because clearly Andy was tired of it."

Despite the sympathetic reaction from many of the women in attendance, others there viewed Martha in a negative light. One of them said later, "We felt she was nothing but an ultra upscale Betty Crocker. There seemed to be tears in her eyes, almost as if she were an actress. Indeed there were tears in her eyes because of course her husband had just left her, and she told us all the story. She said he couldn't stand her perfection. Then she said, 'I've had such a terrible day. I've been out tending my chickens.' And she actually said, 'I was wiping their bottoms and putting them back in their basket.' And I thought, 'Wow! Wiping little baby chicks' bottoms.' The part she wasn't telling was that it looks cute and was probably photographed.''

Martha spent most of that emotionally draining day and evening at Barnard virtually epoxied to her friend Wendy Supovitz Reilly; they actually shared the same chair at the table for most of the day. Reilly said she was shocked at the animosity that she felt their classmates had toward Martha.

"When she went to the bathroom, they were making carping statements about her—'Oh, she's so full of herself. . . . She has *too* much hubris . . .'—but I didn't agree with them. Martha worked hard. She achieved something. So why shouldn't she be proud of it? Why should she play it down? She's just Martha.''

Business as Usual

Through the end of 1988, all 1989, and into the summer of 1990, the Stewarts' divorce battle raged behind closed doors. Motions were lobbed back and forth like grenades by the two deeply entrenched warring sides.

Andy demanded the return of his personal property, particularly certain of his photographs, which he said were "important for professional purposes.''

Martha ordered that the scope of discovery be limited so as not to cause her "embarrassment and damage.'' She was particularly concerned that the details of her Kmart contract not be revealed.

Andy filed a motion for contempt of court, charging that Martha had failed to comply with an order to allow appraisal of personal property, which included "all antiques and objets d'art."

Martha objected to producing certain documents that she claimed were "confidential."

They fought over division of their various properties: the famous "Martha Stewart House," at 48 South Turkey Hill Road, and the adjacent lots at 50 and 54 South Turkey Hill Road; the old "Adams House," in Westport, which was to be the subject of restoration in *Martha Stewart's New Old House* book and video, and became the focus of a local scandal; the Middlefield house; and undeveloped land in Salem, New York.

At one point Martha's attorney wrote hopefully: "There are numerous economic issues that we are vigorously attempting to resolve . . ." and he "anticipated conclusion" of the litigation within a month. But the conflict raged on for another six months, and there were skirmishes for years after that.

On May 10, 1988, a New York *Daily News* gossip column reported, under the headline SHE'S DINING ALONE, that "cookbook queen Martha Stewart and hubby, Andrew, so lovey-dovey in her new video cooking tapes, have separated. Word is the Connecticut hostess is also taking up a pad in the city." While the item was true, it infuriated Martha, who firmly believed that her marital problems provided "a field day for gossip columnists. They love to report that I'm dining alone now."

Actually Martha had already purchased, renovated, and furnished a six-hundred-thousand-dollar-plus fifth-floor apartment in a chi-chi building at Seventy-second Street and Fifth Avenue, across from Central Park. To decorate the place, she had hired the ultra-upscale David Easton— "a *fabulous* guy," Martha told *HG*'s Charles Gandee. Easton had worked on billionaire John Kluge's Albemarle Farms, a five-thousand-acre country manor in Virginia. She also retained the equally upscale architect Walter Chatham

to oversee the design. Afterward, though, Martha spent little, if any, time at the apartment, which her friends and
colleagues found odd. Rather than stay nights there when
she was working late in Manhattan, she chose to be driven
back to Turkey Hill. She used the Fifth Avenue digs mostly
for photo shoots and as an occasional pied-à-terre. Plus she
was now in a social club that demanded its members have
at least one Fifth Avenue address. For Martha, the apartment's purchase and renovation were part of doing business, of fitting in.

However, it was Martha's acquisition of real estate in
tony East Hampton, dubbed Malibu East, that generated the
most interest and had the greatest impact. In East Hampton
she hosted an annual cocktail party that drew big-name celebrities and became fodder for the gossip columns. In East
Hampton she also did battle with neighbors and zoning officials.

"There's a saying that goes, 'When you get divorced,
you go to the Hamptons,' " Martha once said. But it was
not the kind of highfalutin how-to advice she would have
ever offered in her books, which had strong appeal in the
Midwest and especially the South, where folks don't cotton
to such talk.

Initially Martha wanted a contemporary beach house,
"which I couldn't afford," so she was forced to settle for
a twelve-bedroom Victorian cottage, built in 1878 for a
minister from Brooklyn. The Talmadge house was the first
home constructed on Lily Pond Lane, one of East Hampton's most exclusive addresses. Martha reportedly paid $1.6
million and spent another cool million on improvements.
Why such a big place for a single woman? "Oh, I just want
one," she said. "It's *fun*."

Martha's new neighbors included high rollers like *U.S.
News & World Report* and New York *Daily News* publisher
Mort Zuckerman and Cannon towel heiress Frances Ann
Dougherty. The renovation was done by a contractor who
did the homes of other Hamptons luminaries, such as Billy
Joel, publishing magnate Chris Whittle, and Madison Av-
enue advertising guru Jerry Della Femina.

However, one East Hampton abode wasn't enough for

Martha, so she bought a second, more prestigious place designed by Gordon Bunshaft, the architect known for stark modernity. The price was more than three million dollars for the one-story, three-room contemporary, and Martha bought the house practically unseen. "My motto is," she declared, "if you love it, buy it."

Martha said she was at a cocktail party when she overheard two young architects talking about the house, and the moment they mentioned it she knew she wanted it. She said she came in with a low-ball offer, which started a bidding war—"not very nice for anyone"—and wound up paying three million for the place. "No matter! The place was mine."

The fact that Martha, known for her country living style, had bought a Flash Gordon–style house provoked curiosity and controversy. *The New York Times* wrote about it, and it was of more than passing interest to *New Yorker* editor Tina Brown, who immediately dispatched Brendan Gill, an acquaintance of the late Mr. Bunshaft's, to find out what was up. The ensuing piece, connecting Martha to Bunshaft, was worth the house's hefty purchase price to Martha in publicity alone.

The last time *The New Yorker* had noted Martha's existence was in a biting Roz Chast cartoon titled "Martha Stewart Takes Over the Universe," which showed the lifestyle queen ordering up a formal dinner for twenty-four on Mars, a Sunday brunch for eight on Pluto, and a Christmas feast for two hundred on Alpha Centauri. "Don't forget the personalized finger bowls!" Martha advised.

In his piece Gill, who showed a fondness for Martha even though he noted that her "genius" was to create "an imitation" of an "imaginary happy family life, and to market its trappings convincingly . . . ," expressed wonderment about why the Martha Stewart of "warmhearted, cozy domesticity" would buy the "severely modernist retreat, whose façade an architect critic once described as resembling the death-row wing of an especially desolate penitentiary. . . ."

Martha had a ready answer. She convinced Gill that she had been a Bunshaft aficionado dating back to the early sixties, when, while spending time at Yale where Andy was studying, she had watched the Bunshaft-designed Beinecke Rare Book Library being erected on campus, and that later as a stockbroker she had been enthralled at the sight of the Bunshaft-designed Chase Manhattan Bank building she passed on her way to the office.

But intimates of Martha's who read the piece snickered, believing Gill had been snookered. "Knowing Martha," said a pal familiar with the way her mind worked, "I'd say she stayed up all night reading about Bunshaft and prepared responses to all possible questions he might ask, knowing all the while that her answers would have to be erudite, literate, and educated for *The New Yorker*. It worked."

The Bunshaft architecture, members of Martha's circle also agreed, was secondary to the house's strategic location overlooking Georgica Pond, the most exclusive area in East Hampton, where Martha could rub shoulders, network, and do deals with high-powered neighbors like Steven Spielberg, Calvin Klein, and Ron Perelman.

But Martha eventually found herself in a feud with at least one neighbor and with East Hampton village officials, involving both her homes there. She split the zoning board in half when she asked for a variance to build a swimming pool at her Lily Pond Lane place just eight feet from her neighbor's property line instead of the regulation twenty-five feet.

After the board vetoed her application, Martha found another location for the pool on her one-acre property. But she then went ahead and built a nine-and-a-half-foot rose trellis around the pool without seeking proper permission. The zoning board considered the trellis a fence, and fences in the exclusive neighborhood were limited to a height of only six feet. Martha won this battle, though, convincing the "property police" that the trellis "was neither conspicuous nor an eyesore." Declared the victorious lifestyle guru: "A trellis is not a fence—at least not at my hearing."

Martha got into another dispute, this time with her next-door neighbor on Georgica Close Road, Harry Macklowe, a millionaire businessman. The two became embroiled in a disagreement over plantings along the border of their properties. Macklowe said he needed to put in plantings because Martha had cleared trees and undergrowth. Martha had previously accused him of "trespassing, illegal planting, and illegal obstruction, and illegal construction of overheight fencing" on her property. The matter went to court and was still being decided in early 1997.

Around the time she joined East Hampton society, Martha had become acquainted with the writer Kurt Vonnegut through his photographer wife, Jill Krementz, who had invited Martha to drop by the Vonneguts' place in Sagaponack. Martha had seen fit to boast that it was the Vonneguts who had been her entrée into Hamptons society—"they took me to all the parties"—and that she had repaid the favor by whipping up some of her delectables and rolling up her sleeves to clean the novelist's office studio. She made it appear that it had been a longtime stay.

"It was just a long weekend she spent with us—three or four days that's all," Vonnegut countered, noting that before and after he hadn't read any of Martha's books. "One morning I walked into my studio, and she had mopped the floor for me, and I just found that quite wonderful. She's also liable to pull weeds. I guess she's compulsive that way. I think she cooked a meal or two, and anytime anyone's willing to go into the kitchen, that's nice."

Later the friendship between Martha and Jill Krementz became strained, mutual friends said, and the relationship cooled. Whatever the case, Martha had made certain that she had been linked in print to the well-known author.

By the fall of 1990 Martha's ninth book, the fifty-dollar *Martha Stewart's Gardening, Month by Month,* which she claimed had taken her four years to photograph and write, made the best-seller list. The first press run of 250,000 copies grossed $12.5 million, giving Martha about $1.5 million in royalties. Martha called it "the best thing I've ever done . . . the best gardening book ever." By then her books in total had sold more than 2 million copies—"As long as I'm alive I'll be writing," she declared—and had grossed more than $70 million for her publisher. "*I* support Clarkson Potter," she boasted.

By the early nineties Martha had a personal income of about two million dollars a year. But she claimed, "I'm not rich. What do I do with my money? I put it back into my work. I don't have a big stack of gold in the closet. I'm very frugal. I don't have fancy things."

Martha had become a cash cow. *She* had become the product. That fact was underscored when Laraine Perri, the director of product marketing at CBS Records, decided that the masses should get a taste of the label's classical music list. How, she wondered, could she generate interest and sales? Like Kmart's Barbara Loren-Snyder, Perri thought of Martha Stewart. "People kept saying to me, 'I'm having people over to dinner. Do you have any tapes?' Then, instead of having liner notes, I thought recipes would be fun."

The finished product was the "CBS Masterworks Dinner Classics," a collection of CDs and cassettes designed as background music for special occasions and meals, such as *The Sunday Brunch Album* and *The Viennese Album*. Perri declared the collection a success, saying that each album was selling "far beyond a traditional classical album . . . beyond anyone's expectations." *Sunday Brunch*, in fact, quickly jumped onto *Billboard*'s classical chart because the disks and tapes were sold where Martha Stewart wannabes shopped.

One project that had to be completed posthaste was the *Secrets of Entertaining* videotape series, which had been thrown off course for a time by Andy's departure. Despite her problems with Martha, Kathy Tatlock had hung in, even though Martha was, according to Tatlock, nickel-and-diming her to death. Because of Tatlock's proposal and pitches, Crown had agreed to fund three videos. But Martha constantly argued with her over money.

"I said, 'You just can't not pay me, Martha. It's all in the contract.' And she said, 'Well, I'm not paying you for any more creative services.' I said, 'Martha, you're the star. You said the words. But I designed the entire program according to the proposal that I originally wrote. I planned the entire thing from start to finish. I'm not saying you didn't contribute to figuring it out. You got the recipes and decided which ones you would do. But I did the work. I should be paid, don't you think?' And she said, 'No, I'm *not* paying you.' "

Meanwhile working with Martha on the set during production and editing had become hellish for Tatlock and Dick Roberts, the line producer-cameraman-editor. "She had this very mercurial personality," Roberts noted. "She'd change from being the sweetheart. I once dropped a piece of ice cream on the kitchen floor while we were shooting, and she just blew up. I'd been doing this kind of work for thirty-five years, so I just knew to walk very, very gently, be careful. If I said the wrong thing, did the wrong thing, belched at the wrong time, I'd be in trouble. She would have these blowouts with Andy, and it would show on her face, and then somebody who was in her inner circle—either her mother, or her sister Laura, or whoever—would come out to the set and say, 'Watch out, Martha's in really terrible shape today.' But my God, she'd get on the set, the lights would go on, and she'd be Martha Stewart, no matter what. Then after the take, the phone would ring, and it would be Andy, and she'd have this terrible argument with him in front of everybody."

Members of the staff recalled that Martha was "ripping people's heads off" during the production, which was mostly shot in her studio kitchen, where the temperature hovered around a hundred degrees because of the television lights and cooking ovens. At nearly every break Roberts ran to an open door to breathe fresh air, and he had started wearing an iced towel on his head to avoid heat stroke.

Martha's disposition didn't help matters. "She was sour. She was unpleasant. She was angry. It was horrible," a crew member said. "Martha was a nightmare."

As all hell was breaking loose around her, Tatlock was trying to direct Martha so that the final product would look professional. But Martha wasn't always cooperative. "Martha left Kathy Tatlock in shreds," Dick Roberts noted. Tatlock's biggest problem had to do with Martha's style of speaking and her on-camera attitude. "Martha had what is known in acting circles as an academic tone, that lofty tone of the intelligentsia that people adopt," she explained.

"She also had a very clipped delivery. She had very *intentional* good pronunciation. She clipped her consonants. She popped her *P*'s and *B*'s. She gave a hoity-toity delivery. I told her, 'Martha, you're giving a message to the common people. You have to be able to talk to people as one of them, not as someone high-and-mighty.' If she was in a lousy mood, she'd say, 'Well, this is who I am, and this is the way it is. Don't you correct my grammar. Don't you correct my speech.'

"It was the same with her accoutrements. I'd say, 'Mom and Pop, who will be watching this tape at home, are not going to be able to afford that hundred-and-fifty-dollar pan to poach fish, and it's going to cost another one hundred dollars for just the fish.' And she said, 'No, I want to give people something special. This is what I do, and I want it to be beautiful and unique.' "

Things got even worse in the editing room. During important screening sessions, when final editing decisions were made, Martha sometimes fell asleep. Someone would have to rouse her and ask for her opinion, and she would groggily say, "It's wonderful, it's marvelous," and fall back asleep. Later she'd criticize the work and place the blame on others for screwing things up. (Two edits that Martha did oversee from start to finish were the excision of "Robyn Fairclough floral consultant" from the credits of *Secrets* and the deletion of Andy's name from the dedication and acknowledgments in *Entertaining*.)

Despite all the problems, the difficult video project was completed, and *Martha Stewart's Secrets of Entertaining*, like all her products, sold briskly, despite mixed reviews. Diane White, a columnist for the Boston *Globe*, who earned a reputation for writing a series of humorously scathing pieces about Martha over the years, wrote: "Men who never watched a minute of Julia Child have been known to take a sudden, uncharacteristic interest in cooking when a Martha Stewart special airs on PBS. It's understandable, I thought, watching as she tossed her blonde mane, raised her big brown eyes to the camera, grasped a cucumber, and instructed viewers to slice it 'thick enough to pick up but not too big to put in your mouth.' "

While the New York *Daily News* noted that the tapes were filled with "practical, everyday tips" and "sensible cooking and entertaining suggestions," its critic pointed out that those tips and suggestions might be of value only to "viewers who—like Martha—have herb gardens in the plural, commercial ovens, plenty of help, the patience to cut heart shapes out of bread and cucumbers. . . . [T]he video context in which these recipes are offered is so opulent it's offensive: Martha Stewart is possessed by her possessions, and amorally oblivious of reality. The tapes will simply make a lot of viewers feel inadequate, as if they can't cook pork roast unless they have service for 24."

Kathy Tatlock, who was excited at the beginning of *Secrets* because Martha wanted her to work on future TV and video projects, had gotten the ax when she demanded that she be paid the money owed her under their contract. Tatlock was forced to hire a lawyer to get the $33,741.17 in fees, not including promised royalties. In the end Tatlock was so devastated by her experience that she decided not to pursue the matter further and settled for Martha's final offer of about eighteen thousand dollars.

"Kathy really felt that if she had pursued a lawsuit with Martha, her life might have been in danger," Clare McCully asserted. "Other people who have seen Martha as this happy homemaker would think, 'Oh, that's just sick on Kathy's part.' I don't think so. For me, that's not a leap. I feel Martha could do harm."

Tatlock said she never felt physically threatened, but she did find Martha frightening at times. "I must say I was afraid of her when we were starting to have problems because she would just be so fierce but so pulled back at the same time. To me that's the most scary kind of rage. If someone gets up and screams and yells and makes a scene, I understand that. But if somebody's eyes are just speaking rage and frustration and hatred, and it's all pulled into themselves, I think that's frightening, and that's what I saw in her.

"After this had all happened, she called me one day out of the blue and asked me to go out to lunch. I said, 'Martha, I don't know what you're thinking. Why would I want to go out to lunch with you after what you did to me?' And she said, 'Well, I thought it would be fun.' ''

Dick Roberts, who remained on good terms with Martha after Tatlock's departure, signed a contract to produce and direct a series of thirty-second Kmart TV spots called "At Home with Martha Stewart." The concept had been conceived by Barbara Loren-Snyder for Kmart as a marketing and advertising tool.

"We did these commercials on a very low budget because Martha would always get her pencil out," Roberts said. "I had to work very quickly, and because we were working fast and on the cheap, we didn't have a generator, and we'd keep blowing out the power lines, and the power company was always being called out. Martha's neighbors had already been infuriated with all the disruptions, so we had to be very, very quiet about what we were doing."

Meanwhile on the set Martha was playing the role of glamorous star, regaling the young men on the crew with provocative stories about her bachelorette adventures at New York parties. For instance, she told them how she had run into Warren Beatty "and wouldn't have minded fucking him." The crew guys found her manner off-putting and embarrassing. On other occasions she tried to entertain them with risqué jokes. One, about a "blow job," made everyone in earshot uncomfortable.

One member of the crew, who had come to the job knowing and liking Martha, was the Broyards' daughter, Bliss. "I thought of her as a wonderful example of the confident, aggressive, successful woman," she said. A year younger than Lexi, Bliss Broyard had just graduated from the University of Vermont and had gotten the month-long TV gig through Dick Roberts, also a friend of the Broyards'.

The young woman's main job, besides gofering, was to act as Martha's hand double. Martha's hands were in terrible shape after years of yard work, and Roberts felt they weren't attractive enough for television. Whenever a close-up was required of Martha's hands, Bliss Broyard's were shot instead.

After a few weeks of working closely with Martha, Broyard's positive feelings began to change, and she came away from the project thinking of Martha as a strange, insecure, and sad woman. "She was a perfectionist," Broyard learned early on. "It was difficult to do things the way she wanted. I was taking things from her house to decorate the set, and she was obviously concerned about getting them back in the right place. She even suggested I take Polaroid pictures before I removed something, so I'd know where to put it back. Her life was so regimentally scheduled that she didn't really have time for a lot of niceties. She was intimidating, *very* demanding, and could be *really* bitchy. Occasionally I had to put on her clothes for these hand shoots, and she was perfectly rude. She'd say, '*This* is a seven-hundred-dollar Donna Karan alligator belt, *just* so you know.' I had never known her before as a celebrity, and she would vacillate between feeling entitled to a lot of attention and being insecure."

Despite the fact that Martha intimated that she had a glamorous life, Broyard came to believe that she "didn't have a lot of *real* friends" and led a rather lonely life. That fact was underscored one afternoon when Martha asked her to fetch something from her bedroom upstairs at Turkey Hill.

"There were four bedrooms, and each was beautifully decorated, but none had any evidence of someone actually living in them. They all looked like gorgeous hotel rooms. I said, 'Martha, which room is your bedroom?' And she said, 'Oh, you know, I sort of sleep in all of them, not one in particular.' And that seemed sad to me, her not having one bedroom of her own. I saw her as being lonely and not somebody who would spend a lot of time in a beautiful corner of her house with a book.

"The whole house was furnished like a museum. While her whole business was creating a sense of home, she didn't seem too comfortable in her own home, in the way one would think. She was always so busy developing projects, so ambitious, that she never slowed down enough to want to enjoy the comforts of home. But yet this is the thing that she sold, this kind of warmth and family."

Tuna on Toast

Like Martha, Frank Kostyra was creative and had an entrepreneurial bent, though nowhere near the Himalayan scale of his sister. For a time he operated a little picture frame shop, and he made a modest living as a handyman, builder, and contractor. But he constantly was thinking of ways to make *big* money—much like their father, and now like his sister.

When Martha became the "five-million-dollar" spokeswoman for Kmart's housewares division, Kostyra thought he saw an opportunity for himself and other members of the Kostyra clan to start "a little cottage industry" and cash in on some of the wealth that only Martha was accruing.

Kostyra's idea, which looked good on paper, was to design and produce a line of logo aprons—"Look Who's Entertaining with Martha Stewart," "Look Who's Cooking with Martha Stewart"—and sell them exclusively through Kmart. On his own Kostyra spent money and time researching the manufacturing process. He also found a source for secondhand embroidery machines that could be picked up "dirt cheap" in a third world country, and he located an idle plant in the Carolinas where the schmattes could be inexpensively manufactured. Even with the manufacturing costs and overhead, he figured that the profit would be "outstanding, unbelievable," on a sale price of $19.95. "People will buy them up because they already have Martha's books," Kostyra predicted at the time.

With all his research completed, Kostyra pitched the idea to Martha. "I laid it at her feet and told her that Laura could be involved, that Mom could get involved, that it would help the whole family, and that we would all come away filthy rich."

But Martha wouldn't bite. "No one in this family is going to come riding in on *my* coattails," she snarled, according to Kostyra. "You're not coming in on *my* success." When he described his sister's response to their mother, she shrugged knowingly. "Well, Frank, you know how she is: *Martha's Martha.*"

Eventually, Frank's simmering anger toward Martha boiled over. Envious of her success, hurt by her rejection, he took the road many scorned relatives of the rich and famous have taken: In 1996, he sold tell-all stories about his sister to the tabloids. "The family is very disappointed in his inexplicable behavior," a spokesman for Martha said in response to a *New York* magazine gossip item headlined MARTHA'S LIVING NIGHTMARE.

Martha's Martha. That was the same conclusion to which a number of executives at Kmart came after having several years of sticky dealings with their star attraction. But to those outside looking in, particularly the news media, which gave extensive coverage to the ironic upscale Martha Stewart–downscale Kmart alliance, everything looked as cheery as the Martha Stewart–brand percale sheets and towels that were nice but weren't exactly leaping off the shelves.

In fact the upbeat corporate statements and the confident public performances by Martha masked an ongoing internal war. "She never really did do the job that she was supposed to do," declared Barbara Loren-Snyder, who brought Kmart together with the domesticity diva. "From the very beginning Martha's attitude was that she didn't want to have Kmart as the force behind her. She wanted a better, bigger, more substantial company, with a better image. What she was saying for public consumption wasn't the way she really felt and wasn't the way she acted within the company. I had frequent meetings with Joe Antonini because it disturbed me greatly. Jaclyn Smith would get on a TV show and talk about her fabulous clothes and show great pride in her product and talk about Kmart. That was the way I had hoped Martha would be. But that never worked.

"Martha actually did a disservice to the company in the way she acted about Kmart. She never talked about the company if she didn't have to. There are dozens of memos to and from Joe Antonini about Martha and how she wasn't promoting the company publicly the way we wanted her to. If she went on a TV show and talked about one of her Christmas projects, she should have referred to the fact that the products were available at Kmart. She would never do that.

"Martha liked the Kmart money. Martha did not like Kmart. And there was nothing we could do about it. I quickly learned that Martha Stewart was a very dishonest person. She would lie and manipulate to get what she wanted, and she would do it right to your face."

Others within the company also were having problems with Martha on a variety of issues. Of particular concern was Martha's use of corporate travel and entertainment. If Kmart required her presence for an in-store appearance in a certain city, Martha arranged to schedule an unrelated engagement in that same city, for which another party also was paying her travel and expenses. That kind of double-dipping infuriated the Kmart people, who believed that for the money they were paying her and the promotion they were giving her, Martha owed Kmart exclusivity and loyalty.

"In those instances Martha was collecting double, and that happened a number of times," asserted Marilyn Gill, then Kmart's divisional merchandising manager for home fashions and the day-to-day overseer of the Martha Stewart promotion. "The contract itself was kind of loose in some areas, and Martha knew the loopholes. And because it was so loose, there were a lot of wars."

One of the most blatant examples of apparant avarice on Martha's part involved a lunch that she served to several executives during a meeting at Turkey Hill. Martha laid out a simple spread of tuna sandwiches, iced tea, and fruit. Then she submitted the tab to Kmart—for a whopping one thousand dollars.

"*That* was pure Martha," Barbara Loren-Snyder, who was present for the lunch, chuckled later. "Martha doesn't pay for anything, and she would bleed a stone if it was possible. She wanted to get whatever she could get out of Kmart. Martha abused almost everything. If she came into headquarters for a day and a half, her personal telephone bill would be two hundred dollars. Sometimes she wouldn't stay overnight and would leave when she could have given us more time. Martha wouldn't do anything for free. When I was involved with her, I didn't know of one charity event that she ever did for free. For a while Kmart had her do March of Dimes events and she got her three thousand dollars apiece from the company. When she traveled, she'd have cars pick her up. She'd reserve the best hotel suites. She flew first class."

Marilyn Gill said another problem was that Martha sometimes violated the terms of her travel agreement with the company by bringing along her attorney or an assistant and billing Kmart for their fares. "There was a big brouhaha over all that because there was nothing in her contract that said she had to travel first class or that we had to cover paying for anyone traveling with her."

When the woman who was in charge of checking Martha's expense account questioned her charges, "Martha would rip her from one end to the other," a Kmart official recalled.

Early on Kmart had retained the Manhattan advertising firm of Calet, Hirsch & Spector, Inc. to carry out the planning and ad campaign for the Martha Stewart–Kmart alliance and produce a series of television commercials starring the new spokeswoman. The Park Avenue South shop had handled image-making spots and advertising for politicians like Jacob Javits and big corporations such as Corning and Westinghouse. Peter Hirsch, the creative director and one of the firm's partners, thought Kmart's decision to go with Martha Stewart was "brilliant." As a neighbor of hers— he lived in Fairfield, next door to Westport—he was inti-

mately aware of her reputation for perfection, going back
to her days as a caterer, and he thought her books were
beautiful. But he also was aware of how Martha's greed
was causing dissension and feared that it would injure her
within Kmart.

"Her pettiness caused a lot of friction," Hirsch maintained. "I talked to Martha about this several times. But
she had come from this poor Polish family in New Jersey,
so she would charge Kmart if she used a napkin. She would
bake pies for the marketing director for use at a charity
event, and she would charge them a lot of money for the
pies. Martha believed that she should get paid for every
word that came out of her mouth, for every morsel of food
that she served. The Polish New Jersey person came out. I
think she thought she was going to be starving to death
tomorrow, so she wanted to make money, and she wasn't
sensitive to, or didn't care about other people's take on her.

"I said, 'Martha, you're being foolish. You have in the
palm of your hands a multimillion-dollar public relations
campaign to promote yourself nationally, and you're screwing it up because you're charging them for a tuna fish sandwich. For eighty-nine cents you're going to blow millions.
These guys aren't used to dealing with strong women, and
you're shooting yourself in the foot by doing this. They're
going to get angry at you and turn off the money faucet.
You're going to become famous with *their* money; you're
not using *your* money. So don't charge them for all these
little petty things.'

"She listened to me, and I thought I got somewhere with
her. So the next thing she did was cut the cost of her pies
to Kmart to twenty dollars apiece. It's funny. She just
couldn't stop herself. I couldn't believe it."

Martha's treatment of people also raised eyebrows and
caused problems for her with the Kmart hierarchy. "Everyone below Joe [Antonini] and above me hated the Martha Stewart program, and they hated Martha," Marilyn Gill
said. "They felt she wasn't a real person. If Jaclyn Smith
came in, she was so sweet. If Martha came in, her attitude
was: 'Who the hell are you?' They didn't like her because
she didn't care about them. If you were in the rest room

and Jaclyn came out of one of the stalls, she'd say, 'Hi! How are you today?' and talk to you. If Martha came out, she'd fix her makeup and walk out. She'd talk to Joe because Joe was in power and had the authority. But the rest of them she didn't care about. Other than Joe, no one wanted Martha there. It was a constant war.''

Peter Hirsch also had observed that Martha tended to treat people shabbily, and it wasn't always Kmart executives who took her heat. One of Martha's assistants was her sister the widowed Laura Herbert (who remarried in 1990). On location in Miami to shoot a Kmart spot Martha had viciously lit into Laura, leaving those in the party shocked and horrified.

"A bunch of us were having dinner at Joe's Pier, and we all were having a drink before dinner,'' recalled Hirsch. "When Laura ordered a second drink, Martha snapped at her sister and said something really nasty, and Laura just broke down sobbing. It was an embarrassing situation. Martha certainly was mean to her. It was terrible. Laura was working for Martha, and Martha laid a lot on her sister and put her through pure hell, bossing her around, treating her like the maid, always being very sharp with her. For Martha to do that to her own sister in front of people from a production company, an advertising agency, and the client was a little nuts.''

Hirsch worked closely with Martha, liked her, and thought she worked diligently on the commercials "even though she talked like a WASP but wasn't really a WASP.'' But he came to the conclusion that while she was "very creative and very inventive and brought a modicum of taste to the Kmart line,'' she also was "an absolute control freak,'' which he saw was causing constant friction with just about everyone at Kmart headquarters below the level of Joe Antonini. And he noted that unlike Jaclyn Smith, Martha had absolutely no loyalty to Kmart.

By the late summer of 1990, the third year of Martha's five-year contract, Kmart had spent $27.9 million to market her, not including product cost and royalties that had been paid out. But 1989 sales had totaled only $12.4 million.

Clearly, those dismal numbers had not escaped the atten-

354 *Martha Stewart*

tion of key Kmart honchos and advisers. "The sales seem inadequate for the investment . . . Martha Stewart overall represents a very small, almost insignificant volume for Kmart," a consultant's memo stated. "What it represents is an image builder; a unique product for our customers. If we fail we will have questions to answer from customers, from press, from manufacturers. . . ."

A lot of people at the top of Kmart, Joe Antonini included, were clearly worried about how the Martha Stewart program was being handled. As the memo pointed out, ". . . sales to date are small, investments large! Does Martha Stewart make sense for Kmart?"

Martha, the memo stated, should be the umbrella for the chain's whole bed and bath area, and as the spokesperson she should be used to bring customers into the department. But Martha, the memo continued, was partly to blame for the program's initial failure.

> Martha very early on alienated Kmart people by her cold, haughty exterior. She turned off buyers and merchandisers with her attitude. She is a difficult person to work with but as with all talented people we needed to prove to her we had the talent to do what we had promised to do. Additionally, she turned off those most prepared to help push the program by her greed, thoughtlessness, lack of concern for costs, and her inability to use the words Kmart when being interviewed, to interject Kmart when the opportunity presented itself on television, in print, in lectures.

With two years remaining on her contract, which eventually was extended, Kmart began testing a Martha Stewart magazine, with eight-page inserts in women's magazines. Planning had also started on a direct-mail Martha Stewart–Kmart catalog. The catalog would not have a Kmart logo but would have the appearance of being Martha's, with a warm, friendly, and informative editorial focus.

There was a strong push for the catalog idea because Martha had already put out the word that if Kmart wasn't interested, she'd use the concept with her next corporate partner, Time Warner.

The Adams House

In the early summer of 1990 Martha had become embroiled in a cause célèbre that so infuriated a faction of the citizenry of Westport that eggs were hurled at one of her homes. The target of the angry assault was the facade of her historic teal and white Adams house, which was to be featured in *Martha Stewart's New Old House,* her tenth book, published in 1992, and her fifth how-to video, *Martha Stewart's Decorating with Style,* released around the same time.

Martha telephoned the Westport police late in the afternoon of June 18, 1990, to complain angrily that a "large amount" of eggs had been thrown at the front door, and she expressed fear that there might be more harassment and vandalism.

The attack, Martha believed, had come as a result of what she termed "negative press reports" about a three-week-long, highly publicized, and very glitzy decorator showcase that she had sponsored at the house during the previous month. The advertised beneficiary of that event had been Paul Newman's Hole in the Wall Gang Camp Fund, a charity for children with life-threatening illnesses.

Suspicious townspeople, familiar with the ways of Martha Stewart, had begun questioning how much of the money actually would go to help the poor and sickly kids. A number of volunteers—decorators, artisans, craftspeople—who participated in the event also were dubious about the expenses Martha claimed she had incurred.

Meanwhile few, if any, were aware that the restoration of the house hadn't cost Martha a red penny. The money had actually come from vendors affiliated with her corporate sponsor, Kmart. Martha had then contracted her brother George Christiansen, a local builder, to perform the labor, the process of which was photographed inside and out, and filmed, for Martha's forty-five-dollar Clarkson Potter book and her video, which was sponsored by Murphy's oil soap. As usual, both the book and the video sold extremely well.

After the physical restoration had been completed, Martha got artisans and craftspeople from as far away as California to volunteer their time and talents to decorate the interior and grounds for the charity showcase.

Once finished, the 1838 Federal–Greek Revival farmhouse was opened to the public for three weeks, and as many as three hundred people a day trooped through, paying fifteen dollars a head to Homestyles, the trademarked business entity that Martha had set up especially for the event. Naturally that too raised a question in the minds of those involved in the project and the paying customers, who thought it curious that the entrance fee wasn't paid directly to the Hole in the Wall Gang.

Then, before the spackle was even dry from the removal of one decorator's sconces, and while a number of artists were still striking the showcase set, Martha shocked everyone by plunking down a "For Sale" sign on the front lawn. After having publicly expressed so much fondness for the old place, she was suddenly selling it—now that it was restored by others—for a whopping $1,350,000, more than twice what she had paid for it. The $535,000 purchase had also been made with someone else's money, an interest-free loan from Kmart.

For years before the renovation and controversial showcase, Martha had had her eye on the Adams place, the former residence of a prominent Westport educator, Ebenezer Adams, headmaster of the Adams Academy, a preparatory school for boys. By the mid-eighties, with only Esther Ruth Adams, the eightyish retired Westport reference librarian and a great-granddaughter of Ebenezer Adams, in residence, the house had begun to look "sadly down at the heels," Martha later noted.

"Miss Adams had little interest in the house other than a roof over her head," Martha writes in *New Old House*. "Clearly a frugal spirit, she had no plans to restore the house, and she lived there until she could no longer cope with the maintenance and upkeep of the place. The house was in dire need of attention, and since no other family members wanted to assume responsibility, Miss Adams reluctantly decided to sell. . . . I wanted very much to save the Adams house, to put it to rights, to return its history to it, to make it livable again."

In fact Martha's bargain-hunting instincts had kicked in when she heard the place was up for grabs, and the tag sale shark had begun swimming around old Esther Ruth Adams like the great white in *Jaws*. "Martha's hope was that she could pick up the place for a song from the old lady," one friend recalled. "Her plan was to fix it up and sell it for a profit. As with everything she does, she saw the renovation as a photo op, and she got the idea for the book, the video, and the showcase. It all started coming together for her. The wheels were working in Martha's head, and she saw dollar signs."

The first time Martha walked into the house to see if she could strike a bargain with the Adams woman, she could hardly believe her eyes. Other than the small portion of the building that the elderly lady was occupying—the kitchen, a bedroom, and a bathroom—all the other rooms were brimming with antiques and collectibles.

"I was amazed at how much stuff one family could accumulate in a period of 150 years," Martha says in her video. "Every room was stacked from floor to ceiling with just an *amazing* amount of stuff."

Martha thought she had died and gone to heaven. Her goal now was to get the house *and* all its contents as a package for a bargain price.

"Martha said she wanted to buy it, and she needed a million dollars to restore it," Barbara Loren-Snyder said. "She proposed making a video of the restoration project and then selling the tape through Kmart. Joe [Antonini] and

I looked at each other, and we thought it was a pretty dumb idea because Kmart consumers weren't going to spend money to buy a tape about renovating a house. Joe looked at her and said, 'Martha, what would you do if I turned you down? Who would you go to?' And she said, 'Well, probably to my publisher.' And Joe said, 'You know, a million dollars is a lot of money, and it wouldn't really make sense for us to do it. So I think you should go to your publisher.' "

But Loren-Snyder felt she knew Martha better than Antonini did. "This woman had no conscience," she observed. "If she got turned down by Kmart, I felt she would go to someone like Home Depot, one of our competitors, and make a deal with them. So I developed the 'At Home with Martha Stewart' campaign—a series of thirty-second television commercials that would be paid for by Kmart vendors, not Kmart, and would generate approximately fourteen million dollars in revenue. From that amount Martha got her money. Each vendor would pay three hundred thousand or five hundred thousand, or whatever, and over a period of a year each would be given certain time slots when his commercials would run. At the same time *Family Circle* would run eight-page Martha Stewart inserts. The magazine material and the TV commercials, for example, would show Martha giving tips on painting—using the old house or her house on Turkey Hill Road as the setting—and touting particular products. The open and close of those spots would say, 'At Home with Martha Stewart, brought to you by Kmart.' "

In July 1987, as one of their last husband-wife acts together, Martha and Andy Stewart bought the old Adams place, using the interest-free loan from Kmart. This was three months *after* Andy had officially taken his leave from Martha. At Martha's behest Andy had even shot an extensive series of photographs of the Adams house's decrepit interior and exterior, for use as background material for the planned book and video project.

Almost from the moment the contract was signed, Martha began complaining to Adams and others that the purchase price entitled her to the antiques that were in the house. But the bill of sale did not include the house's contents. Kathy Tatlock, who designed the book and video concept for the *Old House* project as writer-director, said, "Mrs. Adams didn't want to talk to Martha. She didn't want to deal with Martha. She didn't want to *see* Martha. Mrs. Adams thought Martha was trying to steal things from her."

The Kmart vendors who were footing the bill for the Adams house renovation also began to think they were being taken for a ride. As Barbara Loren-Snyder put it, "Martha really was such a greedy human being during this campaign." According to other Kmart executives, Martha got a list of the vendors and was constantly calling them and demanding materials, everything from paint to lightbulbs, to be used in the Adams house and elsewhere. "We'd get calls from a vendor who would say, 'Martha Stewart just called and wants thirty gallons of paint,' and we had to ask her to stop calling the vendors directly," Marilyn Gill recounted.

"These vendors had not agreed to give her unlimited supplies. They were paying for the commercials. I called her and said, 'Martha, I need you to quit calling the vendors with your demands. I think I can handle it better.' She was making similar demands for her signature products. She'd ask for thirty tablecloths, or six dozen sheets, so many sets of dinnerware and flatware. This is Martha, you know."

Another executive said, "For every vendor, she was extremely demanding. She demanded that she had to have at least two of everything sent to her, two of everything that was going to be promoted, plus everything that was necessary for the commercial production. If it was telephones, she'd say, 'Send me up a box or two.' "

The production of the forty-three commercials for the "At Home with Martha Stewart" campaign also caused grief for Westporters who lived near the Adams house and Turkey Hill and had to contend with the mess. The Westport *News* reported that residents complained about the Kmart trucks and film crews "swarming in and out" of the Adams house, which was across the street from a church. Because of the complaints, a zoning inspector filed letters with his department, one from a gentleman who feared "there will be an accident" because of "all the cameras, trucks, and lighting" at a busy four-way intersection nearby. "It's a danger spot," he declared, "because people are looking around. . . . One day there are tulips, another a gazebo. . . ."

In January 1990, with the renovation of the house finally completed, Martha formally announced the benefit designer showcase, called "Homestyles—Trends and Traditions." Martha said the idea for the event had been "brewing" in her mind for several years and reflected her conviction that "the 1990s would bring with it a renaissance of American and European decorating techniques with more homemakers than ever before becoming personally involved in restoration, renovation, decoration and landscaping. The interest in how-to is at an all-time high."

In late March the Westport Planning and Zoning Commission met to question Martha on whether she would personally benefit from the fund-raiser. She claimed for the first time that having the showcase was *the* reason why she had bought the Adams house, which she called "temporary art." She told the commission, "What I'm trying to do here besides raise money for the Hole in the Wall Gang is to propagate the idea of the home being a place to nurture your family." In making her case that what she was doing was purely out of the goodness of her heart, Martha claimed to the commissioners that between 1982 and 1990 she had donated a whopping ten million dollars to charity from the revenues from her writing and lecturing. Intimates of Martha's were shocked by her statement. As one confidant observed, "She has the first dollar she ever made."

On May Day 1990, Martha's showcase had opened, displaying the work of some three dozen decorators and a dozen landscape designers, from as far away as California and England. Manhattan decorator to the rich and famous Mario Buatta was the honorary design chairman.

When an artist friend of Norma Collier's mentioned that she had volunteered to do a mural in the house, Collier gave her a warning to be careful. "I said, 'Martha's not going to pay for it. She's going to stiff you, and you're not going to be able to remove it because it'll be on the wall.' So she did it on stretched canvas. When it was over, she said, 'Thank you for the warning.' Sure enough, Martha said, 'I'm not paying for this, and you can't take the wall.' And my friend said, 'No, but I can take the canvas out.' And she said to me, 'Oh, God, thank you for warning me about Martha.' ''

Another friend asserted that Martha borrowed copper pots from Williams-Sonoma for use in the show house kitchen. When the event was over, Martha cooked a celebratory dinner using the pots. Afterward, the friend maintained, Martha tried to return the used copperware. ''I came into the store, and the clerk said, 'Your friend Martha tried to bring back all the pots, and she had used them, and we told her she had to pay for them because they were only loaned for display. Now we can't sell them because they've been cooked in.' Martha finally paid, but she just has this attitude where she feels she's above the regular rules and laws of society, and she can do whatever she wants to do.''

A couple of weeks after the event Martha put the Adams house on the market. ''The value of her property was enhanced by the permanent design work of local artists in the showcase who stenciled floors and painted sophisticated trompe l'oeil illusions on the stairwells, baths and bedrooms,'' Westport *News* reporter Susan Malsch wrote at the time. ''Local landscapers donated decorative kitchen and vegetable gardens in creative designs using dwarf lilacs, conifers and boxwood and hundreds of tulips and primroses.'' Malsch emphasized that Martha was ''reluctant'' to give out the final tally on how much money the event had raised. She quoted her as saying, ''We don't have to declare publicly how much we are giving to the Hole in the Wall Gang Fund. It's our business. We don't have to toot our own horn.''

Martha's secrecy infuriated residents of the town, and angry letters started arriving at the Westport *News*. ''Martha Stewart's uncharacteristic modesty in discussing proceeds of her recent Homestyles decorator showcase gave me a good laugh,'' wrote one local resident, whose comments typified the view of many townspeople. ''Martha has tooted her horn loudly and clearly at every opportunity, and many of us who paid $15 for what we thought was a charity affair would love to know just how much of that $15 did, indeed, go to The Hole in the Wall Gang Camp.''

In an article headlined SOME EYEBROWS RAISED OVER SHOWHOUSE RECEIPTS, Malsch quoted the Hole in the Wall Gang Camp's attorney, Leo Nevas, as saying, ''I can't imagine anyone being concerned. . . . Mrs. Stewart is not making any profit. Only a twisted mind would think that Mrs. Stewart would try to take a tax deduction on this.''

Some volunteers also complained that they had been treated rudely by Martha's staff. A spokesperson for Martha said later, ''I don't think it's true. I know that some women were told to watch a particular room because we were afraid of theft, and they would leave. Another problem was that women were told not to wear high-heel shoes because we didn't want the floor damaged, and some would show up in them anyway.''

The barrage of stories and letters infuriated Martha, who angrily telephoned the Westport *News*. ''She just started screaming at me,'' recalled Malsch. ''She said, 'I don't have to blow my horn to you. You're nothing but a local paper. Forget it.' It was a riot. I just sat there and listened to her and took notes. She had quite a temper, and she's got that arrogance mixed in too. I just don't think she felt she owed anybody any explanation. I just don't think she felt any responsibility to be accountable to the people. She didn't want to be bothered. In the end I felt her motives were mixed. It was partially done to enhance her own property and to raise money for a good charity. The feeling I had about her was that she felt these people were to be used—the artists and craftspeople. Then people threw eggs at her door, and she felt the media were out to get her.''

In a later press account, in which Martha was asked about the flap over proceeds, she declared, ''I don't think we should give the dollar amount. They all got $15 worth of information out of that house. Think of it this way: It's like going to the movies.''

At the end of June, some six weeks after the show house event had concluded, the town finally got some answers in the form of a press release from Martha's sister-in-law Rita Christiansen, George's wife, who was business and finance manager for Martha Stewart, Inc.

Christiansen denied that Martha had personally profited or benefited from the work performed by the designers and artisans. She also asserted that Martha had not received any compensation for her time and efforts and had not gotten "any effective tax benefit" for running the event. In all, Christiansen said Newman's charity had received "in excess of $210,000 net after expenses. Paul Newman and the camp were very pleased with Martha's efforts." She concluded by saying, "This event was a great success, and I think that it is a shame that so many seem to have lost sight of the goal." A few days later Christiansen told the New York *Post:* "People like to criticize Martha. I don't know why."

Martha's initial efforts to sell the Adams house failed, and the place stayed on the market for a considerable amount of time. The property also became an arguing point in her divorce battle with Andy. Finally, after six years of controversial ownership, Martha sold it in April 1993 to a couple for $862,500, a profit of $327,500.

Lexi as Trump Card

A little more than two years after Andy had filed for divorce from Martha, the court issued a final decree in the summer of 1990, formally ending the Stewarts' marriage of twenty-nine years, which included the period of their

acrimonious separation. Martha got to keep the contents of
Turkey Hill, which were appraised at almost nine hundred
thousand dollars, cash, and securities. She also kept an expensive Connecticut house that the Stewarts had bought for
Martha's mother and her sister Laura to live in. (Martha
Sr., according to family members, had to use the proceeds
from the sale of the Kostyra homestead in Nutley to repay
her daughter for her half of the new house.) Martha also
kept Andy's valuable books, photographs, and *objets*. Andy
came away with the couple's undeveloped acreage in up-
state New York, and he got the Middlefield cottage.

But Martha kept stalling on giving Andy the $1.5 million
plus interest she still owed him for his half of Turkey Hill,
an amount stipulated by their divorce decree. Andy waited
and waited and finally recommenced a lawsuit against her,
one of several contempt of court proceedings he had to
bring to get her to comply with the terms of their settlement.

Some five years after their divorce, Martha finally agreed
to pay up after Andy took the extreme measure of starting
foreclosure proceedings on Turkey Hill, which would have
been publicly embarrassing for the lifestyle queen.

The day Andy arrived at the house to pick up the big
check, though, Martha had deducted several hundred thousand dollars, which she said she planned to give to Lexi.
Andy was livid. He told Martha he would be happy to give
his daughter help, money, and support, but she had to start
communicating with him. And furthermore, he would be
the one to give his money to Lexi, not Martha, whom Andy
didn't trust. After a heated early morning fight, Martha gave
in and the battling couple drove to the bank where Andy
demanded a certified check, refusing to take one of his ex-
wife's personal checks.

But their legal wrangling continued. In October 1996,
Andy filed a civil suit against Martha in U.S. District Court
in New Haven, Connecticut, claiming she owed him more
than one hundred fifty thousand dollars from a pension fund
that was established when her business, Martha Stewart,
Inc., was incorporated in 1979—eight years before the couple separated. Their divorce decree had stipulated that he

receive the money from the fund. Andy decided to sue after Martha claimed his vested interest in the plan was zero, and questioned his eligibility. It took the sheriff weeks to serve Martha with court papers because she continually dodged him. The case was expected to drag on—possibly into the twenty-first century.

The most painful sticking point, however, remained twenty-five-year-old Lexi, the Stewarts' only living possession. Lexi had sided with her mother when her father left.

Lexi, who had grown into a beautiful young woman (after graduating from Barnard, she modeled for a time like her mother), was emotionally devastated by the parental split. As a result, mother arranged for daughter to go into therapy. In fact all of the Stewarts separately sought treatment for their emotional pain.

But Martha's fury never abated. She was determined to see that Andy was punished for leaving her, an act that she later claimed for public consumption had taken her "five miserable years to get over." Privately, however, Martha remained in a constant state of agitation. As her own mother acknowledged in the fall of 1995, "I don't think she'll ever get over it."

As late as the spring of 1996 Martha said, "I felt rejected, stupid and failed. I should have just gotten on [with my life]. Somebody told me that, and I didn't listen. I should have."

Some six months after their divorce became final, Martha, in what sounded to many like a spiteful boast, declared that Andy's "punishment" for leaving her—she actually used the word "punishment"—"has been that our daughter doesn't speak to him, hasn't spoken to him for four years. Which is a disgusting punishment, I would think. I know he cares about his child very much, but she can't forgive him his behavior. It's sad. It's not like he got on a motorcycle and rode off into the sunset . . . it's the same life, only it's miserable. I mean, I don't know, I imagine it's miserable. He doesn't have a wife, doesn't have a daughter, doesn't have the dogs, the cats, the house, the gardens, you know . . . I think that's pretty miserable."

But in fact Andy did have a new life: He had Robyn

Fairclough, whom he planned to marry. He had the fellowship and support of most of the Stewarts' old friends. He had his publishing career. And he had a beautiful farm in New England, with pets and livestock, and many, if not all, of the amenities he had had at Turkey Hill. "Once he left Martha and got over the initial shock, Andy never felt better and healthier, both emotionally and physically. By divorcing her, it was as if he had removed a cancer from his system," a longtime confidant remarked.

One of the few statements Andy has ever made publicly about the decline and fall of his marriage is that he and Martha had done "a poor job as parents." He said, "We were too involved in our professional lives and fixing up the house. We were always making the home into a mythological place. But it wasn't a home—we didn't spend enough time with Lexi."

On several occasions during the separation and after the divorce Lexi and her father inadvertently ran into each other on the streets of New York, but few, if any, words passed between them. Andy told friends he was saddened and depressed because of the severed connection with his only child. He wasn't invited to her college graduation, and he never received an invitation to any of her birthdays after he left Martha. Lexi herself has acknowledged that she had found her parents' separation and divorce "very, very difficult" to deal with.

Lexi has said little publicly about her relationship with her father, but the words she has voiced have been tinged with anger and bitterness. "If he was a nice man, I would talk to him," she said about a year after the divorce. A couple of years later her view of her father had not softened. "I don't think he's a very nice person," she declared. "There are bad people, and there are good people, and just because you're related to them doesn't mean you have to tolerate bad behavior." At a Christmas party in 1995, at Indochine, a chic Manhattan restaurant, Lexi told her old high school flame Nick Dine that she had no intention of *ever* resuming her relationship with her father.

"It's a source of tremendous pain for me," Andy said. "I think of her [Lexi] every single day, many times." He said he felt that if he'd had to do it all over again, he would have discussed the separation with his daughter before he left, but "I never had a chance to do that. She saw her mother hurt, and she thought I was uncaring. One way or another she got the facts wrong as well as the interpretation."

Members of the Stewarts' inner circle were mystified. Why, they wondered for years after the split, had Lexi turned against her father? Most of them had always viewed Andy, not Martha, as the loving, doting, and giving parent. To them, it made no sense whatsoever that Lexi had taken Martha's side.

There was speculation among Stewart intimates that Martha had in fact bought her daughter's loyalty and allegiance by plying her with money, clothing, a fancy Upper East Side apartment, and European jaunts. "That would not be a shocker because Lexi is Martha squared," stated a member of the inner circle. "Andy wouldn't have given his daughter a mink coat when she was in college. Martha did. Lexi liked that. Like her mother, Lexi likes having stuff." Thus longtime Stewart friends perceived that Martha constructed what one called "a Berlin Wall of money" between her daughter and her father.

Lexi became a jet-setter of sorts and was hanging out with what one friend described as "the Manhattan-Euro brat pack—rich kids who partied and traveled." At one point Martha planned to spend a few weeks in Europe with Lexi, who already was there, visiting a boyfriend in Italy. When a friend asked Martha whether she planned to meet Lexi in Rome or in Paris, Martha offered an intriguing response. "She said, 'No, no. Lexi is going to come home first.' And I said, 'How can she come home when you're leaving for Europe in a few days? Why don't you just meet each other there?' And Martha said, 'Well, Lexi says there's nowhere to do her laundry in Italy, so she wants to come home first and do it here.' "

Martha also installed Lexi in a brownstone apartment in the upscale Manhattan neighborhood near Madison Avenue and Ninetieth Street, picking up her rent and paying for the furnishings.

"The apartment was extremely tasteful but cold," a friend of Lexi's said. "It wasn't a warm, cozy young woman's apartment. It looked more like a show space. Everything was uncomfortable, including underfoot—because she had those hemp rugs. What was startling was that in her bedroom, which had lots of eiderdown and pillows on the bed, there wasn't a single chest of drawers. Lexi kept *all* her clothes—and everything was black, white, or beige—meticulously folded on shelves. It looked like a store. It was the most anal apartment of a twenty-something-year-old girl I'd ever seen in my life."

Lexi's room at Barnard had been decorated much the same way, a college pal recalled. "It was white-on-white-on-white—sterile as a hospital room." Lexi herself acknowledged that "except for the cross, my room looked exactly the same" as a convent.

Through the years, Martha continued to bestow gifts on Lexi—who had taken to calling herself a "poor little rich girl"—and helped finance various of her daughter's business ventures, the first of which—a diner in Bridgehampton—ran into problems with the old guard.

For fifty thousand dollars Lexi bought a railroad car–size stainless steel diner in a Boston suburb and had it transported to the town of Bridgehampton, near where her mother owned property. Lexi's plan was to call her restaurant the Delish Diner and have a big neon sign on the roof. The concept infuriated townspeople and officials, much the way Martha's catering operations had rubbed officials the wrong way in Westport. "If I had been Mr. Jones from one of the old East Hampton families [instead of the daughter of a nouveau riche high-visibility celebrity]," Lexi said later, "it might have been easier."

Her next effort, which did take off, was the trendy, ten-unit, $245-a-night (in season) Bridgehampton Motel, where guests were supplied with spa-quality bathrobes, goose down comforters, and Egyptian cotton Frette sheets. "I don't sleep on anything other than cotton sheets and I don't expect my guests to," the young hotelier declared, sounding more and more like you know who.

Buying, renovating, and operating the motel was Lexi's

first real job. She was twenty-eight years old. "I hadn't had a *real*, real job," she admitted. "I didn't *have* to do anything," a fact that made her focused and driven mother "very unhappy" about her daughter's lack of direction.

The week the motel opened, Martha said of the place, "These are her ideas, not mine. Alexis has always been an independent child. She *wouldn't nurse*! She would have died in the old days. She's very self-directed. And believe me she's her own person."

Whatever their relationship, having Martha Stewart as her mother helped Lexi promote her new venture. Before the motel even opened, trendy *New York* magazine and the "Styles" section of *The New York Times* did extensive feature stories on the place, publicity that Martha had arranged through her network of high-powered media pals.

After several years Lexi grew bored and put the motel on the market for more than a million dollars. "My life has just gotten too busy," she declared, sounding like Mom again. "I don't know what I'm going to do next."

Together with several trainers, Lexi opened the East Hampton Gym, a once-grubby fitness center, which she jazzed up. She also bought an East Hampton shop called Yard Sale, to hawk the tchotchkes that she collected, all of which had prompted *New York* magazine to ask, "Is Alexis Stewart . . . plotting Hamptons domination?"

Friends said the real answer was that Martha had bankrolled Lexi's businesses to keep Lexi in her corner and out of Andy's. "After her parents' separation, Lexi was having problems with men and dating, and I would often say to Martha that it would be wonderful if Lexi could resume her relationship with her father," Janet Horowitz said. "I would tell Martha that it was a loss for Lexi not to have contact with Andy, and Martha agreed with me—*verbally*. She knew I was right. But in actuality she did *not* want Lexi to have a relationship with Andy because Lexi was Martha's trump card. Lexi was the only thing she could hold over Andy, the only thing Martha had that she knew that Andy really wanted, so she could play Lexi, and she has played Lexi."

The Horowitzes remained in Andy's corner, which particularly upset Lexi, who had been extremely close to Janet. At a party in New York City following the Stewarts' divorce, Lexi made a scene by venting her anger. "Lexi was violent to me," Horowitz asserted. "She said, 'Drop dead. Fuck you.' She really lashed out at me, and it hurt and horrified me. She called me 'two-faced' because I remained Andy's friend. I sent Lexi a card afterwards, but she sent it back with a vicious note."

The fact that Lexi sided with Martha didn't necessarily mean that mother and daughter had finally forged a bond after years of squabbling. The two had never been particularly close, and that didn't change with Andy's departure. "It's a constant battle," as Lexi herself acknowledged about her relationship with her mother. "But we're all we have for each other. We're like good friends. I don't think my mother *ever* thought of me as her little girl. It's like the movie star with the boyfriend and nobody knows who he is. That's me. It's the dichotomy of 'Why aren't they taking my picture?' and '*Thank God* they aren't taking my picture.'"

Martha and Lexi often fought, and the coldness existing between them continued through the mid to late nineties. Lexi once remarked that her mother was a difficult taskmaster who "might come over and torture me because the floor's not clean or the television in my office had dust on it. She's controlling, but it's all right. She doesn't mean any harm."

Lexi saw through Martha and let her know that fact at every opportunity. For instance, when Lexi read her mother's books and the sunny anecdotes about Stewart family life, she often laughed aloud at what she viewed as their falsity. "I mean, it's very funny to read those books," she said. "My friends and I sit around and giggle. I mean I don't care. I don't have to go on tour with her to Iowa, so nobody asks me. Is it in large part fantasy? Well, no, it's not really. Because it's really the way she sees it. She really does. I mean, my attitude is much different than my mother's, so I can't argue with her about it because if that's the way she thinks it is, it's not the way I think it is."

Mother and daughter were at odds over everything, even

down to Martha's published fantasies about Lexi's wedding day—if she ever got married. Martha dreamed of a wedding for Lexi "under apple trees, in the spring, coming up the front of the house." Lexi, on the other hand, saw her nuptials "in the winter, in a restaurant, at night." The message she communicated to Martha was clear: "You're not doing anything, so there's no need to get excited."

Always private and seemingly withdrawn, Lexi began to open up about life among the Stewarts, complaining about her childhood in Westport and putting down her now-famous mother. "Getting up and going to antique shows when you're eight is not every kid's idea of fun," she observed. "I didn't like Connecticut. People are so closed-minded and preppy. I didn't fit in. I didn't have enough Fair Isle sweaters to compete."

Like her father and her parents' friends, she said she had found the famous Turkey Hill house uncomfortable and virtually unlivable because of the constant renovation and her mother's drive to turn the place into a museum. "It was 'Don't sit on the comforter, turn it down before you sit on it.' As an only child you get all this shit and you get all the good stuff, too." She recalled the letters from her mother when she was at camp and the fact that Martha always included "a list of words I'd misspelled" in letters Lexi had sent home. It was amply clear that mother and daughter were *not* happy campers together and would never be.

Martha's emotions regarding her daughter have risen and fallen like badly baked bread: Over the years since the divorce she's made contradictory public comments about their relationship. In the spring of 1993, for instance, Martha stated, "Lexi is a good friend to me as well as a benign critic, and I think I'm the same to her." Three years later she admitted, "I'm *always* wrong with my daughter. She's very strong, and impossible. She stands up to me all the time."

Nevertheless, Martha tried to bond with Lexi by playing more the role of girlfriend than mother. For example, Martha took to offering Lexi curiously liberal advice about her sex life. "Martha told me that she wanted Lexi to have a

lot of glamorous experiences,'' Bliss Broyard recalled.
''She told me Lexi was going to Rome to model, and Martha said, 'I told her to go have an affair in Rome because that's a great thing to do as a young woman.' ''

Martha also proudly displayed to Broyard and others a series of daring photographs that had been taken of Lexi, supposedly for a European fashion magazine. ''The pictures were from a lingerie shoot and were *very* sexy,'' Broyard said. ''They showed Lexi just kind of leaning over in a bra, and Martha was really proud of her. I thought it was odd in a way that she would show those pictures of her daughter because they *were* erotic, and Martha was aware of that.''

On another occasion Martha showed Kathy Tatlock ''a very sexy cover girl kind of picture'' of Lexi supposedly taken for a calendar. ''She looked very beautiful, and sexy, and sort of a different Lexi than I had ever seen,'' observed Tatlock, a mother of two daughters. ''Frankly I was tickled when I saw the picture. I thought, 'Well, Lexi is finally going in her own direction, doing her own thing. *Hallelujah.*' ''

Like other friends of the Stewarts', Tatlock thought that Lexi had become a pawn in her parents' marital wars. Over the years, for instance, she noted that whenever Lexi was angry at her father, ''Martha took advantage of that'' to pit her daughter against her father. ''So when Martha and Andy separated, my heart went out to Lexi because she was totally a victim of their mess. My heart also went out to Andy.''

By 1997, Lexi still had not married and appeared to be having difficulties with at least one man in her life, an ex-boyfriend. Two days after Christmas 1996, Lexi reported to East Hampton, New York, police that he had beaten her. A police detective, Robert Mott, said, ''Miss Stewart has a very swollen cheek and has pressed assault charges.''

Lexi was quoted as saying, ''I was hit in the face. We had split up, and I told him I didn't want to see him again. But he didn't listen. He began to argue with me. Suddenly and without warning, he hauled off and hit me in the face. It totally stunned me and I fell against a door. My face is bruised. I'm never going to talk to or see this man again. I don't believe a two-hundred-and-fifty-pound man has the right to go around hitting women. I called my mother, who is out of the country at present, to tell her what happened.''

Finding Mr. Right

While Martha has claimed that Andy's exit shattered her, she immediately began working on changing her look so she could be sexier and more appealing to other men. Despite what she declared about the paralyzing impact of Andy's departure, Martha didn't waste a lot of time before beginning the hunt for the next Mr. Right.

''She moved away from that soft, sweet look to the powerful, sexy woman, so she could attract men,'' a close friend pointed out. ''She started wearing more plunging necklines and shorter hair. She went from that sort of coy, coquette, wholesome *Seventeen* model thing, which she played until she couldn't possibly get away with it anymore, to the look of a grown-up, *seriously* hot woman. And Martha started playing it to the hilt. She loved to be tall and look powerful, and she felt *that* was sexy. She would wear this ankle-length mink coat that she looked monstrously striking in.''

Martha's brother Frank Kostyra felt that his sister's image change made her appear more formidable—even, he thought, masculine. ''When a woman takes long hair like she had, and all of a sudden gets a divorce and then chops her hair off, she's putting on the pants. It's not only psychological but actual in her case,'' he observed.

In January 1990 *Avenue* magazine, a hip chronicler of New York's movers and shakers, photographed the new, improved Martha. She looked nothing like the way she did in her books or on television. No L. L. Bean preppy khaki pants and work shirts here. One shot was of her standing next to the stove at Turkey Hill, her mink coat draped below her bare shoulders, her bosom barely covered by the bustier top of a slinky, short black cocktail dress, her legs sheathed in black stockings, her feet in four-inch dominatrix heels. There was a seductive, come-hither look on her face; her mouth was pouty; her hair tousled and wild-looking. NO ONE'S IN THE KITCHEN WITH MARTHA, the caption blared. ''Now that she's divorcing, Martha is breaking out of her calico cocoon.''

To look svelte, Martha was up at daybreak daily to work out with her female trainer, putting in two rigorous hours of stretching and weight lifting, swimming, biking, and using a StairMaster. She was taking a thousand milligrams of vitamin C every day, plus calcium, magnesium, and an all-purpose vitamin. She drank fruit juices and herb teas and ate vegetables, but she stayed away from butter and all fried foods, and she used olive oil on virtually everything. Everywhere she went she carried bottled water. She drank little if any alcohol, smoked not at all. But despite her workouts and diet, she remained a size twelve.

Once she felt she looked hot and buff, Martha began her search for a suitable guy. (She even had transformed the studio barn at Turkey Hill into a guesthouse, explaining coquettishly, ''I don't like any guests in this house unless it's a boy guest.'')

One of the first men Martha pursued was her onetime colleague from Wall Street Brian Dennehy, who by the late 1980s had been appearing in Hollywood features and made-for-TV films for a decade.

During the time they worked together, Martha and Dennehy had had a strong mutual attraction, which Martha had revealed to Kathy Tatlock while they were working on the *Secrets of Entertaining* video project. ''After Andy left, Martha tried to get in touch with Dennehy,'' Tatlock recalled. "I felt she had this fantasy of hooking up with him and showing Andy that she was still viable. She said she always thought Dennehy was a very attractive guy."

As Dennehy remembered it, he and Martha accidentally "bumped into each other" in New York City when he was in town for the premiere of a film starring one of his agent's clients. Martha told Dennehy about her separation and how it had "enormously affected" her. "But it's very hard to tell with Martha because she's really good at disguising her feelings," he observed. "She's a good actress and a tremendously strong person, who's *not* going to appear terribly vulnerable."

Martha, who was interested in going out with Dennehy, did get her wish. She accompanied him to the premiere and the party afterward, and while Dennehy was in town, he and Martha "kind of hung out" together. Dennehy said he found her even more "vivacious, interesting, and fun" than he had remembered her from the old days on Wall Street. "We spent some time together. But it wasn't *that* kind of relationship. I've always liked Martha. To have her on your arm is not such a bad thing. But it was never anything more than that. Martha is one of those women who intimidate the *shit* out of men."

Nevertheless, Dennehy realized from their conversations that she was interested in meeting a suitable man. "There was this attitude in those days," he noted, "that my God, there's got to be *somebody* out there for Martha." So the actor tried to fix her up with a Left Coast–Right Coast power broker, Dennehy's pal and sometime employer Michael Fuchs, then the head of HBO and Warner Music, part of the Time Warner conglomerate.

"I was doing a picture, I think it was another one for Fuchs, and I said, 'God, Martha, I got a great guy for you.' But they never did go out because she's about a foot taller than him," said the hulking Dennehy. "Fuchs, who I like a lot, has this thing about people trying to fix him up and get him married off, which he's not really interested in doing. Martha and Michael laughed and agreed that it was an interesting idea that would never happen."

In the late eighties to early nineties Martha, her fame and

power growing, joined the ranks of New York's glitterati, and her name began to appear regularly in boldface in the gossip columns. When she began house hunting in the Hamptons, the details were duly reported. When she ran into Lee Iacocca during a business meeting at Kmart's Michigan headquarters, a gossip column noted the fact that she had given him her latest compact disk of music to eat by. Her cocktail parties became fodder for the tabloids too, mainly because of the impressive guest list: the Calvin Kleins, the Jann Wenners, the Morton Janklows, Herb Ross and Lee Radziwill, among others.

About a year into her separation she found a prime date-mate candidate, prominent New York art dealer Richard Feigen, a member of New York's nouvelle society, with whom she had a brief but for the most part dispassionate romance. "We started as friends. We ended up as friends. And in between there was a romantic involvement that didn't last very long," Feigen acknowledged. "Was it a long, enduring romance? No. We went to a couple of places together, but at that point she was not as tremendously busy as she became. It was never one of those until-the-end-of-time, marriagelike things. I don't get involved in those mad, passionate affairs. Personally I have not had very many long, enduring romantic involvements. Martha's an attractive woman, and she's a dynamic woman, and that dynamism amplifies her attractiveness. At least it did for me."

According to Feigen, who also dated multimillionaire socialite Ann Bass, Martha spent a good deal of her time kvetching about how Andy was trying to hold her up for more than his fair share of their joint holdings in their divorce battle.

"I wasn't privy to what went on between them," Feigen said, "so I had kind of a one-sided view of it from Martha. But she said she was undergoing considerable pressure from him for money. She told me there were a lot of legal problems. But she didn't—and she doesn't—talk a lot about her emotional life. I suspected that she was shocked by the breakup of their relationship, and the way it verbalized itself was through resentment of his demands for money and his pursuit of her money.

"I don't know what his contribution could have been that would have made him merit a substantial sum of money. Knowing her and the way she conducts her business, I would think it was pretty much of a one-woman show. And I can't imagine anybody's having done anything to merit a substantial chunk of what she was doing."

While Fuchs and Dennehy were washouts and her relationship with Feigen fell into the realm of "an enduring friendship," Martha's first *real* romantic interest in the wake of Andy was with a member of "royalty" of sorts, a good-looking Jewish businessman who had earned the title of Baseball Card King of Westport.

Dan Shedrick was extremely wealthy, recently divorced, and in his late forties. Like Martha, he had worked on Wall Street. But in the early seventies Shedrick had gotten into the lucrative business of sports marketing. An entrepreneur like Martha, he had put together a live syndicated TV network of college basketball games, had packaged some major tennis matches, and had worked in sports promotion and public relations.

Beginning in the eighties, already a millionaire many times over, Shedrick made another bundle hawking Sportsflics, multidimensional magic motion cards for kids. He hit it really big, though, by cashing in on the growing collector and investment craze in baseball cards, selling them through one of his companies, Major League Marketing, which he built in just four years into a $150 million cash cow: ergo the Baseball Card King. Shedrick was a go-getter who had locked up exclusive deals with players who were high on collectors' lists: Major League Marketing's Nolan Ryan card, for example, showed him delivering his record five thousandth strikeout pitch. Some cards became hot investment items, leaping in value 300 to 400 percent in the go-go days of the market.

Martha and Shedrick met at a Christmas party on Park Avenue, and he never forgot the magical moment. "Martha has a very beautiful face," Shedrick reminisced. "She holds herself beautifully. She's athletic, and I like athletic women. She's been criticized a lot for being a very cold, impersonal-type person, but I found her to be a very caring, loving person. She's intelligent and well read, and we could talk on a myriad of subjects: foreign policy, society, art. She likes to laugh, and she laughs easily. I found Martha to be a fun gal.''

Martha introduced her new man to old friends by ordering several bottles of expensive champagne delivered to her special table at Westport's fashionable Sol e Luna restaurant, where she took everyone by surprise by glibly toasting her "engagement" to Shedrick.

Earlier that day Martha's friend Diane Sappenfield had called to say she was in town visiting from Washington. "Oh, I want to have dinner with you," Martha exclaimed. "Can we do it tonight?" Sappenfield explained that it might be touchy because she and her husband had already made dinner plans with Janet and Len Horowitz.

"At that point the Horowitzes had really made a choice that they were going to side with Andy," Sappenfield noted. "But Martha said, 'Diane, I *desperately* want to see them.' I said, 'Let me check this out and see if it's going to work.' I called Janet, and she was *very* uncomfortable with the idea. Martha really loved Janet, I guess because she never was a threat to her, and that's probably the reason why she's always been friendly to me. I said, 'Janet, you were such a close friend of Martha's. There are two sides to everything. Why don't you just come?' And Janet said, 'Well, if you really want to do it.' ''

Martha and Shedrick were the first to arrive, and they were already seated when everyone else got there. "They were drinking Dom Pérignon when we arrived," Sappenfield recalled. "We probably had three bottles that evening, and we were supposedly celebrating Martha and Dan's engagement. The Horowitzes were really uncomfortable, and I think they were shocked that Martha was making this out to be some sort of engagement party. They sort of took it as a put-on and went along with it. Then Martha said it was all a big joke. But the Horowitzes were really upset by the way Martha was acting. It was the first time Martha had seen them in a while, and I think that's why she was doing this engagement thing. It was sort of like 'Let's be actors.' It was one of the *strangest* dinners I've ever attended.

"Dan was one of those people who are big talkers, a lot of ego, boastful, and it was interesting because we could tell that Martha actually *liked* that about him. I thought, 'It would be hard for most males to adapt to her. He's probably one of the few who isn't intimidated by her, and maybe that's why they could have a relationship.' "

Some years after that dinner Shedrick, an easygoing, friendly fellow, described Martha's talk about an engagement that night as "just spoofing." He and Martha had dated for quite a while, and after the romance faded, they remained good friends, but he came away from the relationship convinced that it would be virtually impossible for Martha to find a suitable mate.

"It would be very difficult because she's *so* tough," he observed. "Martha has her own agenda, her own game plan. She's an incredibly focused person. She's intelligent, she has great inner direction, she's goal-oriented, so the combination of those multiple strengths—plus the fact that she's attractive, and charming, and beguiling—place her in a very rare area. She creates an aura, and it's that aura that *really* is her personality. It would be difficult for someone to fit in a niche where he would find a comfort zone with her."

As she did with Feigen, Martha complained often and bitterly to Shedrick about the one man who had survived almost three decades with her. Shedrick thought that Martha had become obsessed with every aspect of the divorce proceedings. "The most difficult thing for her was the property issues," he stated. "It was constant. She didn't delegate responsibility to anyone. She was right on the firing line all the time, and I think that worked against her because it became a burden for her. It was eating her up. It created an emotional tailspin for her. Sometimes it's easier to just let go, but she couldn't. With a marriage of that length and given the nature of the divorce itself, a lot was at stake emotionally, and it was very difficult for her to separate the rational, intellectual part from the emotional part. Given the partnership that they had through their marriage, the separation and divorce were a very difficult thing for her to digest. The divorce was an ever-present part of her life. It just didn't come and go."

When she *could* get Andy off her mind, Martha and Shedrick shared good times, attending parties and going to cultural and sporting events. "They were definitely a handsome couple, and they were very close for a while," said a friend of Shedrick's. At the time the noncelebrity Shedrick meant more to Martha than the well-known walkers with whom she was linked publicly. One was blustery conservative TV talk-show host John McLaughlin, who squired her to some Clinton inaugural events and an Academy Awards presentation. McLaughlin also had Martha as a guest on his show. During a surprisingly caustic question-and-answer session, he suddenly asked why she had earned the nickname Martha Dearest. Clearly embarrassed, Martha went on to describe her "perfectionist mood" during which she admitted she "rants and raves" at people. Later, questioned by *TV Guide* about the incident, Martha asserted, "I'm not a fanatic, but I am a hard taskmaster." *New York Times* Washington columnist Maureen Dowd once noted that she had run into Martha—whom she described as "so scary, like Big Nurse with a pastry bag"—at one of the Clinton inaugural parties, accompanied by the loudmouth McLaughlin. ". . . that was unnerving, too," Dowd declared. "It conjured up the image of the carnivorous talk-show host bounding into the lissome life-style guru's perfect kitchen with a perfect linen napkin tucked into his shirt, bellowing, 'PAPAYA, JÍCAMA AND AVOCADO SALAD, MARTHARINO—UP OR DOWN?!' "

Martha also had a few dates that made the gossip columns with then *Late Night with David Letterman* coexecutive producer Robert "Morty" Morton, a decade younger than she was and known as a ladies' man. The two became acquainted during Martha's humorous appearances on the Letterman show. Talk-show host Charlie Rose, who also interviewed Martha on a couple of occasions, squired her briefly, but like the others, they were just friends. The press even linked Martha to Mort Zuckerman, a Hamptons neighbor who Martha once hoped would buy her idea for a magazine.

For a time it appeared to some observers, including Martha-watching publications ranging from the *National Enquirer* to *Vanity Fair*, that she had become romantically involved with Dr. Sam Waksal, a New York immunologist, businessman, and investor. Martha had first met Waksal when she catered an event for a charity he was involved with. He then met Lexi, and they dated for a while. But Waksal was fifteen years her senior and a few inches shorter. Lexi had little in common with the man, who once described himself as "a closet intellectual" who read Spinoza in his spare time.

But Martha had remained friends with him, which led to gossip that they were an item. When his pal the British actor Terence Stamp came to New York for a visit, Martha put the two of them up, and the threesome made the rounds of parties. "[E]verytime they see me with Martha and Terence," Waksal said with a wink, "they think—well, who knows what they think." Later she helped Waksal find a place in the Hamptons. "Her loyalty paid off," *Vanity Fair* reported, pointing out that Waksal had invested in one of Lexi's ventures.

Of the men she dated after her separation, Dan Shedrick was probably the one with whom Martha came closest to falling in love. They had much in common: for instance, a love of the sea and fishing.

In her reminiscences about growing up, Martha wrote about the wonderful times she had had fishing with her father off the New Jersey coast and with her brother Eric at a Nutley watering hole. Andy also loved the sea, was an avid sailor, and had taught Martha the ropes. The Stewarts once sailed with friends from Halifax to Boston through horrendous weather, and Martha was one of the few of the six aboard who didn't get sick, and the group included a couple of veteran yachtsmen.

Around the time of their breakup, when they were searching for something to bind them together, Andy and Martha seriously considered taking up sailing on a regular basis. The squabbling Stewarts had even applied for membership in the exclusive Pequot Yacht Club, on a pretty harbor, in Southport, Connecticut, and went shopping for a boat. Martha had her eye on an old forty-foot sailboat, whose hull she planned to paint green, adorned with darker green sails.

Pequot was a quiet, conservative club, made up mostly of bankers, lawyers, businessmen, even a dean of admissions at Yale. But there were no celebrities like Martha. The last one to apply was Phil Donahue, but his application had been rejected by stuffy board members who were said to be disturbed over the way he comported himself on his talk show.

So when Martha applied, at least one club member, her friend Sandy Broyard, was concerned that the lifestyle guru might transgress the club's bylaws, which clearly stated that no commercial activities were permitted on premises. "Martha was telling me about buying this beautiful sailboat," Broyard said, "and I envisioned her bringing out photographers for photo op picnics at sea, and that sort of thing, because everything she does has a commercial twist to it."

The devilish Broyard said she didn't feel compelled to tell the other club members about Martha's commercial proclivities because "I would have enjoyed the spectacle of seeing Martha hang herself when she got into trouble. But she might have charmed them and gotten away with it because she has the ability to get away with certain things, and she has." It all became irrelevant, however, when Martha and Andy dropped out of the admission process with the breakup of their marriage. During the period immediately after the separation, when Martha was still trying to woo Andy back, she told people that she bought Andy a sailboat as a gift and named it *Andy's Garden*. But no such boat ever actually existed.

As it turned out, Dan Shedrick belonged to several exclusive fishing clubs whose membership consisted of high rollers who chartered boats and went after big fish such as tarpon off the coasts of Costa Rica and Belize. When Shedrick mentioned to Martha that he was about to go on such a trip, which he described as "your basic male bonding—

card games, cigars, good food, and lots of fishing,'' Martha's face lit up, and she asked to go along.

"She was the only woman there, and it was a four-day trip," Shedrick said. "It was *awesome*. She was really one of the guys and was a real player and a lot of fun, and everyone had a good time. She played cards with us. She hung out. On the last day she caught a hundred-ten-pound tarpon, and she was really annoyed that it was *only* one hundred ten pounds, as if it should have been a hundred fifty pounds. Anything over ninety pounds of tarpon is a great, great sports fish, and she brought it in rather quickly, and she did a masterful job. But she was unenthusiastic about the fact that it was only one hundred ten pounds."

Despite their common interests, Shedrick realized Martha wasn't the kind of woman with whom he could settle down because of what he called "her unrequited appetite" for business and career. "You'd think when she's at her places in the Hamptons she'd be relaxing, but it's just the opposite. She'd be working out early in the morning. She'd have people over for breakfast to talk business. She'd be doing a final edit on a book. She'd be doing photo selections for the magazine. She'd be working on some business negotiation. Then, late in the afternoon, she'd be making food for some charity event. I'm not exactly sure what it is with her, but she's *so* driven, so *totally* driven. She's unbelievable."

Martha's search for Mr. Right continued. "I don't especially enjoy being single," she acknowledged. "It's not nice to live in an empty house. Prince Charming will show up one day."

The Big Score

The first action Time Warner executives took when Martha approached them with her idea for a magazine on lifestyle was to conduct a highly secret in-depth background investigation to find out what her personal lifestyle was all about. Rumors about Martha's vindictive actions in the wake of Andy's split had circulated in publishing and social circles and had reached the ears of the executives at Time Inc. Ventures, which was seriously considering getting in bed with her in what they believed would be an ultimately profitable but highly speculative and expensive publishing operation. Before they committed their money, resources, and respected corporate name, they wanted assurance that their future partner was as pristine a family values person as she portrayed herself to be in her best-selling books, television specials, and other enterprises.

As one major Time Warner player later said, "The biggest risk was personal endorsement. We were nervous because we *never, ever* did anything that had somebody's face or name on the cover. Who's to say that person won't go out and tarnish the reputation? What if we had put O. J. Simpson on as the spokesman for *Sports Illustrated*? So those kinds of things can go sour.

"Here we were talking about putting Martha on the cover and naming the magazine after her. We saw that as a *big* risk. I don't think Martha ever knew we did an investigation, which included getting a copy of her divorce

settlement, which was *pretty* ugly. Right in the settlement
it said that she was not allowed to come within, I think,
two hundred yards of his [Andy Stewart's] then residence.

"Also, at the time when we did the deal with her we
discovered that Martha and her daughter were not on speaking terms. And Martha had to amend that. She wasn't stupid. She knew we were going to ask, 'What about your
kid?' What was she going to say? 'I have a daughter, but
we don't talk to each other or don't get along very well.'
So she had to fix the image thing there. When the magazine
started, Martha put Alexis on the masthead [as associate
style editor and later as a consultant]. I think it also was a
way of trying to build a bridge to her daughter.

"At that point we knew pretty much what everyone
didn't know about Martha Stewart, and we had to make a
judgment on whether or not the details would ever surface,
and we presumed that some of them would. Mainly we
wondered whether it would matter, and we presumed it
probably wouldn't. In the end we felt that the great American public wouldn't care."

Martha had developed the idea for *Martha Stewart Living*—a natural spin-off of her books—after her publisher
Crown and later Time-Life Books had rejected her proposal
to start "my own little publishing company." She had gone
to them with a list of all the books she had wanted to
produce, and they had said no.

The road that ultimately led Martha to Time Warner and
her own magazine and multimedia empire—at least in
name only—started with another idea, a signature line of
affordable quality gourmet foods. Her partner in that deal
was her ex-brother-in-law George Friedman, a shrewd,
high-powered businessman, who had been the second of
Andy's sister's three wealthy husbands. As one family wag
put it, "Martha and George got together because each of
them had been rejected by a Stewart sibling."

Be that as it may, Martha saw that Friedman could be of
enormous help to her career, and Friedman saw Martha's
ideas as a potential gold mine for him. In the end, though,
it was Martha who benefited the most from their ex-familial
alliance.

While Martha was still hawking hot dogs at Nutley High School football games, Friedman, a Brooklyn College graduate, had started his business career as an adman. On Madison Avenue he worked for Doyle, Dane & Bernbach; Foote, Cone & Belding; and Young & Rubicam. In 1968 he left the gray flannel suits behind to begin a very close and financially rewarding relationship with Estée Lauder. Starting as managing director of Aramis, Inc., he eventually became group president for Aramis and Clinique.

By the mid-seventies he believed he knew enough about the cosmetics game, a business he had learned from Mrs. Lauder, to sell himself big time. He took his ideas to Ralph Lauren and Warner Communications. Their ultimate joint venture was called Warner Cosmetics, a company that created a number of highly successful fragrances: Polo, Lauren, Vanderbilt, and Picasso, among others. When Warner Cosmetics was sold to Cosmair Inc., the U.S. licensee of L'Oréal S.A., Friedman became a very wealthy man. He stayed with Cosmair as an executive, and as a consultant to L'Oréal.

Around the time he hooked up with Martha, Friedman had started a company called Gryphon Development, a joint venture with The Limited, to create, develop, and manufacture fragrances and toiletries. Later, when The Limited purchased the shares of his company, Friedman became even wealthier.

Besides fragrances, Friedman's Gryphon Development was always on the lookout for lucrative new ventures, and when he heard Martha's idea for a signature line of preserves, mustard, salad dressings, and frozen foods—sixty different products in all—he thought it would be a winner. While Friedman saw that Martha could make a decent living from her books and related ventures, he always believed that the really big payoff for her would come from some form of package goods. Martha's gourmet food line idea meshed perfectly with his thinking. His immediate goal was to create a company around Martha's products and sell them to retail outlets. Naturally his first target was Kmart, where Martha had an exclusive contract. Working together,

Martha and Friedman created the packaging, advertising, displays, and promotion.

They then had a series of meetings with Kmart honcho Joe Antonini and members of his kitchen cabinet. Initially the Kmart people loved the idea, and a deal was about to be struck, but at the last minute Kmart refused to give the Stewart-Friedman combine a one-year agreement to leave the products in a hundred or so stores, with a defined unit of space—they wanted about twenty feet—for a market test.

Martha, who thought she had a done deal, was shocked by Kmart's last-minute rejection and furious that Antonini and the others didn't see the same dollar signs that she and Friedman had envisioned because the whole concept of affordable quality gourmet food was just beginning to boom. In her eyes the Kmart executives were "boobs and idiots" who didn't get what she really was all about.

With the food project down the disposal, Martha now refocused her energies into making her dream of having her own magazine come true. Again she sought her brother-in-law's help.

Socially, and through business connections, Friedman knew billionaire media mogul S. I. Newhouse, and he suggested that Martha pay him a visit. As it turned out, Newhouse was familiar with Martha and her ability to sell products. Her publisher, Clarkson Potter, had become an imprint of Random House, which in turn was part of Newhouse's Advance Publications. That entity comprised the Condé Nast magazine group, which included *Vanity Fair* and *The New Yorker*. Newhouse immediately saw the uniqueness of Martha's vision and assigned Rochelle Udell, then in corporate marketing, to develop a prototype. Udell, later editor in chief of *Self*, was no stranger to Martha either. They knew each other socially; Martha had even included a photo of Udell's wedding invitation in her *Weddings* book; and Udell's husband, *Family Circle*'s creative director Doug Turshen, had designed *Martha Stewart's New Old House*. He also worked with his wife on Martha's magazine dummy.

"Martha and I spent an initial session brainstorming

ideas, and then *I* went off and did it,'' Udell said. ''We visualized and brought to life the concept of Martha Stewart in magazine format. It didn't take very long to do—this was not brain surgery—because what Martha had done in her books was easy to translate into a magazine format.''

The philosophy of the prototype was ''information and inspiration.'' From the beginning everyone agreed that Martha should be on the cover, and a number of names were considered, including Lily Pond Lane, the address of one of her East Hampton homes.

But in the end Newhouse passed on the project. ''At first he wanted my name on the magazine,'' Martha explained ''and then he said that after a lot of thought he couldn't put my name on the magazine. And I said, 'That's all right.' But he was really worried about that.'' Martha made it seem that Newhouse rejected her idea mainly because of a concern that his other top editors—*Vogue*'s Anna Wintour, *Vanity Fair*'s Tina Brown—might want their names on their covers too. But that *wasn't* Newhouse's prime fear about the project.

His biggest worry was over how Martha's magazine would be positioned. Would it be a mass book or a small class book? Would it ever have more than a million circulation? His final analysis was that it could never be a mass-circulation magazine. He gave Martha the prototype as a gift and wished her luck shopping it elsewhere. As Martha acknowledged later, ''*Martha Stewart Living* didn't fit into Condé Nast.''

Next stop, Rupert Murdoch's News Corporation. But the Australian-born media baron had bigger fish to fry. ''He loved it,'' Martha said, ''but he was selling [off] his magazines.''

At that point George Friedman decided to call on his old friend Steve Ross, the flamboyant onetime funeral director and parking lot magnate who had engineered the historic and behemoth fifteen-billion-dollar Time Warner merger, which had occurred around the time Martha had begun pitching her magazine to prospective publishers.

Friedman, who knew Ross from his highly successful

Warner Cosmetics days, had lunch with his old pal and told him about Martha's terrific idea.

The timing could not have been better. The philosophy of synergism—the interaction of elements that when combined produce a total effect greater than the sum of the individual elements or contributions—was alive and well at the new Time Warner, and Martha's world was definitely synergistic: If handled right, Time Warner could produce her magazine, her television programming, eventually get control of her book publishing contracts, develop and sell her product lines, put her in cyberspace. The horizon was limitless.

Ross thought Martha's idea, as proposed by Friedman, was dynamite. He saw that it wasn't just a magazine that was being pitched but rather a whole range of products that could cut across the entire Time Warner firmament. Ross bought it. It also helped that his third wife, Courtney, was a Martha wannabe who loved decorating homes, buying expensive art, having a place in East Hampton, rubbing shoulders with celebrities, and dominating her husband.

Ross called in Nick Nicholas, Time Warner's chief operating officer, who agreed that the idea sounded like a winner. Ross and Nicholas then put Martha in touch with the right people within the organization—the entrepreneurial new ventures group—and Friedman helped shepherd Martha through some of her earliest meetings. But he stepped out when it became clear that none of his ideas for Martha Stewart products, such as the gourmet food line, was getting a positive reception, and that's where Friedman had hoped to make *his* buck.

In the end it was Martha who grabbed the Time Warner brass ring. "Time Warner was initially open to *Martha Stewart Living* because Steve Ross *declared* it was a good idea," said a highly knowledgeable participant. "That was the *only* reason she got the deal. The *Time* guys were never really comfortable with her or the magazine. In fact they probably hated Martha. Women weren't really important in the *Time* culture. Martha's a tough, smart woman, and she's not easy. She can rub people the wrong way, so they had problems with her from the start. She's very strong-willed, very demanding, and single-minded, and that's how you get things done. The *Time* guys were not used to that. Everything had to go through committees, and that's not the way to deal with Martha. These guys were difficult. It was the old WASP school. Nobody was really hungry, and nobody made waves, and suddenly they were enveloped by this entrepreneurial group of people, the Warner–Steve Ross group. Martha was in the right place at the right time.''

Later Martha revealed that during her early discussions the main question posed to her by the Time Warner people—whom she described somewhat bitterly as ''all men, only men''—was ''How do we know you're a team player?'' She said she told them, ''Give me a chance.'' Then she added angrily, ''It was a *stupid* question.''

It wasn't the best time to start a new women's service magazine, and Time Warner was bucking a definite trend, taking a big chance. The combined circulation of the seven big women's magazines—*Ladies' Home Journal, Redbook, McCall's, Woman's Day, Better Homes and Gardens, Good Housekeeping*, and *Family Circle*—had declined by eight million during the eighties. Every year at least a million homemakers were joining the work force, leaving fewer women at home who had either the time or money to do the complex cooking, decorating, and entertaining projects Martha advocated. Even bleaker was the fact that magazines were dying left and right, as Martha was well aware. ''Some people think I'm nuts to start a magazine in a climate where magazines are closing and suffering,'' she admitted on the eve of the launch of the first test issue of *Martha Stewart Living*. ''But I think this is the best time to start a magazine. It's a challenge.''

The initial Time Warner negotiations with Martha and her attorney were described as difficult. It seemed that every offer the *Time* people put on the table was not good enough, and the talks dragged on. ''We had a major ego to contend with,'' said one of the players.

Meanwhile, confident that an agreement eventually would be worked out, *Time* executives began introducing Martha to potential advertisers. Because she wasn't involved romantically, the *Time* people often arranged for a gentleman to accompany Martha to those advertiser-related functions. "We could usually get somebody for the first date," one executive recalled, "but they rarely wanted to go out with her a second time."

When Martha was instructed to make another appearance at a formal dinner to be attended by key advertisers and *Time* brass, she announced, for once, that she'd get a date on her own. The party in question happened to coincide with a very touchy stage in Martha's negotiations with *Time,* a period when she was very upset that she wasn't getting everything she was demanding.

That night Martha stunned and angered about a dozen *Time* honchos and potential advertisers seated at her table by arriving with the handsome date she had personally chosen. His name was Peter Eldredge and he was the publisher of *Time*'s biggest rival, *Newsweek.* The *Time* guys went ballistic. "We didn't have the first deal signed and she was trying to use whatever leverage she could find. Martha thought it was a way of playing hardball to get back at us guys," said a *Time* executive who was present. "What went through my mind was 'Can this really be happening?' Everybody was so uncomfortable. It was unbelievable that she would do that, bring a guy from *Newsweek.*

"What she demonstrated that evening was that she didn't know the game and that she wasn't as sophisticated or as slick as she probably thought she was. Our immediate questions were: Why would she have such bad judgment and bad taste? Is this what she thinks is going to be a negotiating ploy by making us all look kind of silly? And does she have something actually going with this guy that we should know more about? Because, if she does, some of the inner secrets are going to be shared in pillow talk."

Despite Martha's "quirkiness and demands," the *Time* people thought she had the entrepreneurial drive and instincts to make the magazine a success. Finally, after some months, a contract was hammered out that gave Martha a starting base salary of $450,000 a year. With bonuses if she met certain advertising and circulation targets, she would receive more than $500,000 a year in compensation. Moreover, she was given a slew of perks: a chauffeur-driven car, a clothing allowance that eventually reached $50,000 annually, a hair and makeup budget, and expenses to cover business operations at her homes in East Hampton and Westport. The perks were good, but not extraordinary; most top editors at women's magazines got similar or better benefits. But they *were* rare for Time Inc. editors.

Martha also reportedly demanded, but did not get, a loan from *Time* for the purchase of her first Hamptons home. But several years later she was said to have been given a two-million-dollar loan to help finance her three-million-dollar purchase of the Bunshaft house, in East Hampton. (That loan was viewed as "a way of keeping Martha at bay and placating her" at a time when she was threatening "to take her toys and walk" if she wasn't given a major equity stake in her operation, a *Time* executive asserted.)

When word of Martha's initial deal began circulating within the staid *Time* organization, a number of editors and executives expressed anger—and envy. "There was an undercurrent of resentment and jealousy," one of them acknowledged. "People were asking, 'What are we doing besmirching our good name by getting in bed with somebody like this? She's *not* an editor.' There was definitely some backbiting."

Time executives believed they had given Martha, whom they viewed as unproved as both an editor and a businesswoman, a good deal. But from the start she expressed dissatisfaction, believing she should own a piece of the pie.

Instead she was offered phantom equity, which meant that at a certain point in the future, either five years or nine years—she chose the latter—*Time* would have a third party appraise the gross value of the business, and Martha would receive a check for 15 percent of that valuation. From the beginning of their relationship *Time* executives told Martha a fact of life she didn't want to hear, which was "*You're* not going to make money until *we* make money." For a time Martha went unhappily along with that corporate mantra.

Meanwhile it was clear to everyone involved in the project that the magazine's success or failure depended mainly on Martha Stewart's name and visual recognition. "I must maintain a presence," Martha declared. "My reader really likes seeing me wearing a work shirt and digging in dirt."

In actuality the hands-on editing of the early issues was done by a woman named Isolde Motley, whom Martha had brought with her. *Time* executives viewed Motley as the "key ingredient" who could produce the magazine as envisioned by Martha. They also thought she was "the one person who could organize and tame the wild beast."

Said one executive: "When Martha started out, she told Isolde, 'Look, you're the professional. I'll follow you. I'll be the inspirational muse.' But then Martha wanted to do some top line editing. Eventually that took its toll on Isolde. It all became a little too much, and she eventually left.

"Martha got involved as an actual editor on a very selective and quirky basis—for example, when she felt something wasn't right that she wanted to change or when she felt that something hadn't been treated the way she specifically thought it should be. But then she might go away again."

On November 12, 1990, the first five hundred thousand copies of *Martha Stewart Living* appeared on newsstands across the country, with her picture on the cover. The magazine was targeted at what *Time* executives were calling the new grown-ups, boomers with kids, making forty thousand dollars a year and up.

Like her books, the pilot was practically vacuumed off the racks by Martha's loyal followers. Only about a fifth of the magazines were returned unsold to the distributors, despite the fact that the cover price was three dollars, compared with one dollar or two dollars for other women's magazines.

Martha and her first staff immediately got to work on the second and final test issue, which hit the racks in March 1991. A main feature story was about Lexi's collection of tchotchkes and her cool 1870 carriage house, which she described as looking like "a happy soda shop." The layout, showing all her neat stuff, her dog, her four-wheel-drive vehicle, and her classic sixties red Mustang convertible, was enough to make any struggling young woman reader jealous.

The second issue of *Martha Stewart Living* sold even better than the first and had even more advertising pages, despite some negative press comments. "Although it purports to be a practical guide to a stylish home, *Martha Stewart Living* portrays a fantasy world where women have time to play croquet, kids are clean, and checks don't bounce," observed *The Wall Street Journal*. On his radio program Don Imus called *Martha Stewart Living* "the whitest magazine I've ever seen—all these white people, running around in white clothes."

Martha acknowledged that some of the articles in the first two issues were a bit over the edge—tips on how to print personalized gift wrap and sewing an organdy Easter dress didn't seem part of the real world—but she expressed confidence that the magazine would demonstrate that such information was not impractical or unrealistic. "I really want people to get out their sewing machines again," she maintained. "I know we don't have time, but just thinking about it is a step in the right direction."

By May, Time Warner had internally declared the test of *Martha Stewart Living* a success based on sales and advertising. On June 17, 1991, both sides signed a ten-year contract for regular publication of the magazine and the production of television programming, videos, and books derived mainly from the magazine.

Before the ink was even dry, a *Time* executive, who was to work closely with Martha for the next several years, remarked to a confidant, an advertising executive, "My biggest fear, and I told Martha so, is that 'I don't want to wake up one morning and see on the cover of the *New York Post* that you have run off to an island with an eighteen-year-old and embarrassed the company.'" The ad person, a woman, rolled her eyes. "I thought that was *hysterical*," she said later. "I told him, 'You *really* don't understand Martha at all.' Many of them still had lingering concerns about her."

In fact, the people at *Time* did view Martha as a gamble, even a loose cannon, and only black ink on the spreadsheets would change their minds about her.

"The deal," *Advertising Age* noted, "marks one of the

most ambitious attempts to exploit the combined resources of Time Inc. and Warner Communications since the companies merged. . . . The home entertainment guru fits into Time Inc. Ventures' strategy of tapping into the perceived return of family- and home-oriented values among aging baby-boomers.''

Plans were made to publish a third issue in July, a fourth in September, and a fifth in November 1991. Beginning in 1992, *Martha Stewart Living* would be a bimonthly.

Time Warner also worked out a tie-in advertising campaign with NBC's *Today* show. It gave Martha a regular weekly six- to eight-minute segment on the most popular morning show on television. Her appearances had to be based on editorial material from the magazine. Time Warner envisioned shooting footage for the *Today* segment and ultimately pulling it all together for a full-length TV show that would lead to the creation of marketable videos. However, *The New York Times* wondered, ''Is there such a thing as too much exposure? There may be a saturation point even for someone as effective as the glamorous Ms. Stewart. . . . But for the time being Time Warner is betting that there is not.''

Meanwhile one of Martha's earliest *Today* segments became an embarrassment for her and the show.

CAN THIS ADVICE, was the headline over an item in the New York *Daily News* about the segment in question. *Today* cohost Bryant Gumbel had asked Martha if it was necessary to add some lemon juice or vinegar so that the tomatoes she was instructing viewers how to can attained the proper level of acidity. Martha said no, explaining that tomatoes were solid acid and nothing else was needed. The phones immediately rang off the hook at *Today*'s offices, letters poured in, and Gumbel was forced to make a disclaimer. ''We got a lot of calls from food safety experts,'' he said, including one at Cornell University who said that one should ''always use a little bit of lemon juice to avoid the possibility of botulism.''

Despite her faux pas, Martha quickly became a hit on the program, and rating points usually rose on the mornings of her appearances, the dates of which were advertised in her magazine's soon-to-be parodied feature called "Martha's Calendar."

"People are into their homes these days and they connect with her," explained *Today* executive producer Jeff Zucker of Martha's success on the show. "Sometimes she [does] topics, like designing your floor, that we thought were crazy—and yet millions of Americans [are] fascinated. She's selling lifestyle. She tells people they can do things themselves. But if they can't, they live vicariously through her experiences."

Some members of the *Today* crew came to dislike Martha, finding her manner imperious and dictatorial. Martha usually brought a personal entourage to help her set up for her weekly appearance. On one occasion, according to *Today* lore, Martha stepped out of the makeup room, was displeased with the presentation on her set, and slapped the person responsible—in front of the show's horrified regular crew.

Another chef who made a number of appearances on *Today* asserted that "the set crew, the set design people, the people who have to work with Martha's crew get yelled at by her all the time, and they *hate* her."

TV Guide, which took a critical look at Martha now that she was a morning prime-time regular, observed:

> The real problem is that Stewart's projects are endlessly time-consuming. . . . When Stewart creates a perfect table setting, it's with the help of a personal assistant, three stylists, three gardeners, a housekeeper, and the entire staff of her television show. [Martha herself admitted her crew might spend an entire day making a shot of an apple look perfect.]
>
> . . . [S]ometimes Stewart seems curiously out of touch. When asked why couples busy with children and full-time jobs should be interested in the best way to make risotto, she snaps, "What's so important about an eight-hour-a-day job? What I'm teaching is meaningful because it's gratifying."

Viewers don't turn to Martha Stewart to get a new recipe

or a tip on gardening so much as a view of what the perfect life should look like. She's a cross between an old-fashioned woman of leisure and a new-style back-to-nature guru.

Time Warner soon packaged a weekly television show based on the *Martha Stewart Living* concept, with Martha, of course, as chief cook and bottle washer. With the program her celebrity would have seemed nearly complete. But Martha wanted more.

She had been hoping that NBC, which she viewed as highly prestigious, would pick up the series because she already was an element of the network's *Today* program. But NBC passed. Instead Time Warner cut a syndication deal with very aggressive Group W Productions for a weekly half hour that would air on cable's Lifetime network and eventually on more than 150 local stations around the country, reaching as many as 85 percent of U.S. households. *Time* quickly sold its fifty-two-week inventory of commercial airtime to five sponsors.

(Martha had a long, successful run with *Today*, but in January 1997, she defected from the still top-rated early-morning show to the lowest rated—CBS's *This Morning*—part of an overall deal under which she contributed segments to other CBS news programs.)

Meanwhile the magazine's readership was growing enormously—it tripled in two years to 750,000—and advertisers were lining up. But editorial and production costs were escalating too. Martha "spent money like mad on staff and production," a Time executive said, and the magazine, which *should* have been profitable, was swimming in red ink at a time when she was aggressively pushing for equity. Naturally her bosses were getting a bit miffed.

Then there was a dark cloud on the horizon called competition. Just like the intense late-night ratings wars between Jay Leno and David Letterman, a lifestyle magazine battle appeared to be shaping up. Martha's old chum Mary Emmerling was about to enter the field with *Mary Emmerling's Country,* with the substantial backing of The New York Times Company. There were also reports that Hearst

Magazines might test-market a *Ralph Lauren Magazine*. Martha and Emmerling were billed by the Chicago *Tribune* as ''Dueling Divas of Decor.'' (In the end, though, Ralph Lauren stayed with clothing racks rather than magazine racks. And Martha outlived Emmerling's effort and continued to dominate the genre.)

Originally Martha's editorial offices were in the prestigious Time-Life Building, but her superiors quickly moved her into less opulent digs on West Forty-third Street. ''We got her into some cheap space,'' said a former *Time* executive. ''Our intention was to not have her in the Time-Life Building. It was too expensive, and we didn't want her to develop bad habits. She already had a champagne taste on a beer budget, so we kept her pretty much at arm's length.''

Feeling the pressure, Martha was willing to try almost anything to bring in more revenue, and in the process, she alienated others in magazine publishing with her methods. At a trade convention in Bermuda, for example, she declared that she was willing, even anxious, to create special issues for advertisers. For instance, if the BMW people told her they would fork over a million dollars for a one-shot buy to attract Martha's yuppie readership, she vowed, ''I would put out a supplementary issue, focusing on travelling across America, in which the advertiser would sponsor the entire issue. You don't even have to show the car in the editorial.''

Other publishers and editors who witnessed her presentation were appalled. ''I try to keep my editor out of sponsor considerations,'' declared Jack Kliger, publisher of *Glamour*. Jackie Leo, editor in chief of *Family Circle*, which previously had a tie-in with Martha's Kmart promotion for her old-house project, called Martha's suggestion ''a terrible idea . . . the editor reports to the reader!'' Stung by the criticism, Martha claimed she might not have used what *Inside Media* termed ''industry buzz words,'' and she vowed to follow American Society of Magazine Editors guidelines to the letter. Others in the industry heard her excuse, and her pledge, and sniffed, ''Yeah, right.'' They thought of her as ''a walking advertorial.''

Martha turned up her nose at the criticism. "The food world is a club. The author world is a club. The magazine and TV worlds are clubs. So, I don't care. I sort of swim over the top. I don't feel I have to be smart or creative or introspective about this kind of business."

Private Lives

For Martha, 1991 was a very special year. Not only had she fulfilled her dream of starting her own magazine, but she had come to a major milestone in her personal life. That August, as she was furiously working to turn out the next issue of *Martha Stewart Living*, America's queen of domesticity celebrated her fiftieth birthday—for the most part alone.

Despite all of Martha's phenomenal career accomplishments, she was not the happy homemaker she publicly portrayed. Her life continued to be her work, which was one of the reasons why Andy had left her and apparently why there was no other man in her life. Her relationship with her daughter remained strained. She continued to squabble with various members of the Kostyra family. She had trod over many of her close friends along the way, and they had dropped out of her life. And her battle with Andy was ongoing. To close observers, deep down Martha was in the dumps.

However, by the time of Martha's "big five-O" she and her old friend Norma Collier, after numerous spats and disagreements over the years, were again on speaking terms, although Collier saw little of Martha because of her extremely busy celebrity-executive schedule. In 1988, when Collier turned fifty, Martha had graciously called to wish her happy birthday and had given her a bouquet of roses. Collier decided to return the favor in August 1991, particularly after a close mutual acquaintance had informed her that Martha "had no friends, was all by herself, had only a few hangers-on to talk to, and was very depressed and miserable."

Collier telephoned and invited Martha to lunch to celebrate the very special occasion, suggesting a nice Spanish restaurant close to Collier's office in Westport. But Martha said she wanted to go to a place in Fairfield for the salad. That posed a bit of a problem for Collier, who had a limited amount of time. "But I thought, 'I extended the invitation, I'll do it.' "

On the morning of the planned celebration Martha called to say, "I don't want to go to Gregory's anymore. I want to go to Meson Galicia. And we have to eat at a quarter to twelve because I have a friend coming up from Manhattan and I have to pick him up at the train at one-fifteen. Now *don't* be late." Naturally Collier was peeved. "By this time I'm thinking, 'Why did I ever do this? I'm trying to be nice to her, and I'm getting screwed over again. Am I stupid or what?' But I called and changed the reservation."

Collier arrived on time and waited for Martha. And waited. The birthday girl finally showed up forty-five minutes late. "She comes running in wearing a T-shirt and jeans, her hair pulled back, no makeup, all in a dither, sits down, and starts saying, 'That son of a bitch Andy . . .' " Martha proceeded to tell Collier that she had been on the phone all morning with her lawyer, still doing battle with Andy over financial issues of their divorce. "He's so *mean* to me, but I'm going to *get* him," she said, then rushed through lunch, flashing a sweet smile only when someone came over asking for an autograph.

"She threw down her lunch and said, 'Have to run,' and she just got up and left the restaurant. And there I was sitting alone, and I thought, 'I don't care if I *ever* see Martha again.' "

Collier got her car and pulled into traffic, which was quite heavy. At a stoplight she looked over to see Martha sitting in her big black Mercedes. "She was screaming into her car phone. I could see she was absolutely beside herself, extremely agitated. She didn't even notice I was next to her watching this crazed scene."

Because she had lost so many good, old friends, Martha had taken to surrounding herself mostly with sycophants, a few of whom she would even put on the payroll of *Martha Stewart Living*. As one observer at Time Warner noted, "As it often happens with celebrities, Martha had to have her handlers constantly around her to protect her and fawn over her, and yes her to death. And a few began sucking off the Time Warner tit."

Martha's closest pal, it appeared to many, was her personal and corporate publicist, Susan Magrino, an attractive, unmarried blond PR wizard, whose company, the Susan Magrino Agency, appears on the masthead of *Martha Stewart Living*. The two met when Magrino landed a job in Crown Publishing's publicity department shortly after *Entertaining* was published. To hype one of Martha's subsequent books at a booksellers' convention in New Orleans, Magrino went all out, throwing a party for two thousand guests in a building that she had had wrapped in white satin. A decade later Magrino left Crown and founded her own firm with a client roster headed by Martha, Dominick Dunne, New York hairstylist Frederic Fekkai (who gained fame in 1993 by clipping Hillary Rodham Clinton's mane), Elizabeth Tilberis (the editor of *Harper's Bazaar*), and the Hard Rock Café, among others.

When the press attacked Martha—and that became increasingly common in the nineties—it was Magrino who defended her and put out the fires. When Martha needed a publicity fix, it was Magrino who planted gossip column items or made anonymous positive responses to negative stories. But her forte was arranging for big-time coverage, such as a mostly flattering October 1995 cover story in *People*, another Time Warner publication. That piece, headlined THE REAL MARTHA STEWART, exemplified what Magrino could do, and the clout she wielded.

"Susan set it up for Martha and then tried to control *People*'s coverage from start to finish," a Time Warner magazine executive asserted. It also was said that Martha went to the top at Time Warner and demanded and received permission to preview the story and make revisions before it ran, which is not journalistically kosher.

From the beginning of their relationship Magrino was absolutely devoted to Martha's professional success and consistently lavished praise on her. "Before Martha wrote *Entertaining*," she once said, "there had never been anything like it before. Martha was a pioneer. It was a lush, lifestyle cookbook, all color, and expensive, but also warm and genuine. It defined a lifestyle of opulence yet ease and practicality—Martha's lifestyle. It's been an unbelievable inspiration to women. The proof is in the sales and her soaring popularity. Martha clearly knows what women want."

Magrino was devoted to making Martha's personal life happier too. When Martha traveled, it was Magrino who often accompanied her on a number of business and pleasure trips. "Martha and Susan are like the Bobbsey Twins," maintained a mutual friend. "They're inseparable."

For instance, when Martha needed to get away for a breather over Christmas 1991, the end of her hectic first year of running the magazine, Magrino went along as company. Their destination was St. Bart's, the Caribbean playground for the rich and famous. There Martha was a guest at a bizarre New Year's Eve party thrown by advertising mogul Charles Saatchi aboard his yacht. It was a very discreet affair because only those who came dressed as the opposite sex were permitted aboard, and privacy was important because a number of the prominent guests were gay or lesbian and were still in the closet. Saatchi promised there would be no publicity. That evening Martha partied with Barry Diller, David Geffen, Jann Wenner, Fran Lebowitz, Diane von Fürstenberg, Quincy Jones, and Kelly Klein, whose designer husband, Calvin Klein, declined the invitation because, as one participant later told the *New*

York Post, "Calvin's smart. He wouldn't be caught dead in drag."

As Martha was tanning in St. Bart's, the trade publication *Mediaweek* toasted her success in New York, declaring "... forget that Martha's described as a harridan, forget that she calls buyers of her Kmart–distributed housewares Kmartians. She still puts out one hell of a magazine."

Since Andy left Martha six years earlier, his career had also undergone drastic changes. In 1988 he sold Stewart, Tabori & Chang, which had been undercapitalized from the start, but stayed on with the company for another four years as the salaried chief executive officer and publisher. While he actually owned only about 20 percent of the publishing house, he came away with a significant chunk of change from the multimillion-dollar sale. He also started running Chanticleer Press, which published nature field guides, and for a time he oversaw the operations of both companies. By the early nineties Andy was worth seven figures and was financially comfortable, but he had nowhere near the monetary resources, nor did he lead the glamorous lifestyle, of his former mate.

Andy's personal life had changed dramatically too. In July 1992 he and Robyn Fairclough had quietly become engaged after what friends described as a sometimes rocky on-and-off romance. "There were several periods when they had an intense relationship and several periods when they had no relationship whatsoever," one confidant said. "There was a point when Robyn moved to San Francisco and another when she went to Iowa to study. During those times, and even when they lived near each other, they went out with different people. It was not always an exclusive, steady relationship. But they both felt strongly about each other, and eventually they came together for good."

Another friend said, "Robyn knew it would be difficult living in Martha's shadow. That's why she had qualms about marrying Andy."

But on May 15, 1993, a sunny Saturday, Andy and Robyn were joined in holy matrimony in a simple ceremony performed by a justice of the peace. Some seventy-five guests, including friends of Andy's dating back to his days at Putney, were present for the nuptials, held at the quaint Four Columns Inn, not far from Andy's Vermont farm, where the couple were to live. Hors d'oeuvres were served outdoors, and the guests sat down to dinner in the dining room. It was a romantic and beautiful setting that Martha would have been proud of. In fact the security was tight that day because the lifestyle queen's specter hung over the ceremony and celebration. Because there still were a number of unresolved financial issues pending between Martha and Andy, because their level of mutual acrimony was at as high a boil as ever, and because Martha had made it clear that she hated Andy and Robyn with a passion, the bride and groom, and some of their guests, were fearful that the woman who had written the book on weddings might make a surprise appearance.

"I'm still afraid of her constant anger," Andy told one of his chums just before he placed the ring on Robyn's finger. "Any way she can mess up my life, I think she'll do it." He also told friends that Martha continued to "haunt" him long after the initial odd and scary events that occurred in the year or so after their split. He said he and Robyn had been plagued by telephone calls and were forced several times to change their numbers or get them unlisted. They could never identify the caller. For a time Andy lived in a small house in Redding, Connecticut, and he had spotted Martha cruising by. Martha also was seen driving slowly by Robyn's Westport apartment.

With all that as background, several of Andy's pals volunteered to stand guard at the wedding just in case, keeping their eyes on the inn's driveway for any sign of Martha's black Mercedes 300 SDL Turbo, or her black Ford Lariat pickup, or her black Chevrolet Suburban. But Martha never made a showing, and the celebration went off as scheduled.

She did, however, make an unexpected and unwanted appearance at an unhappy Stewart family gathering later that same year. Almost six months after the joyous wedding Andy's mother, Ethel Stewart, who was in her eighties, died. At the time of her passing, on November 5, 1993, Andy and his sister placed a notice in *The New York Times* that underscored how deeply they had felt about her. They described her as "beautiful, elegant, strong, creative, wonderful, spiritual and witty" and made mention of the fact that she was a "lifelong student of Christian Science and member of the 3rd Church of Christ Scientist, New York City and The Mother Church." The death notice noted that "her unique and dignified presence was felt by many on Madison Avenue. Her wisdom and loyalty were cherished by all she knew. Her love of beauty, and of this City will be expressed by the planting of trees in Manhattan. . . ."

About a week after her cremation friends and family members gathered in Ethel Stewart's small apartment on East Sixty-third Street to pay their respects. Andy, who planned to offer the main eulogy at the informal service, was standing in the crowded living room, chatting with other guests, when he suddenly looked up to see Martha, who had not been invited, march into the apartment with her mother and sister Kathy Evans in tow. Robyn, who was standing next to Andy, gripped his hand tightly when she saw Martha, shocked that she had actually made an appearance and fearful she might cause a scene.

While everyone was dressed conservatively for the solemn occasion, Martha, who had closets full of conservative Armani, arrived wearing what a number of those present thought was an inappropriate miniskirt. She brushed off an attempted greeting by Andy, who was visibly shaken by her appearance, and angrily demanded to know, "Why didn't you invite me?" Later Andy told a friend that the only thought running through his mind at that moment was that Martha had rudely hung up on his mother the last time they had talked, not the first time she had treated Ethel Stewart shabbily.

Andy hurriedly conferred with his sister. He told her that Martha's presence had made him physically ill, that he feared misbehavior on her part, that he didn't think he could speak as planned, and that he thought he should leave. She was emphatic. Martha, she said, should be the one to go. But when she asked her to leave, Martha refused.

Meanwhile Andy greeted Martha Sr. and Kathy Evans, both of whom he had always liked. To others present, the

two women appeared embarrassed and confused by what
was happening. Apparently they had accompanied Martha
to the gathering with the understanding that she had been
invited. As one guest said later, "They just had no idea
they were intruding." Finally, because Martha's presence
had become so uncomfortable for Andy and his sister, a
relative persuaded Martha to leave, and she stormed out
without ever once offering her condolences to Andy. A
family friend described Martha's actions that day as "re-
volting."

It's a Good Thing

The way some Time Warner brass saw it, Martha's increasingly vocal demands for equity in her money-losing
magazine were sparked because she was "trying to keep
up with the Joneses": the Steven Spielbergs, the Billy Jo-
els, the Calvin Kleins, and the other monstrously wealthy
superstars who had become her neighbors, acquaintances,
and party guests. One Time Warner honcho observed,
"Martha realized about three years into the magazine's life
that the public presence that she created was, indeed, equal
to a lot of the new friends she acquired in Hollywood, but
that those people were worth tens and hundreds of millions,
and she felt she didn't have anything substantial to show
for all her efforts. And it was driving her crazy. Her friends
would go off and make an album and earn ten million dollars, or make a movie and earn fifteen million, and she was
still working off a basic income of around a half million

dollars. She realized she was never going to make *big* money. That's when she went in to renegotiate her deal, and that's what opened the Pandora's box.''

Starving for a bigger piece of the pie, Martha began playing hardball by retaining the services of one Allen Grubman, dubbed by the press as a ''high-powered entertainment attorney,'' to represent her interests in negotiations with Time Warner. After all, Martha *had* actually morphed from entertaining *expert* to entertainment *diva* in the thirteen years since *Entertaining* became boffo in the bookstores.

Of Grubman, she once said, ''Bringing in someone who had not 'grown up' with me was the best thing I did because people who knew me before just considered me good old Martha—really, even the Time Inc. people. From day one, Allen knew what I was—*a star*. He looked at me from the standpoint of this-level-up-here instead of down there. Allen is the king of schmooze, and then when you see him negotiate, you know that the schmoozing is, in his words, foreplay. But I'll tell you, he is the best negotiator I ever saw. I've learned a lot about that. It's wonderful what he does.''

In his early fifties Grubman, of Grubman, Indursky, a New York firm, was a man of enormous confidence and ego, who once was quoted as saying that no one but he should be included on a list of top entertainment attorneys. Pointing with pride at himself, he declared, ''This is it, *bubeleh*.''

Grubman also was a high roller, and with clients like Madonna, Bruce Springsteen, Elton John, Mariah Carey, David Geffen, Rod Stewart, and Martha Stewart, he could afford to be. When his daughter got married, about the time Martha had sicced him on Time Warner, he paid an estimated half million dollars for the affair at the Pierre Hotel. The Village People (one of Grubman's disco-era clients) provided some of the entertainment, twelve thousand dollars were spent for the Beluga caviar served from a dripping sturgeon ice sculpture, and the room was filled with ten thousand white roses, plus a lot more. As one guest noted, ''You could tell Martha Stewart didn't cater this one. It was more Don Corleone than Darien, Connecticut.'' In any event, Martha was among the more than four hundred guests in attendance and was photographed by *The New York Times* conferring with the father of the bride, who boasted he had made the whole event, including twenty pounds of Italian white truffles, possible.

Martha needed a powerhouse like Grubman in her corner because her support at Time Warner appeared to be eroding. At the beginning her biggest champion was S. Christopher Meigher III, who headed Time's new ventures group. But he left after losing a power struggle. (He subsequently set up his own very successful company, Meigher Communications, and his first magazine, *Garden Design*, was kind of a faux *Martha Stewart Living* about the gardening lifestyle.)

Meigher was replaced by Robert Miller, who set up shop in California rather than New York, ''which gave Martha a free hand to run up costs and expenses in Manhattan,'' a former Time executive asserted. When Miller's job evaporated in a corporate restructuring, Martha had no real rabbi remaining within the organization. She then came directly under the thumb of Time Inc. president and CEO Don Logan. As a member of his executive circle noted, ''Don is a bottom-line Alabaman, a real gentleman—but tough. He didn't buy Martha's charm. He didn't buy Grubman's schtick. He wanted profits, and *Martha Stewart Living* wasn't producing them.''

Martha was critical of Logan and found his management style ham-handed. It was Logan who had pushed out Bob Miller and closed down the ventures group. Worse, Don Logan wasn't a connoisseur of the Martha Stewart style of living. His favorite repast? Meat patties flown to New York City from a hamburger joint in Decatur, Alabama.

When Martha brought in Grubman to represent her interests, the feeling at Time Warner was ''Oh, shit, this is awful,'' a former executive said. With Grubman handling her business, Time Warner sweetened Martha's deal somewhat to keep her at bay, bringing her salary, bonuses, and perks to over one million dollars annually. Time Inc. also established a new division called Martha Stewart Enterprises, encompassing the magazine, the magazine's merchandising, multimedia, and television spin-offs. Martha was given the title of chairman, in addition to editor in chief of the magazine.

But Don Logan and the corporation firmly resisted granting her the equity she desperately wanted and felt she deserved. As *The Wall Street Journal* put it in a front-page story headlined DOMESTIC ICON WANTS EQUITY IN HER EMPIRE—OR ELSE . . . "SHE REALLY LIKES CONTROL"— ". . . the ultimate arbiter of modern homemaking . . . has also become a world-class headache for Time Inc, the Time Warner publishing unit that for five years has bled plenty of red ink to bankroll her ever-expanding empire."

By the spring of 1996 Martha had begun shopping around for a new backer, with thoughts of buying back her magazine, taking it elsewhere, and running it herself with venture capital. She seemed to have an attractive package when she walked in the door: The total Martha Stewart empire reportedly generated two hundred million dollars a year, with the magazine accounting for about a quarter of that amount. Ad pages had soared more than 50 percent over 1995, and circulation was up to about 1.2 million a month. But the magazine still wasn't turning a profit, and the subsidiary ventures weren't generating big money either.

Still, there *was* outside interest. Among those courting her were bankers, publishers like Si Newhouse, and even her old boss at *Time*, Chris Meigher. Condé Nast president Steve Florio said at one point, "If *Martha Stewart Living* ever went into play, we'd be very interested. It's more than a magazine. It's a media phenomenon with magazines, a syndicated TV show and books."

But after talking to her, everyone who showed initial interest passed. The bankers wondered, "Is this really proved yet? Is a single-title magazine company the way of the future?" One publisher said, "Martha got courted by everybody, but she got more of a cold bath than she expected. No one did the deal because her demands were just too great."

Another businessman revealed, "She wanted equity that

would be twice what we would normally give somebody. Fifteen percent is considered normal, and some of the great ones might get up to thirty percent if they hit every kind of target or benchmark that you set for them. But Martha wanted in excess of that, and she wanted to have full control over both the editorial operations and the publishing operations. We saw the same problems she has with Time Warner, so it's a kind of nonstarter. She was being sadly unrealistic. She knew a lot more about the editorial process than she once did, but *not* a lot more about the publishing formula. She's working under the theory that somebody's going to fall in love with her and say, 'This is going to be fun. I'm famous. I made all my money building shopping centers. I'll hitch my star and bank account to Martha Stewart.' ''

Back at Time Warner, according to another scenario, Martha attempted to mend bridges. For example, she was said to have met with Reg Brack, chairman of Time Inc., telling him that they should be on better terms. Brack was charmed. When Martha learned that Brack's daughter was getting married, according to one account, she offered to oversee the entire shindig. "He was a guy who was against the magazine," one Time Inc. executive said. "And then all of a sudden he was smitten with her."

By early October 1996, however, someone else had become smitten with her too, or at least that's what Martha revealed. She claimed she had found an outside backer and was involved in secret negotiations to end her troubled relationship with Time Warner and take over full control of her operations.

"The sixty-four-dollar question for anyone who goes into business with her is, When does the American public catch on that Martha Stewart is a bit of a sham?" said a former high-ranking Time Inc. official. "If she's not making much money today, which she is not on a huge amount of revenue that probably approached sixty million in fiscal '96, then is there ever going to be any *real* profit in all of what she does?"

In January 1997, after more than a year of sometimes tedious discussions and hardball negotiations, Martha cut the umbilical cord that held her to Time Warner by agreeing to pay upwards of $75 million for control of her magazine and subsidiary operations. As part of the deal, Time Warner got to keep a piece of her action—under 20 percent. By the end, Time Warner was happy to see her go, although Don Logan maintained, "We didn't want out, Martha wanted out. . . . She wanted to be in control of her own destiny." Martha boasted that she didn't have to borrow a penny, using what she called "internally generated funds" to get back her baby and fly solo. She named her new company Martha Stewart Living Omnimedia, an umbrella for all of her related ventures: the magazine, the books, a new syndicated TV show, a new syndicated newspaper column called Ask Martha, a catalog–mail order operation called Martha by Mail; new endorsement deals with her first corporate sponsor, Kmart, and with Sherwin-Williams paints; and even the twenty-five thousand dollars a pop she charges for each personal appearance. "It's mine," Martha declared triumphantly. "I can control very clearly what I want to do and where I want to go." One of Martha's assertions to a reporter boggled the minds of associates: "I'm not out to make a buck," she declared with a straight face.

Around the time Martha was making her new big deal, she had become embroiled in another bizarre skirmish with Andy, this time over his ability to father children.

It began in the late summer of 1996 when Liz Smith published an item in her nationally syndicated gossip column trumpeting a forthcoming cover story in the October *McCall's*. Smith reported that "the queen of home planning and gracious living . . . the glamorous domestic deity" had revealed, "The only regret I have in my entire life is that I don't have more children. That is a very serious regret. My husband had cancer that precluded him from having more children. And I didn't want to adopt. It was stupid. I'd give *anything* to have a son right now." Martha of course never disclosed to *McCall's* that she long ago decided not to have more than one child, nor did she reveal that she had a hysterectomy while her biological clock was still ticking.

"When Andy heard about Martha's statement, he was furious. I've never seen him so livid," a close associate said. "Andy's cancer [in the late seventies] *never* precluded him from fathering children, and Martha knew that. She's still so angry with him and clearly jealous of his happy life with Robyn. All of us who knew the real story were shocked and horrified when we read Martha's words and wondered how she could be so evil to say something like that."

Andy consulted an attorney about taking possible legal action against the magazine and Martha. At the same time he spoke with Sally Koslow, the editor in chief of *Mc-Call's*, and demanded a retraction, which was refused. Koslow, who said she stood by writer Gail Collins's story, told him he could write a letter, which might be published, and she also requested medical proof regarding his claim. One concession on Koslow's part was that she hadn't realized, until Andy told her, that there had been a twelve-year gap between the time Alexis was born and the time of Andy's cancer, plenty of time for Martha to have had another child if she had wanted one.

In a letter to Koslow in mid-September, Andy asked for but was refused a full and prominent correction. "Could it be," he wrote, "that you fear the consequences of Martha Stewart's rage?" In the letter he called Martha's statement "utterly false. I had cancer, it was cured, and it in no way interfered then or interferes now with my ability to have children." He went on:

> The honest reason why Martha Stewart and I did not have more children is that our marriage was strained and painful and it provided an unhealthy atmosphere in which to bring up children. Our careers dominated, and we devoted far too little time to the child we had. We would have been even greater failures as parents if there had been a second child. Martha made it very clear at the time in many conversations between us and in conversations with friends that she did not want another child . . . to put a more sympathetic spin

on her personal story at my expense, she untruthfully offered my cancer as the reason.

Caught lying, Martha retracted. In a letter published in the January 1997 issue of *McCall's,* she wrote:

> With respect to my interview in your October issue, I would like to clarify that my former husband, Andrew Stewart, and I did not have more than one child for personal reasons, not because of any medical disability on Mr. Stewart's part. As far as I am aware, there is no such medical disability.

Andy's assertions and Martha's admission proved to be true. On March 19, 1997, two months after Martha's retraction was published, Robyn Fairclough Stewart gave birth to two beautiful, healthy twin girls. Earlier she and Andy had adopted an infant boy. "Andy's the proudest father I've ever seen," a friend said. "He's so happy. For once, he feels his life is complete."

Whatever her shortcomings, the journey of Martha Kostyra Stewart from blue-collar New Jersey to the pinnacle of wealth, power, and success as America's premier arbiter of style and taste has been a phenomenal one. Her strength, spirit, grit, chutzpah, and beliefs are remarkable, if not oftentimes curious, or downright bizarre. Martha Stewart truly is an American original. After her decade and a half on the national scene, loyalists and detractors can agree on one fact: that the *public* Martha is a superwoman, a description she herself has promulgated successfully.

Superwoman, or something more?

At the height of her success an eerie corporate manifesto somehow slipped out of Martha's offices and made its way from one Time Inc. executive's desk to another and eventually from a Xerox machine to the outside world.

It spoke of "Shared Values" and of "Founding Beliefs." It discussed something called the "Underlying Value Proposition." And all of it focused on "Martha's Way."

From its wording, some wondered whether Martha's

world was more gentrified Jonestown than happy home-maker. The white paper, replete with what was described as an incomprehensible flow chart, declared, in part:

> In Martha's vision, the shared value of the *MSL* [*Martha Stewart Living*] enterprises are highly personal—reflecting her individual goals, beliefs, values and aspirations. . . .
>
> "Martha's Way" can be attained because she puts us in direct touch with everything we need to know, and tells/shows us exactly what we have to do. . . .
>
> MSL enterprises are founded on the proposition that Martha herself is both leader and teacher. . . . While the ranks of "teaching disciples" within *MSL* may grow and extend, their authority rests upon their direct association with Martha; their work emanates from her approach and philosophies; and their techniques, and products and results meet her tests. . . .
>
> The magazine, books, television series, and other distribution sources are only vehicles to enable personal communication with Martha. . . .
>
> She is not, and won't allow herself to be, an institutional image and fiction like *Betty Crocker*. . . . She is the creative and driving center.
>
> By listening to Martha and following her lead, we can achieve real results in our homes too—ourselves—just like she has. . . . It is easy to do. Martha has already "figured it out." She will personally take us by the hand and show us how to do it. . . .

Notes and Sources

EPIGRAPH

Page

xv "There are no skeletons. There are no secrets": Martha Stewart, Conversations with Charlie Rose, lecture series, March 26, 1996, 92nd Street YM-YWHA, New York City.

PART I
FATAL ATTRACTION

Page

5 "He told me Martha": interview, informed source.

6 Hair-pulling incident: interviews, Kathy Tatlock and informed source.

INTO THE WORLD

Page

6 1:33 P.M. on August 3, 1941: birth certificate, New Jersey Department of Health, Trenton, New Jersey.

6 Christened at St. Ann's: interview, Estelle Kostyra Bukowski Burke.

7 "Leo birthday party": "Martha's Calendar," *Martha Stewart Living*, July–August 1995.

7 Despite the *Jersey Journal*'s: *Jersey Journal*, August 2, 1941.

7 A gasoline curfew: ibid.

7 *The Bride Came C.O.D.*: ibid.

415

7	At 33 Stagg Street: birth certificate; interviews, Kostyra family members.

7	Kostyra's Tavern: interviews, Kostyra family members.

7	The Sparrow Hill: Jersey City Public Library, New Jersey.

8	Eric's birth on: interview, Eric Kostyra Scott.

8	Remembering the moment: interview, Burke.

8	"My sisters and brothers": interview, Scott.

8	"I kept that secret": interview, Burke.

8	"I knew Eric": interview, Diane Carey.

9	"If your grandmother": interview, Scott.

9	The shotgun wedding: interviews, Kostyra family members.

9	Eddie had met Martha: ibid.

9	"They ran off": interview, Clementine Ruszkowski Carriere.

9	"Dad joked that": interview, Scott.

9	"Eddie and Martha said": interview, Burke.

10	On September 7: interviews, Kostyra family members.

10	"To my mother": Martha Stewart, *Martha Stewart's Menus for Entertaining* (New York: Clarkson N. Potter, 1994).

10	"1994 was an important": Martha Stewart, *Special Occasions* (New York: Time Publishing Ventures, 1994).

11	"Martha *sponsored* the party": interview, Frank Kostyra.

11	"Our parents had eloped": ibid.

11	"She said it was a shotgun": interview, Burke.

FROM POLAND WITH LOVE

Page

12	Franz Josef Kostyra: Biographical information and anecdotal material, interviews, Kostyra family members.

12	Medieval kingdom of Poland: Britannica CD 2.0 (Chicago: Encyclopaedia Britannica, 1995).

13	A cafeteria chain: Kenneth T. Jackson, *The Encyclopedia of New York City* (New Haven and London: Yale University Press, 1995).

14	A family of storks: interview, Hank Kostyra.

14	Edward Rudolph: Biographical information and anecdotal material, Kostyra family members.

14	"She babied him along": interview, Kostyra.

14	"Grandfather would hold": interview, Scott.

14	Jersey City history and Frank Hague biographical information: Joan Lovero, manager, New Jersey Room, Jersey City Public Library, New Jersey.

15 "Dad worked hard": interview, Kostyra.

15 Society of Sons of Poland: *Jersey Journal,* December 27, 1943.

15 Hudson County Democratic Association: ibid.

15 Hague-Kostyra relationship: interview, Kostyra.

16 "By that time": ibid.

16 "He didn't have me sign": i bid.

BEING THE MAN

Page

18 "He had what you'd call": interview, Hank Kostyra.

18 "Eddie was a walking": interview, Estelle Kostyra Bukowski Burke.

18 "We have a talent": interview, Frank Kostyra.

19 "Music hath its": Dickinson High yearbook, 1929.

19 A high school gym teacher: interviews, Burke and Hank Kostyra.

19 Details about Edward Kostyra's college years: interviews, Kostyra family members.

20 "Eddie would go": interview, Kostyra.

20 "Everything he read" ibid.

20 "Eddie just wasn't": interview, Hazel Wacker.

20 "He said he met": interview, Hank Kostyra.

21 "The race is not always": Panzer College yearbook, 1933.

FINDING A MATE

Page

21 "There weren't an awful": interview, Hazel Wacker.

22 "Eddie tried to make the best": interview, informed source.

22 "Eddie's father had his own": interview, informed source.

22 "Actually, our parents": interview, Clementine Ruszkowski Carriere.

22 Family history of Ruszkowskis: interviews, Carriere and Kostyra family members.

23 "She talked about her": interview, Frank Kostyra.

24 "It was boy, girl": interviews, Kostyra family members.

24 Details about Edward Kostyra's wartime experience: interview, Hank Kostyra.

24 "When I asked Dad": interview, Frank Kostyra.
25 Letters of administration: Docket #58, Case #115129, Book 200, page 68, Hudson County records, Jersey City, New Jersey.
25 "Mom took it over": interview, Hank Kostyra.

A DYSFUNCTIONAL FAMILY

Page

26 "It was the perfect job": interview, informed source.
27 His first job was: interviews, Kostyra family members.
27 "But if another": interview, Hank Kostyra.
27 "At one company": interview, Eric Kostyra Scott.
27 "Special professional service": Nutley *Sun,* undated.
28 "Dad doctored us": interview, Frank Kostyra.
28 Eddie Kostyra boasted: interview, Hank Kostyra.
28 Thirteen thousand dollars in his best year: Martha Stewart, Conversations with Charlie Rose, lecture series, March 26, 1996, 92nd Street YM-YWHA, New York City.
28 "Eddie felt he never": interview, Clementine Ruszkowski Carriere.
28 "Dad was physical": interview, Frank Kostyra.
29 "My father fancied himself": interview, Eric Kostyra Scott.
30 "In many ways": interview, informed source.
31 "My Father, for instilling": Martha Stewart, *Entertaining* (New York: Clarkson N. Potter, 1982).
31 "For being my first teacher": Martha Stewart, *Martha Stewart's Gardening* (New York: Clarkson N. Potter, 1991).
31 "Drilled into my head": Martha Stewart, "Remembering," *Martha Stewart Living,* December 1993.
31 "An art form": Martha Stewart, "Remembering," *Martha Stewart Living,* October 1994.
31 "Dad fished for food": Martha Stewart, "Remembering," *Martha Stewart Living,* April–May 1993.
32 "Dad's favorite purveyor": Martha Stewart, "Remembering," *Martha Stewart Living,* April–May 1992.
32 "Severely punished": Martha Stewart, "Remembering," *Martha Stewart Living,* February 1995.
32 "Including his fiery temper": Martha Stewart, "Remembering," *Martha Stewart Living,* April–May 1993.
32 "He was a real ogre": interview, Gail Hallam Charmichael.

33 "Guilty of perpetuating": Martha Stewart, "Remembering," *Martha Stewart Living,* February–March, 1993.
34 "We walked to school": interview, Diane Carey.
35 "We were friends": Martha Stewart, "Remembering," *Martha Stewart Living,* December 1992–January 1993.
35 "You didn't see Martha's": interview, Miriam Mendelson McRob.
35 "When I was in scouting": interview, Scott.
36 "Martha and I fought": interview, Frank Kostyra.
37 "Very difficult, very demanding": *Manhattan, inc.,* January 1989.
37 "My father took me under": *New York* magazine, January 28, 1991.
37 "Crazy force in the family": Conversations with Charlie Rose, March 26, 1996.

SCHOOL DAYS

Page
38 "Martha Senior was a sweet": interview, informed source.
38 "When I would read": interview, Judy Churchill Stothoff.
39 "Beautifully groomed": Martha Stewart, "Remembering," *Martha Stewart Living,* September 1994.
40 "I remember getting up": ibid.
40 "Martha was a very": interview, Irene Weyer.
41 If Martha didn't go home: interview, Stothoff.
42 "Our best friends": Martha Stewart, *Martha Stewart's Pies & Tarts* (New York: Clarkson N. Potter, 1985).
42 "She had *nothing* to do": interview, Estelle Kostyra Bukowski Burke.
42 "The bowl that she": interview, Frank Kostyra.
42 "Dad said Mr. Maus": interview, Eric Kostyra Scott.
43 "Well, because you're making": *New York* magazine, January 28, 1991.
43 "I guess I was the only": interview, informed source.

PUBERTY AND PRIVACY

Page
44 Years later she was still bothered: Martha Stewart, "Remembering," *Martha Stewart Living,* February–March 1993.
45 "Laura's birth caused": interview, informed source.

45 "I was forever dusting": ibid.
45 "White onion on white": *New York* magazine, January 28, 1991.
46 Being somewhat wall-eyed: interview, informed source.
46 "She was staying with me": interview, Clementine Ruszkowski Carriere.
46 "Coveted": Martha Stewart, "Remembering," *Martha Stewart Living,* February–March, 1993.
46 "When I grow up": interview, Estelle Kostyra Bukowski Burke.
47 Two Guys from Harrison: interview, Frank Kostyra.
47 "Martha saw me wearing": interview, Judy Churchill Stothoff.
47 "My appetite for reading": Martha Stewart, "Remembering," *Martha Stewart Living,* October–November, 1992.
47 "Already curious": ibid.
48 "They were more her style": interview, informed source.
48 "Martha's room was very": interview, informed source.
49 "Martha had about as much interest": interview, informed source.

HIGH SCHOOL DAYS

Page
50 "I sat next to her": interview, Barbara Rubin Oliver.
50 "She had a focus that": interview, Barbara Viventi Howard.
51 Were considered simplistic: interview, informed source.
51 "I tried to show my": interview, Maxine Hoffer.
52 "A lot of our friends": interview, Lynn Sherwood Kaneps.
52 Eddie Kostyra had warned: interviews, Kostyra family members.
52 She served as: 1958–1959 Nutley High School yearbooks.
53 Most of her activities: interviews, informed sources.
53 "He helped her with": interview, George Christiansen.
53 "In the winter": interview, informed source.
53 "I'd scream, 'Stop,' ": interview, informed source.
54 "Martha's mother, *not Martha*": interview, Howard.
54 "I recall reading": interview, Eleanor Watts Flavin.

THE MODEL HUSTLE

Page
55 "Dad pushed Martha": interview, Frank Kostyra.
55 "I went with her": interview, Lynn Sherwood Kaneps.
56 "Martha wanted to do it": interview, Barbara Viventi Howard.
56 "I remember modeling": *New York* magazine, January 28, 1991.
57 "She was seen climbing": interview, Gail Hallam Charmichael.
57 "We all thought": interview, Eleanor Watts Flavin.
57 "In Nutley in those days": interview, Barbara Rubin Oliver.
58 "We'd be in math class": interview, Mike Geltrude.
58 "Everybody was in awe": interview, LeAnne White Ritchie.
58 "Martha's modeling was a big thing": interview, Mariette Vandermolen.

HIGH SCHOOL BOYS

Page
59 "Martha was very closemouthed": interview, Nancy Teischman DeGrote.
59 "I'm always surprised": interview, Lynn Sherwood Kaneps.
60 "She was *too* attractive": interview, Ansis Girts Kaneps.
60 "The guys didn't think": interview, Gail Hallam Charmichael.
61 "My folks *loved*": interview, Mark Hallam.
61 "We were not looking": interview, Lynn Sherwood Kaneps.
61 "Martha immediately took to": interview, informed source.
61 "It was supposed to be very": interview, informed source.
62 "Martha kept things": interview, Lynn Sherwood Kaneps.
63 "Peter used to laugh": interview, Peggy Mylod Farabaugh.
63 "She thought Peter was": interview, informed source.
64 "Martha made the dress": interview, Diane Carey.
64 "Unlike my house": ibid.
65 "Connie Francis's brother's": interview, DeGrote.
66 "I always got the impression": interview, informed source.

HIGH HONORS

Page
66 "I had little choice": *New York* magazine, January 28, 1991.
66 "If she had": interview, informed source.
67 "Dear Ellie, I've just": interview, Eleanor Watts Flavin.
67 "Stairway to the Stars": *Maroon and Gray,* June 4, 1959.
68 "Like Martha, Peter": interview, Lynn Sherwood Kaneps.
68 "She wanted to stand": interview, Diane Carey.

BARNARD, BERMUDAS, AND *GLAMOUR*

Page
69 "My best friend": Martha Stewart, "Remembering," *Martha Stewart Living,* July–August, 1995.
69 "It was really exciting": interview, Wendy Supovitz Reilly.
71 "Dress Code Horror": *Barnard Alumni Magazine,* Fall 1995.
71 "Martha and I were totally": interview, Reilly.
73 "I lived home my first year": *New York* magazine, January 28, 1991.
73 "Martha's life wasn't": interview, Caroline Fleisher Birenbaum.
73 "Martha was very knowledgeable": interview, Marlene Lobell Ruthen.
73 "Very short time": *American Photo,* July–August, 1996.
73 "Martha didn't have": interview, Reilly.
74 IT'S A GRAND NEW FLAG: *Glamour,* August 1960.
75 "A very big deal": interview, Barbara Stone.
75 "Martha was excited": interview, Norma Collier.

FEW COLLEGE MEN

Page
76 "My boyfriends had been": *People,* April 14, 1980.
76 "I was not as beautiful": interview, Wendy Supovitz Reilly.
77 "There could well have been": ibid.
77 "Martha was very picky": interview, Rosemary López Roca.
78 "Martha wanted to marry": interview, Reilly.

78 It began in a Greek: interview, Diane Stewart Love.
79 "Excuse me, but": ibid.

PART II
ANDY

Page
83 Profile of Andy Stewart: interviews, informed sources.
83 Profile of George Stewart: interviews, informed sources.
84 Owned a seat: New York Stock Exchange records.
84 "My father had been very impressed": interview, Emanuel J. Matkowsky's daughter.
85 Profile of Ethel Gilbert Stewart: interviews, informed sources.
85 "Looked like a sultan's": *New York* magazine, October 7, 1991.
85 "Ethel put up": interview, informed source.
85 "Other than my family": *New York* magazine, October 7, 1991.
86 "You could practically not": interview, informed source.
86 Never exchanged birthday presents: interview, Gene Levy.
86 When Andy was just a child: interview, Diane Stewart Love.
86 Right after the war: ibid.
87 "I don't like to be a copycat": *New York* magazine, October 7, 1991.
88 "None of us wanted": interview, informed source.

MEETING ANDY

Page
89 "Andy was always looking": interview, Jack Rosenblum.
90 "I lived in the servants' quarters": *New York* magazine, January 28, 1991.
90 Martha made an impressive: interview, informed source.
90 "She wasn't embarrassed": interview, Wendy Supovitz Reilly.
90 Meeting of Martha and Andy: interviews, informed sources.
91 "We fell in love": *New York* magazine, January 28, 1991.
91 "I think the ladies": interview, Reilly.
92 "She started coming": interview, Rosenblum.

93 "She talked nonstop": interview, informed source.
93 "Their relationship": interview, Rosenblum.

A SHAKY ENGAGEMENT

94 "I was raised a strict": Martha Stewart, Conversations with Charlie Rose, lecture series, March 26, 1996, 92nd Street YM-YWHA, New York City.
94 "There was church": interview, Eric Kostyra Scott.
94 "The Catholic Church": interview, Eleanor Watts Flavin.
94 "I was kneeling down": interview, Frank Kostyra.
95 "Andy had many discussions": interview, informed source.
95 Eddie Kostyra was clearly: interviews, Kostyra family members.
96 "We were young and innocent": *People,* April 14, 1980.
96 "He stood outside": ibid.
96 "He told me I was crazy": ibid.
96 "That half Jew": interview, informed source.
96 "Eddie certainly was": interview, informed source.
97 "We moved from Jersey City": Philip Roth, *Portnoy's Complaint* (New York: Vintage, 1964).
97 "Because she would have said": interview, Estella Kostyra Bukowski Burke.
97 " 'You know my sister's' ": interview, Gail Hallam Charmichael.
97 In the 1930s: interviews, Stewart family members.
97 "I *never* knew": interview, informed source.
98 "She said she felt": interview, informed source.
98 "Can you imagine my real name": *USA Today,* December 18, 1989.
99 "We decided to raise": Martha Stewart, "Remembering," *Martha Stewart Living,* December 1992–January 1993.
99 "I don't think she ever": interview, informed source.
99 "I knew Martha was looking": interview, informed source.
99 "Andy was well fixed": interview, Charmichael.
100 "Mother and Dad": Martha Stewart, "Remembering," *Martha Stewart Living,* March 1995.

TYING THE KNOT

Page

100 Their first squabble: interview, informed sources.

101 "That incident should have set off": interview, informed source.

101 "We found out at the last minute": interview, Lynn Sherwood Kaneps.

101 "Martha was sewing": interview, Ginny Stager Diraison.

102 "I was late . . . really late": *USA Today Weekend,* March 20–22, 1987.

102 "In a bit of an unsophisticated": Martha Stewart, *Martha Stewart Weddings* (New York: Clarkson N. Potter, 1987).

GUILFORD HIATUS

Page

103 "We both had summer jobs": Martha Stewart, *Martha Stewart Weddings* (New York: Clarkson N. Potter, 1987).

103 "Had a crazy fantasy": interviews, informed sources.

104 "They parked their car": interview, Hank Kostyra.

105 "As the man I most liked": interview, John Carswell.

105 "I went back to sleep": Martha Stewart, "Remembering," *Martha Stewart Living,* November 1994.

106 "I'm sure Martha would": interview, Carswell.

106 "I had very little": interview, Kyra Carswell.

114TH STREET

Page

107 "Eddie [Kostyra] made Andy feel": interview, informed source.

107 "A miserable little": interview, informed source.

108 The place looked: interview, Hank Kostyra.

108 "It took some thought": Martha Stewart, "Remembering," *Martha Stewart Living,* Spring 1991.

108 "When I was *your* age": *USA Today Weekend,* March 20–22, 1987.

109 "The tub was so long": Martha Stewart, "Remembering," *Martha Stewart Living,* February–March 1993.

109 "Just a year into": interview, informed source.

109 "It's interesting": interview, informed source.

110 "My actual diary": Martha Stewart, "Remembering," *Martha Stewart Living,* June–July 1993.
111 One extremely upsetting: interviews, informed sources.

RIVERSIDE DRIVE

Page
112 "Martha had big dreams": interview, informed source.
112 "We were trying": Martha Stewart, "Remembering," *Martha Stewart Living,* February–March, 1994.
113 The Stewarts subsequently: interview, informed source.
113 "Crowded . . . huge country trestle": ibid.
113 "Martha and Ethel's personalities": interview, informed source.
113 "Wrapped up in the excitement": ibid.
113 She began feeding: interviews, informed sources.
114 "In those days": interview, Norma Collier.
114 "Was Martha destined": interview, Barbara Stone.
115 As much as thirty-five thousand dollars: *Time,* December 19, 1988.
115 "That's another one of": interview, Collier.

A LITTLE STEWART

Page
115 "On a purely intellectual": interview, informed source.
116 "There was nothing dramatic": interview, Florence Libin.
116 "Martha was a very": ibid.
116 Chigi . . . "best friends": Martha Stewart, "Remembering," *Martha Stewart Living,* Spring 1991.
116 "Martha was always": interview, informed source.
117 "Even learned to answer": ibid.
117 Martha virtually fell: interviews, informed sources.
117 "But for some": interview, Libin.
118 At the time: interview, Paul Elfenbein.
118 "Delightful-looking, all-American": interview, Kathy Tatlock.
118 "Martha fucked me upside": ibid.
119 "Pat theories, avuncular anecdotes": *Washingtonian Magazine,* 1975.
119 "Martha wanted to raise": interview, Norma Collier.

119 "I'm afraid what Ginott": interview, informed source.
119 "All of a sudden": interview, Gene Levy.

MIDDLEFIELD LIFE

Page
120 "We were in ecstacy": Martha Stewart, *Martha Stewart's New Old House* (New York: Clarkson N. Potter, 1992).
121 "We took turns": Martha Stewart, "Remembering," *Martha Stewart Living,* December 1994–January 1995.
121 "Andy learned carpentry, plumbing": Martha Stewart, *Martha Stewart's Quick Cook* (New York: Clarkson N. Potter, 1983).
121 Despite Martha's fairy-tale: interviews, informed sources.
121 "Martha and Andy devoted": interview, informed source.
122 "A totally devoted husband": interview, Paul and Florence Libin.
123 "It was *so* ritualistic": interview, informed source.
123 "Anal and controlling": interviews, informed sources.
123 "I thought Martha was really interested": interview, Emily McCully.

MASTERING THE ART

Page
124 Julia Child biographical information: *Current Biography,* 1967.
125 "Martha was always big": interview, Norma Collier.
126 "Absolutely everyone we knew": Martha Stewart, *Martha Stewart's Christmas* (New York: Clarkson N. Potter, 1989).
126 "Invented on the spot": Martha Stewart, *Martha Stewart's Hors d'Oeuvres* (New York: Clarkson N. Potter, 1984).
126 "Out of the blue": interview, Lynn Sherwood Kaneps.
126 "She never, ever": interview, Elizabeth Hawes.
126 "Her relationship with little": interview, Emily McCully.
127 "I'd scurry around": Martha Stewart, *Entertaining* (New York: Clarkson N. Potter, 1982).
127 "They all wanted": interview, Alexander Cortesi.
127 "She was strong": interview, Roger Hooker.
127 "My take on her": interview, Hawes.
128 "She was smart and ambitious": interview, Hooker.
128 "It was a time of": interview, McCully.
128 "My husband and I": interview, Collier.

129 "There was a lot": interview, informed source.
130 Andy later told: interview, informed source.
130 "Martha Stewart a swinger?": interview, informed source.

PART III
THE STOCKBROKER

Page
134 "Martha told me that": interview, Norma Collier.
134 "It was either that": *New York* magazine, January 28, 1991.
134 "To sort of gamble": Martha Stewart, Conversations with Charlie Rose, lecture series, March 26, 1996, 92nd Street, YM-YWHA, New York City.
134 "She just made": interview, Andy Monness.
135 "We were kicking": interview, Kenny Sidel.
135 "Andy watched me": interview, Brian Dennehy.
135 "I taught Brian Dennehy": *USA Weekend,* March 20–22, 1987.
136 She was formally registered: New York Stock Exchange records.
136 "I was making about a hundred thirty-five thousand": *New York* magazine, January 28, 1991.
137 "Martha very much": interview, Sandy Greene.
137 "Martha was a vastly": interview, Kathy Tatlock.

A NEW LIFE

Page
138 The school was based: John Davy, *Rudolf Steiner: A Sketch of His Life and Work.*
138 "Martha was an ambitious": interview, Florence Libin.
139 "The only big mistake I ever": Martha Stewart, Conversations with Charlie Rose, lecture series, March 26, 1996, 92nd Street YM-YWHA, New York City.
139 "Martha felt that one": interview, Libin.
139 "Martha said they weren't going": interview, Kathy Tatlock.
139 "I learned how to be really": Martha Stewart, *Charlie Rose* TV interview, 1995.
140 "When Pietro's ceased to exist": Martha Stewart, *Martha Stewart's Quick Cook Menus* (New York: Clarkson N. Potter, 1988).

141 "My daughter, Alexis": Martha Stewart, *Martha Stewart's Quick Cook* (New York: Clarkson N. Potter, 1983).

141 "Martha": interview, informed source.

RED ROSES

Page

141 "Martha called me": interview, Norma Collier.

142 Martha was standing at a pay phone: interview, informed source.

142 "Politics' Bad Boy": *New York Times,* June 28, 1988.

142 "A not-so-subtle toupee": ibid.

142 "Andy said that at first": interview, informed source.

143 "In those days": interview, Andrew Stein.

143 "It wasn't a big thing": interview, Collier.

143 "There was almost": interview, Andy Monness.

143 "In truth": interview, Sandy Greene.

144 "Andy had distinct designs": ibid.

144 "Martha was my dream girl": interview, Monness.

144 "In those days": interview, Brian Dennehy.

145 "I was the young wife": interview, Blue Magruder.

MORE CHANGES

Page

146 By the end of 1969: interviews, informed sources.

147 "Felt very pressured": interview, Sandy Greene.

147 "She was *always* complaining": ibid.

148 "What the hell are we": interview, informed source.

148 "All starry-eyed": interview, Kathy Tatlock.

148 "My skirt was": ibid.

149 "To start with": ibid.

A STEPFORD WIFE

Page

150 "We were very surprised": interview, Florence Libin.

150 Lifestyle choice and an investment: interview, Paul Libin.

150 "We had all been": interview, Elizabeth Hawes.

151 "We thought we'd fix": *New York* magazine, January 28, 1991.

151 "Westport is and was": interview, informed source.

153 "When they lived in Manhattan": interview, informed source.
153 "She became a very pouty": interview, Norma Collier.
153 "Something had started to go wrong": interview, informed source.
154 Privately, Andy began: interview, informed source.
154 "It was a major": ibid.
155 "Just look how beautiful": interviews, informed sources.
155 Slept with another man: interviews, informed sources.
155 "Andy wondered how": interview, informed source.

THE CRASH

Page
156 "She was working her butt off": interview, Ken Sidel.
157 "For us . . . it was a *huge* order": interview, Sandy Greene.
157 "She wasn't a gambler": interview, informed source.
157 "Stunningly beautiful": interview, Sandy Broyard.
158 "Speed addict": Jill Robinson, *Bed/Time/Story* (New York: Random House, 1974).
158 "Who really rescued me": interview, Jill Robinson.
158 "Martha was everything": ibid.
158 "I found her attractive": interview, Alan Bomser.
159 "Andy and Martha": interview, Jill Bomser.
159 "We had a fifty-five-foot": interview, Alan Bomser.
160 "One afternoon": interview, Greene.
161 He strongly advised her to quit: interview, informed source.
161 "When the business started going": interview, Brian Dennehy.
161 "Lost a lot of my money": interview, Norma Collier.
161 "We gave a bunch of it": interview, Emily McCully.
162 "Martha felt the pressure": interview, Andy Monness.

FLOUNDERING

Page
163 "I was a nervous wreck": *New York* magazine, January 28, 1991.
163 "Martha had a nervous breakdown": interview, George McCully.
163 She took the required test: interview, informed source.
164 She was frenetic: interviews, informed sources.

164 Painted the entire house: interview, informed source.
164 "That took on such": interview, Alan Bomser.
164 "I'd go over there": interview, Janet Horowitz.
164 "For many years I resisted": *New York* magazine, January 28, 1991.
165 "Well, that's Martha": interviews, informed sources.
165 "I once went over": interview, Ann Brody.
165 "We would sit": interview, Horowitz.

MOMMIE DEAREST

Page
166 "The first basket-weave": Martha Stewart, "Remembering," *Martha Stewart Living,* April–May, 1994.
166 She has told readers: Martha Stewart, "Remembering," *Martha Stewart Living,* August–September, 1992.
166 "Genuinely surprised": Martha Stewart, "Remembering," *Martha Stewart Living,* June–July, 1993.
166 "Many hours": Martha Stewart, "Remembering," *Martha Stewart Living,* September 1995.
167 "Waited serenely in bed": Martha Stewart, "Mother's Day Lunch," *Martha Stewart Living,* April–May, 1993.
167 "Martha was *not*": interview, Janet Horowitz.
167 "I like to think": interview, Jill Bomser.
168 "She likes housework": Bridgeport (Connecticut) *Post,* May 1975.
168 "There wasn't a lot of love": interview, Bomser.
169 "She was asking whether": interview, Blue Magruder.
169 "When Lexi was the star": interview, Ann Brody.
170 " 'I'm going to come to your house' ": ibid.
170 "Martha said, 'Well' ": interview, Gail Leichtman-Macht.
170 One afternoon: interview, informed source.

THE UNCATERED AFFAIR

Page
171 "Martha retired to a world": interview, Brian Dennehy.
171 "Martha taught kids": interview, Norma Collier.
172 "If Martha thought Lexi": interview, Ann Brody.
172 "Was born under my nose": interview, Jill Bomser.
174 "She *worked* at being": interview, Brody.

174 "Contained every modern": Bridgeport (Connecticut) *Post,*
    July 29, 1976.
175 "We were investigating": interview, Brody.
176 "We'd go shopping": interview, Collier.
177 "Oh, no, that's not": interview, Collier.
178 "Martha told me": interview, informed source.

THE MARKET BASKET

Page
180 "It was a nice little": interview, John Macht.
180 "One day": interview, Gail Leichtman-Macht.
182 A number of the respondents: interviews, informed sources.
183 "Martha often got involved": interview, informed source.
183 On a bitterly cold: interview, Vicky Negrin.
183 "Vicky was like Martha's": interview, Macht.
183 "Martha was like": interview, Leichtman-Macht.
184 "I was like the little": interview, Negrin.

"THE *GNOMES* COOKBOOK"

Page
185 When Bangor Punta's: interview, informed source.
186 "Vicky had this beautiful": interview, Ujala Hsu.
186 "I just figured": interview, Vicky Negrin.
187 A shrewd publisher: interviews, informed sources.
187 "Martha's idea was": interview, Negrin.
188 Levin hit the ceiling": interviews, informed sources.
188 "Who else could do": interview, informed source.

DARK CLOUDS

Page
189 Andy had always been: interviews, informed sources.
189 "We were extremely close": interview, George Christian-
    sen.
189 Christiansen was twenty-five: ibid.
190 The river was extremely rough: interviews, Christiansen and
    informed sources.
190 He discovered a lump: interviews, informed sources.
190 "He was in the hospital": interview, Eva Wiener.
190 Radiation, amputation: interviews, informed sources.

190 "This is sort of so": interview, Gail Leichtman-Macht.

191 "Martha collapsed": interview, George McCully.

191 "Prior to his illness": interview, Ann Brody.

192 "Like shit": interview, Jill Bomser.

192 One Mother's Day: interview, informed source.

192 "Don't *ever* get married": interview, informed source.

192 As the Stewarts drove home: interview, informed source.

193 "She treated him like a dog": interview, Frank Kostyra.

193 "Of course, she wasn't": interview, McCully.

194 On another occasion: interview, Gene Levy.

194 " 'Well, the only reason' ": interview, McCully.

195 "One day, when we had": interview, Norma Collier.

195 "Martha said something strange": interview, Wendy Supovitz Reilly.

195 One Martha arranged: interview, informed source.

196 "We were told": interview, Mary Emmerling.

196 "She told him many times": interview, informed source.

THE PROPRIETOR

Page

197 "I don't know how they found out": interview, informed source.

197 "A full working kitchen": interview, Leichtman-Macht.

197 "She always had to be": interview, Dick Goldman.

198 "Any catering jobs": interview, Pat Goldman.

198 "In the end": interview, John Macht.

198 The coup de grace: interviews, Florence Fabricant and Leichtman-Macht.

198 "We thought the story": interview, Leichtman-Macht.

199 Keeping her dismissal: interviews, informed sources.

FAMILY AFFAIR

Page

199 MARTHA STEWART CATERS, *People,* April 14, 1980.

200 "She asked us to dress": interview, Barry O'Rourke.

201 A sad and sullen child: interviews, informed sources.

201 "I'm going to kill": interview, Mary Emmerling.

201 Lexi was crying and complaining: interview, informed source.

201 With Lexi in tow: interview, informed source.

201 "There was a lot of": interviews, Naiad Einsel.
201 Various physical ailments: interviews, informed sources.
202 Several boarding schools: interviews, informed sources.
202 "Laura's relationship with": interview, informed source.
202 "I don't want money": interview, Frank Kostyra.
202 The situation had become: interviews, informed sources.
203 Failed to get a college: interviews, informed sources.
203 "She had come from a": interview, informed source.
203 "They'd go back and forth": interview, informed source.
204 "We had a very pleasant": interview, Digby Diehl.
204 "Laura did have a breakdown": interview, Kostyra.
204 "Our relationship has been": part of statement faxed to author by Laura through Martha Stewart's publicist, Susan Magrino.
205 Drinking heavily: interviews, Kostyra family members.
205 A bizarre concoction: interview, informed source.
205 "Ed was killing the pain": interview, Eric Kostyra Scott.
206 Martha exploded with annoyance: interview, informed source.
206 August 31, 1979: interviews, Kostyra family members.
206 "I've never experienced": interview, Father Edward Haber.
207 "It was really embarrassing". interview, informed source.
207 "I was ready to go up": interview, Estelle Kostyra Bukowski Burke.
207 "I was shocked": interview, Haber.
207 "I think in some respects": interview, Kostyra.
208 "Martha didn't look": interview, Sandy Broyard.

COOKIE CUTTERS

Page
209 "Martha wanted a deal": interview, Eva Wiener.
209 "Too greedy": interview, informed source.
210 "Inside was a layout": interview, Joanne Barwick.
210 "A royal bitch": interview, informed source.
211 "They came off *publicly*": interview, Naiad Einsel.
212 "Martha was sitting in the backseat": ibid.
213 "Martha said, 'Oh' ": ibid.
213 "She just had us trapped": interview, Carolyn Halsy.
214 "It sounded good": ibid.
214 "I had a migraine": ibid.
214 "I was pretty": interview, Tony Halsy.

215 "This is the food we served": interview, informed source.
215 "The next day people would say": interview, informed source.
216 "We had *such* problems": interview, Mary Emmerling.
216 "To me . . . it was so": interview, Barry O'Rourke.
217 "But Martha wanted": interview, Joe Ruggiero
217 "At parties she catered": interview, Clare McCully.
217 "I know she stiffed": interview, Einsel.

PART IV
ENTERTAINING

Page
222 "The most unusual": *New York Times,* December 19, 1982.
222 "I was lucky to be there": interview, Alan Mirken.
223 " 'We don't do those' ": interview, Mary Emmerling.
223 "Because *High-Tech*": ibid.
223 "Martha was really, really": interview, informed source.
223 During intense: interviews, informed sources.
224 "It was *so*": interview, Carol Southern.
224 History of cookbooks: Britannica CD 2.0 (Chicago: Encyclopaedia Britannica, 1995).
226 She saw herself: interviews, informed sources.
226 "Martha did *Entertaining*": interview, Richard Sax.

THE GHOST AND MRS. STEWART

Page
227 "Martha paints her own landscape": interview, informed source.
227 "Mrs. Stewart carries": *New York Times,* August 30, 1987.
228 "We were actually broke": interview, Elizabeth Hawes.
228 "This is going to be a fifty-fifty": ibid.
228 "I called Martha Stewart": interview, Roberta Pryor.
229 "As I recall": interview, Hawes.
230 "I did no research": ibid.
230 "If you can make me understand": interview, Alan Mirken.
230 "We were just relieved": interview, Carol Southern.
230 "Liz did a great": interview, Mirken.
231 "Martha did *no* writing": interview, Hawes.
231 "You'd better give in": ibid.
232 "Liz was the writer": interview, Southern.

AUTHOR! AUTHOR!

Page
232 "They were very cautious": *New York* magazine, January 28, 1991.

232 "Martha was *always* pushing": interview, Carol Southern.

233 "One of the things": interview, Alan Mirken.

233 On the one hand: interviews, informed sources.

234 One evening: interviews, informed sources.

234 "Martha wanted Andy": interview, informed source.

235 Martha's actions: interview, informed source.

235 "Andy and I were walking": interview, Norma Collier.

STOP, THIEF!

Page
236 "That's what my public expects me to wear": interview, informed source.

237 "It was *so* funny": interview, Sandy Broyard.

237 "Martha's underlying philosophy": interview, informed source.

237 "She's a real screamer": interview, informed source.

238 "Golden Dartboard Award": *Village Voice,* November 26, 1996.

238 "Somebody mentioned the party": interview, Elizabeth Hawes.

238 "I was sort of dumbfounded": interview, Ann Brody.

239 "Martha was great": interview, Diane Sappenfield.

240 "Mere amateur": interview, informed source.

240 "Martha told me that Craig": interview, Dorian Parker.

240 "Very few of the recipes": ibid.

240 "Well, you know what": interview, Norma Collier.

241 "One day I got": interview, Barbara Tropp.

241 "I was shocked because": ibid.

242 "The first to expose Martha": interview, Richard Sax.

242 "Was very kind of": ibid.

242 "Maybe Barbara Tropp": Chicago *Sun-Times* quoted in New York *Daily News,* December 7, 1983.

243 "Martha's saying that": interview, Sax.

243 "These weren't recipes": interview, Tropp.

243 "Now *that* upset me": ibid.

244 "Sweet-and-hot": *New York* magazine, January 28, 1991.

245 "I telephoned her": interview, Richard Jeffery.

ALL THE NEWS THAT FITS

Page
246 "We spent a lot of time": interview, John Hilts.
246 "I'd report the calls": interview, Marinda Freeman.
248 "*That Marian Burros*": interview, Clare McCully.
248 "She was horrified": interview, Marian Burros.
249 "It was the first time": interview, Bryan Miller.
249 "We had to reprint it": *New York* magazine, January 28, 1991.
250 "I was hired": interview, Anne de Ravel.

FAMILY SECRETS

Page
250 As a consequence: interviews, informed sources.
251 "The PMS poster": interview, informed source.
251 "She said Martha had been": interview, Dorian Parker.
251 "I always felt Martha": interview, Vicky Negrin.
251 "My breeding days": interview, Clare McCully.
252 "She just didn't want": interview, Parker.
252 "We were in the car": interview, Janet Horowitz.
253 "But no one went": interview, Parker.
253 "We connected by phone": interview, Marinda Freeman.
253 "We're pouting because he's away": *New York Times*, December 19, 1982.
254 "Practically baby-talk": interview, informed source.
254 "Not health spa": interview, informed source.
255 "From my vantage point": interview, Rafael Rosario.
255 "As successful as": interview, Clare McCully.
255 "Lexi didn't talk": interview, informed source.
255 "Wasn't considered cool": interview, informed source.
255 "She always worked": interview, informed source.
256 "Martha and Andy": interview, Nick Dine.
256 "I was there when": interview, George McCully.
256 "She did exactly as she pleased": interview, Parker.
257 Black basketball player: interview, informed source.
257 "They were pretty relaxed": interview, informed source.
258 "I wrote her": interview, George McCully.
258 Lexi was angered and offended: interview, informed source.

A MARKETABLE COMMODITY

Page
259 "We made a deal": interview, Carol Southern.
259 "We knew we had something": interview, Alan Mirken.
260 "The people at Crown": interview, Dorian Parker.
261 "It was a big job": interview, Carrie Donovan.
261 "Martha was hard to find": interview, Bryan Miller.
262 "Martha basically used *Times* money": interview, informed source.
262 "Produced, and what she": interview, Donovan.
262 "The copy person was": ibid.
262 "Martha loved it": interview, informed source.
262 "She felt that she": interview, Clare McCully.
263 "Martha was there": interview, Richard Jeffery.
263 "I just thought she was going": interview, Donovan.
264 While on location: interviews, informed sources.
264 "*Input* from Martha": interview, Mirken.
264 "We would sit in her kitchen": interview, Elizabeth Sahatjian.
264 "Andy told me": interview, Jeffery.
265 "*Outdoor Pleasures* clearly": interview, informed source.
265 "Very unpleasant, difficult": interview, informed source.
266 "We were very smitten": interview, Elizabeth Kent.
267 "Martha's contract with Crown": interview, Brooke Dojny.
267 *Newsweek* did a feature: *Newsweek*, December 1, 1986.
267 Martha called the: Hartford *Courant*, April 5, 1987.
267 "It was incredible": interview, Kent.
268 "I called Andy": interview, Cyrus Harvey.
268 "The last thing in the world": interview, Kent.

TURKEY HELL

Page
269 Descriptions of Martha's actions: interviews, informed sources.
271 "Martha was very angry": interviews, Kostyra family members.
271 "My initial take": interview, Marinda Freeman.
271 "Martha would try to hedge": interview, Rafael Rosario.
272 Freeman claimed: interview, Freeman.
272 "Within the first six months": ibid.
272 "The letters *were* upsetting": interview, informed source.

272 "There were periods": interview, Freeman.
273 "All of a sudden": ibid.
273 "She started a stink": ibid.
273 "Well, people are dying": interview, Clare McCully.
274 "Martha had a lot of": ibid.
274 "They're my little gay": ibid.
274 "Martha's a bright woman": interview, Rosario.
275 "I don't know if AIDS": ibid.
275 When Martha mentioned: interview, informed source.
275 "He was enthusiastic": interview, informed source.
276 "They were all very conscientious": interview, McCully.
276 "Like a dog turd": interview, informed source.
276 "Andy was sort of this": interview, informed source.
277 "Go talk to Robyn": interview, informed source.
277 "She was really going after him": interview, informed source.
278 "Within five minutes": interview, McCully.
279 The Stewarts' zoning battle: reports in Westport (Connecticut) *News*.

I OUGHT TO BE IN PICTURES

Page
282 "I'd trade my mother": interview, informed source.
282 "I told Peter": interview, Norma Collier.
283 "When *Entertaining* came out": interview, Peter Murray.
283 "She was a crazy": ibid.
283 "Every countess in the place": ibid.
284 "Peter had what was": interview, Ward Chamberlain.
284 "Martha didn't approach TV like": interview, Murray.
285 Duck in the fireplace: ibid.
285 "Shitload of money": interview, Geoffrey Miller.
285 "It was . . . one of the worst": ibid.
286 "This guy went berserk": interview, Murray.
287 "Reneged on the whole deal": ibid.
287 "A window during which": interview, Michael Cunningham.
287 "Christ, I wish": interview, Chamberlain.
287 "She was determined": interview, Alan Mirken.
288 "Laura and Kimmy were": interview, Janice Herbert.
288 "She was very able": ibid.
290 "A hysterically funny": interview, informed source.

290 "Leave my property this minute": interview, informed source.

291 "Suddenly she's going around": interview, informed source.

291 "A truly weird experience": interview, informed source.

292 "The mike had already been": interview, informed source.

292 Housewife-humorist, New York *Daily News*, November 25, 1988.

293 "The object now is to get": Hartford *Courant*, April 5, 1987.

WEDDINGS

Page

294 "Like this week": Hartford *Courant*, April 5, 1987.

294 "I'd much rather": ibid.

295 "I wanted Liz": interview, Carol Southern.

295 "I wanted to be sure": interview, Elizabeth Hawes.

295 "We knew *Weddings*": interview, Southern.

296 "In some cases": interview, Hawes.

296 "To get that one": ibid.

CHAPTER 50: ATTENTION, KMART SHOPPERS

Page

297 All of the material in this chapter is based on extensive interviews with Barbara Loren-Snyder and confirmation from knowledgeable sources.

303 "Many strange combinations": *New York Times*, August 23, 1987.

PART V
THE SPLIT

Page

307 Several times in the early to mid-eighties: interviews, informed sources.

307 "Martha just went nuts": interview, informed source.

308 "She lost it": interview, informed source.

308 "Andy couldn't believe": interview, informed source.

308 "It was a disaster": interview, informed source.

308 "They were having a huge": interview, informed source.

309 "The hard work." Hartford *Courant,* April 5, 1987.

309 Later Frank Kostyra: interview, Frank Kostyra.

309 "Even though cover credit": interview, Elizabeth Hawes.

310 "Together they were": ibid.

310 "At the last minute": interview, Carol Southern.

310 "She was a perfectionist": interview, Alan Mirken.

310 "A fifty-dollar, five-pound": *New York Times,* April 4, 1987.

311 "I try to write about": *New York Times,* August 30, 1987.

312 "If you're planning a wedding": *Oprah,* April 8, 1988.

312 "The irony was too much": interview, informed source.

312 "It was a troubling thing": interview, Mirken.

313 "I was walking Andy": interview, Kathy Tatlock.

313 "I left her": interview, informed source.

313 "The breakup happened": interview, Clare McCully.

GETTING EVEN

Page

314 "After Andy left": interview, Janet Horowitz.

315 "Martha's need to control": ibid.

315 "It was the worst": *New York* magazine, January 28, 1991.

316 He specifically returned home: interview, informed source.

316 "Martha went back and forth": interview, Kathy Tatlock.

317 "When Martha realized": ibid.

317 "Andy visited us": interview, Clare McCully.

317 "Well, you haven't even asked": interview, informed source.

318 Gave Martha some marijuana: interview, informed source.

318 "Martha was not sleeping": interview, Tatlock.

319 "Sometimes she would cook": ibid.

320 "That was one of the landmarks": ibid.

HELL HATH NO FURY

Page

322 "Andy knew it would be difficult": interview, informed source.

323 "What Robyn found": interview, Clare McCully.

324 "I learned about Robyn": interview, Kathy Tatlock.

325 "She was so goddamned angry": interview, informed source.

325 "I didn't slap him": *New York* magazine, January 28, 1991.
326 "[H]e did a lot": ibid.
326 "During my separation": Martha Stewart, *Martha Stewart Living,* June–July, 1993.
327 "Andy told me": interview, informed source.
327 "She looked at me": interview, Frank Kostyra.
328 "Martha told me": interviews, Kostyra and informed sources.
328 "It was very disturbing": interview, Clare McCully.
328 "If Andy had any": interview, George McCully.

FEAR OF ERICA

Page
329 "Midlife memoir": Erica Jong, *Fear of Fifty* (New York: HarperCollins, 1994).
330 "I didn't know she viewed me": interview, Erica Jong.
330 "After the split": interview, Wendy Supovitz Reilly.
331 "Writing, yoga, dogs and cooking": Jong, *Fear of Fifty.*
331 "People were cavorting": interview, George McCully.
331 "Tortured me": interview, Clare McCully.
332 "Martha spent the whole": interview, Jonathan Fast.
332 "Erica thought Martha": ibid.
332 "We were at a dinner party": interview, Jong.
332 "I had a little baby": ibid.
332 "He used to do these comic": ibid.
333 "I always heard that *she*": ibid.
334 "I heard that Erica *did*": interview, Fast.
334 "Andy was really upset": interview, informed source.
335 "All of a sudden": interview, Caroline Birenbaum.
335 "We felt she was nothing": interview, informed source.
336 Martha spent most: interview, Reilly.

BUSINESS AS USUAL

Page
337 "A field day for gossip": *Yankee,* February 1989.
337 "A *fabulous* guy": *HG,* May 1990.
338 "There's a saying that goes": *New York* magazine, January 28, 1991.
338 Another cool million: ibid.
338 "Oh, I just want": *HG,* May 1990.

339 "My motto is": *Chicago Tribune,* October 24, 1991.
339 "Not very nice": *New Yorker,* October 16, 1995.
339 "Martha Stewart Takes Over": *New Yorker,* June 25, 1990.
339 "Imaginary happy family": *New Yorker,* October 16, 1995.
340 "Knowing Martha": interview, informed source.
340 But Martha eventually found: *New York Post,* May 7, 1990.
340 "A trellis is not": *New York Post,* June 19, 1991.
341 "They took me to all the parties": *New York* magazine, January 28, 1991.
341 "It was just a long weekend": interview, Kurt Vonnegut.
341 Later the friendship between: interviews, informed sources.
341 "The best thing": *Avenue,* January 1990.
341 "As long as I'm alive": *New York Times,* August 3, 1987.
341 "*I* support Clarkson": *Avenue,* January 1990.
342 "I'm not rich": *Dallas Morning News,* November 18, 1992.
342 "I said, 'You' ": interview, Kathy Tatlock.
343 "She had this very": interview, Dick Roberts.
343 "She was sour": interview, informed source.
343 "Martha left Kathy Tatlock": interview, Roberts.
343 "Martha had what is known": interview, Tatlock.
344 "It's wonderful": interview, informed source.
345 "Practical, everyday tips": New York *Daily News,* May 15, 1988.
345 "Kathy really felt": interview, Clare McCully.
345 "I must say I was": interview, Tatlock.
346 "We did these commercials": interview, Roberts.
346 "And wouldn't have minded": interview, informed source.
346 "I thought of her as": interview, Bliss Broyard.
347 "She was a perfectionist": ibid.
347 "There were four bedrooms": ibid.

TUNA ON TOAST

Page
348 "A little cottage industry": interview, Frank Kostyra.
349 "I laid it at her feet": ibid.
349 "No one in this": ibid.
349 "The family is very": *New York* magazine, January 20, 1997.
349 "She never really did": interview, Barbara Loren-Snyder.
350 "In those instances": interview, Marilyn Gill.
351 "*That* was pure Martha": interview, Loren-Snyder.

351 "There was a big": interview, Gill.
352 "Her pettiness caused": interview, Peter Hirsch.
352 "Everyone below Joe": interview, Gill.
353 "A bunch of us": interview, Hirsch.
353 "Even though she": ibid.

THE ADAMS HOUSE

Page
357 "Martha's hope was": interview, informed source.
357 Martha thought she had died: interviews, informed sources.
357 "Martha said she wanted": interview, Barbara Loren-Snyder.
358 Martha and Andy Stewart bought: Westport, Connecticut, real estate records.
358 Andy had even shot: interviews, informed sources.
359 The bill of sale did not: interview, informed source.
359 "Mrs. Adams didn't": interview, Kathy Tatlock.
359 "Martha really was": interview, Loren-Snyder.
359 "We'd get calls": interview, Marilyn Gill.
359 "For every vendor": interview, informed source.
360 "The interest in how-to": *The Hour,* Norwalk, Connecticut, January 22, 1990.
360 "What I'm trying to do": Westport (Connecticut) *News,* March 21, 1990.
360 "She has the first": interview, informed source.
360 " 'Martha's not going to pay' ": interview, Norma Collier.
361 "I came into the store": interview, informed source.
361 "The value of": Westport *News,* June 6, 1990.
362 "I don't think it's true": *The Hour,* June 22, 1990.
362 "She just started screaming": interview, Susan Malsch.
362 "I don't think we should": *The Hour*, June 22, 1990.
363 "People like to criticize": *New York Post,* June 30, 1990.
363 For $862,500: Westport, Connecticut, real estate records.

LEXI AS TRUMP CARD

Page
365 "Five miserable years": *McCall's,* October 1966.
365 "I don't think": *People,* October 2, 1995.
365 "I felt rejected": Martha Stewart, Conversations with Char-

lie Rose, lecture series, March 26, 1996, 92nd Street YM-YWHA, New York City.

365 "Our daughter doesn't": *New York* magazine, January 20, 1997.

366 "Once he left Martha": interview, informed source.

366 "A poor job as": *People,* October 2, 1995.

366 "Very, very difficult": *Newsday,* June 24, 1993.

366 "If he was a nice man": *New York* magazine, January 28, 1991.

366 "I don't think he's": *Newsday,* June 24, 1993.

366 At a Christmas party: interview, Nick Dine.

366 "It's a source of tremendous": *People,* October 2, 1995.

367 "That would not be": interview, informed source.

367 "A Berlin Wall": interview, informed source.

367 "She said, 'No' ": interview, informed source.

368 "The apartment was extremely": interview, informed source.

368 "It was white-on-white": interview, informed source.

368 "Poor little rich girl": *Newsday,* June 24, 1993.

368 "I don't sleep on anything": *Avenue,* Summer 1993.

369 "These are her ideas": *Newsday,* June 24, 1993.

369 "My life has just": New York *Daily News,* July 19, 1996.

369 "After her parents' ": interview, Janet Horowitz.

370 "Lexi was violent": ibid.

370 "It's a constant battle": *Newsday,* June 24, 1993.

370 "Might come over": *TV Guide,* August 7, 1993.

370 "I mean, it's very funny": *New York* magazine, January 28, 1991.

371 "Under apple trees": ibid.

371 "Lexi is a good friend": *Newsday,* June 24, 1993.

371 "I'm *always* wrong": Martha Stewart, Conversations with Charlie Rose, lecture series, March 26, 1996.

371 "Martha told me": interview, Bliss Broyard.

372 "The pictures were from": ibid.

372 "A very sexy cover girl": interview, Kathy Tatlock.

FINDING MR. RIGHT

Page

373 "She moved away from that": interview, informed source.

373 "When a woman takes": interview, Frank Kostyra.

374 To look svelte: *Longevity,* August 1991.

374 "I don't like any guests": *HG*, May 1990.
374 "After Andy left": interview, Kathy Tatlock.
375 "Bumped into each other": interview, Brian Dennehy.
375 "Kind of hung out": ibid.
375 "There was this attitude": ibid.
376 "We started as friends": interview, Richard Feigen.
376 "I wasn't privy to what": ibid.
377 "Martha has a very beautiful": interview, Dan Shedrick.
378 "Oh, I want to have": interview, Diane Sappenfield.
378 "They were drinking": ibid.
379 "Just spoofing": interview, Shedrick.
379 "It would be difficult": ibid.
379 "The most difficult": ibid.
380 "They were definitely": interview, informed source.
380 "I'm not a fanatic": *TV Guide*, August 7, 1993.
380 "So scary, like Big": *New York Times*, July 30, 1995.
381 "[E]verytime they see me": *Vanity Fair*, March 1993.
381 The Stewarts once: interview, informed source.
382 "Martha was telling me about": interview, Sandy Broyard.
382 "I would have enjoyed": ibid.
382 *Andy's Garden*: interview, informed source.
382 "Your basic male": interview, Shedrick.
383 "I don't especially enjoy": *San Francisco Chronicle*, November 5, 1990.

THE BIG SCORE

Page
384 The first action: interview, informed source.
384 "The biggest risk": interview, informed source.
385 "My own little publishing company": *New York* magazine, January 28, 1991.
385 "Martha and George": interview, informed source.
387 "Boobs and idiots": interview, informed source.
387 "Martha and I spent": interview, Rochelle Udell.
388 "At first he wanted": ibid.
388 "*Martha Stewart Living* didn't": Martha Stewart, Conversations with Charlie Rose, lecture series, March 26, 1996, 92nd Street YM-YWHA, New York City.
388 "He loved it": ibid.

389 "Time Warner was initially": interview, informed source.
390 "All men, only men": ibid.
390 "Some people think": *San Francisco Chronicle,* November 5, 1990.
391 "We could usually get somebody": interview, informed source.
391 "We didn't have the first deal": interview, informed source.
392 "A way of keeping": interview, informed source.
392 "There was an undercurrent": interview, informed source.
392 "I must remain": *Wall Street Journal,* March 28, 1991.
394 "Although it purports": ibid.
394 "The whitest magazine": ibid.
394 "I really want people": ibid.
394 "My biggest fear": interview, informed source.
394 "I thought that was hysterical": interview, informed source.
394 "The deal . . . marks one": *Advertising Age,* May 20, 1991.
395 CAN THIS ADVICE: New York *Daily News,* June 30, 1991.
396 "People are into their": *TV Guide,* August 7, 1993.
396 "The set crew": interview, informed source.
396 "The real problem": *TV Guide,* August 7, 1993.
397 "Spent money like mad": interview, informed source.
398 "We got her into": interview, informed source.
398 "Industry buzz words": *Inside Media,* November 4, 1992.
399 "The food world is a club": *Inside Media,* April 14, 1993.

PRIVATE LIVES

Page
400 "Had no friends": interview, Norma Collier.
400 "But I thought": ibid.
401 "As it often happens": interview, informed source.
402 "Susan set it up": interview, informed source.
402 "Before Martha wrote": *Yankee,* February 1989.
402 "Martha and Susan are like": interview, informed source.
402 St. Bart's event: *New York Post.*
403 "Forget that Martha's": *Mediaweek,* December 2, 1991.
403 Sometimes rocky: interviews, informed sources.
403 "There were several periods": interview, informed source.
403 "Robyn knew it would": interview, informed source.
404 "I'm still afraid": interview, informed source.

IT's A GOOD THING

Page
406 "Trying to keep up": interview, informed source.
406 "Martha realized about": interview, informed source.
407 "Bringing in someone": *Working Woman,* June 1995.
407 "This is it": *New York* magazine.
407 "You could tell Martha": interview, informed source.
408 Twenty pounds of: *New York Times,* November 19, 1995.
408 "Which gave Martha": interview, informed source.
408 "Don is a bottom-line": interview, informed source.
408 "Oh, shit, this is": interview, informed source.
409 DOMESTIC ICON WANTS: *Wall Street Journal,* April 10, 1996.
409 "Martha got courted": interview, informed source.
409 "She wanted equity": interview, informed source.
410 "He was a guy who was": interview, informed source.
412 "When Andy heard about": interview, informed source.
413 An eerie corporate manifesto: published in *New York Observer,* February 6, 1995.

Index